Maurice Sugar

Maurice Sugar

Maurice Sugar

LAW, LABOR, and the LEFT in DETROIT 1912–1950

Christopher H. Johnson

Wayne State University Press   Detroit   1988

Library of Congress Cataloging-in-Publication Data

Johnson, Christopher H.
     Maurice Sugar : law, labor, and the left in Detroit, 1912–1950 /
Christopher H. Johnson.
          p.   cm.
     Bibliography: p.
     Includes index.
     ISBN 0-8143-1851-7 (alk. paper). ISBN 0-8143-1852-5 (pbk. :
alk. paper)
     1. Sugar, Maurice, 1891–1974.   2. Lawyers—Michigan—
Detroit—Biography.   3. International Union, United
Automobile, Aerospace, and Agricultural Implement Workers of
America—History.   4. Trade-unions—Automobile industry
workers—United States—History.   5. Trade-unions and
communism—United States—History.   I. Title.
KF373.S78J64   1988
344.73'0188'0924—dc19
                                                             87-34636
                                                                  CIP

All the photographs in this volume, except those otherwise labeled,
are used by permission of the Archives of Labor and Urban Affairs,
Wayne State University.

For Ernest Goodman and in memory of my mother, Janice Thompson

Other names crowd memory; I must stop playing favorites. But not before reverting to Maurice Sugar. "Maurice Sugar really was Mr. CIO in Michigan," Carl Haessler wrote me. "Any story of CIO without Sugar is incomplete." Agreed—except that Sugar's influence radiated much further. We felt it in Washington. On this trip I found it still widely felt in CIO though, under the victorious Walter Reuther, Sugar was no longer UAW general counsel. Whatever brains conceived CIO, it was born in the labor struggles of the workers—notably those in Auto, for whom Sugar was counsel and advocate from the first. Attorney for unions since 1914, Sugar stood high in labor and progressive circles from long before CIO. His service to UAW capped a career marked by both legal talent and a deeply principled and philosophical attachment to the labor movement.

—Len DeCaux

THE HEMLOCK
To Maurice Sugar

High above the swamp, rugged, noble,
It stands aloof, limbs outstretched meeting
The sun and the wind head-on, proof to
Cedar, pine and tamarack below
That roots sunk down deep will brace a tree
To overcome burn, the ice storm's woe,
The fungal growth, rust and density.

Its rings mark off each wedding to a year,
Concentric configurations of
Pride and joy and accomplishment.
Its limbs dance pavanes for the dark,
Its needles sing songs to the wind,
It drops its cones and it sheds its bark,
Incendiary fuel for all of mankind.

—M. Furay

✤ CONTENTS

✤ ILLUSTRATIONS

✦ PREFACE

Half a century has passed since protests against unemployment and evictions and early Depression strikes sparked the movements that culminated in the organization of the United Automobile Workers (UAW) of America. From its inception as a Committee for Industrial Organization (CIO) affiliate in 1936, the UAW went on to take its place as the largest and, in many respects, most vital union in the United States during the decade between the Great Sit-down and Taft-Hartley. It is forty years since the passage of that act, which put labor on a defensive course it has not yet reversed. Nineteen forty-seven, too, was the year that Walter P. Reuther gained full control of the UAW, emerging from the bitterest and most widely publicized factional fight in trade-union history with the support of a clear majority of its membership. The passions generated by that battle have begun to subside, but the historiography of automobile unionism has remained deeply divided. However, in the public mind, as always, the winners have a decided edge.[1]

Maurice Sugar, Detroit's most prominent labor lawyer and UAW general counsel from 1939 to 1947, was a key leader of the losing side. One of the aims of this study is to understand the perspective of those defeated in 1947. The point is not to attack or to open old wounds but to reassess the entire process and to examine the goals and ideals of the losing coalition from the vantage point of one of its intellectual guides. It is, further, to shed light on the historical forces that precipitated the rise and fall of the old Left and its broad group of allies as the dominant elements in the UAW. In looking at the Left and labor before the victory of Reuther and his conception of trade unionism, we are dealing with a sharply defined era in U.S. labor history, one that began with the Depression and ended with the Cold War.

Few figures allow us to come to terms with this era more clearly than Maurice Sugar, and few places in the United States provide a more appropriate setting than Detroit. Stretching back to his colleagiate conversion to socialism in

11

1912 and forward to 1950, Sugar's active life presents a remarkable journey along the intertwining paths of the Left and the labor movement. He seemed to be continually on the frontier—at first in the literal sense, born in a timber boomtown near Sault Ste. Marie and then at many of the critical junctures in the struggle of working people for justice in American society.

One of the first labor lawyers in the United States, Sugar spent the years immediately following his graduation from the University of Michigan Law School in 1913 battling against injunctions and antipicketing laws for Detroit American Federation of Labor (AFL) unions. Sugar and his wife, Jane Mayer, joined the leadership of the Michigan Socialist party. Although classified as a "yellow," an anti-Bolshevik, Sugar was among the handful of Michiganders who went to jail for their refusal to register for the draft. This experience, copiously documented, encouraged his shift from yellow to red, although he did not join the Communist party, which was organized in September 1919. Indeed, Sugar refused to join any political party after the Michigan Socialist party was dissolved in 1919. This resolve held firm throughout his career, allowing him, as an independent Marxist of generally pro-Soviet leanings, to serve both the labor movement and the Left in a way that would otherwise have been impossible. In this he was typical of a group of individuals (including Sugar's friends, Scott Nearing and Carl Haessler) who played similar roles.

Reinstated to the bar with the aid of Frank Murphy in 1923, Sugar returned to the defense of labor unions and took on civil-liberties cases, especially those involving racial discrimination. Beginning with the Depression, his activities diversified substantially. Virtually every significant movement or event engaged his energies: the antieviction struggles of the Unemployed Councils, the Ford Hunger March of 1932, the fight to release the Scottsboro Boys and Tom Mooney, and dozens of new labor and civil rights cases. Then, as lawyer for the pathbreaking Mechanics Educational Society of America, a candidate for judge and city council who garnered vote totals amazing for a loudly denounced "red," and the reigning authority on the mechanisms of antilabor strategy practiced by the companies and public officials, Sugar became the Midwest's most prominent defender of labor's interests on the legal and political fronts. Finally, as lawyer and advisor during the sit-downs of 1937 and as general counsel for the UAW after 1939, he emerged as a labor leader of national stature.

While it would not be accurate to call Sugar's period of involvement simply the "pre-Reuther era," since Walter, his brothers, and their comrades were significant actors in the UAW almost from the beginning, the union's center of gravity was George Addes, who served as secretary-treasurer from 1936 to 1947. The broad Addes coalition, which grew out of the anti–Homer Martin Unity caucus of 1937–38, included Communists and various political associates from Popular-Front configurations along with a great mass of militants like Ed Hall or Paul Miley who were vaguely Left but were tough trade unionists above all. They put together majorities throughout the decade, although after 1941 they sometimes agreed only on their opposition to Reuther. This was Sugar's crowd.

Sugar was the highest-placed friend of the Communist party within the UAW. Although he never followed "the line" slavishly, he generally adhered to its principles. The Nazi-Soviet pact tested his loyalty, but the business of organizing the Ford Motor Company, auto's last great citadel of resistance, so preoccupied him that the agony the pact caused so many never surfaced in his public or private utterances. As general counsel, Sugar was also the keeper of the union's constitution and hence the main day-to-day defender of rank-and-file interests. This role he perhaps relished above all others. It was only in a fully democratic union that socialist principles could make their weight felt. Union democracy and Marxism: for Sugar they fit hand-in-glove. Many others on both sides thought they did not. The complexities of their interrelationships and Sugar's activities in defending both constitute, perhaps, the unifying theme of the entire book.

A number of critical issues in recent U.S. social and political history may be examined through Sugar's biography. Bert Cochran has rendered grudging testimony to the activities of the Communist party in CIO organizing, particularly in the automobile industry. But he and most writers on this subject seem preoccupied with showing the mistakes, limitations, and myopia of the Communists; even pro-Communist writers, in aggrandizing the role of the Party, remain concerned with evoking an idea of what might have been had certain other courses been taken. There is an assumption running through much of this that the Communists were in a position somehow to have led a class-conscious American working class, if not to revolution, at least to a substantially stronger position than was achieved had they only done it right. Although the evaluation of errors and "wrong turns" still has its place, a more urgent task is to understand the historical significance of the Communist party during the decade of its greatest influence and particularly in a context away from regular contact with its leadership. Sugar's role as a witness to the process and as a liaison who often revealed the mechanisms of Communist influence in a major union is important indeed. As a sympathetic nonmember, he typified the world of the "fellow travellers" (an honorable term in the pre-McCarthy era), a much larger and more stable community than the Party itself. Hardly "dupes," they unquestionably influenced the Party as much as it influenced them. Sugar's vantage point, I would argue, represents the perspective of the U.S. communist movement much more than the vacillating pronouncements of Party leaders or even the activities of the rapidly changing Party rank and file.[2]

Another important problem is the relationship of the law to the labor movement (particularly the place of constitutional rights, the product, after all, of a bourgeois revolution) in the struggle for a socialist transformation of the United States. Sugar's thought and action in this regard may well be his most important contribution. In his mind, the courtroom was a forum from which to educate the working class and the public at large about the injustices perpetrated by the capitalist system. At the same time, the very constitutional rights supporting the economic interests of the ruling class could often be turned against it in

13

defense of the proletariat. What better illustration of the dialectic, of the unity of opposites, could be found? Sugar was able to pose sharply the inherent contradictions within U.S. law between property rights and human rights. His classic statement of this problem was his discussion of the "legality" of the sit-down strikes of 1937, which reached tens of thousands of radio listeners in the nation's industrial centers. The law as an instrument of capitalist domination also remained a constant theme in Sugar's work. In hundreds of court cases, but perhaps above all in the great legal struggle against the Ford Motor Company, Sugar demonstrated the historic prejudices of the law in favor of capital, while simultaneously utilizing concepts from the common law, such as the doctrine of "unclean hands," to challenge them.

Sugar's activities also carry us into the fight for legislative reform of labor law and into the manifold consequences of "labor's bill of rights," the Wagner Act. The increasing role of government in labor disputes (whether through the National Labor Relations Board [NLRB] or direct presidential intervention), the regularization of labor relations by legal strictures promoting "labor peace" through collective bargaining, and the whole problem of the no-strike pledge and the War Labor Board were all questions that engaged Sugar's detailed attention. Through his eyes, therefore, we can witness the growing place of the government under the New Deal in relations between capital and labor and the growing dependency of labor on the law. The very law that protected it initially increasingly limited its alternatives. Finally, with the Taft-Hartley "revision" of the Wagner Act in 1947, the law became a virtual prison. No person in the United States, with the exception of his close friend, CIO Counsel Lee Pressman, was in a better position to observe this development—moving forward with the logic and irony of a Greek tragedy—than Maurice Sugar. The U.S. version of the class struggle grew with the law only to be stifled by the law.[3] And the ultimate rationale for its stifling, in the form of Taft-Hartley compliance by labor's officialdom, was anticommunism.

Nineteen forty-seven was the climax of Sugar's life. He lost the factional fight against Reuther and was removed as general counsel. That year also saw the waning of a particular style of trade-union politics. Some called it factionalism, others called it anarchy, but many called it democracy. The roaring convention battles, complete with fistfights, name-calling, and outrageous factional songs, the "flying squadrons" of the various factions, the daily plotting, the massive factional political campaigns in every local in the nation, and the labyrinth of deals made among leaders at all levels have become part of the lore of labor history. The Reuther regime put an end to all that; the last convention smacking of the old ways was in 1951, at which Reuther consolidated his power. The order and respectability of the UAW in the 1950s and the leadership of a "labor statesman" should perhaps be seen as compromises with the realities of the Cold War United States that saved as much for labor as could be saved. But just as obviously, something important was lost. Factionalism ensured that the ranks,

14

whatever their opinion, could speak out: lots of members may have hated the nasal New Yorkese of Communist whip Nat Ganley or the gravelly brogue of Association of Catholic Trade Unionists (ACTU) spokesman Henry McCusker, but their presence and recognition meant that all others could be heard as well. The essentials of the union constitution under which such democracy was possible was developed by Maurice Sugar and George Addes, who also remained the ongoing watchdogs of the constitution. All internal conflicts relating to local elections, antiunion behavior, spying, seniority, grievance processing, and so on passed through their offices. They, and especially lawyer Sugar, were the keepers of the seal, which in the UAW of those years meant the keepers of the faith in union democracy. This strand of the story, the changing place of the ranks in the UAW, may be the one with the deepest meaning for Sugar—and, perhaps, for today. Union democracy of the old sort disappeared, as well, in the fog of anticommunism.

And so did a unique coalition of the Left and labor, whose special character grew out of its geographical location. Detroit was not New York, nor was it Washington. Time and time again, Communists and their friends in Detroit and in auto generally acted in ways not appreciated by the central leadership. Time and time again, UAW leaders and followers irritated the center of power in the CIO. But for the 1930s and 1940s, there is a real question about where the center was. Was it not in fact in the coal fields, in Akron, Cleveland, Pittsburgh, Detroit, even South Bend—the places where industrial unionism flourished? And everywhere, what happened in the community at large was critical to the success of industrial unionism. Very often the stimulus for community support came from the activities of the Communist movement. Nowhere was this truer than in Detroit. Several local unions there were founded in International Workers' Order halls, for example. More broadly, community awareness and mobilization on behalf of unionism grew through demonstrations, drives, political campaigns, single-issue formations, lectures, artistic presentations, and a host of other public manifestations of prolabor sentiment. This whole phenomenon may be explored in depth through Sugar's biography. Through his political campaigns as "labor's candidate," through his countless lectures, through his role as public spokesman for unions in the course of their strikes, through his exposure of spies, paramilitary right-wing groups, and mobsters and the complicity of local government in protecting them, and through his ability to capture the deepest meaning of the struggle in his famous labor songs, such as "The Soup Song" and "Sit-down," Sugar encompassed a whole range of involvements that brought the public and the labor movement together. A careful exploration of how the wider Left community in Detroit contributed to the advance of the labor movement is therefore a crucial element of this book.

Maurice Sugar was an important figure. His list of accomplishments is impressive. But more essential is the way that Sugar draws together, in his life, so many of the fundamental threads of the history of the Left and labor in the first half of the twentieth century. There were dozens of other local and middle-rank leaders like him, but few had the special blend of experiences that seem, almost, to summarize an era.

At first glance, it might seem unusual that a French social historian should write a book about a rather specialized aspect of U.S. labor history, so perhaps an explanation is in order. Shortly before Christmas in 1977, I received a telephone call from Ernest Goodman, Detroit's most renowned civil-rights lawyer, whose firm had won a variety of landmark decisions over the years and whose name inspires reverence in the heart of anyone who has taken a chance with the law in the name of justice. In my case the connection was direct, since he had defended my wife and me (and several dozen others) in a case arising from our participation in a march that violated Governor George Romney's declaration of martial law after Martin Luther King, Jr. was assassinated. Acting on the suggestion of Philip Mason, creator and director of Wayne State's Labor History Archives, Goodman wanted to know whether I might be interested in writing a biography of Maurice Sugar. I vaguely knew who Sugar was—author of "Sit-down," founder of Goodman's firm, original organizer of an annual Left fund-raising extravaganza called the Buck Dinner, and a folk hero of the old Left in Detroit. His funeral in 1974 was a major event. I also was fascinated by the many tales I had heard about the battles within the UAW, had read most of the standard works on Michigan labor history, and had even directed a Master's thesis on the formation of the Great Lakes steelworkers' local. Goodman promised me access not only to the then unauthorized and unclassified Sugar Collection recently turned over to the archives, but to other materials still in the possession of the family and the firm as well as help in setting up interviews. No strings were attached, and I would have carte blanche in thematic development and interpretation.

We agreed to all this in a subsequent letter—this is in no sense an "authorized" biography—and I set to work. I quickly discovered what a massive amount of research would be required and drew George Colman, former Presbyterian minister, Detroit activist, and bona fide historian (he was my Master's student mentioned above) into the project as oral historian. As it turned out, George carried out a number of marvelous interviews and other research activities in the early stages, but other commitments took him away from Detroit. I cannot thank him enough for his contributions and for the intellectual stimulation he provided.

The most important sources for this study are the papers of Maurice Sugar, which can be divided into three unequal categories. The first is the Sugar Collection at the Walter P. Reuther Library for Labor and Urban Affairs, Wayne State University. Now cataloged into 117 cartons (one of the archives' largest series), these materials range from Sugar's earliest writings in the Detroit Central High School literary magazine to his voluminous correspondence as general counsel for the UAW. The amount of documentation on Sugar's political devel-

16

opment, particularly his role in the Michigan Socialist party before 1920 and his place in Left politics in the 1930s, is impressive. Sugar's tracking of the growth of the UAW (along with a distressing unconcern about his role in it) gives us one of the best sets of clippings, position papers, and marginalia that we have for the period from 1936 to 1947. It is especially important in that the volume of material picks up precisely where the valued Joe Brown Collection begins to fade—and remains significant throughout the period. Finally, the originals of Sugar's songs, several hundred personal letters, and a wide range of important memorabilia are located in the Sugar Collection.

Legal scholars will be disappointed in the collection, however. When Sugar cleaned out his office on his retirement in 1950, he kept only those briefs and related materials that provided a legal record of the political and factional battles before and after the establishment of the UAW. Hence one finds his investigative notes relating to the post–Hunger March arrestees and a commentary on the grand-jury whitewash, large holdings concerning the Black Legion, the paramilitary fascist organization that slated Sugar for assassination, and the multiple legal documents relating to the fight against Homer Martin in 1938–39, but few briefs for his many labor cases, including such critical ones as the Chrysler sit-down injunction hearing of April 1937.

Many of the later cases (from 1934 on) remain in the files of Goodman, Eden, Millender, and Bedrosian (the firm Sugar founded), which, along with several private files retained by Jane Sugar, constitute the second general category of Sugar papers. Photograph collections developed by Jack Auringer and a number of personal letters were quite useful in clarifying aspects of Sugar's biography. Especially important, his correspondence with Bud Reynolds during the 1960s provided valuable retrospective information on Sugar's view of the law and its role in the class struggle during the late twenties.

The third principal source is Sugar's incomplete autobiography. It informs virtually every page of the first five chapters of this book. In the early 1960s, at the urging of friends and colleagues, Sugar undertook to write his memoirs, focusing above all on the cases he felt best illustrated his pathways in labor law. His intended readers were, above all, young lawyers with a thirst for social justice and an interest in the labor movement. As with so many people his age, he was also able to recall his childhood in vivid detail. The result was a headache for any potential publisher but a gold mine for the historian. In thirty-four chapters totaling more than twelve hundred pages that barely reach 1935, Sugar recounts hundreds of incidents and dozens of cases in the form of fascinating and insightful ancedotes. Sugar did not finish his autobiography, in part because of failing health and, I think, in part because of the amount of pruning that would have been necessary for publication. In fact, he would have been forced to rewrite everything he had already done, perhaps in a totally different style. Unhappily, therefore, he did not get to what many would consider the most important years of his life, the time with the UAW. But he did leave several vignettes about particular events and personalities (among them the Flint sit-down and "my relations with Walter Reuther") that are of great interest. A copy of all this material, although originally made available for my exclusive use by Ernest Goodman, is now in the Sugar Collection at Wayne State.

Beyond Sugar's personal papers, I have drawn information about him and those with whom he interacted from a wide variety of sources. The Burton Historical Collection of the Detroit Public Library houses copies of the manuscript censuses (above all, for 1900), business directories, and descriptive materials that allowed me to fill in the context of Sugar's early days in Brimley, while photographs and a visit to the place provided an image of the physical setting. Sugar's peculiarly "American" Socialist perspective, which he shared with Eugene Debs, was rooted in this context, and I needed to understand it clearly. Secondary works, especially Richard Dorson's classic *Bloodstoppers and Bearwalkers* made sense of the lore of the timber country and helped me to appreciate Sugar's love of the north and his sense of humor. His early Detroit experience was set in the era of the city's growth as an industrial center. Besides a variety of Wayne State theses and dissertations, the most useful secondary works were Melvin Holli's *Reform in Detroit,* Olivier Zunz's *Changing Face of Inequality,* and Steven Meyer's *Five Dollar Day.* Sugar's legal education at Michigan was placed in perspective by the early chapters of Jerold Auerbach's masterly *Unequal Justice.*

The microfilmed papers of the Socialist Party of America, the rare collection of materials (including the only copy of the *Michigan Socialist* newspaper) in the Robert Westfall Papers in the Labadie Collection at the University of Michigan, and the unexcelled *Detroit Labor News* (Reuther Library) provided the main primary documentation (besides Sugar's papers) for chapters 2 and 3. I found Ray Ginger's *Debs,* James Weinstein's *Decline of Socialism,* Robert Murray's *Red Scare,* and Theodore Draper's *Roots of American Communism* to be the most influential secondary works—despite my substantial reservations about each—in developing my understanding of the larger picture. Nick Salvatore's *Debs* has also had an impact. For the specifics of the local labor scene and factional Socialist conflicts after the war, several holdings at the Reuther Library—above all, the materials relating to the Auto Workers Union and Justice Department spy reports recently obtained via the Freedom of Information Act—provided important data. Sugar's pamphlet, *The House of the Masses Trial,* and assorted Reuther Library materials relating to the post-Palmer-raid situation in Detroit illuminate a little-known chapter in the splintering of the U.S. Left in 1919–20, the origins of the Proletarian party, and help us to understand the longstanding enmity Sugar and a host of other Marxists in the area felt toward members of the new Michigan Socialist party.

Although the forthcoming study by Joyce Peterson will do much to fill the gap, there is no general work on the economic and social history of Detroit in the late twenties and the early Depression years. For the auto industry, we have Robert Dunn's classic, *Labor and Automobiles* (1929), for race relations and the Sweet case, David Levine's *Internal Combustion,* and for the politics of the early thirties, Sidney Fine's *Frank Murphy* (vol. 1). On the early relationship between

18

the Communist party and auto workers, I relied heavily on Roger Keeran's dissertation, now published. But most of the difficult work of reconstructing Sugar's life and milieu during the period between his reinstatement to the bar and the Ford Hunger March was drawn from his autobiographical sketches and other writings; personal interviews with Jane Sugar, Jack Tucker, and several others; and the manuscript and printed materials in the Sugar Collection. Although the other series at the Reuther Library generally do not become important until after 1932, a number of oral histories (especially that of Phil Raymond) and the Joe Brown Collection shed light on various aspects of early Depression developments.

Paucity of documentation and secondary literature disappears as a limitation after 1932. If anything, the problem is the reverse. Of the scores of commentaries and histories consulted, the most influential were (more or less in order of importance) Bert Cochran's *Labor and Communism,* which appeared as I was beginning my research and served as a marvelous counterpoint to a number of my then naive conceptions of the role of the Communist party in the CIO; Keeran again, who worked my thinking in the other direction; Sidney Fine, *The Automobile under the Blue Eagle,* an immense storehouse of information on the 1933–35 period (and which I found more satisfying than his more famous *Sitdown*); Mark Naison's study of communism and community in Harlem, which I read as I was developing my thesis on the Left community and union consciousness in Detroit; Meier and Rudwick's *Black Detroit and the Rise of the UAW,* a godsend, again appearing in the midst of my researches (although I think they underestimated the significance of the Left, and specifically Maurice Sugar, in developing links between blacks and industrial unionism in the city); *The Many and the Few* (1946) by Henry Kraus, which still captures the spirit and the meaning (if not all the details) of the Flint sit-down better than any other book, although we anxiously await the published results of Neil Leighton's massive oral-history project; Ray Boryczka's articles on the early years of the UAW and Nelson Lichtenstein's book on shop-floor relations and rank-and-file militance during the war, which were important in guiding me through the thicket of vituperation between Reutherites and anti-Reutherites that obscures so much of the history of the auto union from 1936 to 1947; the contemporary journalism of Louis Adamic and Carl Haessler, which provided insights on a variety of specific issues, and a different kind of observer, Clancy Sigal, who evokes the bitter war of 1946–47 better than any historical work in his novel, *Going Away;* and finally, Steve Nelson's autobiography, which introduced me in detail to the kind of Communists that seemed to abound in Detroit, who, while loyal Party members, often deviated from the line, especially if the line seemed to conflict with rank-and-file workers' interests.

In an area where the bibliography is exploding, there are a number of books, besides Lichtenstein's and Naison's, that were not yet out when I began my research. Fortunately, dissertations or articles were available, so the basic arguments of Harvey Klehr on communism during the 1930s, Maurice Isserman

19

on the war years, and Howell Harris on new management strategies could be appreciated if not always fully accepted.[4]

The endless source materials, both printed and manuscript, in the Reuther Library provided the main foundation for chapters 5 through 10. The Sugar Collection remains the principal series but is now joined by the remarkable UAW collections. The key one for me was that of George Addes, the most important figure in the UAW before Walter Reuther's rise to power. He served as secretary-treasurer of the UAW from 1936 until he was defeated in 1947 by the Reuther juggernaut. Sugar was his main correspondent, especially after the attorney took over officially as general counsel in 1939. He was also Addes's most trusted confidant and advisor on all sorts of matters, the *éminence grise* of the union's broad Left coalition that Addes led. The papers of Homer Martin, Carl Haessler, R. J. Thomas, Walter Reuther, Emil Mazey, UAW Public Relations, the Wayne County AFL, UAW War Policy Division, the Association of Catholic Trade Unionists, and UAW locals Dodge 3, Bendix 7, Plymouth 51, Briggs 212, and Ford Rouge 600 were the most important collections for my purposes, although references to Sugar and correspondence with him were found in several dozen other collections. The UAW Convention Proceedings, the executive board minutes (verbatim after 1946), Sugar's own clipping collection, and various newspapers, especially the *United Auto Worker,* the *Wage Earner,* and *Labor Action* were the principal printed sources used.

Despite the voluminous source material, the observant reader will note that the biography loses much of its personal flavor after 1938 (see chapter 8). Sugar, though more prominent in his role, becomes more elusive as a person. It is especially difficult to trace his political opinions or to observe precisely how he related to political organizations, particularly the Communist party, after that date. The practical reason for this is the paucity of documentation—no political writings, no personal papers or letters, and above all none of the autobiographical reflections that give such life to the first two-thirds of this book. Moreover, Sugar's friends and colleagues were reluctant to talk about his private views on a variety of politically sensitive issues if they were not absolutely certain of his opinions, and even then, specifics were hard to come by. After taking on the job of general counsel in 1939, Sugar made it clear that that would be his life—it was the culmination of his career. His position made him the representative of all the union and therefore public or even repeatable private political comment might be regarded as unacceptable for one serving in his function. He was immensely popular and respected in virtually all quarters of the union. Why should he undermine that trust by appearing closely associated with any group? This closed-mouth attitude also meshed with his natural diffidence and was strongly reinforced after he failed to get a conviction for libel against a man who accused him of being a member of the Communist party in July 1939. What we see, at least until the trying struggle of 1946–47, is the public Sugar, fighting the legal battles of the UAW and defending its constitution. This lacuna is a shame, for it is clear from what evidence we have that he was dismayed with the course taken by the U.S. Communist party from 1939 on. A detailed chronicle of his disappointment or, better, a running critique would have allowed us to carry forward the story of that side of his life. What we have instead are fleeting glimpses only, largely as they relate to UAW policy. Only on the question of *anti*communism was Sugar clear and vocal: he would not tolerate it and fought against all initiatives, whether from Homer Martin, Richard Frankensteen, or Walter Reuther, to exploit its political benefits.

The other major element among the sources for this book was the oral interview. The collection in the Reuther Library was only of marginal use to me although the long narrative of Carl Haessler was illuminating. George Colman and I therefore conducted a number of interviews, the importance of which can be gauged from references to them in the text. They were all conducted in 1978 and 1979. For personal information and details on Sugar's younger years especially, four long interviews with Jane Mayer Sugar and her sisters Gertrude and Emma Mayer were invaluable. Unquestionably, my four interviews with Ernest Goodman gave me the greatest insight into Sugar's mind, his personality, and his legal and political principles. Their agreement on issues—after Goodman joined Sugar's firm in 1938—was virtually complete, and thus it was possible to quiz Goodman on certain questions almost as if he were the man himself. Obviously the historian can offer such evidence only for what it is, but in the case, for instance, of Sugar's view of the Nazi-Soviet pact, Goodman's remarks ring true. Goodman was also my mentor in matters of the law, procedural detail, and the like, and in the interpretation of several of Sugar's written passages.

George Addes was my next most important source. In two long interviews, he confirmed again and again his close cooperation with Sugar and emphasized the latter's general role in the history of the UAW as traced in this book. He also stressed his perception of Sugar's distance from the Communist party—as a sympathetic outsider who took his own positions on issues as they came. Addes also provided fascinating insight into his own place in the history of the UAW, especially the crucial questions of the election for president at the Cleveland Convention in 1939 (from which office he backed away), the response of the International to the wartime strikes, and the grinding conflict with Reuther in 1946–47. Sam Sweet, long-time education director for Plymouth Local 51; Percy Llewelyn (recently deceased), the first president of Ford Local 600; Sheldon Tappes and Christopher Alston, two of the great black pioneers in UAW history; and George Burt, regional director for Canada until 1950, all provided long and detailed interviews focusing on specific issues relating to Sugar's biography. We were unable to obtain a requested interview with Emil Mazey.

Among those without formal UAW affiliation, we interviewed Larry Davidow, first Sugar's friend in the Socialist party, then his enemy, who provided important new information on Sugar's status and role in the Flint sitdown strike. LeBron Simmons, a Detroit activist attorney, gave us an excellent picture of how Sugar was viewed in the black church-related community in

1935; his interview was a critical turning point in our assessment of Sugar's role in developing a prounion consciousness among black people in Detroit. Stanley and Margaret Nowak, important figures in the Polish Left community and in women's political activism, provided a wealth of material on issues ranging from the early Proletarian party to the organization of cigar workers and the Women's League against the High Cost of Living. An interview with William Weinstone, district organizer (DO) in Detroit from 1934 to 1938 and currently official historian of the U.S. Communist party—carried out in New York in March 1979—allowed me to pursue a number of questions about Sugar's relationship with the Communist party (he made it perfectly clear that Sugar was not a member) and about the origins of Sugar's misgivings concerning Walter Reuther, a story followed up in some detail in chapter 6. Finally, early in the process, Colman and I spent several delightful and fascinating hours with Saul Wellman, also a DO in Detroit who, as he put it, "oversaw the dissolution of the Communist party in Michigan" in the 1947–54 period. Saul provided all sorts of information and made numerous suggestions about lines to pursue. I thank him for the stimulation he provided and the warm welcome he gave to me.[5]

Virtually all our main interviewees graciously invited me (or us) into their homes and spent long hours sorting out often distant and not always pleasant memories. I cannot thank them enough. Many others contributed to this book as well. My three Master's students who wrote on topics related to this study, Michael Kroll on George Addes, Joseph Fardella on ACTU, and Scott Craig on blacks, communism, and auto organizing, provided insights and information that I never would have seen otherwise. Dozens of people in Detroit talked about Sugar and this history with me—for a while, new ideas sprouted weekly. To try to name them all would be to risk forgetting someone special. But I must thank those who read all or parts of the manuscript. Melvin Small, Robert Zieger, Tom Klug, Steve Babson, and Seth Wigderson shielded me from many errors and offered a number of important insights. The logic, organization, and readability were improved by Sándor and Carol Agócs, Nancy S. Macy, Austin Johnson, and Lois Johnson. Besides discussing hundreds of problems with me, Lois also typed the entire first draft, turning my hieroglyphics into English. The amazing Ginny Corbin, who never makes a mistake, typed two further drafts and saved me from dozens of misspellings. As for Gertrude and Emma Mayer, whose support was so crucial as the research was proceeding, I just hope that the final product will put to rest their numerous concerns about the manuscript. They obviously contributed greatly to the book and it would be sad to think it a disappointment to them.

But finally, and above all, I thank the man who made this book possible and in whom the spirit of Maurice Sugar lives on, Ernest Goodman. I ask him to share the dedication of this volume with the person who got me interested in the whole business long ago.

1 ❖ AN AMERICAN RADICAL

Brimley

In September of 1889, Kalman and Mary Sugar arrived with their two small children in a little logging village then called Superior, a whistle stop on the Soo line to Marquette. Standing in the rutted, unpaved main road, the Sugars could see a few scattered clapboard and split-log buildings separated by stretches of grassy open space and a few clumps of second-growth conifers. To the north was Waiska Bay (Kalman thought it was called Whiskey Bay), and across it lay a grey line of buildings, scaffolding, and smokestacks. That was Bay Mills, an impressive complex of sawmills connected with Superior by a long trestle. In all other directions stood dark evergreen woods. Winding out of them was a deep stream named, like the bay, for the great Chippewa leader who had conquered the Huron. Thousands of tons of timber rode its currents each spring and spilled into the bay, forming a moving island, and was then pulled toward the sawmills.

The train trip from nearby Sault Ste. Marie ended a long voyage that began on the shores of the Baltic Sea a few years before. Kalman Sugar and Maria Berman were Lithuanian Jews. In 1881, when he was twenty-three, Kalman came with his brother Isaac to Baltimore and was followed in 1884 by Mary, whom he soon wedded. Sugar was a peddler. Why he and his new wife decided to move west is not known, but Detroit's reputation as a developing commercial and manufacturing center must have influenced them. Pearl, their first child, was born there in 1886. Hard times soon pushed them on—north to the timber kingdoms of the Upper Peninsula.

Kalman first tried his hand as a traveling salesman of foodstuffs and dry goods working out of St. Ignace, where their second child, Lawrence, arrived in 1888. He peddled his wares in lumber camps and fishing towns all over the Upper Peninsula until he discovered Superior, where he immediately recognized the opportunities for a general-provisions merchant.

23

Maurice Sugar was thus the son of pioneers, an unusual circumstance for a U.S. Jewish radical. He was born on August 12, 1891 in the bedroom above the new store next to the railroad tracks. His mother's dearest friend, Minnie Belanger, wife of a French Canadian lumberjack, attended her. Two years later, when Mary delivered the last Sugar child, Victor, the store was larger and a stable had been added. The town was developing rapidly, boasting two hotels, a restaurant started by Mrs. Belanger, four barbers and—a sure sign of settling down—Mme. Sordan, a dressmaker. It also had a new name, Brimley.

The town's only immigrants from Russia remained prosperous. By 1900, the Sugars owned their place free and clear and employed a fifteen-year-old French Canadian servant girl. Also living with them was Charles Main, a Russian-born Jew and a traveling salesman. They owned two horses, one for dray and a fancier pleasure horse, Nancy, whom little Maurice loved dearly. The store itself was spacious, sported the traditional pot-bellied stove, and sold all the essentials of life in the north woods. Like all country stores, it was the gathering place for townspeople to exchange gossip and tell stories.

Maurice's early education owed as much to his north woods experiences as it did to the formal schooling he received in Brimley's two-room schoolhouse. A school picture reveals a sturdy nine-year-old—a son of the north. Arms folded confidently, face open and engaging, he looks healthy and happy. Sugar retained a roseate vision of those early days. Swimming in the buff in the freezing waters of the bay, spinning logs like "river hogs," fishing for whitefish, and dozens of other outdoor activities dominated his memories. School was not a high priority, although books were important. His father read some, particularly a multi-volume world history, and was reputed to have a strong knowledge of the Bible, and Mary had an abiding interest in music.

Overall, if the Brimley years did not contribute significantly to his intellectual growth, they were immensely important in defining his essential nature. Here Sugar acquired characteristics and attitudes that differentiated him from many of his left-wing intellectual friends but matched those of lots of Detroit working people. Although he did not exactly spring from the working class, the conditions of his life and the associations made in Brimley's rough-hewn environment were certainly remote from anything that might be described as bourgeois. Sugar could think of little from those years that might have influenced his decision to become a Socialist. The only Socialist in the area was Gus Bertram, who was thought to be a little odd. But the whole experience of life in Brimley was set in a context of *them versus us,* and the Sugars, typical of most shopkeepers or barkeeps dependent on working-class customers, sided with labor.

The other side consisted of the International Paper Company and Hall and Munson Lumber of Manistique. Their owners lived far away and representatives were few and far between. Only two company superintendents, one bookkeeper, four sawmill engineers, and five foremen resided in Brimley. One more man should be added to the list: J. Parsille, manager of the company store founded in 1895 by International Paper. Significantly, he was also the postmaster, the only government official in town. Rounding out the "bourgeoisie" of Brimley were a doctor, a druggist, two preachers, two schoolteachers, and a freight agent. Against this handful of gentlefolk, the census of 1900 listed 348 people who worked with their hands or catered to those who did. Brimley was a working-class town. Its main category of workers was "laborers," meaning lumberjacks and mill hands.[1]

The Waiska Valley was among the last areas in Michigan to be logged, in part because its marshy terrain produced less pine than it did "scrub" or "popple" —balsam, cedar, hemlock. and other softwoods. The companies were perfectly happy to turn them into pulp; many real lumberjacks, who had "followed the pine" from Maine to Saginaw to Seney, moved on to the Pacific Northwest rather than waste their skills on timber that "cut like butter."

This may explain the more settled nature of Brimley when compared to the fabled timber towns like Manistee or Seney. In contrast to Seney, for example, where they dominated the population, the itinerant bachelors who created the image of the lumberjack constituted less than a third of Brimley's laborers. Sugar remembered many family men among the Brimley jacks. These "solid citizens" were hardly immune, however, to the delights and disasters that accompanied reentry from the long, celibate, normally abstinent, and certainly cold campaigns in the woods, for the town always burst into "sudden, wild, roaring life" at that moment.

Young Maurice was fascinated by the work and the lore of lumberjacks. Their work life had two distinct phases. First was the main work in the woodland camps during the winter, followed by the river drive after the thaw. The second covered more varied summer activities. Many jacks went to work at the sawmills for the same companies that jobbed out the logging operations in the forest. The work in the mill enthralled Maurice:

> When the floating logs reached the mill, they were steered . . . to pronged chains [that] ran up out of the water to the singing circular saws. The saws cut the logs into shortened lengths, which then were pulled upwards into a trough. Intermittently there were openings in its walls, fitted with chutes running down to the hatches of the waiting freighter. On one side of the trough were platforms upon which men stood . . . holding their pickaroons. When a log arrived at the chute, a man hitched into it and pulled it into the chute. . . . Here was a fascinating operation. We kids never tired of watching it, and frequently the men let us handle their pickaroons and make a try of it. We got to be pretty good at it, even though we frequently got stuck on logs and had to let them go by.

The workingmen who made up a majority of Brimley's population were craftsmen in one of the proudest and most demanding occupations in U.S. history. While Maurice never actually witnessed lumberjacks at work, he heard dozens of stories about them. His sense of humor, evident in his later courtroom presentations, speeches, letters, and especially songs, owed much to these tales. Their essential characteristic was to intrigue the listener with a confusing or improbable set of circumstances and then conclude with an outwardly rational but totally outrageous explanation or resolution. Sugar worked with the twists and turns of such humor, juxtaposing irrational situations arising from social reality with the foolish answers given by the system. His most famous use of the idiom occurred in the "Soup Song" (1931), in which each grim verse is answered with the ironical "Just give them a bowl of soup."

Unlike the commercialized versions of lumberjack legend (Paul Bunyan, etc.), the stories collected from real woodsmen put little emphasis on the work itself. As Herculean as their work exploits may have been, their work life was assumed; as the core of their identity, it was fundamentally private. Such discreteness also marked their attitudes toward sex, about which, too, no tales were told. "Scrupulous decorum" was the key characteristic in their relationships with women, even prostitutes. Work and relations with females were part of a rigorous code of ethics that one writer compares to "the cult of the medieval knight in providing standards of valor, honor, justice, and chivalry." But unlike the knight, the lumberjack worked prodigiously, relentlessly, and with profound respect for the object of his labor and a curious selflessness about his own well-being. The ultimate disgrace was to be fired because it was assumed that his skills had failed him. "The stigma would follow him to hell. Other jacks remembered the man who had once been fired, talked about him slurringly, and avoided his company."[2]

It is fascinating to consider such characteristics and values in relation to Sugar's mature personality. His enormous capacity for plain hard work and his reputation as a perfectionist in the preparation of law cases were legendary. He also expected the same from his staff. He had no use for slackers. Pride in work well done was matched by a reticence to boast about it. Moreover, friends later remarked about his "courtly" bearing, which gave a well-mannered, polite, and pleasantly diffident character to his relationships with all, but particularly with women. This was part of his charm, of course, but was sometimes seen as a distant, even ascetic, manner. The personality of Paul Wooster in Clancy Sigal's *Going Away* is a caricature of Sugar as the austere, single-minded, icy leader of the anti-Reuther caucus in the struggle for the union in 1947. Such traits are easy to magnify for dramatic purposes, and it is useful to remind ourselves of their probable source: the north-woods individualism, chivalry, and reserve of the lumberjacks and not, as Sigal was implying, a steely and highly disciplined "Party" mentality.[3]

Sugar learned from the lumberjacks his first lesson in the power of labor united. The nature of their work required intense cooperation, and living in the camps under such extreme conditions enhanced group solidarity. They could idolize their camp boss, whose strength and skill legitimized authority, but they also knew when they were being exploited. As one Upper Peninsula ditty put it:

26

Oley Olsen is a jobber,
Who will go to hell some day,
For working men long hours,
and cutting down their pay!

Lumberjacks normally went on strike not for union recognition or the right to bargain collectively on a permanent basis but because they were angry. Resistance arose when they were "fed up," being worked too hard, or paid too little at a particular moment; they then determined to "change things." The first Michigan strike—in Muskegon in 1881—arose out of such circumstances. The strikers won their ten-hour day and that was the end of their "union." Collective bargaining contracts were not the issue; power, some money, and control over one's own life were.

Brimley had a strike and young Sugar witnessed it. It was called by the hold men at the sawmill.

They had been receiving thirty-five cents an hour and they asked for forty. They had no union. The increase was refused and one day, quite suddenly, they all quit work. I soon learned that a strike by these men meant virtually a strike by the town of Brimley. A couple of days went by, and nothing happened. It was then that I learned what a "scab" was. Listening to the talk in our store and about town, I heard that a number of scabs had been hired. They were recruited from Sault Ste. Marie. The first talk I heard about the scabs was merely that they could never do the work. No experience. And that made the work too dangerous. A day or two later the talk had changed.

To reach the mill you had to walk about a half mile on the trestle. Now there was nothing to prevent anyone from walking on the trestle. And early one morning, when the strike was but a few days old, some scabs who were walking out on the trestle to go to work ran into a number of strikers who happened to be there just when they came along, and who were apparently unfriendly. There was some jostling. The scabs ran back towards land. They traveled as fast as they could, but were impeded by the crossbeams of the trestle which [had] considerable space between them. One of the scabs fell into the deep water and had to be pulled out by some strikers.

The next day none of the scabs showed up for work. The following day the strikers went back to work at forty cents an hour. All Brimley was pleased.

Sugar's early learning about labor, social relations, and class conflict was rooted in experience. His parents knew nothing of socialism. Kalman Sugar finally joined the Socialist party, but he did so in 1918 under the influence of his son, not vice versa. In the 1890s he was a staunch supporter of William Jennings Bryan. Nevertheless, from life in a harsh environment where hard work was only a fragile barrier against poverty, from the association with an entire community of working-class people and poor farmers, in suffering himself from an education

27

that taught him to read and little more, and in absorbing the timber tradition of collective, proud, and awe-inspiring labor, Sugar certainly learned important lessons for socialism.

He learned a great deal more—about fighting and drinking, about guns and hunting, about the joys of singing, dancing, and reading. He also learned about himself, his family, and their place in the community and in the United States.

The lumberjacks' return from the woods was an exhilarating and fearful time. The tales told about exploits with bottle and fist were fine for the public and for the receptive imaginations of boys like Maurice, but for the wives and children of hell-raising jacks, perhaps the stories came too close to reality. The yarn about Joe Donor of Eckerman, who drank himself into oblivion, crawled home, passed out under the dripping eave, and awoke in the morning encased in a frozen shroud was amusing enough but also a frightening reminder that the most frequent victims of accidental death in that part of the world were frozen drunks. The legend of P. K. Small, who would bite the head off of anything from a snake to a pet owl for a drink, got lots of laughs; but he stirred thoughts of the pitiful plight of the old alcoholics who hung around in every town.

The Sugars had their own experiences with drunken lumberjacks. One remained vividly ingrained in Maurice's memory and is worth recounting, for it captures an aspect of Brimley life and perhaps contributes to the explanation of why he remained a light drinker all his life. Bill, a father of three, had just returned from the woods and, recognizing the temptations in store for himself for the next few days, asked Kalman to keep a portion of his pay packet for him in his safe. Under no circumstances was he to let Bill have the money. A day passed. Late in the evening came a thunderous pounding at the door; it was Bill, dead drunk and demanding his money. He careened through the store, swearing and screaming. Finally he unleashed a stream of anti-Semitic epithets that terrified Maurice, who watched the whole affair from behind the counter. But his father prevailed. Limp and pale with frustration, the sodden lumberjack left the store. The following day a sober and chastened Bill claimed his money and thanked "K" from the bottom of his heart.

This incident underlines the harsher side of the often glorified milieu of the whiskey-soaked lumberjack. There is no romance here. Nor, in fact, was there a great deal in the other enterprise that preoccupied the story-tellers—fighting. Unreal as might seem the tales of T. C. Cunnion, the man-eater from Petersborough, who reportedly warmed up for a fight by eating babies for lunch, or of the grizzly lynching and mutilation of the McDonald boys by the denizens of Menominee's Frenchtown, they came perilously close to the truth. Sugar was horrified by the vicious fights he observed as a child. One was a family-grudge match in which sons, seconded by their fathers, tore at each other until one finally got the other down and smashed his defenseless opponent in the face again and again before he "managed to grunt: 'Nuff! The victor rose slowly, looking at his left hand. His thumb was hanging by a shred of skin." This rough-and-tumble world, where legend and reality melted into one another, became a permanent fixture in Sugar's mind.[4]

So too was the immigrant world he lived in. Brimley was a meeting ground for people from remarkably diverse origins. Three-quarters of the town's 179 household heads were born outside the United States, although about half of these came from English-speaking Canada. Among the minority of "Americans," half were born in Michigan and a third in the lumbering Northeast. Most were of Yankee extraction, although three were second-generation Irish, and three German. A majority of them had probably worked in the industry in the lower peninsula ("valley boys") and had now finally settled down. They largely married younger women of Canadian background (both English and French) who came from the more populous Soo area. For their part, the English-speaking Canadians had followed the pine in a similar fashion across their country. A quarter of these "English" Canadians had Scottish- or Irish-born parents (with the nod to the latter) and many others possessed Scottish and Irish surnames. Many Brimleyites thus spoke English with a brogue. A Congregationalist and a Catholic church were quickly established to serve their (and others') religious needs.

The largest single ethnic group in Brimley, however, was French Canadian, which accounted for about a quarter of the total population. A smattering of other immigrants (Scandinavians, Finns, and Germans) also found a home in Brimley, but the *Canadiens* stood out statistically and in Sugar's memory. His best boyhood friend was Tom Belanger, whose large family lived close by. Tom's father was a naturalized citizen who had come to Michigan as a boy. He worked along with three of his sons in the sawmill and lumberjacked in the winter. The Belangers were typical of the French population of Brimley in many respects and lived close to their compatriots. Only in the length of their U.S. residence were they somewhat exceptional. Like most of the other "Frenchies," the Belangers did not own their own home. The father was poorly educated and Minnie was just seventeen (only slightly below the French average) when she married him. Most of the French had large numbers of children and experienced tragic rates of infant mortality. In the case of Minnie Belanger, only seven of her eleven children had survived as of 1900.[5]

Members of the other significant national group in the area were all born there. While only a few Chippewa resided in Brimley itself, some two hundred lived in Bay Mills. As Sugar remarked, "Indians were a common sight to us— they evoked no more interest than anyone else." Although this was the era nationally of the final onslaught against Indian power and self-respect, the Chippewa of this area still retained much autonomy, continuing to hunt and fish at will (despite restrictions) and to move as they pleased in the Whitefish Bay hinterland. Most also retained their Ojibwa names. In a few short years the "Indian Mission" would change all that, bringing them something called civilization.

Maurice's little universe, while socially homogeneous, was thus culturally complex. The store rang with a half dozen different accents every day, and at dusk men would sit around and start telling their tall tales. Sugar would later describe the scene in a short story: "Outside the snow whirled . . . the night was so dark that, as the good-natured village storekeeper said: 'You couldn't see your handt behindt your pack.' Around the little stove sat a group of unique characters. . . ." And the yarns unfolded—"Ze Skunk," or how Eve was a French-woman; Finnish tales of Jussi the Workman or the sharp ironies of Lapatossu jokes; Eric Ericson taking *resources* for *racehorses* on his tax return; or John Lufkins, the Chippewa Brimleyite who played halfback for the 1898 Carlisle football team, telling about the gift-bearing white missionary, who, when asked if he would go look after a sick woman, answered "yes, but will the presents be safe in the teepee?" "Oh sure," was the response, "there's not a white man around for forty miles!"[6]

While we do not know precisely who all the regulars at the Sugar store were, it appears that Kalman served the less-favored elements of the community. In his memoirs Maurice speaks of French Canadians, Swedes, Finns, Irish, and Indians and says nothing of Scottish, English or Scotch-Irish, save a mention of Orangeman's day and anti-Catholic rhymes. It makes sense that a Jewish peddler would build a clientele among the more "foreign" and poorer elements of the growing community. This was undoubtedly a source of Sugar's later concern for the plight of the foreign born and of racial and religious minorities.

The Sugars themselves were foreign born, religiously distinct, and, in the terms of reigning late-nineteenth century "scientific" theory, of a separate "race" as well. The Sugar family was conscious of its differentness. There were no other Jews for miles around. But their situation was not unique. The American diaspora carried many Jews to the farthest reaches of the land and left them dotted, often in isolation from one another, across the countryside as tailors and other craftsmen or as small-scale merchants. While they may have maintained contact with other Jews, their religious experience was largely familial and day-to-day friendships were inevitably with Gentiles.[7]

It is thus easy to see why the Sugars were strongly assimilationist in their view of their place in the United States. Both Kalman and Mary sought and gained citizenship as quickly as possible. While Mary and Kalman spoke Yiddish early on, they soon abandoned the use of their native tongue even in speaking to each other, and the children, from eldest to youngest, knew less and less of the language. As time passed, the family discarded most religious practices as well. "We were taught no religious precepts," wrote Sugar, "notwithstanding that my father presumed to be a student of the Bible, and in the early years performed the traditional rituals of the Jewish Holidays." Sugar remembered them only "as a strange and puzzling show." Mary Sugar did keep a kosher kitchen in those days, however; her husband rationalized it on the grounds of good health. "My observance of pig sties around town," Maurice remembered, "made it easy for me to accept, but I did wonder why it was that Jews were destined to be the only healthy people."

While Sugar would retain a Jewish identity, growing up in a largely non-Jewish environment created in him a strong melting-pot outlook. But his family associated mainly with fellow immigrants of non-English backgrounds and hence did not seek assimilation in an "Anglo-conformity" manner, to borrow a phrase from sociologist Milton Gordon. On the other hand, it was not possible for them, like the Irish or the French, to participate in a subsociety of their own ethnic group. They therefore put a premium on interethnic ties through which they built their identities as Americans. If many ethnics did not melt in accordance with the myth, the Sugars, in effect, had to do so in order to work and live where they did.[8]

Nevertheless, they and young Maurice were reminded in unpleasant ways that they were different. Racist attitudes toward Jews found their way to Brimley, and dealing with them could be a trial. Maurice, in thinking back on those days, recalled the banter of his playmates:

> I used to hear boys say: "I had a piece of pork and I put it on a fork and I gave it to a curly-headed Jew, Jew, Jew." To them this was highly appropriate in my case, as I *was* curly headed. Sometimes I heard: "Holy Moses, jumpin' joses, all the sheenies have big noses," and this in spite of the fact that none of the four kids in our family had a nose that could be considered exceptional in any way.
>
> It would not be true to say that I did not resent these thrusts by my companions. I did. But to me, as it was to them I am sure, it was intended as good-natured ribbing. As I see it now, it must have had its origin in a longstanding prejudice, not in the boys, but in the totality of the environment. I believe that it had the same significance, coming from Tom, as my shots at the French which was in his heritage, such as "Pea soup and Johnny cake make a Frenchman's belly ache." There was no ill will in what to him was fun, and for his fun he was drawing upon the only sources which were open to him in the given setting. In truth he had an excellent sense of humor which was a delight to me and which reduced to the trivial any feelings that his jibes generated in me. I was his favorite pal and I knew it.

The reader can sense in this an attitude that might be described as defensive indifference. In reality, the boy (and the man remembering) had little choice about the matter. What is described here is obviously part of "melting": you had to "take it" from time to time if you were to get along. Sugar would encounter anti-Semitism in more virulent forms in his later life and would vigorously combat it. But his assimilationist mentality provided a degree of latitude, an understanding of the prejudices of others less likely to be found in more easily bruised persons from tightly sealed ethnic environments. For them, the first encounters with racism could be truly traumatic, cause them to retreat back into an ethnic shell, and even form deep reactive hatreds toward other groups. Moreover, Sugar's early experience of interethnic contact no doubt contributed to the ease with which he later related to workers from widely varied backgrounds and to his ability to act as an important liaison between groups. The mature Sugar was viewed as rather specially "American" in that while it was generally understood that he was a Jew and that he welcomed close relations with other Jews, he seemed to blend various traditions, both immigrant and indigenous. The Brimley melting pot, with its monoindustrial working class, whose craft was regarded as somehow specially "American," too, was fundamental in the formation of this man.

The Brimley years also saw the formation of three permanent passions that are important in understanding Sugar: hunting, song, and reading.

While a love for hunting is hardly unusual for a north-woodsman, it was rather remote from the normal experience of most Socialist intellectuals and more than a few of them opposed it on principle. On the other hand, plenty of Detroit workers, Socialist or otherwise, whether Finns or Anglos from the Michigan north, Poles or Italians from the coalfields of Pennsylvania, or Scotch-Irish from Appalachia, had also been weaned on rifles. Although some of the middle-class leftists who went to the first "Buck Dinner" that Sugar organized in 1929 were surprised that the name derived not from the funds that were to be raised for various causes but from the food they were to eat, many were intrigued by a Marxist who was also a deerslayer. The seriousness with which Sugar took hunting can be measured by the following story. In September 1939, at the height of the legal battle with Homer Martin's renegade UAW-AFL, Sugar wrote CIO general counsel, Lee Pressman, that in setting the final trial date, they would have to wait until after the end of November. Why? Hunting season, of course. "It is part of my religion," he said, "to go deer hunting every fall."

As a boy, Maurice learned to shoot without the blessings of his parents. He bribed friends who had twenty-twos with "a handful of caramels or chocolates or lozenges" and went off a-shooting at virtually any target, animate or inanimate. His first deer hunt took place in secret with kindly Gus Bertram leading him back to town. More public was a shooting contest the boy entered for a dime. Lo and behold, with the contest apparently over, he had won a Thanksgiving turkey! But since there was still one shot left in his group of ten, an old man, who had not been there to preregister for the contest, asked if the rules might be bent a bit so that he might enter. The organizers said it was up to Maurice. "I suddenly found myself faced with one of the most critical decisions I was ever to make in all my life." It was victory and ego versus sportsmanship. Sportsmanship won, and so did the old man: "His bullet drove the tack!"

Sugar wrote at length about such experiences in his autobiography. Clearly, they represented something significant for him. A complex combination of manual skill, knowledge, intellect, and a feel for nature constitute the challenge of the deer hunt. It is important to give some stress to Maurice Sugar the hunter and the man in nature because such individualistic impulses are often ignored in the U.S. Left tradition. Scott Nearing, Sugar's long-time friend, who always stayed with him when he came to Detroit, represents that tradition in an even more obvious way, finally carving out his own world and sense of being from the woods of Maine.[9]

It is not surprising that a man who is remembered almost as much for the "Soup Song" and "Sit-down" as he is for his role as a labor lawyer and left-wing activist should have embraced music at an early age. But not just any kind of music. Although Sugar's mother had visions of his becoming the next Pade-rewski, a classical piece identified only as "Meditation" was the only thing he ever mastered on the piano. Instead, his interest focused on the little dance hall above Scribner's store, and he would listen to the strains of "Turkey in the Straw," "The Irish Washerwoman," "The Arkansas Traveller," "The Girl I Left Behind Me," and dozens more as they wafted across the railroad tracks to his open bedroom window; on occasion, he managed to dance, clap, and sing with the music on the spot. The saloons also blared out lively tunes from their gramophones, and Maurice would sit outside and listen for hours on end. "Neither my father nor my mother responded as I did to the music of the woodsmen." But its cadences, the tight rhyming of the lyrics, and the ironical twists of the story lines captured his imagination.

Young Sugar also loved to read. The books were generally of the nickel-novel variety, though occasionally rising to the level of Horatio Alger or even Mark Twain. "My reading was usually done at night, and for the most part surreptitiously, by the light of a kerosene lamp. It went on for hours after I was sent to bed and the lamp had been blown out, only to be relighted by me when the house became quiet. My trouble lay in my inability to put down any story until I had finished it." The boy was often listless after these late-night sessions and his parents even called in the doctor, who found him out. But Maurice continued to play the same game. Reading was his passion, and that was that.

The Brimley years were thus remarkably rich and varied. The work life in timber country, a working-class environment virtually untouched by bourgeois amenities, a complex mixture of ethnic influences and a family that of necessity related to the less-favored elements, and the emergence of a mentality that owed something, certainly, to the Jewish tradition but a good deal more to its assimi-lation into a broader current of cultural interpenetration: these features of that experience stand out most clearly as forces in the formation of Maurice Sugar. He was hardly thinking such things, however, during the lengthening days after his school picture was taken. Instead, he thought, with mixed emotions, about the move the family was about to make. Brimley, Tom, logs, fiddlers, and the warm smells of K. Sugar, General Merchandise, were soon to be things of the past.

Detroit

In July 1900, the Sugar family arrived in Detroit on the most practical mode of summer transportation from the far North, a big side-wheeler that regularly sailed between St. Ignace and the city. Despite Maurice's thirst for knowledge, he and his brothers and sister were being ill-educated in Brimley and their parents were determined to seek better schooling for them. Detriot had an enviable educational reputation in those days. Kalman Sugar found it possible to relocate the family there while maintaining the store up north. They moved into a brick house near the northern boundary of Detroit, at 212 Harper Avenue, four blocks east of Woodward, the city's main thoroughfare. It was a new, middle-class neighborhood and put the children within walking distance of prestigious Central High School.

Maurice found the new environment rather foreign. For a boy who saw his first lawn mower from the boat and his first flush toilet in a Detroit hotel (brother Lawrence convinced him that it was a fire alarm), to move into a neighborhood where he played with Edsel Ford was quite a change. The boy from the north proudly announced when he matriculated at Farrand Elementary School that he was to be a fifth-grader. A week later he found himself in the third grade. The decision to come to the city seemed vindicated. It put some strain on normal family life, however, since Maurice's father had to travel back and forth between Brimley and Detroit.

Detroit in 1900 stood on the brink of major-city status. With a population of 285,704, it ranked thirteenth in the nation. Its industrial character had been established for two decades. Older consumer-goods industries such as textiles and cigar-making had given way to iron and steel, foundry and machine-shop products, locomotives and railway cars, carriages and bicycles. Pharmaceuticals, too, emerged between 1880 and 1900. As with all burgeoning industrial cities, Detroit attracted large numbers of immigrants, now, above all, Eastern Europeans, who had replaced Germans as Detroit's dominant foreign-born element by 1900. For example, 14 percent of the city's hundred thousand immigrants were Poles. Such changes combined with the effects of the depression of 1893 to create social and ethnic tensions of unprecedented proportions. Dozens of conflicts occurred during this period, but the Conner's Creek rising was the worst. Some five hundred Polish workmen used fists, picks, and clubs to reject the shift to piecework on a public-works project. Three people died in the battle. Violence of this sort fueled the anti-Catholic American Protective Association's racist condemnation of immigration and even stimulated the *Michigan Catholic* (run by Irish and Germans) to denounce "savage mobs of howling Poles."

Hazen Pingree, Detroit's mayor, had been radicalized by the spector of mass poverty and left the fraternal halls ringing with anticapitalist language: "Vast accumulations of wealth are more dangerous to the liberties of our republic than if all the Anarchists, Socialist and Nihilists of Europe were let loose on our shores." To the dismay of the business community, Pingree initiated social measures and municipal reforms that caused him to be viewed as the champion of the poor. Most important, he had not, like many self-anointed progressive reformers, assumed that "immigrants" equalled "corruption." Indeed, as historian Melvin Holli has noted, "the municipal government of Pingree's period was probably one of the most successful institutions [in the nation] for channelizing ethnic hostilities, sounding out urban discontent, and redirecting human energies." Pingree left a pervasive inheritance and would be regarded by Michigan Socialists as an important precursor.

In 1900, however, the striking fact of Detroit life was its skyrocketing economic growth. The Sugars had moved from boomtown to boomtown. If the automobile did not take hold immediately upon their arrival, by 1908, 72 hundred Detroiters worked in the various branches of the industry. Eight years later, over 100 thousand found employment in auto. Detroit's population doubled every decade after 1900. It was the progress of "Dynamic Detroit," not the struggles of its workers and their unions, that impressed the boy on Harper Avenue. But it appears that he also felt alienated from his new environment. The richness of his memories of the North is matched by the barrenness of his pre–high school Detroit recollections. He might have appreciated the nice house and the good school, but the atmosphere of gentility dampened his spirit. The Sugars' neighbors were businessmen and professionals with English, Scotch-Irish, and a few Irish names. Slavs and Italians on Harper lived well to the east and there was not a Jew in sight.

Detroit had its Jewish neighborhood. Indeed, when debating the location of the new Central High building after its original downtown site burned down in 1893, the school board rejected a location perilously close to it, arguing that the thrust of "better" Detroit was to the north; hence, the semirural site at Warren and Cass. Less than 3 percent of Detroit's total population in 1900 was Jewish. This still represented an immense increase during the last decade. Detroit's original Jews were German. They were rapidly outnumbered by immigrants from the vast world of the Pale. In fact, 88 percent of all Russian immigrants in Detroit were Jews. The *Detroit Sunday News-Tribune* delineated "the ghetto" in a story published in September 1896: "In a rectangle formed by four streets, Monroe, Watson, Brush, and Orleans, the larger portion, by far, of all the Jews in Detroit have made their home. Of this whole district, Hastings Street is the business thoroughfare. Around that street and those that adjoin it pretty much all that is orthodox and distinctive of the Jewish race [*sic*] in Detroit clusters." Besides serving as a minor document in the history of racism, this quotation underlines the tendency toward geographical concentration among more recently arrived ethnic groups.[10]

But the Sugars were not part of this process. In light of their earlier experience of ethnic isolation, their strong assimilationist views, and their rejection of religion, this is not surprising. It does not mean, however, that young Sugar was oblivious to the realities of anti-Semitism, particularly in these worst of times in his parents' native land. This was the age of Pobedonostsev, of the Black Hundreds, of the Protocols of the Elders of Zion, of the pogroms that sent hundreds of thousands of Russian Jews to the United States. Sugar remembered a chilling conversation that he overheard on the streetcar. That very morning, a story had appeared in the papers about a pogrom in Russian Poland in which hundreds of Jews had been murdered. One of the men said, "I'm just as much against these Jews as anyone, but I don't go for this killing them. That's going too far."

"Yes," said the other, "they shouldn't do that."

"Sure," said the first. "What they ought to do is put them all together and keep them somewhere by themselves, but this killing them—no, that's going too far."

The boy was dumbfounded. "I had liked the looks of these men," Sugar wrote. "I could tell by their appearance, their quietness, and their friendly attitude towards each other that they were perfectly normal men, 'good' men."

Just as mortifying was Sugar's personal experience in high school. In his last two years at Central, he became a prominent figure. Good-looking, self-assured, and an outstanding student, he was also captain of the junior varsity football team, partner in the "model" debate duo with his brother Vic and captain of the debate team, the most articulate member of Central's mock legislature, and coeditor of the school's famous literary magazine. But he was not to be senior-class president. He undertook an active campaign for the office and engaged the services of Bob Vinton, star basketball player, as manager.

"One day he came to me to report," Sugar recalled, "showing signs of mingled disappointment and indignation."

"The dirty crumbs!" he said.

"Who—what happened?" Sugar asked.

"You know what those guys are doing? They're going around and telling everybody not to vote for you because you're a Jew. And a lot of guys are telling me that they would vote for you except for the fact that you are a Jew."

"They are? And what do *you* say when they say that?"

"Oh," he said, "I tell them that I'd rather vote for a good Jew any day than a crummy white man!" Sugar lost the election by a wide margin.[11]

While much more conscious of racial and ethnic stereotyping than most of his classmates, Sugar himself was not immune to the involuntary use of racist imagery. This can be seen in two or three of his short stories for the Central High School *Student*. He had never seen a black person before he came to Detroit, but derogatory language about blacks had been part of the vocabulary of Brimley children. In his first published piece of writing, a tall tale called "The Handcuff King" (March 1909), Maurice used racist imagery, apparently unaware that he was saying anything inappropriate. The hero tells a tall tale about going off to "darkest Africa," being surrounded by a "tribe of savages," and tricking these "niggers" (and the word is repeated more than once) into chaining themselves to one another in such a way as to bash themselves to death against a tree.

How should such a story be interpreted? In the first place, the violence and sleight of hand in the yarn may well have derived from north-woods tales, quite possibly in this case from one of the many Chippewa stories of Winabijou the Trickster. More important, however, is the evidence of a nonchalant racism in which Africans were "natives" and no one (except blacks) gave a second thought to minstrel shows. That Sugar reflected such a mentality is hardly surprising given his comfortable, all-white environment. After all, even Upton Sinclair, champion of the despised East European ethnics of the Chicago stockyards, was unable to control his pen as he had his black strikebreakers dance around and menace white women during a climactic moment of *The Jungle*.

To transport ourselves back to the days when that passage (like the constant barrage of racism in Jack London's novels) hardly raised an eyebrow among enlightened, often socialist readers, is difficult. It is to Sugar's credit (and to that of the reformed Socialist party when he joined it in 1913) that such prejudices would be squarely confronted and rejected. At the height of his career, Sugar would be an outspoken antiracist and a renowned civil-rights lawyer—risking his reputation and, indeed, his life in defense of black people. From a Marxist perspective, this was the only choice one could make once it was understood, as Sugar later put it, that racism is "rooted in and grows out of the economic basis of the prevailing social system, branching out in a multitude of directions." Racial equality thus became a pillar of belief equal to his faith in the destiny of the working class to recast U.S. society.[12]

In his recollections, Sugar found it difficult to pinpoint high-school experiences that might have developed his orientation toward socialism. But as editor of the *Student,* he already showed signs of a social consciousness. For example, an editorial on snobbery and wealth attacked the prevailing practice of wearing lavish gowns and formal wear to commencement exercises. A "relic of barbarism," it put incredible strains on the families of poorer students. "The love of mimicking the rich," he wrote, "should be suppressed." Sugar also developed a sure grasp of current events. As captain of the debating team, he prepared materials on women's suffrage, freedom of speech, and, significantly, "Emma Goldman's policies." In general, his opinions in the *Student* were moderate, but hints of social rebellion may be found. His first editorial promised that "*The Student* this year will represent [all] the students of this high school; it will positively not be factional." High schools such as Central were normally dominated by cliques of the children of a city's "leading citizens." Sugar denounced this and may have been stung more than once by not really being a member of it. It was, perhaps, more than a little joke that Sugar's "theme song," according to class-day organizers, was "Lonesome."[13]

It was less in school, however, than at home that young Sugar faced the tensions of U.S. society. All during his high-school career, the family struggled to stay solvent. Detroit may have been booming, but Brimley was not. Its decline began in 1903 when International Paper, having digested thousands of tons of pulpwood, abruptly departed, leaving a few scraps of forest for a less voracious enterprise, Michigan Pulpwood Company, to pick over. Brimley's population declined sharply, and Bay Mills virtually disappeared. The number of businesses in Brimley went from forty-one in 1903 to twenty-two by 1909. The decline of itinerants, of wage earners, and of the population in general had its effect on general merchandising. Sugar's father, fearing the worst, left the store in the hands of Lawrence, his oldest son, and invested in a Detroit clothing business in 1905. Depressed conditions in 1906 put the Brimley enterprise on the edge of collapse, and the entire family had to move back north to help save the store. By the fall of 1907, things had stabilized enough for the younger sons to attend high school in Sault Ste. Marie, where Maurice played on the varsity football team. In 1908, Kalman sold the store at a loss. Although the family managed to return to the Harper address, Sugar remembered continued difficulties.

Such problems made it necessary for him to find summer jobs. The one he had in 1910 introduced him to the life and thought of workers. One incident in particular had a profound influence. Sugar worked the grueling twelve-hour night shift at a small machine shop that turned out crankshafts. He was a machinists' helper but was forbidden to do the precision work required of lathe operators. One evening one of them, Frank, was late for work, and Maurice decided to prove his mettle at the lathe, to show the skilled men that he could handle the job, too. Inevitably, he slipped and gouged a costly shaft beyond repair. Sugar assumed that he would be fired as soon as Frank arrived. When he did, the young man bravely went up to him and admitted his guilt. To his amazement, Frank did not go off to tell the foreman. Instead, when the foreman went into his office, he and Fred, another machinist, hauled the shaft out in back and mixed it into a big pile of scrap. "And that was the end," said Sugar, "of my first personal experience in what I later came to know as 'solidarity' among workers. Frank and Fred and I were workers."[14]

A Socialist Lawyer

In September 1910 Sugar entered the law department at the University of Michigan. The family's financial situation made the state university the only possibility, and they looked for the cheapest route to a degree. Maurice's main concern, he admitted later, was "to be a college man." Michigan had three sequences in which one could get a degree in three years, dentistry, pharmacy, and law. Teachers at Central advised law because it would be useful no matter what career he might ultimately pursue.

It turned out to be a fortunate decision. Sugar arrived at a time when the law department was becoming a truly professional and "scientific" program. The case method, taught by legal scholars, had become the measure of a law school's quality. Dean Harry B. Hutchins still complained in 1908 about the "large numbers" of the faculty who remained a "serious embarrassment," for "the old method of teaching by lecture is no longer followed in this or any first-class school." Gone were the days when practicing lawyers would come in a couple days a week and lecture on principles of the law. Besides promoting high standards, Michigan's law department embraced the "Wisconsin idea" of encouraging its professors to contribute to public-policy debate. If Harvard, under Roscoe Pound, best represented this Progressive ideal, Michigan was not far behind. Its next dean, Henry Bates, argued that "the long sneered-at scholar and theorizer is coming into his own"; the "cult of incompetence" was giving way to the age of experts, men who are in a "strategic position" to use their talents "for conspicuous service in the cause of social justice." Law at Michigan would thus epitomize the elitist emphasis inherent in the entire Progressive program.

Sugar had little use for such notions then or later. Indeed, despite the growing reputation of the faculty, he was not particularly impressed by his professors. He learned law and did very well in his courses—making the Woolsack honorary after his freshman year and *Law Review* in his last—but his memories of professors' influences were vague. Nevertheless, they did inspire an appreciation of precision in the practice of the law and a respect for the inherent logic of "legal science" that were of great importance for his future. "Use a sharp pencil" became Sugar's motto. By this he meant that while for general reading, understanding the "main idea" is enough, in the law it is not. "What you are seeking," he noted later, "is not only the main idea but the ideas that are minor or obscure, or entirely lacking. Indeed, the validity of a legal contention may depend upon a sentence construction in which the main idea applies to the facts of your case, but the law does not."

Sugar relished wrestling with the intricacies of the law. In one of his first cases after graduation, he defended a man accused of extortion because he had threatened to kill and blow up the shop of a competitor in the laundry business who started to locate in the same neighborhood. Sugar's client was clearly guilty under the "main idea" of the statute—the rival was being deprived of income because of the threat of bodily harm and of physical damage to property. But the sharp pencil located two loopholes: (1) the statute only mentioned threat of *injury,* not killing; and (2) threats to property in the statute included only property *owned* by the person or close relatives. The state had produced no evidence of ownership at all. The verdict was directed by the judge—*not guilty*.

There was nothing "tricky" about this. It involved an agile mind and artful interpretation, to be sure, but above all it involved mountains of hard work. "Competency in the practice of a lawyer," Sugar wrote, "requires constant labor, often sheer drudgery, that is rarely known to clients." Detailed knowledge, not high-flown phrases and courtroom melodrama, was the foundation of skill, and skill won cases (or lost them less disastrously). Sugar may have used the courtroom as a forum to educate the public about capitalism's injustices and workers' rights, but he also used it to educate lawyers and judges about the law. Dedication and sincerity were fine, but they meant nothing unless they rested upon solid, well-researched, carefully organized, and convincing fact.

Thus the law student readily absorbed the focus on scholarship and expertise that the revolution in the discipline was engendering. But the other half of the progressive lawyers' credo, an elitist reformism that sought, as historian Jerold Auerbach puts it, "to preserve existing institutions by making them responsive to contemporary needs," passed him by. Or rather, he passed it by. For Sugar was soon to be captivated by another sort of principle. Sometime in the fall of 1911 he would read and reread these simple lines: "Law, morality, religion are to [the proletarian] so many bourgeois prejudices, behind which lurk in ambush just as many bourgeois interests." He would also read and reread a scathing attack on his intended profession by a more recent rebel: "The lawyer is exclusively occupied with the details of predatory fraud, either in achieving or in checkmating chicane, and success in the profession is therefore accepted as marking a large endowment of that barbarian astuteness which has always commanded men's respect and fear." *The Communist Manifesto* and the *Theory of the Leisure Class* brought to concrete form a concept that Sugar had only vaguely felt before: that however lawyers might try to "influence" policy, their function in history was to serve as instruments of the ruling class. But he did not come to such a perspective easily.[15]

Socialism had not been a part of Sugar's world. Gus Bertram of Brimley was the only Socialist he had ever known. In Detroit, he led a relatively insulated middle-class existence. Despite recurrent economic difficulties, his parents identified with the U.S. economic system that had, after all, created opportunities unimaginable in their native land. Despite recent reverses, they were glad to be here and rejected most of the old ways. And if we are to believe him, Sugar's initial motivation for going to the circle that met at the home of Otto Marckwardt, a young English instructor, had nothing to do with socialism. It was, instead, "to meet girls."

As it turned out, he encountered something that he had never before experienced—a group of people drawn together to discuss pressing political, social, and philosophical questions who also seemed to have fun doing it. And the socialists in the group actually appeared to be "regular people." Before long, he realized how little he knew about socialism, how much he had swallowed anti-Socialist exaggerations. He continued to question and challenge, but his counterarguments became hollow, because as he read and discussed Socialist ideas, he became convinced that his new friends were right. He also became convinced of another matter: that "a red-headed freshman, a tomboy from Grand Rapids named Jane Mayer" was a very appealing young woman. Her intelligence and wit captivated him. So did her beauty, although at the time—they were reading John Stuart Mill's *The Subjection of Women*—it was inadvisable to mention it.

Jane Mayer was a Socialist. Her parents were Socialists. She had come to Ann Arbor at the urging of the Socialist Marckwardt, whom she knew from Grand Rapids. It was not love at first sight, however. In fact, Jane's first contact with the Sugar family was with Vic, who came to Ann Arbor in liberal arts in 1911 and was her classmate. For his part, Maurice had been dating a vibrant, razor-sharp Irishwoman named Mary Donovan, who later worked tirelessly to free Sacco and Vanzetti and married Indiana's second most famous socialist, Powers Hapgood, the inveterate labor organizer. But as the school year went by,

Jane Mayer emerged as the most important person in Sugar's life. With her he joined the Intercollegiate Socialist Society, one step short of joining the party itself. There they became active in distributing literature, staging lectures on campus, and discussing all manner of issues under the generous tutelage of Marckwardt.

Maurice would marry Jane in April 1914, beginning a Socialist partnership that combined unstinting love with deep respect for each other's individuality. No person exerted a greater influence on Sugar's education in socialism than she. Her background complemented his. Born in Grand Rapids in 1893, she was the third child of Johannes (John) Mayer and Mary Bechtold. John and Mary were both from Württemberg. Although they were born in villages "just an eight hour walk from each other," they did not meet until they had settled in Grand Rapids. John came to the United States in 1884 after completing his apprenticeships and *Wanderjahr* as a cabinetmaker and the requisite military service of the Second Reich. The liberal traditions of his region and the advanced ideas he encountered in a notoriously left-wing trade had developed his socialist sympathies at an early age. A tightening market for skilled men and Bismarck's authoritarianism motivated him to join his brother Friedrich in the United States. Friedrich was working on a farm near Ann Arbor. John moved on to Grand Rapids, the furniture capital of Michigan, and was able to find work immediately. Socialist artisan that he was, he joined the Knights of Labor, probably in response to the eight-hour-day movement. After 1886, John Mayer remained loyal to the Knights and bitterly denounced AFL "scabs." But soon, he had nowhere to go but the International Furniture Workers Union of the AFL. Fortunately, other men like him had joined as well, and the furniture workers remained a bastion of the Left within the federation until World War I. Jane Mayer's mother came from small-owning peasant origins. The Bechtolds' large family could not support, let alone find husbands for, all their daughters, so in 1886 Mary and her younger sister joined their older sister in Grand Rapids. All three found work as domestic servants for the city's prosperous German-American middle class. Mary then realized the dream of many a peasant family: she married a resourceful artisan.

The children came rapidly (six girls and two boys in a dozen years) and John earned decent wages for his work with several of Grand Rapids' famous companies. Like most skilled craftsmen, he possessed an unshakeable sense of dignity as a working man. In 1910 efforts to reorganize work structures and degrade skills at his shop were met with a strike, which failed after several weeks. John lost his job and was blacklisted, creating a heavy burden on the large family at the very time that Jane was going off to college.

The Mayers prized learning. Jane's father read widely and dabbled in writing history—not untypical of German artisan-intellectuals. Her mother had three passionate interests: education, gymnastics, and women's suffrage. Her girls and boys were to have the best schooling possible. She spearheaded PTA activities and worked hard on the tax amendment that financed the creation of

Grand Rapids' first high school. Both she and John were active in the local *Turnershaft,* an institution that combined physical training with German cultural education. Finally, generally sharing her husband's Socialist outlook, Mary spoke out often against female inequality and worked as an organizer for the women's-suffrage movement. These were important influences for Jane and her younger sisters, Gertrude and Emma. All three became teachers of physical education, trade-union activists, and feminists.

Jane Mayer thus came from the very heart of late-nineteenth-century American socialist culture. Otto Marckwardt possessed the same pedigree. Son of a cabinetmaker, his career was diverted from the shops by an accident in which he lost three fingers. His parents sent him to the university, and a Master's degree in literature was the result. He met Jane, who was only six years his junior, at a *Turnershaft* dance in 1911 and encouraged her to apply for a scholarship at Michigan, where he had recently joined the faculty. She received one and embarked on a liberal-arts degree, majoring in German literature. But it was through Marckwardt that the vital aspects of her intellectual life took shape, and this was where her life began to merge with Sugar's.[16]

Marckwardt felt that engaging this young man's full participation in the Socialist cause was as important a task as he faced in the year 1912. That spring he had cajoled a still skeptical Sugar into speaking about the ills faced by U.S. workers at a number of forums, including a campaign meeting for the Socialist mayor of Flint, John Menton, in his unsuccessful bid for reelection against the rising industrialist, Charles Stewart Mott. At the same time, however, renewed financial difficulties in the Sugar family threatened to end Maurice's college career. This set the stage for a letter from Marckwardt that had a profound influence on him and was instrumental in convincing the family that Victor, not Maurice, should sit out a year of school to help with the family business. Unlike any other student, Marckwardt wrote, Sugar's slow and thoughtful movement toward a Socialist world view made him special. "In my mind's eye I could not see the Intercollegiate without you. The things you had to offer were different from those that anyone else in the crowd brought to it. . . . They were also . . . more essential to the life and growth of the organization. . . . Your personality is needed in the organization, needed much more than anyone else's. Don't make any rash plans."[17]

This assessment is important because it is the earliest reference to a quality of mind that would make Sugar a remarkably effective intellectual force: he always thought things through. He mulled, ruminated, set problems in different perspectives, questioned, countered, and then suggested possible alternatives, one of which was obviously the best. Sugar established an intellectual trust in the positions that he took. Many a political activist or union organizer would appreciate this quality. So, clearly, would legal clients and juries.

The world of Marckwardt and Mayer, the comfortable world of immigrant-artisan socialism, now welcomed a man who came to it differently, with much greater effort. But it was not simply an intellectual conversion. Increasingly, he came to understand the contradictions of his own past. A strange system it was that caused drunken lumberjacks to scream anti-Semitic slurs at someone doing them a favor; that stole the pride and self-respect of the Chippewa; that glorified the self-inflicted violence of exploited woodsmen; that allowed huge corporations to devastate the ecology of an area, attract a sizeable population, and then pull out, leaving broken workers and small businessmen in its wake; and that now could push a fifty-year-old couple to the brink of disaster as one "sound investment" after another blew up in their faces. Sugar began to rethink his own life in terms of *them* and *us*.

What sort of socialism did he embrace? The year 1912, the moment of Debs's greatest electoral showing, was a turning point in the history of U.S. socialism. It is impossible today to agree either with liberal historians who see an "eclipse" of socialism due to Wilson's progressive reforms or with romanticists entranced by the Wobbly inheritance, who view the Socialist party after Big Bill Haywood's departure in 1913 as little more than a haven for bourgeois reformers. James Weinstein's fine study of the Socialist party after 1912 shows that the Socialist press and municipal political influence remained strong, that the Left in the party grew, and that it developed important demands in the areas of female and black rights.[18] But what impressed Sugar the most in 1912 was the Socialist critique of capitalist exploitation and of the inequalities inherent in the legal system.

Eugene Debs became Sugar's idol. No one exposed the system's grinding impact on workers better than he. And no one spoke out with a greater clarity on the capitalist biases of the law. "The capitalist court," said Debs, "is an infallible index to the capitalist system. To know the court is to understand the system." The Socialist party had recently fought some widely publicized battles with the U.S. judiciary. The most spectacular was the defense of Haywood, Charles Moyer, and George Pettibone, accused of conspiring to assassinate the governor of Idaho in 1905. In the course of this bitter struggle, Debs locked horns with Theodore Roosevelt after the president virtually pronounced them guilty from the steps of the White House. Roosevelt also labeled the main Socialist newspaper, the *Appeal to Reason,* "a vituperative organ of pornography, anarchy, and bloodshed." Such utterances brought unprecedented publicity to the Socialists. Haywood's aquittal was one of the major news stories of 1907.

Arising out of the same case, Fred Warren, the "fighting editor" of the *Appeal,* was indicted for sending "scurrilous, defamatory, and threatening" literature through the mail. What he had done was to attack the Supreme Court for upholding the extradition of the three to Idaho. Warren finally came to trial in 1909 and was convicted, thus creating another public sensation. Debs crisscrossed the country lambasting the decision and the system that produced it. Only in 1911 did President Taft grant the editor executive clemency. Warren promptly returned the pardon because it did not bear a union label![19]

Such righteous causes could not fail to inspire a Left-leaning law student. But Sugar also began to appreciate how the law served as a critical "secondary defense." Those potential rights of working people and their allies that managed to slip through the "line of scrimmage"—the legislative branch—are "nailed" by the secondary—the judiciary. As Sugar put it in a speech, "Laws prohibiting blacklisting, restricting the power of the courts to grant injunctions, regulating the weighing of coal in mines, prohibiting the use of scrip, and many others have been declared unconstitutional." In short, "contemporary law functions to maintain the present order in two ways: first, by facilitating the exploitation of the worker, and second, by eliminating or minimizing his resistance to that exploitation."[20]

During his last year at Ann Arbor, Sugar studied the contradictions of the legal system under capitalism. How could the Michigan Supreme Court hold that picketing, even peaceful picketing, is illegal because it is "inherently" violent? How could the courts deny a jury trial to persons charged with contempt, as often occurred in trials of radicals and their lawyers, especially when the "very judge who issued the order that they were charged with violating" would render the verdict? How could it be said that one form of social ownership, such as the postal system, is a "social necessity" while denying the case for another, the railroads, whose record of disdain for the public interest, exploitation of workers, and obscene profits were a matter of record? The young man's reputation with his professors grew. One of them, Professor Goddard (an expert on common-carrier liability toward passengers), with whom Sugar had raised the last question, put off a discussion of socialism until a day that Sugar was absent. Sugar hoped it was because the professor was afraid of him.

He may well have been. Sugar diligently read many Socialist classics and, especially, contemporary works that focused on the evils of U.S. capitalist society. The first book he recalled reading was Edmond Kelly's *Twentieth Century Socialism* (1910), a primer for non-Socialists by a Columbia professor. Assuming reader hostility, Kelly presented socialism as both a moral imperative and a logical necessity. Yet his analysis was not really posed in a Marxist framework. The stupidity, wastefulness, and injustice of capitalism were given much greater weight than the class conflict it engendered. Indeed, Socialist Rufus Weeks had to remind the reader in a preface that the two central tenets of the doctrine were historical materialism and class struggle.

But Sugar was impressed. Encouraged by Marckwardt, he went on to John Spargo, the most prolific writer in the Hillquit right-center camp of the Socialist party, and to Jack London. From both he learned hundreds of examples of capitalism's vicious impact on the lives of working people. He was horrified by the system's toll in human life, especially the incredible death rates in U.S. mines. In a speech delivered in Detroit, Sugar reeled off the grim figures and then turned novelist, taking his listeners into the home of a family getting the news that their man was dead. The effect of the audience's tearful response on Sugar was profound. He discovered he could move people.

Sugar also read a great deal in the area of science and socialism and was especially intrigued by evolution and its social implications, digesting Darwin's

Descent of Man and *Origin of Species,* Herbert Spencer's *First Principles,* and Thomas Huxley's main works. In an age when Darwin was perceived by public opinion to be nearly as radical as Marx, and when Marxism strove to be as "scientific" as possible, such preoccupations were not unusual. Certainly he rejected the procapitalist conclusions of people like Huxley but was nonetheless intrigued by wide-ranging studies utilizing anthropology and biology like Paul Lafargue's *Evolution of Property.*

The most important influence on Sugar at this time was Joseph Dietzgen, the Rhenish "worker-philosopher," Marxist member of the First International, and one of the chief figures among German-born Socialists in the United States. He died in Chicago in 1888. Dietzgen's main effort was to develop an epistomology that would challenge Kant's dualism: perceptible phenomena in nature versus empirically unknowable *noumena* (irreducible concepts, such as space and time) that suggested a realm of spiritual being. He did so through the application of Hegelian dialectics to the interplay of thought and the material world and was lauded by Marx and Engels for his "independent discovery of materialistic dialectics." With the publication of his *Positive Outcome of Philosophy* (1887), it became progressively recognized, as the great Dutch Marxist Anton Pannekoek put it, that "Dietzgen [had] raised philosophy to the position of a natural science, the same as Marx did with history."

This positivist thirst for an exact-science understanding of human society, of the operations of human thought, and of all natural processes as elements of an integrated, monistic view of the universe was one given great stimulus by Engels, particularly through his *Dialectics of Nature* (1885), and was a key weapon in the struggle against Bernstein's revisionism. The main idea that Sugar retained from this reading was that Marxism was not just a view of human beings acting in society, but that it held all the secrets of the universe. This is important, because, while Karl Marx himself remained firmly rooted in history and the observation of human behavior, Marxists of Sugar's generation, influenced by the positivist belief that absolute knowledge was possible, were cast in a mold where "scientific socialism" was assessed by how it measured up with trends in mathematics, natural science, and analytical philosophy.[21]

Sugar's socialism was above all nurtured by the meetings and the publications of the Intercollegiate Socialist Society (ISS). This assured that his outlook would be moderate. Promoted by the right wing in the party, the Intercollegiate had been approved in 1905. By 1912, with London and Upton Sinclair leading the way, it had established chapters at forty-three schools. It continued to expand, despite opposition from the party's left-wingers, who thought funds spent on its lackluster journal, the *Intercollegiate Socialist,* were a waste of money. Its articles dealt mainly with tactics and reported on the activities of the Socialist student movement. The quarterly seemed hesitant to pursue ideological questions in depth for fear of losing converts. Still, books and essays on a wide range of questions were reviewed and recommended. Among the works most strongly promoted were those of the muckrakers, both Socialist and non-Socialist. Sugar read dozens of them. Sinclair's *The Jungle* led the way, but Sugar was also impressed by Gustavus Myers's *History of the Great American Fortunes* (which effectively exposed the myth of the self-made man) and *History of the Supreme Court* (which exposed it as the system's ultimate protector) and the works of Charles Edward Russell, who converted to socialism because of his own muckraking. Russell's famous line, "a kind capitalist would soon be an ex-capitalist," became a Sugar favorite.[22]

In stumping for socialism, Sugar was happier describing contradictions of capitalism than he was arguing for its replacement by socialism. In a speech given in Detroit in the fall of 1912, a man in the audience rebuked him for his timidity. In recalling the incident, Sugar exhibited his continuing ambivalence on the question. Is it not better for an audience to digest the facts of the past and present, to understand, and then convince themselves that change is necessary? To harangue people before they are convinced is counterproductive. While Sugar would move far to the left of his Socialist principles of 1912, he never forgot the absolute importance of solid, detailed fact as the basis for the development of Socialist belief. Virtually all his writings and speeches throughout his life were descriptive: clear, carefully organized, well-founded analyses of observable conditions. Even in talking about the Soviet Union after his visit there in 1932, he told his audiences what he saw, contrasted it with what they knew about the Depression-wracked United States, and let them draw their own conclusions. To have gone on about "the realization of the historical destiny of the working class" and the like, Sugar knew, would have put them to sleep. He remained the good lawyer who wins cases with convincing evidence.[23]

Sugar did not and would not become embroiled in high-level theoretical preoccupations. He had to make certain that the Socialist perspective made sense philosophically—hence the exploration of socialism in relation to science and religion—but failed to pursue the internal theoretical debates that sometimes degenerated into a twentieth-century form of Scholasticism. Sugar read many of the Marxist classics during this period, but he seems to have preferred the more practical Engels and his interpreter, Karl Kautsky, to Marx himself. He recalled reading only Marx's *Critique of Political Economy* and *The Eighteenth Brumaire of Louis Bonaparte*. It is significant that he would not read *Capital* until he was in prison in 1918–19. Nineteen-twelve was the age of Debs and of the wide, all-embracing Socialist party. Debates between reformists and revolutionaries there were, tumultuous fights over what Marx really meant occurred, but Debs's pragmatism ruled the day. A focus on practical solutions to practical problems would remain at the heart of U.S. socialism. Armed with such pragmatism, Sugar appeared ready to face the real world. But in facing the real world of work, bosses, strikes, police, injunctions, party factionalism, war, resistance, prison, and the Russian Revolution, he found that theory became increasingly necessary.

2 ✤ LABOR, WAR, AND REVOLUTION

Sugar's career at Michigan was soon to end. In general, he seemed to rank his education in socialism ahead of his legal training. As a committed Socialist, he had taken his stand for justice for the U.S. worker and peace abroad. The latter was becoming problematic, and like most members of the U.S. party, Sugar was troubled by the failure of the European Socialists to make clear their will to resist "capitalist war." His fears were well founded. The war, supported by most European parties, would throw international socialism into convulsions that forever transformed its character. But to the extent that it was also responsible for the Russian Revolution, it gave rise to the world's first Socialist state and new hope to millions of Marxists.

A Labor Lawyer

On the eve of his graduation in 1913, however, Sugar's concerns were more mundane. He was penniless, and his father on the verge of bankruptcy. A small loan from the law school allowed him to buy "a plate of Maurey Sugar" (beans with bread and butter) every day at a local hash house, but no more. Thus, when Dean Bates called him into his office in May and told him of a secure position with a major insurance company, he was sorely tempted. Few of Michigan's graduates found jobs in existing law firms. For Jews it was harder still. Felix Frankfurter might have begun to pave the way to successful careers for a few Jews from Harvard, but the Michigan of Hutchins, Bates, and their fellow sons of the American Revolution had not yet been thus "democratized." Still, Sugar recognized the actuarial purgatory Bates was proposing for him and did not apply.

47

Sugar's first year after he graduated was grim. The recession of 1913–14 had just hit Detroit, and jobs were scarce. Sugar had no connections and thus simply made the rounds to Detroit law offices—to no avail. He even applied for a job teaching extension classes in Milwaukee but was turned down. Finally, Pearl's father-in-law told him about a firm of attorneys that specialized in "commercial indebtedness." The next Darrow became a bill collector for five dollars a week, plus carfare. His customers were almost exclusively working people. All the "depressing incidents," he wrote, "which accompanied my occupation have gone from memory; the sum total of the despondency which they caused has not." Blessedly, this agony lasted only a few weeks, and he managed to tie in with another young lawyer who had graduated from Michigan two years before. Sugar wrote briefs and finally began to get a few minor cases of his own. It was honest work, but hardly remunerative. He made about eight dollars a week at the very time (January 1914) that Henry Ford announced his five-dollar-a-day program. Sugar had to take a second job making out bills at night for the electric company, stretching his work day from 8:00 A.M. until after midnight. On an occasional weekend, he would take the interurban to Ann Arbor to see Jane. They were beginning to talk seriously about marriage, so Maurice was also trying to save money.

Shortly after he began this routine, he had his first civil-rights case. The defendant was Maurice Sugar. One night during his ten-o'clock break at Detroit Edison, he wandered over to Cadillac Square and chanced upon an interesting soapboxer. A burly young policeman soon broke up the crowd and told everyone to move along. Everyone except Sugar did so. "I had studied constitutional law under Dean Bates. I knew my rights. Apparently the officer hadn't taken the same course I had." Sugar was arrested. Having experienced a lineup and spent several hours in jail before meeting bail, he demanded a jury trial. The case was quickly won. Then came a more difficult decision. Should he sue for false arrest? Whom can one sue? Curiously, not the state, for the king can do no wrong. "That," Sugar remarked, "was how far the law had progressed since 1776!" So it would have to be the poor officer. Sugar pursued the matter only to the point of sitting down with the policeman and his lawyer and receiving a formal apology. The situation was terribly frustrating. The policeman had only performed as the system had trained him. He had no idea that he acted illegally. The apology was humiliating, as the man groveled and begged forgiveness. Sugar was enraged at the way the system victimized everyone but those actually responsible.[1]

On April 14, 1914, Maurice and Jane were secretly married in Detroit. Only his mother knew about it. Neither family had been enthusiastic about their marriage, it was said, because of Maurice's precarious economic situation. If their differing ethnic and religious traditions were a factor, nobody mentioned it. Impulsive and romantic it certainly was, but their "elopement" was also the cause of what became a hilarious tradition in the FBI. There was no public announcement of the wedding and the official copy of their license was apparently lost or destroyed. Thus in later years the agency referred to Jane as "his common-law wife" (or worse) in its interminable reports on Sugar. Part of the confusion also derived from the fact that Jane kept her maiden name for professional purposes. Agents simply assumed that the liaison was illicit.

After a honeymoon that consisted of a "walk around Belle Isle," the newlyweds returned to their previous activities, she to her schoolwork in Ann Arbor and he to Detroit. They saw each other on weekends. This long-distance marriage became longer the following spring when Jane got an offer to teach German for a few months in Freeport, Illinois. She was to fill in for peace activist Rebecca Shelley, who took off several months to attend the International Women's Congress in the Hague.

Jane's job lasted only until June 1915. She returned to Detroit, and she and Maurice finally set up house together in a bright new flat on Claremont near Hamilton on the northwestern edge of the city. The rent was twenty-five dollars a month, almost exactly a quarter of Maurice's pay from his two jobs. Jane was unable to find a position teaching in the Detroit system—married women were not being employed. Fortunately, after scoring the highest mark on the civil service examination, she got a job as a teacher for the Department of Recreation.[2]

In the year since their marriage, Maurice had become increasingly active in the Socialist party, spurred on by the atmosphere of unrelenting crisis that marked 1914–15. He developed two specialities for which years of training in thinking on his feet had prepared him: chairing meetings and delivering lectures. The weekly meetings of the English branch of the Detroit Soclialist party, which had a membership approaching two thousand people, took place at Duffield Hall above a saloon in downtown Detroit. Active weekly participants numbered about two hundred. Some fifteen other branches, covering most of the major ethnic groups in Detroit, filled out the local party. Although Sugar's political outlook placed him in the right-center of the party, his tolerance of a wide variety of views and his belief in a broad, nondoctrinaire party, along with a thorough knowledge of Robert's Rules, made him an ideal chairman. The second role was more important. As a lecturer Sugar developed a wide repertoire, "discoursing," as he put it, "on many subjects of economic, social, and political import. All embodied pertinent references to the role of law and legal institutions."

There was plenty to talk about. Since mid-1913, the United States had been in the grips of a recession. The numbers of unemployed working people approached 10 percent nationwide by late 1914. Detroit was especially hard hit. For every man taken in at Ford's Highland Park plant after the announcement of the five-dollar-a-day plan, three were turned away. Detroit was one of several U.S. cities to experience a major demonstration by unemployed workers. On February 12, 1914 some six thousand braved subzero temperatures to register their disgust over Ford's false promises and Detroit's precarious economic situation. Mobilized by the DeLeonite "Detroit IWW [Industrial Workers of the World]," with help from the Socialists, the marchers gathered before a downtown employment office, carrying signs inscribed "Bread or Revolution" and other appropriate Wobbly slogans. They were met by hundreds of policemen, mounted and on foot. A bloody conflict followed. The Detroit press screamed about "foreign radicals" and demanded mass deportations. Arthur Christ, local leader of the IWW, gamely responded that "over half the members of the parade were American citizens," as if, in fact, aliens were dangerous. Predictably, the consequence of all this, besides some severe injuries, was a ban on all IWW activity in Detroit. Authorities also put the Socialists on notice to watch their step.

This event occurred in the midst of a series of outrages nationwide that gave "the class struggle" new meaning. Strikes and demonstrations had routinely been met with official violence, but the string of atrocities—with casualty statistics more appropriate to military combat than labor strife—that stretched from the Paterson strike in January 1913 to the execution of Joe Hill on November 9, 1915 caused Americans to wonder whether the war at home was not as bad as the war abroad.

Paterson left two dead and civil rights in shambles. The Socialist mayor of the city was even arrested. Akron Wobbly-led rubber workers fell before vigilantes and police in February. Detroit's first auto strike—against Studebaker in June—suffered the same fate. Across the forests of the Northwest, lumberjacks, organized by the IWW, fought vigilantes and municipalities. In California the first attempts to unionize agricultural workers—the IWW again—were met with official terrorism and murder. Mining, both coal and copper, witnessed the worst barbarities. The Cabin Creek, West Virginia strike of 1913 left twenty-five dead; saw dozens of activists, including Mother Jones, jailed without charge; and generated the definitive split between Debs and the IWW, which accused him of selling out by arranging a settlement.

The great conflicts of 1913–14 in northern Michigan and Colorado gave rise to the highest death tolls—including the Calumet disaster in which seventy-two children were crushed to death after someone yelled "fire" at a miners' Christmas party, and the Ludlow massacre of April 1914, where militiamen sacked and burned a tent colony of miners' families, killing twelve women and children. Max Eastman, writing in *The Masses* about the latter, described the miners' revenge and concluded:

> I think the palest lover of "peace," after viewing the flattened ruins of that little colony of homes, the open death-hole, the shattered bedsteads, the stoves, the household trinkets broken and black—the larks still singing over them in the sun— the most bloodless would find joy in going up the valleys to feed his eyesight upon the tangles of gigantic machinery and ashes that have been the operating capital of the mines. It is no retribution, it is no remedy, but it proves that the power and the courage of action are here.

In Sacramento, Kelly's Army of the unemployed was brutally repelled by eight hundred deputy sheriffs, who then burned the bedrolls that the marchers dropped while fleeing. Anarchists were rounded up in droves all over the country. A variety of nationalist outrages against foreigners, Jews (this was the age of the Leo Frank case), and blacks occurred. The Ku Klux Klan rode again, and D. W. Griffith was doing research for the racist *Birth of a Nation,* guided, for example, by the studies of that eminent historian, Woodrow Wilson. Even for AFL workers it was a dangerous time. Picket lines became battlegrounds as dozens of strikers all over the country fell before the hail of police, Pinkerton, and militiaman fire. The story that crystalized the entire situation was the arrest, trial, and execution of the Wobbly songwriter, Joe Hill. His drama, which began when he was arrested on January 13, 1914 for the murder of a grocery-store owner and his son, became symbolic of the degradation and the dignity of working people generally and gradually took on the quality of a Passion play.[3]

Detroit during these years was calmer than much of the nation. Mayor Oscar Marx had created the image, if not the reality, of reform in the city. On the state level, a vigorous progressive force had gathered around Republican Chase Osborn, an Upper Peninsula journalist and Hazen Pingree protegé, who was elected governor in 1910. During his two-year term, he pressed hard for legislation creating workmen's compensation, initiative, referendum and recall, and direct election of senators. The legislature even discussed women's suffrage seriously. The most significant measure passed was a watered-down workmen's-compensation bill (1912), largely the work of influential members of the Michigan Manufacturers Association who sought, successfully, to manage the process of reform. This Michigan example of National Civil Federation "progressivism" actually split labor in Michigan, with the state AFL body supporting the final package and the Detroit Central Body condemning it, especially because of suspect enforcement clauses.

Militant though it might be, labor in Detroit in 1914 was a pale shadow of its former self. Few places in the country had been so thoroughly cleansed by the open-shop drive of the first decade of this century. The Employers Association of Detroit, founded in December 1902, helped crush dozens of unions thereafter. Its approach was simple—refuse to renew closed-shop agreements and refuse to sign new ones. Its energetic secretary, John J. Whirl, organized support, both moral and financial, for union-busting bosses, made spies available, brought in strikebreakers, and kept an extensive blacklist. The association's Labor Bureau gathered information on large numbers of workers (forty thousand by 1908) regarding their "reliability," thus creating a pool of potential scabs as well as lists of suspected troublemakers.

The building-trades unions were defeated in strikes against contract non-renewals in 1903, public workers saw their claim to maintain a closed shop declared unconstitutional by the state supreme court the following year, and the powerful printers were brought to their knees in 1905. With wild economic instability in the decade after 1907, the trade-union movement in Detroit remained on shaky grounds. Both branches of the splintered IWW fared poorly in the city. While the Detroit Federation of Labor consistently displayed greater

51

militance than the parent AFL, it remained hamstrung in its efforts because of the remarkable power built by the Employers Association.

Just as important, the character of the work force in the city was changing rapidly during these years. Not only was the population of the city increasing at a rate of 10 percent per year and employment shifting rapidly to automobile and accessories manufacturing, but the demand for low and semiskilled work drew thousands of people from the rural United States and southern and eastern Europe who were generally happy to have a job, whatever the terms. It took a good while before the word *union,* let alone the fine points of contracts, had much meaning for them. Conditions of existence were pleasant neither for them nor for the older immigrant groups who continued to pour in. As historian Jack Russell writes, "Detroit became a jumble of factories and warehouses, old neighborhoods that housed different peoples every few years, and new city blocks which only a month before had been dirt roads and empty fields. Life could be cruel in crowded districts. [For example,] out of every 1000 children born, 186 died in their first year."

Despite militant strikes in 1911 by the butchers and the street-railway workers that momentarily frightened the bosses, labor's decline continued. Still, an important change was occurring. Younger men with some Socialist sympathies were entering the leadership cadres. Most notably, members of Local 18 of the International Typographical Union (ITU), responding to threats to craft autonomy and the collapse of the closed shop, had pushed forward their bright young leader, Frank X. Martel, to take a prominent role in the federation in 1912 and 1913. The national AFL, recognizing the sad condition of labor organizing in the United States' most dynamic industrial city, provided funds and organizational assistance to the beleaguered movement in Detroit in 1913–14. This new atmosphere of hope and respect between labor and socialism hardened into a more intense form of determination as the recession advanced. The Studebaker strike, the unemployment demonstrations, the outrage of those left in the streets after Ford's five-dollar-a-day announcement, and the dismay of the lucky ones facing the murderous pace of production on the inside combined to kindle, by 1915, a renewed sense of solidarity among a number of Detroit working people.[4]

Sugar, as a Socialist lecturer, helped to transform mere discontent into a sharper idea of how the system worked. In so doing, he gained the attention of the more radical elements in the Detroit Federation of Labor. The critical moment occurred one cold evening early in 1916. Sugar had the night off from Edison and had scheduled a speech entitled "Law and the Prevailing Order" at Duffield Hall. This was, in his words, "the speech that started a career."

Sugar developed a penetrating analysis of how capitalism dominated the institutions of U.S. society. Although the term was not then in use, he was talking about hegemony, particularly as established through the law and the professionals—professors, lawyers, and judges—who upheld and profited by it. Influenced by Michigan's famed sociologist, Charles Horton Cooley, Sugar was especially interested in the social psychology of cooptation. How is it, he asked his listeners, that thought—often hard, critical thinking to begin with—is transmuted to fit the needs of the economic system, to justify the prevailing order? Through an elaborate reward system that makes it profitable to conform. The profits are often indirect, coming in the form of honors and prestige, but are real nonetheless. Society is thus split between "the workers and the capitalists with their host of apologists and special pleaders. The producers and the parasites."

His central message was clear and direct. "The law is the most powerful instrument employed for the perpetuation of the rule of the dominant class." It punishes directly, by inflicting physical suffering and confinement, but, more important, the constitutional order punishes those who challenge its accepted meaning through economic privation and social ostracism. Fear of both creates "a world of hypocrites." Bound by fear, workers and legal professionals alike stand in awe before the law as if it were a set of timeless verities. Legal theory defends the capitalist order by playing upon and often distorting values—such as liberty and individualism—sanctified by tradition. To question "the law" is thus to question these values. As a judge in Massachusetts—ruling a 1906 strike illegal because it was unduly coercive—put it, "It is plain that a strike by a combination of persons has a power of coercion which an individual does not have." Strikes threaten individualism. So, Sugar advised his audience, "to be on the safe side, do your striking alone."

While it might be easy to expose hypocrisy before a trade-union audience at a Socialist-sponsored meeting, the average worker, lawyer, judge, or official is suffocated by an entire culture laden with all the proper moral-become-legal arguments about the illegitimacy of collective action by labor and the legitimacy of possessive individualism as practiced in the world of business. Sugar concluded his speech with the transcript of his own cross-examination of the superintendent of police who had denied a group the right to parade because it would disrupt business.

> Q. So you regard it to be your function as Superintendent of Police to safeguard business interests?
> A. And the general public.
> Q. Primarily business interests?
> A. Certainly.

What to do? Ultimately, said Sugar, piecemeal changes in legislatures, courts, or officials will make little difference, for the problem is woven into the fabric of the system. It is the entire system that must change: "The worker is an upholder of law and order. He will support the law that administers in his interest; he will support that order of society which is made to his order. He is fighting to bring about a social system which functions for his benefit, and therefore, for the benefit of mankind." Sugar thus took a stand well beyond simple reformism. The legal violence of the past thirty-six months, the growing tensions over the nation's international position, and the carnage and social dissolution in Europe

53

caused by the war all pushed Sugar and the center of the U.S. Socialist party increasingly toward the Left.[5]

Sugar's condemnation of the U.S. legal system hit home with one group of workers in his audience, the beleaguered printers of International Typographical Union 18. A few days after the speech, he received a call from Bill Fitzgerald, a member of their strike committee and that evening sat down with the leadership of the local. The strike at Joseph Mack Printing Company, which had begun in January, was turning into a major confrontation. Because of Mack's strong connections with the Employers Association, the open-shoppers viewed the strike as a test case, and there seemed to be every chance that it would become the most important struggle Local 18 had faced since the protracted and disastrous strike against Detroit Typothetae in 1905–8.

The union, the oldest local of any trade in Detroit and one of the largest in the ITU with a membership of around five hundred, had had some rough going in the course of the past decade, being a principal target of the Employers Association. Its strikes also produced numerous incidents of police harassment of picketers. Criminal charges against strikers who "provoked" the police or disobeyed injunctions were normal fare. There was plenty of law work to be done, but the men of Local 18 were not happy with Antonio Entenza, their current lawyer. Their president, Charlie Lougheed, put it like this: "Our lawyer is a good one, but what we don't like is that he doesn't fight for us in the court room. . . . We can take the guilty verdicts, but, Goddamn it, we don't like taking them lying down." Speaking to Sugar, Lougheed continued: "Now Fitz here, he says you know what it's all about, and we figure you would put up a battle." The Mack strike began when Joe Mack refused to recognize the union, which was supported by most of his 150 employees. He used the Employers Association's services to import scabs from as far away as Schenectady. As the strike proceeded, a number of brushes between pickets and strikebreakers occurred, creating the excuse for a sweeping injunction issued by Circuit Judge Mandell. This was the point at which Sugar entered the scene.[6]

There was really no such thing as a "labor lawyer" in the pre–World War United States. There were a number of people who took on more cases involving labor disputes than other types, but virtually no one, perhaps with the exception of New Yorkers Morris Hillquit and Louis Waldman, made labor law their specialty. And no college curriculum in the nation offered a course in it.

The reasons for this neglect were not hard to find. In the first place, it did not pay—labor unions operated on a tight budget and hiring legal aid was a last resort. Even then, the fees were laughable. Secondly, the volume of cases was low. The AFL tried to avoid conflict that would lead to the courts, and the IWW disdained legal maneuvering, only calling upon lawyers in cases of dire necessity. Thirdly, legislation defending labor's interests was sparse, so conflicts over rights denied were few and far between; instead, lawyers were normally called upon to defend workers who had pretty clearly broken the law (marching without permits, destroying industrial property, ignoring injunctions, etc.). Hence a problem that no lawyer was happy with: he usually lost the case. Moreover, legal and constitutional theory reflected the interests of big business so overwhelmingly that finding tenable constitutional grounds upon which to file appeals was difficult. Finally, defending workers could be dangerous to one's health. Wobbly lawyers were regularly threatened and occasionally met with physical harm. The practice of labor law thus remained unappetizing and indeed only the passage of the National Labor Relations Act (1935) made it halfway attractive to some lawyers. Before that date, Waldman asserted, "If there were ten lawyers known as union lawyers, I'd be surprised."[7]

Sugar's activities in relation to the Mack strike began with a number of law cases, but soon became a total commitment to a cause. As such, it was typical of much of his work thereafter. The charges in most of the cases arose from illegal picketing or fights between strikers and scabs. Sugar's principal opponent was not a public prosecutor (in those days misdemeanor cases were usually tried by private lawyers named by the plaintiff), but a young attorney who worked for Monaghan and Monaghan, the firm retained by the Employers Association. His name was Frank Murphy, future governor of Michigan during the sit-down strikes, U.S. attorney general, and a widely respected liberal. Sugar and Murphy would become friends and have a number of interesting contacts as the years went by, but for now they were adversaries.

As it turned out, Sugar got the better of him in all but two of the nine cases that they argued. Sugar was no doubt brilliant, but he did have some help. The printers were seasoned veterans in the struggle against the open shop. Their officers were familiar enough with the law to add measurably to a case and were always available for digging up witnesses or needed information. They also knew that espionage cuts both ways.

Sugar's first experience with union agents behind enemy lines was a memorable one. While he was meeting with the leadership one night, a young man came in and reported in detail on the activities inside the Mack Printing Company—orders unfilled, the number of scabs, who among them were detectives, and so on. Soon "there was another rap at the door. It was opened to admit another young man who stepped in and started greeting those in the room. Suddenly he stopped and looked wide-eyed at the first man who had joined us. For a moment he stuttered: 'What the . . . what the . . .' There was a roar of laughter. Lougheed [said], 'Number 7, shake hands with Number 2.' 'Aw,' said number 7, 'I knew it all the time.' 'I had you figured out from the start,' said number 2." In fact, neither had an inkling that the other was a union spy. Both men were from other locals located in areas reached by newspapers where Mack advertised for strikebreakers, and it was normal ITU procedure to send some of their people in to apply. Sugar thought it was an excellent idea: he knew what was going on in the minds of many prosecution witnesses in advance!

Occasionally they even placed people in the strategy meetings with the prosecution's lawyers. In one case, Bill, a union spy, had worked intimately with Murphy in preparing his case. "The next day," Sugar drily remarks, "the case was tried. I did fairly well with my cross-examination of the State's witnesses. And when they put Bill on the stand I tackled him with extra vigor. By the time I was through with him his testimony corroborated that of the defense witnesses. My cross-examination brought me many compliments. It was downright brilliant. I have never equalled it since." And Sugar never did tell Murphy.

Interunion solidarity also entered the courtroom during the Mack strike. One of Sugar's clients was accused of assault and battery by a scab, "a hired thug," and the contest revolved around the printer's claim that the scab picked the fight while the two of them were standing at the bar in a tavern versus the latter's assertion that he just stuck his nose in the door and got smashed, without provocation, in the face. The matter was settled quickly on the testimony of the bartender—a good union man—who supported the striker's story in every detail.

Sometimes helpfulness in the name of solidarity could threaten legal procedures—and the lawyer's integrity. One morning, several members of the butcher's union were tried and acquitted for a misdemeanor. Sugar was their lawyer. That afternoon, in another court, a Mack trial was held, Sugar for the defense again. They ran out of prospective jurors, and the judge decided to impanel members of the audience. One of them was a butcher that Sugar had defended that morning. When asked if he knew the defense lawyer, he responded in the negative, figuring he could give the printers some help. Sugar found himself in a real dilemma. To say nothing was to fail to do his duty as an officer of the court. To expose the man was to betray him and the labor movement. Fortunately, the judge had already sensed something was amiss and adjourned the trial for a week, vowing to "investigate." Later that day Sugar advised the butcher "to disappear" and, as his lawyer, he had the right to conceal his whereabouts. No warrant was served and the judge let the matter drop.[8]

Such problems would arise again and again, and Sugar was normally able to squeeze through them. But when the Constitution and the class struggle refused to mesh, he chose the latter. The first instance was hardly a year away.

While the Mack cases were going on, Sugar led a campaign against the use of the injunction in labor disputes. The injunction gave the judiciary an arbitrary authority that had become management's main instrument in the battle against unions in recent years. "The courts," said Sugar in a speech before the Detroit Federation of Labor, "have become the last bulwark in the fight." The legal argument for issuing an injunction was most often based on the coercion and public inconvenience allegedly caused by picketing. While no state in the union allowed unrestricted picketing, Michigan's statutes had been tightened to the point where for a single union member even to stand silently across the street from a struck plant was considered picketing and therefore, by virtue of an 1898 ruling, illegal because picketing supposedly always provoked violence.

In 1916, the AFL embarked on an antiinjunction publicity drive and designated Michigan as a testing ground. Sugar, besides giving speeches, writing articles, and preparing a brochure on the legal history of the labor injunction, also wrote an antiinjunction amendment to the state constitution and coordinated a petition drive to get it on the November ballot. It read very simply: "No restraining order or injunction shall be granted by any court of the state or any judge or judges thereof, in any case involving or growing out of a dispute concerning employment or the terms or conditions thereof." This was followed with a specific list of activities, such as picketing, that could not be enjoined. The March 10, 1916 issue of the *Detroit Labor News* carried Sugar's photograph and, besides praising his work in the Mack strike, announced that the federation would launch a major drive to amend the constitution using Sugar's proposal and expertise.[9]

Frank Martel of the typographical union became the key labor figure associated with the drive. He and Sugar worked closely together and developed a friendship that lasted for many years. In 1916, at the age of twenty-nine, Martel was on the brink of a long career as an officer—finally president—of the Detroit/Wayne County AFL. Martel's early politics were generally Socialist, although thoroughly reformist and practical. If he had a hero in the Socialist party, it was fellow printer Max Hayes from Cleveland, a representative of the party's pro-AFL right wing. Still, like Hayes, Martel promoted the concept of independent labor candidacies and thus rejected the traditional AFL political formula of "reward your friends, punish your enemies."

Sugar and Martel worked hard on the amendment campaign. Its initial impetus came from the widely publicized Lougheed-Simmons trial for contempt, which came up in April 1916. Sugar argued against Monaghan himself, with Murphy only advising. The case produced several memorable stories. The courtroom was always packed with workers and the word got around quickly. Lougheed was accused of threatening management personnel, particularly a strikebreaker from Cleveland named Tanner. Local 18's president had thumbed his nose at him on one occasion and called him *moonface* on another. Monaghan's brief stated that "vulgar" names were used. Even the judge said he had trouble understanding the vulgarity of *moonface*—"unless you know something I don't know." Titters from the audience became jokes on the outside: Moonface Tanner emerged as an antihero of the Detroit labor movement. Another incident *was* vulgar. Monaghan, a fine lawyer with an eye for drama, began an afternoon session by requesting that the courtroom be cleared of women. The judge granted it and a deputy who had tried to serve a copy of the injunction on one of the defendants during the lunch break was called to the stand. Monaghan asked him what had happened when he held out the injunction. After much hemming and hawing, the deputy reported that the defendant told him, "you can wipe your ass with it." Monaghan, shocked, triumphant, returned to his table. Sugar cross-examined. "Witness," he said, "when he said that to you, what did you do with the paper?" The courtroom exploded and a new folktale entered the annals of Detroit labor. The trial also produced a new name for the Employers Association's favorite lawyer. After Monaghan repeatedly mispronounced Sugar's name, the latter began to call him *Mr. Money-han,* again to the glee of the assembled workers.

Such traditions are often overlooked in attempting to understand how solidarity is built. But anyone who has sat down with workers and explored their experiences knows how important these kinds of anecdotes (often embellished with age) were in forging the culture of the labor movement. The courtroom with its inherent drama was an important arena for generating them.

More immediately, the Lougheed trial (the defendants were convicted but the judge never sentenced them) "broke the camel's back," as the *Labor News* put it, in getting the great antiinjunction drive of 1916 off the ground. In a decision taken at the height of the trial, on April 23, Gompers chose Detroit as the place to kick off a massive national campaign against injunctions. By the end of May, a hundred thousand amendment-petition forms had been distributed to AFL unions throughout Michigan, preparations were being made for Gompers's big speech at Moose Temple on June 2, and Sugar's brochure on injunctions, "Working Class Justice," was ready for distribution. In it and several articles that appeared in the *Labor News,* Sugar made a straightforward socialist analysis stressing the vast importance of breaking this legal stranglehold of capital over labor and laid out the battle plan on the issue. The antiinjunction campaign took off rapidly. The *Labor News* claimed, "It is taking hold of Michigan's working class as no movement ever did." Gompers's speech was preceded and followed by marches and rallies. He was joined at the podium by Max Hayes and by Recorder's Court Judge Edward Jeffries, one of a tiny handful of prolabor judges in the country.

Gompers's visit, while ballyhooed publicly, presented a major roadblock for the petition-drive organizers. Sugar's recollection of his "only meeting with Samuel Gompers" tells the story.

> Frank Martel began to outline our program. Imagine our astonishment when Gompers interrupted him and set about to criticize the entire project. Using the initiative and referendum was foolish. The only way to get results was through the legislature. You've got to elect your friends and defeat your enemies. Besides, "why didn't you come to ask my advice before you started this thing?" This last was said with finality. The conference was over.
>
> We were dumbfounded. For several seconds no one spoke. Then I tried my hand at salvage. I started to explain the political situation in Michigan. Gompers stopped me with a wave of the hand.

At the moment, Gompers was merely "querulous," but as the year wore on, he turned these opinions into policy, thereby seriously undermining the political position of AFL militants in Michigan.

By mid-June a countercampaign of major proportions had developed. The Michigan Manufacturers Association and the Detroit Employers Association placed large advertisements in the press throughout the state, particularly focusing on small-town weeklies. They stressed the freedom of workers to choose to work for whom they wanted when they wanted. Monaghan's closing arguments in the Lougheed case formed the foundation of their message, especially his blunt appraisal of the economic benefits of the open shop: "We have been enjoying a prosperous condition in Detroit for the past ten or fifteen years. This prosperous condition is where the city is run under open shop conditions." To outlaw the use of the injunction in labor disputes would gravely threaten "the man who wants to work in peace."

Most troubling to Sugar and his colleagues on the committee was their inability to keep their plans in any way secret. Virtually the moment they came to a decision, the Employers Association or the Detroit daily press was aware of it and often blocked tactics before they were even tried. As was so often the case, there was a spy in their midst. In an effort to expose him (and future spies) Sugar drew up a proposed city ordinance to regulate and identify all agents of local detective firms. An ordinance committee was chosen, but the spy managed to join it, too. He turned out to be a private detective paid by the Employers Association and at that time an international representative of the International Association of Machinists. The intelligence that he had provided in his many capacities with the local AFL clearly harmed the cause. Spying worked, and labor's counterspies never equalled the effectiveness of the employers' networks.

Whether due to the employers' drive, to the weakness of the AFL in Michigan, or to Gompers's dampening effects, the petition drive fell short of the sixty thousand signatures needed by July 1 to get it on the November ballot. The state body therefore decided to continue to work to get it on the spring ballot. The big push came late in the year, and several strikes and confrontations had marked the intervening months. Police responded to a July cigar-workers' strike with a vicious attack on a picket line in which nightsticks bloodied the heads of a dozen women. A pattern-makers strike in Detroit landed five union men in jail for contempt and created a famous incident. Judge VanZile, who cited them, actually visited their leader, George Krogstead, and promised him his freedom and a clean record if he would "keep away from the struck shops." Krogstead's precise reply was not recorded, but VanZile never tried such a trick again. Fall saw a prolonged round of marches, meetings, and rallies. Forty thousand Detroiters turned out for the Labor Day parade. Late in September the Detroit federation launched a referendum among AFL members throughout the state on whether to call a general strike "in the event that any member of organized labor is committed to jail for contempt of court in any labor dispute."

In the midst of the renewed antiinjunction-amendment drive, a mass rally was held on October 20, 1916. It included a float featuring "Miss Anna Hoffman of the striking cigar girls represent[ing] Justice blindfolded," and a talk by William Rubin of Milwaukee, the nation's foremost authority on the injunction, who spoke the truth when he concluded that injunctions were particularly widespread in Michigan—"because you are not the kind of union men in number and quality that you should be." While the Detroit federation was well organized, possessed a militant press, and regularly supported Socialist positions on various questions, its two hundred associated local unions had a membership of only forty thousand, or about 10 percent of the Detroit work force. Most importantly, the automobile industry was virtually unorganized. It was not until 1911 that the AFL even "recognized the existence of the automobile industry," as economist Robert Dunn put it, allowing the Carriage and Wagon Workers International to seek autoworker members. Even then, AFL craft unions objected to its industrywide claims and sought to limit its jurisdiction. Thus, as of late 1916, a major jurisdictional conflict had arisen to frustrate organizational efforts.

The injunction rally of October 20 nevertheless strove to bring renewed vitality to labor's fight against the open-shoppers. Max Hayes spoke, but it was Sugar's concluding speech that would be reprinted in full in the following week's *Detroit Labor News*. The tone of his speech contrasted sharply with Rubin's schoolmaster lecturing. While Sugar might be critical of labor in private, he saved his public criticism for the bosses and consistently presented positive and unity-building analyses of Michigan labor's potential. Educational psychologists may be divided on the virtues of positive reinforcement, but to make one's listeners feel that their goals are attainable with just a little more effort works better than chastising them for past failures—especially when they have worked hard all day and you want them to take the risks and the time to work for labor's cause in their off hours.

The petition campaign did in fact succeed. Like the English Chartists seventy-five years before, they attached the pages together in a roll two miles long and presented it to the state legislature in early January. The constitutional amendment, however, was abandoned because Michigan treasuries lacked the funds and the national AFL refused to foot the bill. This caused strains within the Detroit organization, and Sugar was disgusted by the decision to throw the issue to the "lap dogs of big business" who dominated Lansing. Inevitably, on April 20, 1917, the antiinjunction bill was killed in committee.

It is difficult to gauge the significance of this episode in the history of Michigan labor. By the time it ended, labor was split over the war, with Gompers supporting and radicals both in and out of the AFL opposing. The president's abandonment of the petition drive may quite possibly help explain why most Detroit unionists were lukewarm in supporting Gompers on the war and generally sympathetic to Socialists who resisted.[10]

Michigan Socialism and the Great War

In Detroit, socialism and the labor movement thus drew closer together in the course of 1916. Sugar served as an effective bridge between the two. He and

Jane Mayer became leaders in the Michigan Socialist party during this year. Their closest friends, Sugar remembered, were largely Socialist workers and intellectuals from all sorts of ethnic backgrounds. Evenings and weekends were filled with meetings, lectures, forums, publication activities, pageants, parades, rallies—"the memory of our activities becomes a blur." The Socialist party in Detroit claimed about half the four thousand members in the state. The party had fifteen separate branches in Detroit, most of which had weekly meetings. Besides the large English branch, there were the east- and west-side Polish branches, two Finnish units, and single branches of Germans, German-Hungarians, Hungarians, Bohemians, South Slavs, Russians, Armenians, Jews, Lithuanians, and Letts. The Detroit Socialists fielded candidates in virtually all elections and covered most offices. For example, they ran thirty-five people for district, county, and city positions in 1916, lacking candidates for only three posts. Their electability was another matter. Compared with New York and Milwaukee or with dozens of smaller industrial cities, such as Reading, Pennsylvania or even Flint, Socialist Detroit's record was weak. Although they came close in city-council elections in two or three wards, they failed to elect a single candidate. Judge Jefferies was the only elected official in the city who sympathized with them.

The party in Detroit worked hard nonetheless. Electoral campaigns became educational exercises. Detroit Socialists sponsored events of all kinds to air their views, but by 1916–17 their ties with labor provided them with their best outlets. Sugar's role was crucial here. He had established a reputation with organized labor—as the *Detroit Labor News* put it—"as a keen student of the labor problem and not as merely a hand-shaking, vote-chasing politician friend." He was a welcome speaker at local meetings, at central-body meetings, and at the weekly Labor Forum. He did not mince words in his presentations. His usual speech revolved around the general evolution of the bondage of working people from chattel slavery to wage slavery. Militant resistance to the injustices of capitalism and its legal institutions were called for, although he stopped short of appealing for violent revolution. Sugar also became Detroit's Socialist impresario, arranging for speaking engagements for prominent Socialists like Debs, Scott Nearing, Fred Warren, and Max Eastman, showing them around and putting them up.

Critical, too, was the Socialist drive to develop a strong presence in the newspaper press. The main local newspapers—the *Free Press,* the *News,* and the *Times*—were virulently anti-Socialist and a weekly, *Detroit Saturday Night,* practiced a form of red-baiting that would become popular in the respectable press only after the United States entered the war. The first breakthrough came with the growing Socialist influence in the *Detroit Labor News.* Founded in 1914, this "organ of the Detroit Federation" shifted to the left in 1916. Julius Deutelbaum joined its staff as associate editor late in 1915; he was a printer, a friend of Sugar's, and a Socialist. Gordon Cascaden, the editor, while described by Socialists as a "syndicalist," opposed the IWW and generally followed Gompers's line. It is unclear just how much influence Deutelbaum and the Socialists had in the paper, but judging from the tone of most articles and from the continuing enthusiasm for the injunction petition drive despite Gompers's opposition, the Left seemed to be gaining the upper hand. Early in 1917, Socialists in the federation exposed a major scandal. James Steele, who had recently barely beaten Martel for the presidency of the federation, had accepted money from the saloon interests during his campaign. Martel and apparently a majority of Detroit Socialists were proponents of Prohibition. Steele was removed and replaced by the vice president, Stanley Anderson, who was in Steele's caucus, but the center of gravity shifted toward the moderate Socialists of the Martel stripe. Deutelbaum became editor of the paper shortly thereafter.

The most significant development in Detroit socialism, however, was the creation of its own newspaper, the *Michigan Socialist*. Sugar, as legal advisor, had organized the corporation that published it and served as one of the five members of its board of directors. Its first issue appeared, appropriately, on Bastille Day—July 14, 1916. The editorial policy of the paper tended to reflect the opinion of party moderates although the editor, Nathan Welch, maintained good intellectual rapport with the more revolutionary elements led by John Keracher. In general, the paper, like Sugar, was Debsian, retaining a clear Marxist militance without rejecting piecemeal change.

In one of its earliest issues, the *Michigan Socialist* supported Debs's stern critique of the national Socialist-party platform on the grounds that it failed to place sufficient emphasis on the class struggle, that it was equivocal on the question of "revolutionary economic organization" (that is, it gave full support to industrial unionism while not condemning the particularism of some craft unions), and that it spoke sheer "hogwash" by exempting "defensive" war from a proposed national referendum on the war issue. Throughout the summer and early fall *Michigan Socialist* reiterated these principles in concrete ways. On war, the paper was uncompromising, condemning right-winger Victor Berger's support for "preparedness," while giving full space to Scott Nearing's analyses of "capitalism's growing crime, the War" and stressing that the "real war" is between capital and labor "right here in Detroit." The arrest and trial of Karl Liebkneckt for his antiwar agitation in Germany was front-page news in August, and the paper reprinted James Oneal's attack on Frenchman Gustav Hervé's concept of "patriotic socialism."

As for the "war at home," the *Michigan Socialist* was particularly solicitous of the efforts being made by the Carriage, Wagon, and Automobile Workers of America (CWAWA) to organize automobile manufacturing on an industrywide basis. This was significant because the AFL, in convention, had recently reasserted the rights of the various crafts associated with automobile making to organize independently and had enjoined the CWAWA to remove the word *Automobile* from its name and to reject industrial unionism. The latter had refused. Detroit Socialists supported the union. Their paper began to publish exposés of the harshness of working conditions and the incredible profits being reaped by the companies: "the automobile plutocrats are working the life out of their men." Sugar spoke on several occasions to gatherings of autoworkers, especially to explain their rights to organize and the intricacies of the legal powers of the employers. It was in this context that he made the acquaintance of William A. Logan, the leader of automobile organizing efforts during the period 1916–21.

In general, the Detroit Socialist line was to the left of the national-party position in 1916 to about the same degree that the local AFL was to the left of the national federation. Socialists had strongly influenced the local labor movement and had forged important links with it. The pages of the *Michigan Socialist* were open to "all trades" in order "to further the cause of labor in Detroit." Among the leadership of the Socialist party, Sugar maintained the closest direct ties with labor by virtue of his work. Most of the key Socialist activists were not involved directly in the trade unions, and, indeed, most were not workers. Dennis Batt was a certified tool-and-die maker and Deutelbaum a printer, but all of the other seventeen delegates and alternates elected to the state Socialist convention of 1916, for example, held various non-blue-collar jobs, ranging from journalists to small shop owners to traveling salesmen. The essential bond among them was intellectual, not occupational. Thus the tie with the local AFL that Sugar had been so important in creating was new and required careful cultivation. And given the national AFL's conservative path, developing the relationship was not always easy.

This helps to explain much of the conflict within the local Socialist party and why Sugar became such an important figure. The Right—those who, like Berger, Max Hayes, Jack London or James Maurer, equivocated on the war issue, opposed industrial unions for fear of alienating the AFL, and tended toward racism—were few and far between in Detroit. Deutelbaum came close, but only Reverend I. Paul Taylor and lawyer Lazarus Davidow shared the characteristics of the far Right. Even so, both of them were at least solid on the war question. The Left was strong and was led by three articulate and tenacious men: John Keracher, Al Renner, and Dennis Batt. Keracher, the state-party secretary, came from a line of Scottish shoemakers and lectured regularly on the intricacies of *Capital* in the back room of his downtown shoe store. His brogue and cheerful but scholarly demeanor gave him considerable charm. Renner, an accountant, was a storehouse of knowledge on contemporary problems. Batt, a former cavalryman with a bull neck and thick shoulders, rounded out the triumverate. He provided the vocal muscle via a huge bass voice and the ability to spellbind a crowd. Together they were a formidable crew. But their approach was purely educational: the workers must be prepared for their revolutionary role by becoming well schooled in the facts of their oppression and thoroughly grounded in Marxist theory. The current trade-union struggles, whether AFL or IWW, were peripheral, and indeed wasted, energy that might otherwise be put into developing a revolutionary consciousness. They did agree with other Socialists that involvement in institutional politics was appropriate, but simply used

63

the electoral campaigns as forums for expressing their revolutionary perspectives. For "immediate demands" they had no use. They could care less what happened to the street-railway system or whether a graduated income tax were intro-duced—piecemeal reforms would only undermine the revolutionary potential.

This issue, in fact, encompassed all the rest. For Sugar and the centrist majority that dominated the Detroit party, the question of working for immedi-ate, limited goals was critical—not only to appeal to the practical interests of the electorate and to the special needs of workers, but because they would pave the way for the revolutionary transformation of U.S. society. Thus, while Keracher and company hoped to set up a "proletarian university" to carry forward their brand of socialism, Sugar, Welch, Robert Westfall, Sam Diamond, Dan Powell, and their allies dealt with the hard realities of the here and now. This meant fights for legislation to counter the employers' power, for changes in the electoral laws, for the five-and-a-half-day week, for the total elimination of child labor, and for a variety of immediate measures to ease the threat of war and to dismantle U.S. imperialism (e.g., freeing the Philippines, abandoning the Monroe Doctrine). In Detroit the issue of immediate demands became the line between *red* and *yellow,* the awkward national designations for left and right. Thus Sugar and the pro-industrial-union, antiwar, antiracist, Debsian center (center-left?) became yellows in the eyes of the Left—and the Justice Depart-ment—and were lumped with a locally miniscule Socialist right wing.

As chairman of innumerable party meetings, it was Sugar's job to keep the reds at bay. Jane Mayer remembered that "he used to go to meetings with Robert's Rules of Order in one pocket and the *Communist Manifesto* in another." He needed them both. The left-wingers, educators that they were, tried to overcome their minority status with long speeches that dragged meetings out past the bedtimes of less ardent members. To the same end, they became masters of parliamentary maneuvering, interrupting procedures with grueling points of order and information.

Sugar learned to deal with them. Robert's Rules did in fact guard against the first problem by its suggestions concerning "dilatory, absurd, or frivolous motions." More important, he handled their parliamentary points of procedure by figuring out ingenious ways to overrule them. One story has become part of the lore of the Detroit Left. Sugar recalled "presiding at a County Convention of the Socialist Party when a critical point of order was raised. My ruling was favorable to the Yellows. Some weeks later I presided over the State Political Convention, and the same point of order was raised under identical circum-stances, but with the opposing parties reversed. This time, too, my ruling was favorable to the Yellows." Dennis Batt leapt to his feet, eyes shining in triumph, and asked in his best voice how Sugar could possibly rule in precisely the opposite manner on the same point of order. "There was complete silence as the body awaited my explanation. 'Yes' I said, 'I do recall that earlier situation. You are right. It was exactly the same situation that we have here. And my ruling was exactly the opposite of the one I have just made here. The fact is, and I say this to

64

you in all fairness'—I was speaking slowly, deliberately—'the ruling that I made at the County Convention was wrong.'" Batt, for once, was speechless.

The reds prided themselves on their knowledge of the Marxist classics. Although not always successful, Sugar loved to find ways to out-Marx them. His favorite tale came from another convention where he chaired the platform committee. The majority naturally wished to list a series of immediate reforms, which they did with little opposition in committee. Sugar suggested that they precede the list with the following sentence: "We socialists fight for the attainment of immediate aims, for the enforcement of the momentary interests of the working class." It passed and the report was sent to the convention floor. In the course of the debate, "a leading member of the opposition" attacked that sentence. "Listen to that! What are we, a bunch of reformers, apologists for the capitalist class, or are we Socialists? Are we here to repudiate Marx?" When he had finished, Sugar calmly opened the *Communist Manifesto* and read the exact words preceding the list to the assembly. The opposition was routed again.

Such would not forever be the case. Nor, indeed, would the good humor implicit in such tales be retained. The Socialist party and Maurice Sugar were heading toward the hardest decisions and the most trying times of their young lives. Late 1916 and early 1917 marked an era of false hopes on the international front and frenetic activity for Detroit Socialists. Local politics became all-absorbing. Sugar had become the biggest vote getter within the local party, having topped the list of delegates to the state convention in 1916. The twenty-five-year-old lawyer was now pressed into service as a candidate for public office—district attorney. He took the task quite seriously, making the rounds to union halls, ethnic gatherings, and large rallies. As the perennial introducer of national figures, he had come more and more into the public eye, and his reputation among the AFL unionists was excellent. While he had no realistic chance of winning, he nevertheless showed himself to be an attractive candidate and captured more votes in Wayne County than any other socialist candidate, outdistancing the presidential hopeful, Allan Benson, by an embarrassing margin, 3,681 to 3,236.

Jane Mayer also ran for office in the spring elections, as a candidate for the school board. Her platform differed sharply from those of the major parties. It focussed on teachers' rights of free speech, their voice in administrative policy, higher pay and smaller class sizes, and the equal-hiring rights for married women and mothers. It condemned the teaching of militarism while seeking greater curricular emphasis on "the social, economic and industrial development of the nations" and "the encouragement of internationalism by the introduction of elective courses on foreign languages in the grades." On February 5, 1917 her husband appeared before the current school board to present a petition against the military-training decision. It was a virtuoso performance. Let us agree, he argued, that the goal of U.S. education was to nurture initiative and individualism. But General Wingate, who introduced military education in New York State, certainly had a strange conception of it: "I want a young man,"

65

quoted Sugar, "when he is spoken to by someone in authority to stand up and look him in the face and then do what he is told without question." Sugar ranged into a variety of other subjects, including the condemnation of the recent militarization of the Boy Scouts whose national chief, Ernest Thompson Seton, had resigned in protest over this trend.

For U.S. Socialists, the involvement of their country in the war was not altogether unexpected. But they were not prepared for the consequences of their decision to take a resolute stand against it. Of all the major Marxist parties in the world, save the Bolsheviks, theirs was the most internationally minded and antiwar. In following their convictions, however, they ran into a buzz saw of hatred, fueled by a government that came closer than any in U.S. history to creation of a police state.

When Wilson took the path toward intervention in February, Socialists joined with Anarchists, Wobblies, and pacifists, as well as liberals like William Jennings Bryan, Robert LaFollette, and George Norris in protest. They all focused on the narrow economic interests that supported U.S. participation. Norris summed it up on April 4: "We are going to war upon the command of gold." For his part, Sugar often quoted a blatant statement by the National Business Alliance (signed by Theodore Roosevelt and William Howard Taft): "Rivalries begin in commerce and end on battlefields. . . . Whatever the diplomatic excuse, every great conflict in modern times had its origin in some question of property rights." The politicians agreed: the vote for war on April 6, 1917 was 82 to 6 in the Senate and 373 to 50 in the House.

While this precise consequence was not expected so soon when, several weeks earlier, the Socialist party called an emergency convention to meet in St. Louis on April 7, it was understood that the debate there would focus on the party's position regarding the war question. As it turned out, the delegates had to face the ultimate issue immediately.

The call for the emergency convention went out on March 15, and delegates from Detroit were elected on April 2 at Duffield Hall by the largest membership turnout in history. Three delegates could be elected (outstate Michigan had four), and Sugar was the top vote getter, followed by chapter president Westfall and state secretary Keracher. The "reds" thus had one delegate, the "yellows" two. Whatever their color, their spirit bordered on revolutionary. The lead article of the *Michigan Socialist* on April 6 began by emphasizing that peace and a truly democratic Europe were close at hand. The March revolution in Russia had overthrown the "bloody Romanov dynasty and has established a democratic republic." German workers were resisting the war as never before and entire segments of the moderate Left were abandoning the Kaiser. And this was the moment the plutocrats decided to go to war! Let them beware. "The recent threats of the eight hour strike and the food riots in the very teeth of the violent flag-waving should have warned these madmen, but it seems the sign was lost completely. The moment war is declared, it will hasten the fall of American plutocracy."

66

Detroit Socialists (all three delegates were on the newspaper's board) thus foresaw the potentiality of revolutionary resistance to the war, the position being taken by the far Left in the party under Louis Boudin of New York and Charles Ruthenberg of Cleveland. The old center (Sugar and his friends) was radicalizing as the tensions at home and abroad intensified. A California jury had just convicted Socialist labor activist Tom Mooney for allegedly blowing up ten people in a San Francisco "preparedness" parade. The IWWs arrested in connection with the Everett massacre—the bloody war between Wobblies and deputies in that Washington town—were coming to trial. Huge demonstrations in Germany, mutinies in the French army, and strikes in the British munitions industry, all considerably influenced by leftists, marked the early months of 1917. Socialists such as Sugar could be proud of their Marxism and feel confident about their ability to have an impact on the course of history. Maybe the revolution *was* coming.

Maurice and Jane took the overnight to St. Louis and arrived in time for the opening of the convention at 10:30 A.M. The only real issue was what the antiwar resolution would say, and thus the main work of the convention was done in the War and Militarism Committee, which met endlessly. This body, with fifteen members, gathered together most of the major voices of the party. It was chaired by Kate Richards O'Hare and included Hillquit, Spargo, Boudin, and Ruthenberg. Sugar was not on the committee and, while fascinated by other activities and enthusiastic about meeting fellow socialists from around the nation, remained isolated from the heart of the convention's activities.

It turned out to be Hillquit's affair. He had no problem with a strong, vigorous antiwar statement. The main thing he wanted to avoid was Boudin's authorship of the final resolution. Boudin and his circle in New York had already made a commitment to the Bolsheviks, especially due to the influence of Russian exile Nikolai Bukharin, whose newspaper, *Novy mir*, had become an important source of left-wing theory. Bukharin had urged the Left to form a new organization (on the Bolshevik model) and thus represented a threat to Socialist unity. Indeed, had it not been for the brief stay of Leon Trotsky in New York, the Left might well have fomented a split. At the meeting on January 14, 1917, Trotsky managed to get a vote in favor of establishing a separate English-language journal expressing the views of the Left but condemning any split. On March 4, Trotsky led the fight, along with Louis Fraina, a gifted young Marxist theoretician and ally of Boudin's, in support of a resolution favoring physical resistance to conscription should war occur. It lost by a narrow margin to Hillquit's somewhat more moderate statement in a meeting remembered by Louis Waldman as the "stormiest . . . I ever witnessed." The struggle for power within the Socialist party was on.

At St. Louis, therefore, Hillquit's key concern was less ideological than political. Once he got the more compromising Ruthenberg to go along with his strong resolution (the one that ultimately became the official party position), the Bolshevik Left, although it had triumphed ideologically, knew it could not control the party. Boudin, to save face, wrote a slightly more radical resolution, signed by only three members. Spargo, a minority of one, wrote a prowar position that emphasized the need to cooperate with the government in order to obtain peace terms advantageous to international socialism, democracy, and the interests of the working class.

When the resolutions were finally brought to the floor on the fifth day of the convention, it was hard for the average delegate to understand what the delay had been all about, especially since the prowar resolution had such little support. Sugar's reactions to it all were probably typical of most of the 176 delegates:

> The debate which ensued left me bewildered. The majority report was vigorously supported by Morris Hillquit, a New York lawyer; and vigorously attacked by another antiwar protagonist, Louis Boudin, also a New York lawyer. Both were able debaters, but I had a great deal of difficulty in grasping the essential difference between them. It appeared to me that Hillquit's arguments represented the skill of a master of advocacy, while Boudin's displayed the erudition of a profound scholar —a "revolutionary" scholar. Perhaps due to a lack of maturity in the consideration of fundamental socialist principles in their application to international affairs, I felt that their differences were largely a matter of phraseology. To me the meat seemed to be the same, the differences being in the cooking. The fact that the two leading cooks were excellent ones tended to make the slight differences appear to be important.

Sugar's appreciation of the events was most perceptive, even though he modestly assumed that there were theoretical profundities that he was not grasping. What he was missing, of course, was the politics of factionalism, a subject that he would later understand more clearly but tolerate no more easily.

The convention's great tragedy for Sugar was Spargo's role. "This was the same Spargo whose books on socialism were among those which I had first read on the subject and which had undoubtedly influenced my early thinking." Sugar voted with the majority (140 delegates). Boudin's resolution got 31—only Keracher from Michigan—and the prowar position won but five votes. Unfortunately, this represented considerably more than that paltry total because many of the party's best known publicists—William English Walling, A. M. Simons, Charles Edward Russell, Spargo, and Upton Sinclair among them—would resign and indeed become more vigorously prowar than many of the key defenders of the administration. Spargo went on to play a particularly inglorious role as a force in the American Alliance for Labor and Democracy, an organization created by the probusiness National Civic Federation and supported by Gompers to counteract the socialist-sponsored People's Council for Peace and Democracy. Russell did him one better by joining the Root Commission to Russia "wearing old clothes so that [he] could talk the Bolsheviks out of their revolution." Sugar did not fully articulate the sense of betrayal that he felt for such turncoats, but there can be little doubt that his ongoing mistrust of bourgeois intellectuals in part stemmed from this experience. At the very least it helped him develop his political definitions. "I was to learn that a large proportion of those who repudiated their previously professed views were such as might, with considerable accuracy, be considered 'liberals.' [Perhaps] they prompted Heywood Broun to say: 'A liberal is a man who leaves the room when the fight begins.' I was to see plenty of this in later years, both in and out of the movement."

The St. Louis resolution was straightforward Marxism. The war was condemned as a violation of the principle of internationalism and the worldwide solidarity of workers. All wars have one consequence: to bring "wealth and power to the ruling classes and suffering, death, and demoralization to the workers." They breed irrational racism and nationalism and destroy political rights and liberties. The resolution urged the workers of all countries "to refuse to support their governments in their wars." And most fundamentally: "the only struggle which would justify the workers in taking up arms is the struggle of the working class of the world to free itself from economic exploitation and political oppression." This was the manifesto that twenty-one thousand socialists approved (with only three hundred against) in the national referendum and became their beacon for the next two years.

For Sugar and for the Detroit movement in general, the heart of the battle became the struggle against conscription. Although not signed into law until May 17, the draft bill had been introduced immediately after the declaration of war. For a nation that had only once, in 1863, known the forced enlistment of military personnel and had been a magnet for immigrants escaping conscription in the Old World, the idea of the draft was shocking. Socialists made it the key antiwar issue. In Detroit, they turned May Day into a massive anticonscription event, which, despite rain, ended with a capacity house at Arcadia Hall. Nightly speeches in all parts of the city followed.

One of the key problems faced by the Socialists was the prowar position adopted by the national AFL. But Detroit local unions did not simply fall into line. Printers Local 18 and Frank Martel on the federation board condemned the war. The Detroit locals of the International Association of Machinists, breaking with national policy, did the same, saying, "If Mr. Gompers wishes to fight, let him do so against [the capitalist] class, *not for* it. Long live the fraternalization of mankind and the fight against exploitation and oppression!" Other pockets of opposition existed as well, and *Labor News* editors Cascaden and Deutelbaum were against the war.

Thus, while a majority of the delegates to the central body were convinced by Gompers that the concessions to be reaped by labor in the war period would outweigh negative consequences, the Detroit labor movement by no means turned its back on the antiwar agitators. Many union halls welcomed antiwar speakers and even allowed Nearing's *The Great Madness* and a new pamphlet by Hulet Wells, *No Conscription, No Involuntary Servitude, No Slavery,* on their shelves. The *Labor News* failed to print pronunciamentos on behalf of the war effort coming from AFL headquarters. In June, the Detroit federation voted to endorse the anticonscription position of the People's Council for Peace and

69

Democracy. Gompers forced them to rescind, but they submitted only at the moment when the federal government was wiping out the council anyway. Finally, the Detroit AFL did not turn its back on its Socialist friends. Sugar, for example, continued to get labor cases. His first job after St. Louis was to defend a fireman at the city-owned Belle Isle power plant who had been "requested" to sign away his overtime rights because of the national emergency and refused. He was then fired. The federation lauded Sugar and wished him well with the case—which he lost.

The Socialists were uncompromising and sometimes tried the patience of their labor allies. On May 25, the *Michigan Socialist* became national news. A huge drawing of a wounded, one-legged soldier captioned "Worse than Death" dominated the upper half of the front page with the following resolution, "adopted by the Socialist Party of Detroit," beneath it:

> The Government of the United States, in the interest of the capitalist class, has now plunged this country into the mad orgy of death and destruction which is convulsing the nations of the old world and has forced conscription on the people of this country.
>
> We, the Socialist Party of Detroit, in joint meeting assembled, reaffirm our allegiance to the principle of international working class solidarity, reiterate our unalterable opposition to the war, and denounce the law just passed to conscript workers into military service.
>
> This law forces into "involuntary servitude" a portion of the population of this country, and we brand it as a violation of the spirit of the 13th Amendment of the Constitution.
>
> In the name of the workers, who will bleed but not benefit, we pledge ourselves to oppose registration for conscription by refusing to enroll on registration day and we call upon all workers to refrain from signifying their willingness to kill the workers of any other nation.
>
> Better freedom of a prison cell than slavery in the interest of commercialism!

This statement was drafted by the Detroit leadership. Sugar's hand in it was obviously important.

But he had more to think about than encouraging others not to register. He was liable for service too. There would be no question about where he stood. Jane gave her full support, although his parents were less than enthusiastic. In one exchange, his father indicated that when Maurice reached his age he might give up his Socialist foolishness. Maurice replied: "You're not so old. Maybe by the time you're as old as Debs, you might see the light."

The Detroit Socialists had a big rally on June 3 and awaited registration day two days later. The party decided not to use force to obstruct registration. There had already been a number of violent exchanges between proponents of peace and "patriotic" citizens, and it was thought that violence would only aid the enemy. As it turned out, registration percentages were high everywhere.

Nevertheless, police began to go to meetings of Socialists (and, indeed, to any place where young people gathered) to check for nonregistrants. The harvest was good. Precise figures have never been assembled, but from accounts in the press, arrests in Detroit over the next year ran into the hundreds. Nationwide, before it was over, arrests for nonregistration and "conspiracy" to prevent registration—which became the charge (under the Espionage Act passed on June 15, 1917) for anyone advocating draft resistance—probably topped ten thousand and the number of convictions reached something like three thousand. The Espionage Act became the basis for wholesale violations of civil rights. Max Eastman summed it up in a piece prepared for the American Union against Militarism. (*The Masses* was destroyed by the government in August–October 1917.)

> I used to say that there was nothing very peculiar about Prussia except that she was organized for war, and that if we organized for war we would turn into another Prussia. But I thought it might take a little time for us to do it. I didn't know we had so much imperial talent already in office. The suppression of the Socialist press has actually been more rapid and efficient in this republic than it was in the German Empire after the declaration of war. And as for our celebrated Anglo-Saxon tradition of free speech—it is the memory of a myth. You can't even collect your thoughts without getting arrested for unlawful assemblage. They give you ninety days for quoting the Declaration of Independence, six months for quoting the Bible, and pretty soon somebody is going to get a life sentence for quoting Woodrow Wilson in the wrong connection.

The public hysteria that accompanied the war and resistance to it is one of the best-known and bleakest chapters in U.S. history. Anything German, from measles to sauerkraut, became suspect and had its name changed. Hundreds of people of German extraction were mistreated, maimed, tarred and feathered, and, finally, a man named Prager was lynched in Collinsville, Missouri. Any opponent of the war, whatever his or her reason, was deemed a traitor and similarly treated. All labor activists and all radicals were assumed to be enemy agents, as were most aliens simply because they were foreign. The "unruly" needed more ruling, and the *New York Times* set the tone when it praised conscription: "The Selective Draft Act gives a long and sorely needed means of disciplining a certain insolent foreign element in this nation."[11]

In such an atmosphere, Sugar's days as a free man were numbered. He was a double violator, a resister and an advocate of resistance. Even before the Espionage Act came to be applied, Nathan Welch, the editor of the *Michigan Socialist,* was jailed, and the June 15 issue was kept out of the mails by postal officials. On June 22 the first Detroit draft resister, Max Goldfarb, was put on trial. Sugar was one of his lawyers, handling all aspects of the failure to register charges. A team of prominent civil-liberties lawyers, led by Ormund Hunt and including William Henry Gallagher, Joseph Seltzer, Joseph Beckenstein, and

71

Walter Nelson, were also involved in the case. Several other young men were indicted and brought into the case, which Judge Tuttle, a harsh but reputedly fair judge, turned into a mass trial. The defense strategy, Sugar remembered (curiously he does not emphasize his own role at all in his memoirs), was to make the prosecution actually prove its case: it is much more difficult to prove that someone did not do something than that they did. Also, it had to come up with proof of age as well. Thus, unlike virtually anyplace else in the nation, the Detroit cases went on and on, much to the amusement of the Socialists—and largely to the satisfaction of strict Judge Tuttle.

Sugar was finally arrested himself for conspiracy to obstruct in late July. This was the first charge that he faced, along with Welch and the three other members of the editorial board. The case became complicated when they realized that Sugar had not registered and he was arraigned for that on August 4. (He had never volunteered his age and had no birth certificate. Minnie Belanger thought that she was doing him a favor when the federal agents came to Brimley and asked about his age. She remembered it perfectly well since her Tom was born just a week later than Maurice.)

The outcome of the trial was a foregone conclusion: on December 7, 1917 Welch, convicted under the conspiracy charge and regarded as the chief mis-leader of youth, got eighteen months at Leavenworth; two others were fined five hundred dollars for conspiring; and Sugar and Sam Diamond received fines plus a year in the Detroit House of Correction for failing to register. The fines-only for conspiracy were part of a deal made with the prosecution for entering a general plea of guilty to all charges. The prosecution thought that it was done with the case and that no appeal was possible because of the guilty plea. But Sugar had discovered that if an "arrest of judgment" motion is made by the defense attorney after the sentence, an appeal may be made. Sugar already had a reputation as a "technicalities" man. This one assured immortality, because his case, *Sugar v. U.S.* 252 F. 79, was appealed to the Supreme Court (though not heard) and would be cited not only in future cases dealing with the constitutionality of the draft, but also in the famous *Shenk v. U.S.* (1919) in which Justice Holmes pronounced the "clear and present danger" doctrine. It also kept Sugar out of jail for an entire year.

While late 1917 and the following year were hard ones for individuals facing the wrath of the government or whipped-up crowds, they were also important years of growth for the U.S. Socialist party. Obviously, plenty of Americans agreed with its war stand and its condemnation of the treatment of labor in face of the gigantic profits capital was collecting from war production. Party membership soared, and in city after city the 1917 elections showed massive Socialist gains. In New York, despite incredible red-baiting and racism, Hillquit piled up 145 thousand votes in the race for mayor while the moderate and mildly antiwar Democrat Judge Hylan was swept in. A vicious prowar campaign had failed miserably. In Detroit, such triumphs were less in evidence. The economy boomed with the war, reaction fed by racism flowered as large numbers of blacks moved in for jobs, and the old coalition of "progressives" and big business held its own. Red-baiting tended to work in this city: Sugar himself helped *Detroit Saturday Night* sell copies on two occasions: one an attack on "Maurice Sugar, the callow emulator of the Russian extremists" and another on the "Bolshevism" of the Detroit Federation of Labor for its willingness to defend Sugar while calling for the boycott of a speech by Theodore Roosevelt.

Nevertheless, the spark between Left and labor remained alive. Sugar's final speech before Judge Tuttle was reprinted in the *Detroit Labor News,* which praised his character and his goals as a Socialist, if not his stand on the war. As he put it, "the only fight for democracy in the world today is the fight by workers of all countries for the ownership of industry—without which democracy of political institutions is a delusion." The hardest blow for Sugar and the one that received the roundest condemnation from the federation, however, was the disbarment proceedings initiated by the Detroit Bar Association a month after his sentencing. Sugar naturally asked for a show-cause hearing, which, after being scheduled before Judge Mandell late in the month of January, led to a flurry of activity in Sugar's support. A resolution approved unanimously by the Detroit federation showed that labor's faith in him was untarnished and emphasized its immense debt to him. "Sugar has served us, and done it well, often without compensation or hope of reward, and in his hour of struggle and trial . . . we must do what we can to save him from being deprived of the right to plead our cause in the future." He also was supported in his cause by ninety of his professional colleagues, who signed a petition encouraging Judge Mandell to overrule disbarment. Mandell hardly listened to the counterarguments. As of January 30, 1918, Sugar could no longer practice law.[12]

The year 1918 was heavily burdened with preparations for the ongoing appeals, but Jane—now working full time as a legal secretary for Joe Beckenstein—and Maurice managed to put their energies behind a renewed attempt to breathe life into the Detroit party, which—despite the relative good will of labor—had not followed the national trend. Its paper was destroyed and its leadership was on trial, out on bail, or jailed. There were rallies and parades, speeches and meetings, but the old verve was missing. Then an idea struck—and grew. What Detroit socialism needed, especially now when renting meeting halls was so difficult, given the political climate, was its own "center," a place for meetings and all sorts of activities. And, as it turned out, there were plenty of available buildings with the proper facilities. Why? Because Michigan went dry early in the year. Prohibition had possibly no other positive consequence. Large meeting halls were cheap, and the German branch of the party knew just the place: Schiller Hall, beer garden of yesterday, at Gratiot and St. Aubin.

Suddenly the moribund party came to life. Ten thousand dollars was raised for a down payment via campaigns, parties, rallies, and raffles. In late April 1918, Sugar and his friends sat down to lay out all the legal language governing the control and ownership of the rambling and inviting building to be christened the *House of the Masses.* A constitution was written—access was guaranteed to all

73

sympathetic groups, but the center was owned by a corporation made up of the Detroit Socialist-party membership. It had a restaurant, game rooms, seminar rooms, and a large hall. It was an immediate force in building the party. Memberships shot back up and their campaigns now had a proper headquarters.

The continuing drive to raise money for the House of the Masses (the total cost was seventy thousand dollars) combined with another activity that would soon dominate the party's concerns: rendering support, both moral and material, to the Bolshevik Revolution. The national party had responded positively from the beginning to the events of November 1917 in Russia, but very quickly the issue of the party's relationship to the war once again became the key issue. Wilson realized immediately that the Bolshevik victory meant an advantage to the Central Powers and within a month had begun to develop the more moderate line that resulted in the Fourteen Points. In doing so, he espoused the Socialist principles of no annexations and no indemnities. This created considerable confusion in the ranks of the party and some (including Eastman) found it possible to support the administration. Moreover, many felt, despite the Treaty of Brest-Litovsk, that the defeat of Germany was necessary to secure the Bolshevik victory. Others, however, staunchly maintained their pacifism while others still sought to utilize war weariness to develop the U.S. revolution. Thus the war continued to hold center stage in socialist debates with the Russian Revolution acting as an exhilerating, though complicating factor. Only by the end of the summer had things sorted out sufficiently (the German defeat appeared imminent while allied intervention in Russia emerged as the greater threat to the revolution), that the Socialist party, characteristically following the lead of Debs, was able to focus clearly on the revolution, declaring through a party secretaries' conference in Chicago its "accord with Revolutionary Russia" and urging "our government and our people to cooperate with it."[13]

The Russian Revolution in Detroit

The new preoccupation with the events in Russia was evident in the Detroit party. The reds, under Keracher, Renner, and Batt, now assumed that the only task was the preparation of the people for revolution, as Lenin had urged in a general way. To this end, they became more ardent than ever in their emphasis on worker education. They had also managed to gain control of the virtually bankrupt *Michigan Socialist* and, after a few weeks, began to issue a largely theoretical paper called the *Proletarian*. One of the chief sources of support for the old Left were members of the Russian branch, associated with the Russian Language Federation and therefore not voting members of the party. As in the Russian Federation everywhere, membership skyrocketed during 1918, and by the time of the state convention in September, the Detroit Russian group numbered around three hundred. A particularly able organizer, identified by

Justice Department agents only as Dr. Rovin, had been sent from New York to develop the Detroit Russian Federation. He spoke English—indeed was reportedly a "brilliant orator"—and therefore also held full party membership.

Another facet of the growing focus on the Russian Revolution were the actions of the federal government. Justice Department agents now increasingly concerned themselves with manifestations of "Bolsheviki" activity, spying on all sorts of Socialist party members' gatherings where discussion of the events in Russia and their ramifications for working-class revolution generally were likely to be discussed. Sugar and his circle, despite their continued identification as yellows, came under regular anti-Bolshevik surveillance during the summer of 1918. We learn, for example, that he had weekly meetings at his house (they had recently moved to a place at 1109 West Euclid, a single dwelling not far from the Clairmount flat) at which "men attending arrive cautiously and leave past midnight." The agent probably fantasized all the mystery, but he did identify "aliens" known to be "fanatics" for the Bolshevik cause. These Sunday evening gatherings would continue for years and served as a kind of round-table group over which Sugar presided; reading and discussion of issues of interest to working people and their advocates was the purpose. It is significant that in mid-1918 Sugar kept his door open to the Left and clearly sought to learn from the Russians. On July 10 another agent attended a general rally honoring Maxim Gorky, at which Sugar spoke. Besides raising money for the House of the Masses, he spent several minutes glorifying the Bolshevik cause and in particular praised Trotsky who "has taught the workmen of America, England, France and other countries how to strengthen social revolution all over the world." Sugar himself remembered speaking on several occasions to the Russian branch, his remarks being translated as he spoke. Overall, the links with Russia and Leninism were beginning to be forged.

Nevertheless, Sugar remained with his old faction. The state convention of the Socialist party was held in the House of the Masses on September 7 and 8. In the absence of surviving local-party records, we are fortunate that it was observed by a vigilant agent of the privately funded but officially recognized American Protective League (APL). Indeed, given the generally literate tone of the report, unlike many by paid spies, the volunteer may have been one of those "upper-crust" folks whom the APL prided itself on recruiting.

Sugar was chairman of the convention again, voted in by a very narrow margin. Left and "Right" were nearly equally balanced. Fifty-six delegates were seated, and Sugar's group largely had their way. The candidates nominated for state offices (including Jane Mayer for the board of education) were yellows. The critical issues at the convention revolved around the level of support to be given to the Russian Revolution and the European revolutionary cause in general. Two resolutions introduced by Keracher and Dr. Rovin became the focus of debate. One stated that the Michigan party would support to the end "the revolutionary working class of Germany, Russia, and all others." Sugar, as chairman, was concerned that such a resolution might be illegal under the Espionage Act and convinced the assembly to table it until the lawyers at the convention could determine this. The second resolution sought "to support the Soviet Government in every possible way and to the last dollar and man." It met the same fate.

It would appear that Sugar, despite his growing interest in the Bolshevik cause, nevertheless was not yet ready to join with his old enemies to support resolutions whose language he felt went beyond the tone of the national party's. Even Debs would not make his famous statement about being a Bolshevik from head to toe until early the following year.

Also, Sugar may have wanted to forestall controversy at the convention because Debs was speaking to its big Sunday afternoon Moose Hall rally on the 8th. The party leader normally drew thousands of non-Socialists to hear his oratory, and one would hate to have the Sunday-morning press blare out new anti-Socialist slanders. (Bud Reynolds, a good friend of Sugar's in later years, remembered that Debs was paid five hundred dollars *by Fair authorities* to speak at the Michigan State Fair in 1914 because he was in such great demand. He gave the money to the Detroit local.) Hundreds were turned away from the Moose Hall speech, and when he took the podium he was greeted by a standing ovation that went on for "30 rounds of applause." The financial results were striking. The Michigan party cleared fifteen hundred dollars from sales of tickets, photographs of Debs, and literature. The money went directly into the House of the Masses fund. Following Debs's speech, Rovin spoke in Russian to an ecstatic response from "four hundred Russians" in the audience.

The convention then went into its final session. Apparently, the earlier issues were not raised again, but the Left had another axe to grind—the financing and general support of the *Proletarian*. Renner introduced the motion that it become, in effect, the official organ of the state party. "Sugar and Bavly . . . fought against this and claimed that 'The Proletarian' did not follow the policy of the National Office. . . . The lawyers and most of the foreigners," especially the Germans, sided with them. The fight went on until midnight with each trying to outlast the other. The final tally was fifteen to thirteen in favor of the yellows—a sorry end, but typical of the virulence of the struggle.

More importantly, the seeds of the future were laid that night. According to the APL's tireless reporter, "a group of the Reds got together and went downtown to a restaurant where they had supper together. The group was comprised of Keracher, Batt, Renner and three other Detroiters, also Sand, Talbott, and Herrlick of Flint, Brown of Pigeon [River], and Early of Benton Harbor." They then went to "the Proletarian Club on John R street" and laid out the plans for "a new organization," the Proletarian University of America. Given the "control of the movement" by the yellows, the reds "[were] drawing off from the rest and this new proposition [was] the result." Their goal was to create a revolutionary educational movement in Oregon, Washington, Ohio, New York, Illinois, and Pennsylvania—the other states where the reds were strong—and before adjourning at 2:30 A.M. on September 9, they had elected officers of the new organization. Renner would be president, and Keracher secretary. This was a frankly renegade move provoked no doubt by the repeated defeats of the Left at the hands of Sugar and his friends over the last forty-eight hours.[14]

As it turned out, the national scope of the Proletarian University never materialized, and the split mentality, whatever the form might be, was too weak, save in the heads of a few intellectuals like Louis Fraina, to produce a separate organization at that point. Moreover, circumstances on both the national and international fronts over the next six months made a split in the U.S. party increasingly foolish, since the Left was gaining power rapidly. In Michigan, this was especially the case, and the national party's decision to allow the Russian Language Federation full voting status in the party changed the left wing's strength dramatically. They came to dominate the local and state party and, as we shall see, would become the "bad boys" of the Socialist Party of America. Nevertheless, it is important to understand the origins of the "proletarian" impulse, and the invaluable Justice Department file reveals a story never before told. We shall have a better appreciation of the renegade Michiganders as they carom crazily through the history of the great Socialist-Communist schism of 1919. And we are forced to wonder what might have happened had their nemesis of the past—who seemed to have almost a lion tamer's ability to control them but who was also increasingly coming to understand their position—*not* been taken out of the fray.

In mid-November, the Supreme Court of the United States refused to hear Sugar's appeal. On November 25, 1918, two weeks after the war had ended, the "dynamo" of Detroit socialism entered the Detroit House of Correction.

3 ✤ PRISON AND POLITICS,
1918–23

Sugar spent ten months in prison. He immersed himself in the daily conflicts of prison life, made friends with prisoners, and helped to improve prison conditions. He also had the opportunity to read much of the social and political theory that he had left aside during the preceding years of constant activity. The year of his imprisonment was marked by massive political upheaval around the world and in the United States. His vicarious relationship to these explosive times allowed him a degree of detachment not possible for many of his contemporaries and meant that he could avoid many of the irreconcilable differences arising from the heat of battle in 1919. Still, his political ideas moved decidedly to the left, causing a permanent break with many of his old allies.

Sugar in Jail

The first weeks, especially, were agony. Jane wrote tender, loving letters. On November 29, she wrote, "I walked the boulevard from Woodward to Grand River this evening coming home from Pearl's. It was a wonderful sight! I wonder if there is a window in your cell so you see the stars. The stars make me think of you—your beautiful eyes." But the real torment was to be at home alone. "If only you were in the big comfy chair beside me, reading your newspaper, so I could tease you and make you kiss me and beg me to sit quiet so you could finish." Finally, Kalman and Mary Sugar moved in with her, giving her more to occupy her attention and relieving some of the loneliness.

There is a delicate, playful sweetness in the surviving love letters between Jane and Maurice. There is also depth and maturity. They were best friends who shared all that they did. "It seemed so strange," wrote Jane, "to attend a mass meeting without you." But the fullness of their romantic love was also obvious.

Because of prison regulations, Maurice could only write to her every two weeks. His letters therefore tended to be more mundane, often including messages to others. His expressions of feeling were rarer and more condensed. Above all, they came in the form of poetry. A flurry of poems reflecting the same sentiments as Jane's letters accompanied his early letters. "You Kissed Me," "Rem'bers," "One Soft Caress," and "A Wish" were some of the titles.

Sugar's outlook in prison remained generally cheerful. In his letters, there were no indications of self-pity, doubts about what he had done, or complaints about his personal comfort. Even in the journal that he began to keep on January 1, 1919, such complaints were likely as not turned into jokes. But there was nothing funny about the degrading conditions in this place. The Detroit House of Correction was built in 1861 for the temporary purpose of housing Civil War prisoners. It was dark and dank and filthy. Sugar's tiny cell had a straw cot attached to the wall, a three-tiered rack in the corner, and a pail for refuse. That was all. The main guard—called only "the deputy"—was a brutish character who carried a huge cane that he swung at the least provocation. The food was slop, punctuated by weekly treats of meat and fruit. Worst of all, prisoners were not allowed to talk to one another. A brief, silent march in the court constituted their daily exercise. Early in his term, Sugar summed up his reaction to the prison in a poem that began,

> This is the place where manhood dies
> And the stricken soul in anguish lies

He vowed that he would change it.

The presence of someone as well known as Sugar, however, put this backward jail under public scrutiny. Sugar made friends easily with other prisoners and also got on well with many of the guards, upon whom he lavished requested legal advice. This helped when he began to act as a spokesman for the prisoners' concerns. Through comments to visitors and sympathetic guards, who told him that many of the "rules" were personal whims of the deputy, he began to draw the attention of the prison board to conditions at the jail.

Sugar also used the moral-uplift lectures sponsored by the board to mock prevailing philosophies of rehabilitation. They emphasized Horatio Alger key-to-success stories and how to cope with society without trying to change it. An organization called *Pathfinders,* developed to assist exconvicts, brought such messages to the prisoners. To take one example, Mr. Wright, its founder, gave a speech about the power of positive thinking. Sugar countered with the story of the barn filled with popcorn and housing a horse. "The barn caught fire. Did the horse burn? He did not. The popping corn popped, the horse thought it was snowing and instead of burning, he froze to death. Ah, the power of the mind!" Sugar's willingness to challenge speakers caused others to do the same, and increasingly a variety of issues were raised, further illuminating both the prob-

79

lems of the prison and the humanity of the prisoners for board members who often came to these gatherings.

Early in February the city chose a new "reform" board. It was headed by Mary Thompson Stevens, a prominent philanthropist. On February 3 came the electrifying news that a noisy period, 5:30–6:30 P.M., would be allowed. On April 13, Stevens announced that the warden had resigned and that she would be acting superintendent. She promised a variety of reforms and lifted the rule of silence in the shops. The assembled prisoners shouted their approval and encouraged Sugar to say a few words. He did so, voicing the appreciation of the inmates and concluding with a call for a vote of confidence for the new board. The response was overwhelming.

In the weeks that followed, the atmosphere in the prison changed significantly. Most of the major health issues were dealt with, and a recreation program, which gave Sugar the chance to play softball and to box, provided the exercise so long denied the prisoners. For Sugar, all of this had a somewhat embarrassing result. The *Detroit News,* always on the lookout for 100 percent "Americans," had interpreted Sugar's speech of thanks as proof that he had recanted his earlier views. His "loyalty" to the prison administration marked the triumph of the new rehabilitation program. Sugar greeted this story more with amusement than with consternation. But a week later, Mr. Wright of the Pathfinders proceeded to take credit for Sugar's return to the path of righteousness. The issue became semiserious when his friend and fellow socialist, Bob Westfall, attacked Wright and his organization in a letter to the *News.* There was nothing wrong with Sugar's character in the first place, he said, and Wright's claim "smacks of cheap advertising." A further exchange followed, and Sugar's reputation as an unreconstructed Socialist was reestablished.

Without question, the most gratifying consequence of Sugar's time in prison was the bond of comradeship that he developed with other prisoners. They often talked about their crimes. Some were proud of their deeds, others contrite, but in general Sugar was impressed with the lack of hypocrisy that he found in almost everything they said. Sugar was surprised by the attitude of most toward women. It was not so much the heavily sexual nature of many of their comments that bothered him, but the indifference they showed toward wives and sweethearts. But, he said, it became understandable "when one sees the number of divorce suits started against men who are in prison." Women who "stick by their man" were regarded as "most unusual specimens."

While it was not universal, "the good humor of some prisoners," Sugar remembered, "was irrepressible. No amount of brutality seemed to dampen it." One of Sugar's best friends was Tom, a big, fifty-year-old Irishman, who worked with him in the shipping room. He and Sugar would get into those situations where the tiniest glance would send them both into gales of uncontrollable laughter. The only problem was that Tom had to load stacks of chairs onto waiting trucks. The game was to try to break him up while he was carrying stacks of chairs. They also sat together in chapel, with inevitable results.

Sugar made no effort to preach socialism to his friends. Yet it was obvious that sympathy for his position was widespread. Sugar was convinced that as his friendships grew a growing respect for 'bolshevism' accompanied them. "It was not long before it had many champions, quite ill-informed, but altogether solid." Sugar loved to tell one story in later years. He and a friend were getting their weekly shave from inmate barbers, when a stubby young tough named Mac—who was just beginning to serve "a life sentence in installments of thirty, sixty, and ninety days"—came up to the door of the barber shed and sneered; "I see you got a Bolshevik in here." "Two," said the man in the other chair, "And what the hell of it?" growled Sugar's barber. "Three of 'em," jeered the man at the door. The other barber made it four and when "the damned little runt" continued his derisive comments, the two barbers turned on him with razors in hand. "Whoa now," said Mac, "there are five of us!" These kinds of incidents and low-key comraderie gave Sugar the untypical experience of actually watching the cause benefit by his presence. Socialist war resisters elsewhere were usually mistreated by other inmates.[1]

Sugar's political outlook did not remain stationary, however. He read voraciously from the moment he arrived (ten novels, a half dozen scientific works, and a raft of magazine articles were digested before Christmas). His nonfiction reading was diverse, but he gave more attention to Marxist classics than he had in the past and even completed all three volumes of *Capital*.

Sugar had already moved to the left before entering prison. The bonds of past friendship more than politics kept him tied to the yellows. But he also felt that the leaders of the Michigan left wing often made the cause look foolish by their bombast and their weakness in cogent argument. To illustrate: Sugar liked Dennis Batt's first articles in an exchange with editor Nimmo in *Detroit Saturday Night*. Then he watched Nimmo get away with stating that Engels had not foreseen the trust, when in fact a whole section of *Socialism, Utopian and Scientific* was devoted to industrial concentration. Batt later allowed the debate to degenerate into mere nitpicking and he was consistently on the defensive. Sugar did not object to the positions Batt was taking, only to his competence.

The development of Sugar's thought in 1919 can be traced through his letters, his prison "order book," and writings while in jail. The first indicator came in mid-February. He revised his speech, "Law and the Prevailing Order," for publication in the *New York Call Magazine*. A number of alterations toughened the language, but the main change was a new ending: "The final struggle has started. The rumble of conflict fills the air as it rolls across the waters of the world. The social revolution is on."

There was good reason to believe this was so. Despite the brutal suppression of the radical Spartakus League by Social Democrat Gustav Noske, the German revolution still appeared to have a chance to materialize as many soviets, including Kurt Eisner's Soviet Republic of Bavaria, continued to hold on. Bela Kun in Hungary was on the ascendant and would soon create another, though highly volatile, Communist regime. In Austria and Bohemia the Left controlled

81

the Social Democratic parties. Italy and England continued to seethe with agitation. In western Canada the One Big Union movement gained ground and craft unions radicalized. The Winnipeg general strike was on its way. On February 2 came the general strike in Seattle. Although it began when the AFL craft unions decided to support striking dockworkers, it turned into an excuse for Mayor Ole Hansen to close down every Wobbly hall in town ("We didn't have any law to do it with, so we used nails"). The AFL pulled out and the strike ended on the tenth. In mid-January there had occurred a huge "Mooney congress" in Chicago, which considered calling a nationwide strike to protest Mooney's imprisonment. While the congress was roundly condemned by AFL officialdom, twelve hundred AFL affiliates from thirty-seven states attended. They set July 4, 1919 as the date for the strike.[2]

Something was afoot, and Sugar knew it. On January 31 he wrote, "If I don't get my article on the League of Nations out pretty soon there won't be any need for it—those darn Socialists are just as liable as not to go and capture international power without waiting for me to tell 'em how to do it." His "Socialism and the League of Nations" was published in May in the *Class Struggle,* Louis Boudin's monthly journal that along with Fraina's *Revolutionary Age* served as the theoretical voice of the left wing. The main argument was that while the League of Nations was presented to the world under the guise of democratic internationalism, in reality it was nothing more than a new mechanism of capitalist international power whose essential purpose was to throttle the international working-class movement. The league, he wrote, "will be the main office of the world's exploiters. . . . Capitalistic institutions have attained such gigantic proportions as to require international administration. The enemies of the workers are wielding a new sword. . . . The international spread of solidarity throughout the ranks of the proletariat generates an international spread of apprehension throughout the ranks of the bourgeoisie. The arrest of the spread of this solidarity must be the principal endeavor of the League of Nations."

The purpose of the League was thus to make the world safe for capitalism. What should be the response of the workers' movement? In the first place, in countries where the workers have captured power, the question of joining the league, in the unlikely event that they should be asked, ought not be "a question of principle" but one of expediency, of "international Socialist tactics." It is quite conceivable that it might be more useful to join whether "from considerations of preservation of the gains of the revolution" or to burrow from within to undermine the stability of the capitalist member nations. The Leninist tone continued in the conclusion, which called for a "Federation of the Proletariats of the World." This body would help worker regimes maintain themselves against counterrevolutions and aid "socialist movements throughout the world" in their drive for power. The presence of British, French, and U.S. troops in Soviet Russia demonstrated the need for an international Socialist army ready to go anywhere. More important, the federation should provide revolutionary movements with financial aid and ideas, particularly the lessons learned from countries where the revolution had already triumphed.

While the Third International was first proposed by Lenin on January 24, 1919, Sugar did not become aware of its goals until he read Robert Minor's interview with Lenin two weeks later, after his article was finished. In an entry in his notebook on February 9, he wrote: "In the same interview, when asked what he thought of the League of Nations, Lenin said: 'They are not forming a League of Nations, but a league of imperialists to strangle the nations.' Now somebody," said Sugar, "has gone and shown Lenin my article."

While Sugar was finishing "Socialism and the League of Nations," the left wing of the Socialist party began to press for power in a way that made either its dominance or a split inevitable. Party membership had grown from 73 thousand in mid-1918 to 109 thousand in January 1919. The left wing benefitted the most because of the influx of pro-Bolshevik East European emigrés. For the first time in the history of U.S. socialism, the foreign-language federations outnumbered the English-speaking membership. The *Revolutionary Age* and the *Class Struggle,* along with a dozen foreign-language journals, spoke for the left wing. The old center of the party was rapidly evaporating. Scott Nearing had become a contributing editor of the *Revolutionary Age,* appearing side by side with Fraina, John Reed, and the other left-wingers. Sugar, Westfall, and Welch (when he returned from Leavenworth in April) represented a similar shift in Michigan.

Despite Lenin's sober reminder to the U.S. in December 1918 that "the revolution in different countries proceeds along various paths, with varying rapidity," the left wing took a European perspective and assumed a revolution in the United States was nigh. It erroneously called the Right "social patriots" and consistently subordinated all other matters to the issue of the "coming revolution." With the Bolsheviks' call for the formation of a third, or communist, International, the left wing became more determined to develop a separate identity. The New York Left produced a separate platform, published on February 8 in the *Revolutionary Age.* On May 17, as the conflict came to a head, Sugar wrote to Jane that he "was quite interested in the 'Left Wing' platform. On the whole I like it, though I do think it is a little rough and crude in spots. That, however, is only natural in a newly defined position. It is valuable in its exclusion of what might be termed the Wisconsin element [Berger and his allies], which has long been a flighty wing of the party. We shall watch developments."

Its main planks called for "year-round agitation" on behalf of the Soviet Republic and the German Left and the encouragement of "mass action of the revolutionary proletariat" in the United States to destroy the capitalist state and replace it with the rule of "federated soviets." The party should engage in electoral politics only for "destructive" purposes. Industrial unions would be the organizational core for developing class consciousness. With the triumph of the revolution, worker councils would take over industry, banks, railroads, and foreign trade. All national debts would be repudiated. This Bolshevik program concluded by demanding that the Socialist party give up its "immediate demands" and "agitate exclusively for the overthrow of capitalism and the establishment of Socialism through a proletarian dictatorship."

Sugar was the least happy with the last point. In the same letter to Jane, he scoffed at the Michigan convention, which had just passed resolutions to expel any member who (1) advocated immediate demands and (2) did not take "a materialist view of the role of religion." Although an atheist, Sugar thought the second was silly: why not subject other "socially determined" phenomena—politics, science, the arts—to the same restriction? The first provision was more difficult for him. His immediate reaction was to chide Dennis Batt. He wondered "if friend Batt has yet been expelled for his support of the Detroit Federation of Labor?" Batt had recently been working hard—and with excellent results—in getting the federation to back industrial unionism in auto and had naturally had to pay lip service to its reformist perspective.

But the "immediate demands" issue was no joke. It would soon be at the heart of the explosion that destroyed the Socialist Party of America. Through March and April, the Left had marched steadily forward. Upon receipt of the word that the Communist International (Comintern) had been formed (March 4), Fraina demanded and got a national referendum on the question of joining it. The vote was 10 to 1 in favor. They then had a referendum to authorize new elections of the National Executive Committee (NEC), dominated by the yellows; the elections that followed should have swept the left wing to power. Fraina, Reed, Ruthenberg, Kate Richards O'Hare, and eight others were elected to the board. Only three right-wingers, including Hillquit, were elected. But the old board unilaterally declared the elections void and called a special meeting for May 24 to deal with the crisis.

Their manner of dealing with it assured that the party would break apart. Three days before, Hillquit had called for a purge: "Let us clear the decks." The first order of business was to expel all of Michigan's five thousand members. Twenty thousand more were removed as seven foreign-language federations bit the dust. The board "suspended" the election results and called an emergency convention to be held in Chicago on August 30. The split was official. Thousands more left-wingers quit the party. In no time, membership had shriveled to forty thousand, thus leaving around seventy thousand unattached left-wing Socialists—the nucleus of the future Communist movement in the United States. Reactions to the coup varied. Much of the leadership of the left wing said good riddance and soon called a rival convention to meet in Chicago at the same time to organize a separate Communist party. Fraina and John Reed, on the other hand, spent the summer trying to line up left-wingers to go to Chicago and try to take over the Socialist convention.

In Michigan, the Batt-Keracher forces had called an emergency state convention on June 15 to select delegates to a left-wing conference in New York. The old center had to make a choice. On June 2, Adolph Germer, the national secretary, wrote to Nathan Welch, who, like Sugar, had represented the O'Hare-

Debs militant center of the party, and asked him to arrange a meeting in Detroit of people sympathetic to the NEC position. Welch, after consulting several other centrists, responded on June 6 saying that he thought the expulsion of the state party was a "fatal blunder," especially at this moment of crisis in U.S. society. The Socialist party needed to move toward "a clear-cut revolutionary platform around which most of us could consistently rally and present an unbroken front to the enemy." The NEC should not hope to gather much support in Michigan. "It is my opinion that the locals and branches who differ from the Keracher group will affiliate with some red local or movement, but will not go along with the national office." Welch personally refused all aid to Germer and the vast majority of Michiganders agreed. In letters and petitions, Michigan Socialists from Hancock to Monroe condemned NEC decisions. Ben Baze of Port Huron put it succinctly: "Down with the Eberts and the Sheidemans [*sic*]. Hail to the Spartacans and Bolsheviks."

Only the English branch of local Grand Rapids gave any appreciable support to the Old Guard. Violet Blumenberg and Charles Taylor claimed that Keracher had stacked the Michigan state convention by denying mileage vouchers to opponents. They were glad the national "house cleaning" was now taking place. But they were even having trouble holding Grand Rapids. Bud Reynolds, a Detroit carpenter working in Muskegon, was making inroads among the Ukrainians there. "He teaches wingery instead of Marx," wrote an outraged Vi Blumenberg. A handful of isolated right-wingers were all that remained of the old party in Michigan. The Detroit yellows had virtually disappeared. Interestingly, Blumenberg wrote Germer on June 13 that "if Maurice Sugar was out of the House of Correction, we would be in a position to put on a strong fight; as it is, in his absence, our side have stupidly allowed the so-called Reds to get a strong hold on our building, The House of the Masses; they have worked a number of their gang in there."[3]

She was obviously unaware of the path her hero was currently taking. Maurice Sugar's immediate reaction was mild enough—but telling. He wrote in his notebook on June 8, "So the National Executive Committee has expelled the Socialist Party of Michigan! That expulsion includes me, both formally and in spirit." The last two words expressed his mood. His prison diary gives a rare glimpse into the mind of a Socialist moving leftward in May–June 1919:

May 1. International Labor Day! A truck driver tells me that there are many policemen around this place. He was told that they were "expecting a crowd of men to come out here and try to get Sugar out."

May 4 (letter to Jane). Truly these are times pregnant with possibilities, [when] workers' thoughts turn to breaking into jails instead of breaking out.

May 4. Said Debs, upon entering prison: "Tell my comrades that I entered the prison doors a flaming revolutionist, my head erect, my spirit untamed, and my soul unconquerable." Kate O'Hare is in, too. Good cheer, Kate.

May 6. During our recess hour I met a man who was given thirty days for selling the *Liberator* (Max Eastman's new journal) on the 1st of May. I am receiving the *Liberator* in here. I met another, an IWW salesman. Of course both of these fellows will go out with changed views, and will become ardent and reliable supporters of law and order.

May 12. Of all the clauses in the treaty presented to the German delegates the one that rivets my attention is the one that compels Germany to give back to Great Britain the skull of the Sultan of Okwawa. Who can say that the war has been fought in vain?

May 13. Says Dietzgen (*Philosophical Essays,* p. 127): "We, too, desire to love the enemy and to do good to him who hates us, but not ere we have effected his unconditional surrender." Says Lenin (*Class Struggle,* p. 177): "History has proved beyond a doubt that in every revolution worthy of the name the new ruling class must reckon with the long, continued, selfish, furious opposition of the deposed class, who for years to come have very real advantages as compared with those of the new ruling class."

May 20. A Washington Methodist preacher would "clean out the Reds from every city, not by moral persuasion, or education, or missionary effort, but clean them out at the end of a rope or a gun." Let us pray. Arthur Guy Emory tells soldiers: "If you feel like fighting, go out and smash a Red—it is a great sport knocking them off their soap boxes." Law and Order.

May 25. The Arkansas legislature has passed a bill compelling the mine owners to establish wash houses. Says the American Alliance for Labor and Democracy: "Passage of this bill is a shining example of what organized labor can accomplish. Every known influence was brought to bear to defeat the measure, which miners have clamored for since 1904." What a revolutionary victory! On with the policy of Gompers! A fifteen year fight to wash up. In fifty years we shall be allowed to take a bath.

Sugar's outrage grew and grew, and his belief in revolutionary solutions increased. On June 1 he asked Jane to order Lenin's *State and Revolution* for him. On June 8 he quoted a long passage from Lenin's "New Letter to the Workers of Europe and America." At the same time, he read Reed's *Ten Days That Shook the World*.[4]

Sugar was at work on the problem of the dictatorship of the proletariat. As the Russian Revolution unfolded, the authoritarian character of the workers' state became obvious. For U.S. Socialists, used to operating out in the open, support for revolution and a dictatorship to shackle capitalism before it struck back meant a marked shift of focus. But the treatment of Socialists during the war, the mounting class conflict across the country since, and the feeling that the worldwide social revolution was at hand made such a shift more reasonable. Between the first of June and mid-August, Sugar carefully put his thoughts in an article entitled "Dictatorship and Democracy."

He began with a standard analysis of why, as the Comintern said, "bourgeois democracy is nothing more nor less than the veiled dictatorship by the bourgeoisie." Through control of established channels of education, the system persuades the worker that he governs himself. The press, churches, and the schools "all move in response to impulses which emanate from the dominant bourgeois state." Only through the exposure of bourgeois cultural hegemony could the workers begin to envision a "new order." The key instruments of change were "working class economic organizations." Craft unionism had played an important role, for it created the very idea of organization. As the economy became more complicated, however, the "lines of demarcation between associated crafts" became blurred and the craft unions had an ever more difficult time in coping with the concentrated power of capitalism. Thus industrial unionism emerged as "the key to the door of the new order."

To make this instrument into a revolutionary force, however, depended on its association with a political movement. Craft unionism corresponded with the politics of bourgeois democracy. It sought reforms through legislation and was represented in politics by liberal, bourgeois "friends of labor." The revolutionary political party emerged as the adjunct of industrial unionism.

"In order to remain an active, living force," Sugar wrote, "such a party must keep in close touch with the workers outside its ranks through an active participation in their economic battles. . . . Such a conception, leading to industrial action, and finally to class action, brings them to the threshold of the social revolution. The permanent revolutionary end must ever be kept to the fore, since it is in its attainment alone that the solution of the struggle lies."

The remainder of "Dictatorship and Democracy" was predictable. With the revolution, the bourgeoisie will not disappear overnight and, indeed, will fight tooth and nail against it. Quoting from *State and Revolution*, Sugar endorsed the concept of the dictatorship of the proletariat. The likelihood of violence is great, but because the goal is "to absorb members of the bourgeoisie into the ranks of the class in ascendency," the process will be inherently less violent than the oppression of the working class under capitalism. "The nature of the means employed is not so much a question of democratic practices as a question of the survival of a state of society where universal democracy is ultimately possible. . . . Such a democracy [will give] birth [to] a beautiful and noble humanity, a humanity genuinely concerned with the enhancement of its own happiness, and, in response to that urge, reaching pinnacles which must lie far beyond the vision of those now struggling for liberation." Sugar's concept of democracy and his sense of the future society under communism reflects the humanism generated both by the glow of the stirring revolutionary events of the day and his reading of the second and third volumes of *Capital*.[5]

Sugar was unquestionably a left-winger. Would he also be a Communist? The answer is *no*, although his respect for Lenin and the Soviet experience remained profound. How and why he kept his distance from the Communist

87

movement is a complicated and not entirely clear story. But we must attempt to sort it out because both the respect and the distance are what make Sugar's political role interesting. His independence put him in a position to deal much more broadly with the Left and labor and to serve in political and professional capacities not possible for Party members. Circumstances both personal and political arising in 1919 and 1920 cast Sugar into his nonaffiliated position.

In his last letter from prison to Jane, written on September 14, Sugar said, "I did read an account of the happenings at Chicago, and it was about as I had expected. You say that some of my friends wonder where I stand in the matter. We'll let them wonder a little while, what do you say?"

Most of his close friends and his family (save Jane) had not evolved toward Leninism. His father in fact had finally converted to socialism, but remained firmly reformist. Vic Sugar, his brother, had joined the army and become a lieutenant, but the experience made him appreciate the Socialist perspective more clearly. In 1919, he became friendly with Maurice and Jane's circle, especially Larry Davidow and his sister Anne, whom he would later marry. But the entire family was preoccupied during the spring of 1919 with the health of Maurice's mother, who had diabetes. Politics, especially for Kalman, remained in the background.

Sugar's best friends were almost all "yellows." In a letter to Jane (May 27) he had closed by asking her to give his "love to Dad, Pearl, Lawrence, the kids, Beck, Wienner, Joe, Larry, Anne, Steve, Dave, Katz, Glad, Seraphin, Charlie, Ben, David, Julius, Frank, Nate, Mac, and such others as may from time to time occur to you." Among other available family and office mates (Joseph Beckenstein, Joseph Selzter, and Henry Wienner) and their wives (Glad and Seraphin), Sugar names Larry, Anne, and Stephen Davidow, Charlie Gildemeister, Ben and David Bavly, Julius Deutelbaum, Frank Martel and Nathan Welch, all of whom, save Welch, remained on the right of the party. Larry Davidow, mentioned in Sugar's letters on many occasions, was a close friend. Sugar recruited him for the Socialist party, argued theory with him, and enjoyed playing billiards with him. He also had great respect for Davidow's abilities as a lawyer.[6]

Conflict loomed. Jane was already encountering problems with their friends. Maurice remarked in an August letter, "In your arguments you find yourself opposed to the united front of the enemy? Hold the fort, Jennie, hold the fort. Soon there shall be reinforcements. And when I arrive—with my 10 months of concentrated learning—watch the foe disperse!" His tone was still quite good natured, however. He obviously was not planning to turn his back on his friends but would convince them of the errors of their ways.

Sugar was isolated from the hardening political lines of 1919, and he did not have to make a concrete decision for this or that party as the multiple meetings in Chicago unfolded early in September. Indeed, he hardly mentions them in his prison diary or his letters. It was clear, nevertheless, that once he got out, Sugar would be put in the position of stating his politics clearly.

With the exception of Dennis Batt, he was probably the most prominent Socialist in Michigan. Even while he was in jail, he had stayed in the news. He had run for circuit court judge from prison in April and received nearly eight thousand votes. In May, he and Davidow cooked up a scheme to get him out of jail and cause the federal bench some embarrassment. It was argued that his sentence actually dated from late April 1918, the point at which his last appeal was denied in the U.S. Circuit Court of Appeals. Sentencing was delayed until after the Supreme Court refused to hear the case. Edward Jeffries, the liberal recorders court judge, agreed to hear the plea and issued an order of habeas corpus for Sugar's delivery to his court on May 2, 1919. Then the fun began. Federal Judge Tuttle, who had originally sentenced Sugar, ordered a U.S. marshall to the prison to prevent Sugar's removal. The lawman actually sat there with a gun. The case became a jurisdictional battle between two proud judges. James Pound, a Darrowesque lawyer from Detroit, acted as friend of the court on Jeffries' behalf and cited precedents stretching back to the sevententh century. The upshot was a lot of newspaper coverage, and Tuttle decided to authorize a two months' reduction in Sugar's sentence. The release date was set for September 25, 1919.[7]

Freedom and Repression

By that time, Marxist politics in the United States had become very complex. The meetings in Chicago created not two, but four, separate parties. The Socialist party, now firmly in the hands of the Right, followed Hillquit's dictum and confirmed the expulsions. The delegates also repulsed an attempt by John Reed and his friends to carry out their takeover strategy. The Socialists nevertheless felt themselves radical enough to vote to seek admission to the Third International. They were finally turned down in 1921 by a famous letter from Zinoviev, who remarked that the Communist International was "not a hotel."

The Communist convention began on September 1. Their perspective was simple enough: prepare for the American revolution and promote the Bolshevik world-revolutionary cause. But there were a number of nettlesome issues, and the Michigan delegation, led by Batt, Renner, and Keracher, was at the center of controversy.

The meeting started off with a bang, as Batt, the official convener, was arrested at the podium for allegedly violating the Illinois antiespionage law two days before. Al Renner was then elected permanent chair. The Michigan people were close to the Russian elements, who dominated the convention. Together they rejected attempts by Reed to negotiate credentials for his group. Only the threatened resignation of much of the other English-speaking leadership prevented the outright expulsion of the Reedites: they could join as individuals if acceptable to the credentials committee. Most refused such charity and went on to form the Communist Labor party.

But Michigan's rapport with the Russians soon evaporated. They rejected the manifesto that the Russians and the *Revolutionary Age* caucus, led by Fraina and I. E. Ferguson, worked out. The main bone of contention had to do with the question of political action. Following their interpretation of Lenin's misgivings about electoral politics, the majority defined all political action as parliamentary and rejected it out of hand. The Michiganders vigorously disagreed. As they put it later, "The Comrades of Michigan, who have upheld *revolutionary political action* in the State Convention over a period of years, regard parliamentary action as but a phase of POLITICAL ACTION, but an important one in countries with a form of government like the United States. . . . The trouble with the dominant elements in our ranks . . . is that they have reverted consciously or unconsciously to the syndicalist position." This was not quite the case, although as Theodore Draper noted, "in practice, the difference was not so great."

When it became clear that their position did not have a chance, the "Michigan Mensheviks," as they were soon labeled, refused to participate in the vote for party officials or to stand for election themselves. Batt and Renner both declined nomination for party national secretary (Charles Ruthenberg won it), and Batt for national editor also, which went to Fraina by default.

The Michigan people had thus given up a strong position in the new party for the role of an outsider carping over an issue that was nebulous and largely unsettled internationally. As it turned out, the U.S. Communist party in its first year was totally paralyzed; had the Michigan group not decided to pull out, perhaps it might have developed a more flexible political position. Batt and his friends came back to Michigan without formally abandoning the Communist party, but neither had they joined it. Soon, however, the Communists officially expelled them, and they formed the Proletarian party, an independent group in which activists such as Stanley Nowak and Emil Mazey received their socialist education. While not ruling out politics, the Proletarians still made industrial-union participation the focus of their activity. Batt, a tool-and-dye maker, was especially interested in the independent Auto Workers Union, and he cooperated with Deutelbaum, Welch, and Martel to keep the Detroit Federation of Labor (DFL), despite national AFL opposition, favorable toward it. On the other hand, the new Communist party, with its support for "dual unionism" and condemnation of the AFL as a "bulwark of capitalism" had virtually no base in the Detroit labor movement. The great steel strike of September was supported by the Party, which hoped it would be the first step toward the revolution, but its official organ, the *Communist,* immediately made its position clear: "trades unionism is the arch-enemy of the militant proletariat; existing trades union organization" must be destroyed. For left-leaning DFL unionists, this simply confirmed their negative opinion of the Party.[8]

For Sugar, the DFL's position was important because its continuing distance from the conservative AFL national leadership and its active fight for workers' goals over the past year convinced him that it remained a crucial force on behalf of Detroit workers in and out of organized labor.

It had consistently supported and promoted overt militance. On May 1, 1919, twenty thousand Detroiters "took the day off" at the urging of their unions and some fifteen thousand showed up that night at the Arena Gardens to hear Wobbly heroes Arturo Giovannitti and James Fisher. Said the *Labor News,* "Where man oppresses man and some live by the sweat of others' brows, the host of labor turned out in mighty demonstration. A new world is in the making and Labor is to be the builder." Strikes by Detroit electrical workers, pile drivers, machinists, carpenters, painters, gas workers, ice-wagon drivers, journeyman tailors, and molders all started that day. Most were successful, and others followed. A new rash of injunctions was served and the war heated up. "The question then is, gentlemen of the employing class," wrote Deutelbaum in an editorial on July 18, "what will you have or what do you prefer? Political action or direct action? It is up to you." In other words, the threat of revolution hangs over every reform resisted. By the fall, the Detroit federation confronted the "red scare," and faced it squarely. "If Bolshevism means progress," remarked the *Labor News* on September 12, "let us have it, since the word is always used to defeat progressive proposals." William Bailey, the moderate president of the federation, echoed the same idea in a widely publicized speech in early October. "Bolshevism and socialism," he said, "are synonymous and interchangeable" and their goal is that "the means of production and distribution shall be cooperatively owned and democratically managed." "Our present social and industrial system," he said, "is insane."9

Sugar was released on September 25, 1919. His liberation banquet brought together all his old friends, within the labor movement and without. His new politics became quickly apparent. While the Davidows, Paul Taylor, and other moderates were shocked (they had assumed that it was Jane who was radicalizing), his labor-movement allies welcomed him with open arms. The DFL officially extended him "a hearty hand clasp" and praised his "unquestionable loyalty to labor."

In particular, Sugar and the local labor movement shared a commitment to a new and exciting phenomenon: the development of the industrywide organization of autoworkers under the auspices of the officially condemned independent, the Carriage, Wagon, and Automobile Workers union, now simply called the Auto Workers Union (AWU). While the AWU could not be a member of the federation, it had wide support in the Detroit AFL. It was hard to argue with success, for membership in the AWU passed from thirteen thousand in 1916 to forty-five thousand in Detroit, the Midwest, and New York in early 1920. Its members were largely skilled men—trimmers, painters, woodworkers, upholsters, and metalworkers. It grew quickly with the boom conditions in the industry of 1919. Many of its leaders were veterans of the labor struggles in Great Britain and its form of organization, based on shop units under stewards, was modeled after the British example. The president of the union and editor of the *Auto*

Worker, William E. Logan, was English-born, hardworking, and a notorious wit. He saved his most withering prose for the Communist party. In the November 1919 issue of the paper, for example, there appeared his article entitled "M'ass Action of the R-R-R-Revolutionary Prowling Terriers," he mocked their hyper-revolutionary stance ("*Don't* change your underwear," for you'll be more "inclined to tolerate the present damnable system") and blasted their apparent ignorance regarding the daily needs of working people and the ways one approaches them. He also feared that their shrill rhetoric would serve as an excuse for governmental repression of the entire labor movement. Logan had ties to the Socialist party, but was above all a trade unionist with decided syndicalist tendencies. Sugar thought he was a most interesting fellow and praised his organizing efforts.

The concept of independent labor representation in a "national Labor party" also found considerable support in Detroit. Conceived by John Fitzpatrick, president of the Chicago Federation of Labor, the Labor party appealed to those seeking "labor power" but uninterested in ideological fine points. According to a West Coast labor paper, it would "fight the battles of labor, whether socialist or non-socialist, whether organized as craft unions or industrial unions" and "work for the solidarity of labor on both the political and industrial fields, with collectivism (Socialism under whatever name) as its chief objective." It was thus to be a large, umbrella party that would bring together a "new majority." On August 1, 1919, the Detroit federation voted to participate in a preconvention conference to be held in Chicago on August 18 and took a straw vote in favor of a Labor party. Over the next two months this "political party of hand and brain workers based upon political, industrial, and social democracy," as the *Labor News* put it, spread its wings in Detroit.

If Sugar did not become involved, especially because "social patriot" Max Hayes headed the party, he welcomed the interest of AFL people in an anti-capitalist program and their abandonment of Gompers's "friends-of-labor" politics. As historian Stanley Shapiro has shown in his studies of the Labor-party phenomenon, the idea of a socialistic party modelled upon the successful British prototype appealed to working people across the nation. Perhaps never before in U.S. history had there been such widespread disaffection with the capitalist system. But labor, however moderate its perspective, was increasingly submerged by the 1919 tidal wave of "Americanism." The bombast of the Communists, the violence of the great strikes, and the prominence of "foreigners" in both radical and labor agitation stimulated the imaginations of many "native Americans," spurred on by the capitalist press, to hideous proportions.[10]

And so, the promise of 1919 gave way to the terror of 1920. Sugar had barely had time to think when the whirlwind of reaction struck. On the night of January 2, 1920 the House of the Masses, allegedly the headquarters of the Communist party of Detroit, was invaded by agents of the Justice Department sent there by Special Assistant J. Edgar Hoover. He had general orders from the White House and A. Mitchell Palmer, the attorney general. Everywhere across the country, "reds" were rounded up, their books and papers sequestered, and their human dignity assaulted. The prize was to find a noncitizen or at least someone who was foreign born.

Large sections of U.S. public opinion supported the move, frightened by the lurid tales in the mass press not only about Socialists and strikes but about race riots as well. The Palmer raids were merely the culmination of a string of official and unofficial violence against the Red Menace. The Centralia massacre, where the killing of four legionnaires storming an IWW hall was followed by the lynching and mutilation of Wesley Everest, started things off. Thereafter, Wobblies everywhere were hounded and beaten by 100-percent patriots as the police stood idly by.

More impressive was the handiwork of the Department of Justice itself. On November 7, 1919, 250 members of the Union of Russian Workers were beaten, then arrested, by federal agents in New York and eleven other cities, including Detroit. On the following day seventy-three radical centers were raided. Whether or not "the nation" was "delighted with the raids," as historian Robert Murray remarks without documentation, the conservative, business-backed press asserted that Palmer's actions brought "thrills of joy to every American" and cartoons villified beetle-browed, unkempt, and dark-complexioned "reds." Then came the discovery that immigration officers were not properly deporting radicals convicted under the federal Alien Law or state "criminal-anarchy" or "criminal-syndicalist" laws. Frederick C. Howe, the Ellis Island commissioner, was forced to resign in disgrace. A few days later the *New York Times* informed the world, "RED BOMB LABORATORY FOUND"—again in the Russian People's House. This brought a further roundup, and on December 21, 249 radicals, mostly anarchist noncitizens, were herded aboard the "Soviet ark," the army transport *Buford,* and "shipped back where they belong." Among them were the famous anarchists Emma Goldman and Alexander Berkmann.

The Palmer raids were the icing on the cake. Prepared carefully in advance, the roundup of members of the Communist party (CP) and the Communist Labor party (CLP) was set for January 2, a Friday night: "your undercover informants [should arrange] meetings" of them. The agents were also instructed not to allow their prisoners to contact anyone until questioning had been completed. That neither the CP nor the CLP had been declared illegal did not seem to cross the attorney general's mind.

The raid on the House of the Masses had the honor of being one of the nation's leading examples of the respect accorded the Constitution by its chief upholder. Eight hundred persons were arrested and herded into an ancient section of the Federal Building. Denied food and adequate toilet facilities, the arrestees remained in dark and stench-filled corridors for anywhere from three to six days. Some three hundred were released "early." These had no connections with Detroit radicalism, having been at the House of the Masses for a social event. Of the rest, some 140 were finally transferred to the Municipal Building and, unshaved and unbathed, seemed the very image of what Palmer thought

93

reds looked like. As he put it so splendidly a few days later, "Out of the sly and crafty eyes of many of them leap cupidity, cruelty, insanity, and crime; from their lop-sided faces, sloping brows, and misshaped [sic] features may be recognized the unmistakable criminal type."

The illegality and immorality of the Palmer raids generally were overlooked by the nation's press, although in Detroit the major newspapers tended to sympathize with the victims. The Justice Department had nevertheless done its work well—the Left in the city was in a state of disarray that matched its ruined headquarters. Sugar described the scene in a brochure written the following year:

> The House of the Masses was raided repeatedly. Doors were smashed, desks broken, equipment destroyed, books confiscated. Persons and papers were indiscriminately loaded into wagons and hauled to jail. Men were picked up in the streets. Homes were invaded, and "suspects" torn from their families. . . . The Detroit movement was paralyzed. Not only were its most active members in jail, but those who were not had no means of knowing at what moment they might be compelled to join them. For many weeks an atmosphere of inquisition prevailed. And so quite suddenly—with the exception of some bolder ones in jail, who defiantly proclaimed their faith to the world—there were no "Communists" in Detroit.

There had been very few of them in any case. The "Communist" presence in this city was largely represented by the Proletarian party and nonsectarian leftists like Sugar and Nate Welch. They cooperated with Communist party members as best they could. The old Michigan left wing remained in contact, and all the groups used the House of the Masses. Al Renner, a Proletarian, was its manager, but Boleslav Gebert, a CP organizer, held meetings there.[11]

The Proletarians suffered most severely from the Palmer raids. They were, in the eyes of the Bureau of Investigation, as "Communist" as anyone they were looking for. They displayed the *Manifesto* and *Program of the Communist International* prominently for sale in the House of the Masses and proclaimed themselves loyal Bolsheviks. Renner, although native born, was a prize catch and was not released on bond until Friday afternoon, the 9th. At eleven the next morning, I. Paul Taylor, Larry Davidow, and one Alex Riebe came to see him at the House of the Masses. It was not a social call. Instead they delivered a document that would create between all elements of the old left wing and the new Socialist party in Detroit an ongoing bitterness matched in few cities in the country. It was a formal notice that, as 100-percent Socialists, the recently (yesterday) constituted board of directors of the "only legal" Workers Educational Association, the governing body of the House of the Masses, demanded to take possession of the building. Renner told them to get out, and on Monday they filed suit to effectuate the takeover.

What was going on? It was a sordid story. The Socialist party was short of funds and its home-office overseer and legal protector, Seymour Stedman, had been casting about for several months for ways to recoup. Sometime in November, his eye fell upon the big building at the corner of Gratiot and St. Aubin in Detroit. Who owned the House of the Masses? Or, put another way, who owned this structure purchased for seventy thousand dollars whose value had doubled during the boom times of 1919? This was a good question. The hundreds of people who used it daily and the group who operated it were mostly the same people who had done so since it was originally occupied in July 1918. More to the point in a capitalist society, the people who had bought shares in the corporation that administered it, the Workers Educational Association (WEA), were overwhelmingly the same people who continued to be involved in its direction. They had a board of directors and a manager, Mr. Renner. However, the original set of bylaws, drawn up by Sugar, had said quite clearly that all members of the WEA had to be members of the Socialist Party of America. So who owned the house when all members of the Socialist Party of America in Michigan were expelled in May 1919? The Socialist party had been "reorganized" in June with Violet Blumenberg's little clique in Grand Rapids and her husband, Ben, virtually alone in Detroit, leading the way. In the summer and fall, Detroit people actually belonging to the Socialist party were few and far between. Neither later stalwarts Paul Taylor nor Davidow, for example, had rejoined and Sugar was trying to convert them to his point of view all during that autumn.

Unfortunately, we have little exact information about relations between Sugar and his friends and family in late 1919. Immediately after his release, he and Jane went north for a camping trip and first scouted out Black Lake, where they would later obtain some property. Shortly after their return, tragedy struck. Mary Sugar died on November 16, 1919. Maurice's mother had been a stabilizing influence in the family, particularly in her support of Maurice and Jane and the way they wanted to live. Her loss may have created a dynamic within the family whereby Jane became more isolated—and easier to blame for Maurice's political transgressions. His propaganda with friends and family did not take. Davidow and Taylor rejoined the Socialist party sometime in December. So, at their urging, did Kalman Sugar. While Maurice was saddened by this turn of events, there was no reason to think that their decision was based on anything but their analysis of the current scene. After all, Kate O'Hare and Debs stayed with the party.

But by the end of the month, there was reason to wonder about the timing and stipulations of their rejoining. Another clause in the Sugar's ironclad bylaws of the Workers Educational Association was that to be eligible for office, one had to have been a member of the Socialist party for three years. No one from Michigan, whatever their situation, could fill that bill, since everybody had been expelled on the previous May 25. Thus when Stedman informed all reborn members of the party that they had never been expelled, Sugar's suspicions grew. But it took the Palmer raids and their ugly aftermath to confirm them. To be sure, he did not know that Ben Blumenberg had written Stedman at the very

95

moment a second round of raids on the House of the Masses was going on (January 5, 1920) that the time for the "repossession" had arrived. "Lazarus Davidow is our attorney," he wrote, "but we are also informed that you have the matter in hand," and added that he had heard "that the Communists were recently offered $140,000 for the property." But Sugar was well aware that Taylor, this new "Paul, disciple of Stedman," was out scouting for membets who could qualify for the three-year rule. "He got them. On the ninth day of January they organized their board of directors and elected their officers. Of the board, only one had ever been a member of the corporation. They elected him [Alex Riebe] president." They then proceeded to serve notice on weary Al Renner, poking about in the shambles that had been his office, the next morning. The irrevocable line of treachery had been drawn. The very idea that the Socialist party would grub for property in the midst of one of the grossest violations of civil rights in U.S. history was incredible. An irreparable breach in the Detroit Left—and in the very heart of the Sugar family—had been made.

The court battle that unfolded in June only made matters worse. The Socialists' claim was straightforward: one had to be a member of the Socialist party to be in the corporation owning the House of the Masses, and they all were. Although Davidow did most of the research, Stedman himself acted as their lawyer. Before the case was concluded, he had become vice-presidential candidate for the party and, with Debs in prison, would carry the burden of the Socialist message to the nation. His opponent, suggested by Sugar, was James Pound, the fabled trial lawyer who had once worked on Sugar's behalf. Pound decided to argue the matter strictly on a private property basis and would avoid politics altogether.

Stedman, on the other hand, built his case around the meaning of "Communist," whether the people in the house were such and, if so, what claim they had to be in the house? In so doing, he asked all hostile witnesses whether they were "Communists," which was now really illegal and a deportable offense for noncitizens. Dennis Batt found himself saying, "I am not now and never have been a member of the Communist Party," a sentence as repulsive to have to utter then as it was to be thirty years later. Stedman grilled them on ideology, especially what they thought about "mass action." If he meant violence, *no,* mass organizing, *yes*—and so on. Failing "incriminating" answers here, Stedman often tried to evoke fear of the dangerous alien. "Are you a citizen?" he asked. "I have first papers—" "ARE YOU A CITIZEN?" "No." He also harped on relations with Russians, thus keeping clearly in the judge's head the memories of Bolsheviks and bombs. It was a shameful performance for a member of the party of Eugene Debs.

Pound worked on embarrassing the Socialists. For example, he pointed out that the *Manifesto* of the Communist International, used to prove how "Communist" the occupiers of the house were, was in fact published by the Socialist party (SP). It also turned out that his cross-examination of Socialist witnesses revealed the true political complexion of the new little band of SP members in

Detroit. They were decidedly right wing, embarrassing so for Stedman, who was ideologically a good Debsian. (A few years later, when all of this was forgotten—in Chicago at any rate—Stedman would join the Communist party.) Alex Riebe, the only member of the new Socialist corporation who had been a member of the old one, had been in fact recalled in April 1919 by the members of the "Karl Liebknecht branch" of the party when it was discovered that he had pictures of the Kaiser and Victor Berger in his office and that he supported Schiedemann, Ebert, and Noske, the Social Democrats who had destroyed the Soviet movement in Germany. Essentially, then, only the mildest of Socialists were with the Detroit party in its new beginning. Moreover, they seemed to have no moral scruples.

It took a long time for the stigma to wear off in Detroit. A pamphlet, written by Sugar under the name of "George Hamilton," sought to keep the memory burning. On its front were the words, "And the Socialist Party of the United States stuck a knife in the backs of the workers. It was just a little dig. Indeed, it turned out to be nothing but a scratch. But it left a scar, which is a good thing, because it is something by which the treachery may always be remembered." It was a scratch because, despite Stedman's adventures in red-baiting, the "Communists" won. They won, curiously, on grounds that had nothing at all to do with the merits of the case but which surely drew a wry smile from "Sharp Pencil" Sugar: the Socialists, in bringing the case into the Wayne County Circuit Court and presenting it as they did, were in the wrong court![12]

As much as he might have loved to do so, Sugar could not have been the lawyer in this case. He was banned from his profession and would remain so until late 1923. It is a measure of the conservative turn taken by U.S. society in the early twenties that he had to struggle so long to be reinstated. And even so, he was in the end only allowed to practice in state and local courts. A federal offender, he was forever barred from the federal courts, even after receiving a full pardon in 1933. The age of Harding, this era of "normalcy," Prohibition, flappers, false prosperity, and massive corruption, was for Sugar a trying one but, like his prison year, most productive. He did legal research and wrote briefs for Beckenstein, who had a wide-ranging practice. This work increased his knowledge of the law "many times over" that which he "had acquired as a University student and in my few years as an active practitioner."

In his fight for reinstatement, he learned something about legal politics, too. He was under the opinion that he had a guardian angel within the legal system, Circuit Judge Ira Jayne. Jayne had acknowledged that Sugar had been instrumental in his election to his judgeship in 1918. He had just missed election by a few votes two years before, campaigning without the support of the Detroit Federation of Labor. Although a Republican, he had the reputation of being a liberal on both labor and race and national-origin questions and in 1918 sought federation support. As was normally the case, federation officials asked Sugar what he thought; while hardly overly enthusiastic, Sugar said that he would rather appear in Jayne's court than that of any other candidate. Jayne got the endorsement and won his judgeship handily. Moreover, Jayne knew Jane Sugar personally from recreation-department days. They assumed that he was the judge to whom to direct the petition of reinstatement, which they did promptly on September 30, 1919. He took it "under advisement."

It might as well have been under a rock. Month after month, nothing happened. Obviously, 1920 was not the most politically expedient year to move on the reinstatement of someone of Sugar's background and outlook. Sugar understood Ira Jayne's hesitancy. But they learned a little more when Jane Sugar went to see whether her past associate could help find her a job teaching in the public schools. Judge Jayne graciously took her to lunch, talked about his close friendship with Cody, the superintendent, and then advised that she approach each of the board members individually—she was impressive enough on her own. He did nothing. As it turned out, old friend Otto Marckwardt, now a journalist, knew Cody well. He wrote a glowing letter to him, and in a matter of hours, she got a job teaching grade-school English. More time went by. Ira Jayne was still doing nothing.

He was afraid. Harding had swept into office on a 100-percent "American" platform in which Marxists were labelled the primary threat to the nation. Dozens of patriotic organizations, led by the American Legion and an alarmingly potent Ku Klux Klan, dominated the attention of the media, while open-shop organizations, guided by the National Association of Manufacturers, linked the targets of the superpatriots—reds, blacks, the yellow peril, Jews, and immigrants from the wrong parts of Europe—to the threat of labor and rode with the tide. Civil liberties were trod upon daily. Unpunished lynchings of blacks reached new heights, and Indiana actually elected a known Klansman governor. The clamor for immigration restriction was met with "emergency" legislation in 1921 and with that monument to two centuries of "racial science," the permanent quota system of 1924. To be in favor of much of anything that was not white, Anglo-Saxon, Protestant, draped in a flag, and dedicated to "free enterprise" was politically unintelligent. Judge Jayne, as nice a person as the Sugars continued to think he was, was not about to rush to the rescue of a man who was none of the above.

So Sugar languished. Finally, early in 1923, something happened. "One day," Sugar wrote, "I was walking down Woodward Avenue when I ran into an old legal adversary, Frank Murphy." One thing led to another and Murphy, shocked that a lawyer of Sugar's caliber remained unable to practice, told him that he wanted to help. He got to Jayne and revived the Sugar question. Unfortunately, the judge, who simply needed to hold a hearing on the petition, still found himself torn between humanitarianism and politics. He chose the latter and ordered Sugar to appear before the executive committee of the Detroit Bar—the very body, little changed, that had disbarred him in the first place. Murphy said he would do what he could to "line up its members," while Sugar was forced to reexamine the issues that brought about the original action and then defend himself as he put it, before the "most conservative group of a conservative profession."

As it turned out, the experience was important both for Sugar's self-esteem and in cementing a close relationship with Murphy. The latter worked without a fee and, while preparing to represent Sugar in court, also won his first campaign for public office—recorder's court—in April. This increased the prestige of the petitioner as well. Murphy, in fact, bent over backwards to do everything possible to get Sugar through the committee. But Sugar's performance on the appointed day in May was superb. He did not attempt to justify his actions constitutionally, but argued that they were based on his moral views, augmented only later by constitutional interpretation. Moreover, he now felt that any country under attack would institute necessary measures to defend itself, including draft laws. Note carefully: *would,* not *should.* For Sugar had realized from a Marxist perspective—he certainly did not share this with the corporate and insurance-company lawyers sitting around the table—that the laws of historical development simply necessitated taking whatever action was required to defend the nation-state in the current world system of inherently antagonistic imperialist powers. Morality had nothing to do with it. What he *did* tell them was that "in the event of the enforcement of a draft law in the future his conduct will be one of obedience to the law." By a vote of two opposed, five in favor, and three others in various states of abstention, Sugar's reinstatement was recommended. Finally, on November 7, 1923, Jayne heard the petition and granted reinstatement. The radical lawyer had been returned to the fold by a group of reactionaries and a liberal judge. The catalyst, Frank Murphy let his thirst for justice outweigh his political fears and got away with it. It would not be the last time.[13]

These years had been ones of personal trial but considerable intellectual growth. While at first glance it might have seemed logical that he join the Communist party, Sugar did not do so. Politically, he could agree neither with its hyperradicalism nor, especially, with its positions on political involvement and on relationships with existing trade unionism. Just as clearly, Sugar could not rejoin the Socialist party, given its rightward turn and then the treachery of its few Michigan adherents. The Proletarian position was closer to his, but, unquestionably, old personal conflicts and Batt and Renner's overintellectualizing of their role convinced him to remain aloof from them as well. Sugar thus became fixed in the political stance that he would retain for the rest of his life: an independent Marxist with a deep respect for the Soviet experience and an equally deep respect for the Debsian principles of broad unity of the Left, opposition to ideological nitpicking, full support for industrial unionism within or outside of the existing national organizations, and the building of a true workers' party in the United States. The sectarian splintering that had occurred left him (and others, such as Scott Nearing) without a political home. As he put it when asked by Stedman about his politics at the House of the Masses trial, "I am an outsider."

99

4 ❖ LAW AND THE CLASS STRUGGLE, 1924–32

Sugar had come a long way since he entered the Detroit House of Correction in November of 1918. So had the United States, but they had gone in opposite directions. By the time the election year of 1924 rolled around, the nation had reached a level of conservatism perhaps never witnessed before. Isolationism combined with anticommunism to create for any Socialist a sense that the revolution was farther away than ever. Even in 1920, Debs had still received nearly a million votes. Although it may have been a last gasp, it reminded the world that there had been an important Socialist presence—and a Marxist one at that—in the United States during the previous decade. But in the early twenties, Left politics—certainly in part due to its own vicious infighting exemplified by the House of the Masses battle—became increasingly marginalized and divorced from the main threads of U.S. life.

While documentation is sparse, and memories cloudy, it appears that Sugar reflected this situation personally, keeping political activities per se to a minimum. But his work as a lawyer kept him deeply involved with the labor movement and with civil-liberties questions. Through this work he came to realize what an effective instrument the law, especially constitutional law rooted in the Bill of Rights, could be in defending the worker and in promoting labor's struggle. He also discovered that the Communist movement in the Detroit area seemed to be the most effective political force speaking for the worker and fighting for his rights. Sugar's own perspective deviated little from what it had been in 1919 and 1920, but the Communist party was moving in a direction that he found more acceptable. Its continuing sectarian character meant that joining it remained out of the question, but he would certainly work with it and gladly associated himself with the International Labor Defense, an organization sponsored by the Party and dedicated to the legal defense of the oppressed. He also became active in the John Reed Club and the Friends of the Soviet Union.

At the same time, he retained his ties with other elements of the Left and especially with moderates, such as Frank Martel, within the established labor movement. Especially important in this regard was his work as coordinator and frequent lecturer for the Detroit Federation of Labor's Sunday Forum. Socialists such as Walter Bergman and independents such as Scott Nearing were frequent speakers, along with people more clearly identified with the pro-Soviet orbit, such as Robert Dunn. In this work, Sugar, the voice of Left unity, was in his element.

Sharpening the Pencil

Upon his reinstatement in November 1923, Sugar threw himself into his legal practice. His reputation had not been tarnished by disbarment, and he emerged an even better lawyer. He had, specifically, come to understand the centrality of procedure in U.S. law. In the first few years after his reinstatement, Sugar took on all sorts of cases, labor law continuing to be "hit-or-miss." While his criminal cases were rare, he would occasionally accept interesting ones, particularly if they involved domains of the law with which he was not familiar.[1]

Although Sugar did not know it when the client first came to see him, "lewd and lascivious association and cohabitation" with a person to whom one is not married was a criminal offense in the state of Michigan, punishable by up to one year in jail. Alex Benton, from Ohio, was in the process of getting a divorce from his wife, but it was hung up on the property settlement, she wanting it all, he willing to give half. Benton had spent several months in Detroit working at Ford in Highland Park and was living with another woman. One night a private detective, with a policeman and an arrest warrant in tow, barged into Benton's room. He was in bed with his friend, and the warrant was served on both of them. They were to be tried separately, Benton first. His acquittal meant her acquittal, although his conviction simply meant that she would then be tried. If she were acquitted, his conviction would be reversed. This was a rare offense in which guilt or innocence had to be mutual.

For Sugar, the case mirrored perfectly the state of much law relating to labor. The statute was a relic of mores that were out of date. More important, it took the law into an area where it did not belong—into matters essentially private—while at the same time defending an institution, marriage, that should properly be defined as a social relationship, not a legal one. The prejudice of the law against unmarried lovers was similar to the prejudice of the law against labor; it was the product of a specific set of social circumstances and, in fact, violated abstract principles of justice. The makers and interpreters of the laws in both cases responded to interests, not to concepts of right. But there was a way to equalize the situation to an extent, and it was provided in the very essence of the Anglo-American legal tradition: procedure. In the case of Alex Benton, it

101

was a procedural principle, the rules of evidence, that saved the day. The prosecutor, assuming that he had an open-and-shut case, had been sloppy. After he closed his case, Sugar asked that the judge direct the jury to return a verdict of not guilty because the prosecution had failed to provide evidence, an exhibit or actual testimony going beyond hearsay, that Benton and his bedmate were not married. Everybody knew that Benton's yet-to-be-divorced wife was there in the courtroom, but nobody actually *proved* that they were married. The prosecutor made some desperate attempts to reopen, but the judge—perhaps concerned that Benton was being railroaded by his wife and perhaps impressed with Sugar's cleverness but also perhaps induced, through this exercise in procedural justice, to raise his thought to the inherent injustice of the law itself—ruled in Benton's favor.

It was "procedure" and "technicalities" that made it possible for Sugar to integrate his work as a lawyer under the U.S. constitutional system with his belief in the revolutionary transformation of U.S. society. Can one be a constitutionalist and a revolutionist at the same time? Sugar's answer was an emphatic *yes*. Indeed, without the Constitution, there would be no revolution. The rest was ultraleftist, "infantile" playacting. The sequence of events since the heady days of 1919 had demonstrated to him that the political Right and a whole array of government officials, from the president to sheriffs in dusty rural counties in Alabama, were willing to break the law and ignore the Constitution. It was incumbent upon the Left to expose this whenever possible. The law could be made to work for working people. It might not be the perfect representation of justice, unquestionably it served as an instrument of bourgeois hegemony, yet it was rooted in universal principles of equal justice. The bourgeois revolution itself—the American War for Independence as completed by the Civil War—had proclaimed that all men were created equal and that all individuals had a number of inherent rights that must be protected. The French Revolution and the Declaration of the Rights of Man and Citizen of 1789 had done the same. Constitutions then identified and created the mechanisms for protecting those rights. As time went by, the interpretations of the Constitution naturally tended to reflect the interests of the dominant class, thus tilting the tables away from equal justice. But beneath it all was the bedrock of equality, *procedure,* which specified *how* rights were to be protected.

Sugar's analysis of this question, included in his chapter on the Benton affair and written in the mid-1960s, is a lucid statement of the concept, both legal and political:

> Procedure is important—often vital. Many of the provisions of the Bill of Rights are procedural in nature. The provisions relating to searches and seizures, to self-incrimination, to the right to trial by an impartial jury, to confrontation by the witnesses, and the requirement of due process are all procedural. The concept that one is presumed to be innocent until proven guilty beyond a reasonable doubt is a

procedural concept. And so are the rules of evidence, such as those barring hearsay. . . .

Indeed, it is by procedural requirements that the substance of democracy is preserved. And to the extent that these procedural safeguards are ignored, or denied, or whittled away, whether by legislative, executive, or judicial action, the foundations of democracy are weakened.[2]

Procedure was the equalizer. Its expression in day-to-day legal affairs was the immense corpus of rules and regulations that govern the legal process, popularly referred to as "technicalities." The public mind tends to look with disdain upon lawyers who invoke procedural points to win cases, thus skirting their "merits." They are often regarded, Sugar himself noted, as "shysters, crooks—especially by the losers in the case." The full study of this important thread in the history of American attitudes—its origins, how it has been sustained and by whom, and its meaning as an expression of U.S. culture—has yet to be made. For Sugar, it meant regular attacks by the Detroit establishment press, but in the eyes of the labor movement it was seen as turning the tables on the bad guys, as just revenge for labor's past unequal treatment. Sugar thus played a role in educating workers in the foundations of the law and enhanced the dignity of the "technical lawyer." As he put it after another equally illogical but legally correct victory, a lawyer must "use a sharp pencil!"[3]

Sugar had learned the mysteries of technical law in dealing with dozens of injunctions. While political considerations might cause a judge to give a hearing to strikers, there was in the end no way to stop an injunction "on the merits." So Sugar learned the tactics of delay: "Every bill of complaint, every restraining order, every summons, every service, was scrutinized minutely, dissected carefully in the search for a legal objection which I could advance with some degree of hope." He might thus be able to tie up the hearing for some time, "long enough to win the strike, if possible." The heart of his position was simple enough: "I felt that the legal cards were stacked against labor, so I concentrated on the means of preventing those cards from being played." While a few irate opponents would berate Sugar for "winning cases before they get to the jury," he found that most lawyers respected (and feared) the kind of expertise involved in procedural law. Sugar's cases often drew young lawyers to watch him in action, fascinated by the "technique of the technical."

One injunction case in 1926 suffices to illustrate the training they received. Several small delicatessens on Miami Street in downtown Detroit had been struck by their waitresses, members of the Waiters Union. Their employers moved jointly to seek an injunction against their picketing, which had immediately affected business. The summons was served by the sheriff and a date set for Sugar to "show cause" why an injunction should not be issued. Upon his arrival in court, Sugar, not certain how many people he was representing, asked the judge to read the names of the defendants from the "return of service," a legal document that had to be filed with the court by the sheriff's deputy. The opposing lawyer, Jim Ellman, said, "That's OK, I've got them right here." Sugar said, "Now, now, you know the rules." The judge did not have it. Ellman got an hour's delay and went off searching for the deputy. He was not in his office. Instead he was out serving another summons in far western Wayne County in relation to another case, a case in which the plaintiff was represented by Maurice Sugar! The case would have to be delayed, but the judge's docket was full until the following week. Picketing continued on Miami Street.

On the appointed day, the treasured list was read and the hearing began. Sugar immediately entered a motion to quash because the text of the return was defective. Ellman retorted that Sugar could not file the motion because he had not given prosecution the requisite four days to examine it. Impossible, said Sugar, since the return was just filed the day before. "Do you want the time?" asked the judge. "No," said Ellman, "read the motion." Sugar then pointed out that although the summons was a collective one (three women) the form letter used the singular (*defendant*). The judge would not quash but asked Ellman to do it over correctly. The hearing was delayed another week. Picketing continued on Miami Street. Sugar managed another maneuver worthy of Fabius Cunctator at the next session and got yet another week. By that time Ellman was a beaten man. He agreed to get the restaurant owners and the strikers together to discuss the latter's quite moderate demands.

Sugar then delivered the coup de grace. He called up Frank Martel, now president of the Detroit federation, and asked for a little help. At the negotiation in Ellman's office a few days later, an hour of stonewalling by the bosses had passed when it was announced that Martel had arrived. It was most unusual for a federation president to involve himself with a strike of a member local, particularly one as small as this. After hearing a few more *nos* from the employers, he declared, "Either you sign up right now or we'll throw the force of the entire labor movement of this city into the fight. I guess you know what that means." Capitulation was rapid. The waitresses even won back half the pay they lost during the strike.[4]

While all injunction episodes did not end so happily, it was obvious that the man who had learned to "use a sharp pencil" early on had perfected the game of procedural law—much to the benefit of the class struggle. Sugar felt that the law should be mined for every bit of ore it could yield no matter what amount of dross might have to be stripped away. This would become fully apparent in the cases of the early UAW years when mountains of evidence would have to be sifted often to prove a single instance of firing for union activities or company espionage.

Although Sugar was comfortable with such legalism in the midtwenties, it remained suspect among Communists who, like the IWWs of old, thought it a threat to the revolutionary spirit. This irritated the meticulous and thorough Sugar, who felt it was silly not to milk the law for all it was worth.

One case illustrates the problem well. Early in 1925, Sugar defended Bud Reynolds—the left-winger who had so concerned Violet Blemenberg in 1919 and was now an active member of the Workers party—for violating an injunction issued by Judge Ormond Hunt. Reynolds was president of a carpenter's local in Detroit and a hardworking union man. His politics were of no concern to his members. Such was not the case, however, with William L. Hutcheson, the national president of the United Brotherhood of Carpenters and Joiners of America, especially since Reynolds had supported a reform candidate against him in the national union election a few months before. On January 9, 1925 Reynolds received notification that he had been expelled from the union. His local and six out of seven carpenter's locals in the city condemned the expulsion, and Reynolds ignored it, going on about his normal union business. About a month later, the national office obtained a preliminary injunction against him from Hunt. Reynolds used it to attack "Czar Hutcheson" all the more, waving it at members and saying "you could be next!"

Soon came the show-cause hearing before Judge Hunt, who, it will be recalled, had defended Sugar and his colleagues in the draft case. The current case became famous first because of the massive support given to Reynolds by local carpenters both in the courtroom and in the forums of the labor movement, and then because of Hunt's judgment. In what came to be regarded as a landmark decision, Hunt not only established that due process must be granted in trade-union proceedings against members in good standing but also that his injunction, as Sugar had claimed in his opening response, had been "improvidently made, based upon an assumption of an alleged fact now shown to be unwarranted and unauthorized." As Sugar wrote, what "an unusually unusual judge!"

This was a major victory, but it was incomplete. Sugar had the right to make a cross motion (and Judge Hunt even suggested it) demanding the restoration of all Reynolds's offices, rights, and privileges in the union. But party policy dictated that union issues be fought out in the union and not presented for the determination of "capitalist courts." Much later, in 1964, Reynolds wrote Sugar, "this was a great tactical error and of a piece with a great many leftist attitudes we were plagued with at that time, [all] the while we quoted from 'Leftism—an Infantile Disorder.'" He had recently discussed the question with two old friends:

It was our concensus that the heavy hand of the Russian Federation organizationally and of the Russian Revolution wrenched us pretty badly *out of alignment with our own revolutionary heritage and traditions*. The movement was split, the revolutionary ferment largely drawn out of the trade union movement and many, many Americans, for instance these two individuals and Scott Nearing, while not entirely alienated, were separate and aloof from the organized socialist movement for a whole lifetime.

This is an important assessment. Reynolds was writing to Sugar to ac-knowledge that the latter's view of the law and "our own revolutionary heritage and traditions" was correct. Ultraleftism was out of keeping with the givens of the U.S. system. Sugar remained true to this position and would become impatient with those who would deny the obvious benefits that the law might provide in the name of some untested concept.*

From a Marxist point of view, Sugar's position in 1925 was easy enough to defend in pragmatic terms, but it would ultimately take the writings of philoso-phers like Antonio Gramsci to carry the perspective into the mainstream of Marxist thought. While the proletarian revolution, however it occurred, would have to destroy the bourgeoisie as a class and break apart the mechanisms of its power over the state, this did not mean that all bourgeois culture and institutions must be thrown pell-mell into the ash heap. The dialectical process of revolution-ary change was not simply the replacement of the old order by its total, unim-agined opposite but rather was a synthesis, which in practice meant the *selective* dismantling of the old order. The bourgeois revolution itself had introduced ideas and institutions not only amenable but necessary to the ultimate triumph of the classless society. Chief among these were equality before the law and the mechanisms designed to protect this equality. The Bill of Rights was thus much more than a document defending bourgeois class interest. It was also a legitimate instrument in both the revolutionary workers' struggle and the building of a Socialist society. While much of the Constitution was a class document, it nevertheless contained principles of justice universal in their application.[5]

Such a perspective provided the foundation of Sugar's understanding of the relationship between the law and the class struggle. But in 1925 such philo-sophical considerations were hardly necessary to justify a legal defense of labor under attack. Confronted with an unprecedented solidarity among the bosses sporting their new conception of the open shop—supported with millions of dollars specially put aside for spies and scabs—called the "American Plan," labor leaders tended to pull in their wings. Even a firebrand like John L. Lewis was cautious. The United Mine Workers (UMW) dropped from half a million mem-bers to 250 thousand during the twenties. Gompers died in 1924 and was replaced at the helm of the AFL by a lackluster compromise candidate (who held on for thirty years), William Green, secretary-treasurer of the UMW. The labor movement languished, as leaders, fearing further losses, counseled moderation to members not always in agreement. The gap between top officials and locals in the carpenters' union was hardly unique.

Nor was the role played by people like Bud Reynolds. Communists had a checkered career in their relationship to labor during the later twenties and early thirties, but they became crucial in providing a challenge to the complacency of

*After the Communist party went "underground" in the 1950s, Sugar's successor, Ernest Goodman, was confronted by a similar situation when, in 1953, several of the party members he was defending decided not to pursue their defense on a civil-liberties basis, proclaimed themselves martyrs in the struggle against "American fascism," and went to jail.

AFL leadership. They provided militant leadership in a variety of important organizing efforts (Passaic, New Jersey; New Bedford, Massachusetts; and Gastonia, North Carolina were the most famous in textiles) and kept alive the spark of resistance in many moribund locals. They also caused much trouble in some unions, such as the International Ladies Garment Workers, where the struggle against Socialists became more important than the future of the union.

In the Detroit area, Communist aims were modest but directed with a considerable degree of intelligence. In the middle twenties, the key figure in the city was probably Bud Reynolds. He had been the only Communist president of an AFL local in Detroit. After the injunction fight, the conflict with the national led to the expulsion of the entire local. But it lived on as an independent with Reynolds as its business agent, and Frank Martel of the DFL recognized it as a legitimate union. In one incident, Reynolds and his brother were arrested on a picket line after a fight with a private detective. Sugar brought Martel along to their arraignment. The ruffled detective not only accused them of starting the fight but said that the strike was being carried out by a "bunch of Communists" and that the Reynolds brothers were members of an "outlaw organization" (referring to their local union). Martel countered this in no uncertain terms: "This is a legitimate strike. These men are regular members of organized labor, and anytime I want a god-damn stool pigeon strikebreaker to speak for the Detroit Federation of Labor, I'll notify you to that effect."

An understanding of this link is extremely important, for it meant that the local labor establishment had not succumbed to the blind anticommunism found in much of the AFL. It also meant that the local Party was far more flexible and tolerant of non-Communist leftists within the labor movement than, for example, were their comrades in New York. This idea is corroborated by the memoirs of Communist Steve Nelson who was assigned by the Party to Detroit in 1926. He found local Party policy's independence from the dictates of New York refreshing. Although there were some fluctuations (Passaic hero Albert Weisbord attempted to impose an iron conformism when he became district organizer for a brief period in 1927–28), the Detroit Communist party—perhaps influenced by the continuing popularity of the Proletarian party, by generally positive relations with the federation, or simply by the personalities of local leaders who either hailed from Detroit or were thoroughly familiar with the local scene (such as Reynolds, District Organizer Al Goetz, or Auto Workers Union leader Phil Raymond)—remained flexible in its approach to local politics and organizing.[6]

This "latitudinarian" position of Detroit Communists was unquestionably one factor that helped stimulate Sugar's sympathy for them in 1925–26. But a number of other things contributed as well. The personal influence of Bud Reynolds was important. Born in Detroit of longstanding "American" stock, Reynolds was a Communist whose views on the primacy of militant labor organizing in building the U.S. revolutionary potential coincided with Sugar's. His independence of mind, sharp intelligence, and hearty friendliness appealed strongly to Sugar as well. Reynolds was the local secretary of the International Labor Defense (ILD), a Communist affiliate that arranged for legal defense of party members, labor organizers, workers, and minority people and raised money for the publicity and legal fees connected with the cases it entered. It was deeply involved in widely publicized causes, such as Sacco-Vanzetti, Tom Mooney, and especially the Scottsboro boys. But on a day-to-day basis, the ILD, like the International Workers Order, a friendly benefits organization, and the Workers International Relief, a strike-benefit society, gave yeoman service to ordinary people with often quite ordinary legal problems. Sugar began to take many of their cases, often without fee.[7]

This was the main route by which he became known and respected in Detroit's black community. Most of his major cases involving injustices suffered by black people came during the thirties, but dozens of minor affairs dotted his calendar. One not-so-minor trial drew his participation, though only as an advisor on local questions. This was the famous case of Ossian Sweet, a black physician who with family and friends in September, 1925 defended his newly purchased home against a white mob and mortally wounded one of the trespassers. The main lawyer in the case was Clarence Darrow. This was Sugar's first meeting with Darrow, and he was spellbound by the man's courtroom presence. After a first trial of all eleven people in the house ended in a hung jury, a second—this time against Sweet's brother Henry, who had admitted firing a gun—ended in acquittal on the basis of the good old constitutional rights of bearing arms and defending one's home. Sugar gained the friendship of both Darrow and the Sweet family at this time. Darrow would be a supporter of a variety of Detroit causes (including Sugar's political candidacies), and Ossian Sweet a fellow organizer in a number of campaigns and programs. Henry, who became a lawyer, joined Sugar in several cases during the thirties.[8]

Sugar also agreed with the Communists in Detroit on the need to build a third-party movement. With their support, as well as that of other leftists, he agreed to run for political office in 1927 as a labor candidate in the nonpartisan spring elections for justice of the peace. His campaign literature emphasized the often unacknowledged importance of the office. At the lowest rung on the judicial ladder, the justice court was notoriously slipshod in its procedures. And as it dealt with petty crimes, the malfeasance of its judges was often the lawbreaker's first experience with the law. The justice courts were also the rocks upon which the hopes of many a young lawyer were dashed. As Sugar put it, "In a great number of instances, the very essence of enthusiastic advocacy is crushed. How is the young lawyer to become trained in the technique of the presentation of a case when in the infancy of his practical education his every effort for expression is smothered by impatience, by a lack of comprehension?" As a justice, Sugar would therefore make the court respectable. His candidacy was unsuccessful, although he received several hundred votes. No doubt many citizens of Detroit agreed with Clarence Burton, a local title-company owner and civic leader, who wrote the following remark at the bottom of a campaign circular: "I cannot vote for Mr. Sugar. He was not a good citizen during the late war."[9]

Sugar, Auto Organizing, and the Communist Party

The most important area of mutual concern for Sugar and local Communists was the desire to organize automobile workers. Since its peak in 1919–20, automobile unionism had all but collapsed by the midtwenties. The Auto Workers Union, once claiming a membership of as many as forty-five thousand with thirty-five locals in five states and possessing seven full-time organizers, counted no more than fifteen hundred by 1926. This, however, represented an improvement over the depths reached in early 1922 as a consequence of the depression of 1920–21. The Detroit local had been destroyed by hard times and government and company terrorism. Only two to three hundred skilled men continued to hold cards in Detroit in 1922. The national membership was no more than eight hundred. A brief revival occurred with the upswing of the production year 1922–23, but the espionage mechanisms established by the Detroit Employers Association saw to it that the boomlet was quashed. Later that year, Logan, recognizing the desperate straits of the union, concluded an agreement with Edgar Owens, the Communist district organizer in Detroit: in return for positive comments in the *Auto Worker* about the Workers party, Owen would see to it that fifty communists would become dues-paying members of the AWU. The bitterness of this pill for Logan, the past master of anti-Communist ridicule, was reduced, perhaps, by the Communists' recent shift away from ultraleftism, but if ever one had an example of a successful "united-front" tactic, this was it. While the newspaper folded early in 1924 and Logan and his Socialist comrades gave up hope, the small group of Communists in the union, especially in Detroit Local 127, gave their fullest energies to auto organizing.

In the midtwenties this was both a promising, and a forbidding, task. It was promising because almost no other group in the United States was seeking to organize these (and many other) industrial workers. The IWW was all but dead as a viable organization, having been crushed pitilessly after the war. The Socialist party, moribund and leaderless, hardly had a trade-union policy. The AFL seemed satisfied to retreat behind craft barriers and hope for better days. There was a brief flurry of rhetoric in 1926–27 (the 1926 national convention was even held in Detroit), but the AFL despaired of finding a way to break through the maze of craft jealousies and the ominous power of the companies.

The path was thus open for Communist occupation of an organizational vacuum. But what a forbidding path it was! Robert W. Dunn's masterpiece, *Labor and Automobiles* (1929), describes the growth of the auto giants during the twenties and how they were able to dominate their work force.

Maurice Sugar

The automobile came of age in the United States during the twenties. By 1928, twenty-five million motor vehicles—more than the total number of telephones in use—were on the roads of the United States. Annual production of cars had tripled during the decade with 4.6 million, valued at over five billion dollars, being produced in 1928. Ten billion gallons of gas were pumped that year, while the industry itself consumed "82% of the rubber imports for tires, 63% of the total plate glass production, . . . 60% of the upholstery leather, 14% of the finished rolled steel, 22% of the tin, 17% of the lead, 12% of the copper, 29% of the nickel, and 13% of the hardwood produced in the United States." This country and Canada (largely U.S. companies) accounted for an astounding 90 percent of the total world automobile production at the end of the decade. And of that, despite a wide dispersal of plants nationally, "75% of all cars made in the United States came from Michigan." Within the state, the Detroit area—with Highland Park, Hamtramck, and "Fordson" (Dearborn)—led with a daily car production of around eleven thousand, followed by Flint with fifty-nine hundred, Pontiac with seven hundred, and Lansing with six hundred. Beyond basic auto production, body, part, and accessory companies (some twelve hundred in all) produced myriads of goods. Although figures fluctuated, and companies were notoriously cautious about providing them, the total work force in the industry approached a half million, with some 60 percent of these working in the core area of southeastern Michigan. For some economists, Detroit, now the nation's fourth largest city, had become the hub of U.S. industrial life. Foster and Catchings argued that "no one industry and no one combination of industries in any country has grown rapidly enough to furnish the stimulation to business which the automobile has furnished in the United States."

Autoworkers understood why this was so more clearly, perhaps, than the economists. A simple figure, produced by the Bureau of Labor Statistics, suffices: productivity had increased by 272 percent from 1914 to 1925. "In other words," wrote Dunn, each worker "produced nearly three automobiles for every one he produced in 1914." New technology and generalized rationalization of the productive system accounted for a good deal of this, but speedup, especially as dictated by the final assembly process—the moving conveyor called "the line"—was a significant factor in raising productivity. A 1927 report estimated that since 1919 the speed of the assembly line had increased anywhere from 30 to 50 percent throughout the industry.

Speedup was accompanied by a host of other elements of worker exploitation: constant surveillance, fifteen-minute lunch breaks at one's work spot, hiring practices that mixed uncertainty with favoritism, dependency on overtime for a living wage, annual layoff periods that destroyed any hope of accumulating savings except for the most senior people, and finally—the main reason there were so few senior people—frightful health and safety conditions. The auto industry had the worst on-the-job accident rates in the nation, and health hazards—"dust from sand blasting, polishing, buffing, and woodworking; brass chills, bronchitis and other respiratory diseases; lead poisoning; heat in the

110

forging and other hot processes; fumes from acid dipping and electroplating," not to mention noise pollution—were appalling. Dunn's outstanding analysis of these problems brought to light the "mysteries" behind the incredibly high turnover rate in this "high-paying" industry.

To sustain these profitable circumstances, the automobile companies had created a massive system of labor domination. This meant, above all, the prevention of unionization. While both the National Automobile Chamber of Commerce and the National Automobile Dealers Association carried out extensive union-busting activities, the old Employers Association of Detroit continued to lead the way. On one hand, it operated an employment bureau that had placed an estimated seven hundred thousand workers in the industry by 1929; its chief functions were to assure that "reliable" workers were regularly supplied and to place scabs during strikes. On the other, it promoted the cause of antiunionism with vast sums spent on propaganda, dominated the local chamber of commerce, ran two local periodicals (the *Detroiter* and *Detroit Saturday Night*), and channeled auto money into antiunion activities against other trades.

Labor espionage had become a big business. Exact numbers for the 1920s are not available, but the rapid rate of growth in the private-detective field owed much to these firms' antiunion contracts. Routine work involved posing as workers in the plant and sniffing out union talk. More creative activity, however, involved "preventative medicine." As one Durant worker described in 1926, "Every morning when the unemployed swarm into the employment office we find two or three spies talking unionism, socialism, and radicalism. Here's how it's done. Two of them stay at the doors as workers come in and talk socialism to attract the workers' attention. Later, when the office is about full they talk unionism and the need of organization. If any one becomes interested, or shows any favorable leanings, he is at once reported to the employment manager and does not get hired."

The Ford Motor Company was unwilling to trust union busting to any outside agency. Over the course of the twenties, Ford policy shifted away from the snooping paternalism of the "sociological department" to the totalitarianism of the "service department." The company handbook stated, "The industrial relation between the Ford Motor Company and its employees is purely individual, and every policy is designed with the intention of keeping it so." The atomized "hand" was to be kept that way by legions of internal police within the plants hired, usually, directly out of prison. The key criterion of their employment was that they be tough. Harry Bennett, the group leader of Ford's storm troopers, was an exprizefighter with alleged connections in the underworld. The shop floor at Ford was a tissue of suspicion and brutality. But the system extended well beyond the plants as Ford service men, receiving cooperation from the police (especially those of Dearborn, a city run by Henry Ford like a private domain), rooted out "subversion" wherever it occurred. To speak about unions in your fraternal hall or to wave to a known organizer on the street or to shake the wrong hand in public could mean immediate dismissal from Ford.

The risks involved in entering the battle to organize the auto industry were thus considerable. Undaunted, the Communists had established a solid position in the Auto Workers Union and capitalized on that to build "shop nuclei" in the plants. A tiny number of Communists imbued with the Bolshevik concept of the *vanguard* could make an enormous difference in creating a trade-union presence. Historian Roger Keeran estimates that some four hundred Party members out of perhaps seven hundred in the city were in the plants by 1928. Communist Philip Raymond emerged as the key leader of the AWU, defeating Lester Johnson for secretary in 1926 and recreating a weekly paper, now called the *Auto Workers' News*.

The main work of the union was at first propaganda on behalf of unionism through a series of four-page shop papers (the *Ford Worker, Dodge Worker, Briggs Worker,* etc.). These irregularly published papers were full of news about conditions in the plants, much of it written anonymously by workers, lessons on the nature of the capitalist system, and support for the political goals of the Communist party. The most important thing about them was their clear focus on the class struggle in the plants—the viciousness of the exploitation and the hardhitting response of working people. For example, in the August 1926 issue of the *Ford Worker* there appeared "A Ford Worker's Prayer":

> Our Father Who art in Dearborn, Henry be thy Name.
> Let pay-day come. Thy will be done in Fordson as it is in Highland Park.
> Give us this day our 6 bucks (plus 40¢)
> And forgive us our laziness, as we forgive Thee for speeding us up.
> Lead us not into intelligent thot [*sic*] or action
> But deliver us from all Freedom. For Thine is true slavery.
> Thy power over us forever and ever. Amen.
>
> —From a Fordson Worker

As if to answer it, a poem from Jim Waters in the same issue sang the refrain,

> To hell with you!
> You ain't the whole earth,
> Not by a damn sight!

The constant barrage of condemnation and exhortation in these widely circulated little papers unquestionably had an effect on workers' sense of solidarity.

This Communist effort in the preorganizational stage of the autoworkers movement was significant. By 1929, Communists in fifteen cells in the main auto plants in the city had managed to recruit "several thousand" members for the AWU. Hundreds more had joined locals in Cleveland, Pontiac, and Flint. Sugar was the main lawyer utilized by the Auto Workers Union (when needed) in the two dozen spontaneous strikes to which they gave assistance during the 1927–30 period. Their policy emphasized routine organizational work to help give the walkouts some stability and cohesion. Moreover, as Roger Keeran emphasizes, "the AWU organizers impressed on the workers that a successful walkout demanded racial solidarity and such aggressive tactics as mass picketing." There was no apparent change in this orientation despite the new international focus from 1929 on "red unionism," which called for heightened radicalism and conscious dual unionism. All of this confirmed for Sugar the importance of the work of Detroit's Communists in the struggle for social justice.[10]

With the Depression, their role became all the more significant. The Soviet Party's assessment, made in mid-1928, that capitalism was entering a "third period" (following "stabilization" after 1921) characterized by massive new economic dislocation had proved accurate. Nowhere was this more obvious than in Detroit. The United States' industrial showcase suddenly became an industrial wasteland. Already hurting before the crash, the automobile industry collapsed thereafter. By the late summer of 1931, employment levels in the automobile industry were roughly one-third what they had been in mid-1929. Auto production dropped from 5.4 million in 1929 to 1.4 million in 1932. For those who continued to work, wages had been slashed, and a full week of work was abnormal. Suffering was widespread and severe. The Department of Public Relief found it impossible to serve its hundreds of thousands of applicants. Petty crime flourished. Clayton Fountain, an autoworker, recalled touring wealthy neighborhoods early in the morning to steal milk, and trips to the countryside to pilfer food from farmers were common.

Thousands saw their meager savings wiped out by bank failures. Sugar was directly involved in this aspect of the trauma: "In Detroit there were some thirteen private banks. These were neighborhood banks patronized almost exclusively by workers who had deposited their small savings, accumulated over a long period of time, as insurance against unemployment or adversity. Already, by [the end of] 1930, *every one of these banks had closed its doors*. The savings of 34,330 workers to the extent of $6,250,000 were suddenly wiped out. I represented these depositors in the effort to salvage something for them. I failed." Sugar estimated that another fifteen thousand workers with savings in other institutions lost everything also. While all the fifty thousand were not unemployed, this is a good measure of the magnitude of destitution in Detroit.

Sugar investigated another problem in detail for the AWU. For those lucky enough still to have a job, in addition to lowered wages and to partial workweeks, there was the familiar issue of speedup. As he summarized his findings, "In all their years of employment [autoworkers] had never seen speed-up used with the mercilessness which characterized it [now]." He listed seven forms of speedup: (1) new machinery with faster gearings; (2) conveyor speedup; (3) doubling, even tripling, the number of machines tended by one person; (4) sheer terrorism by foremen; (5) increasing required output units per machine; (6) cutting the time unit to perform a given operation; (7) the "adjustment" of piecework rates and bonus and premium systems of payment. In all, he calculated a range of speedup rates from 50 percent increases in productivity for

113

punch press operators to 400 percent for metal polishers and transmission-gear drillers. The foundations for worker radicalization both outside and inside the plants were thus being laid.[11]

For those inside, however, the initial impact was demoralization. The number of job actions in auto declined precipitously, as did the membership of the AWU. The only important strike in the industry from 1929 to 1933 occurred in Flint in July 1930. Its significance lies less in what happened than in what its legal aftermath tells us about the stance of the law in Michigan toward unions.

The strike arose from cuts in piece rates at Fisher Body Number 1. The demands reflected Depression hardship: withdrawal of wage cuts, the guarantee of a dollar an hour for pieceworkers, the eight-hour day and a five-day week with no overtime. Phil Raymond, Nydia Baker, and former IWW leader Henry Albertini led a group of AWU members from Detroit into the fray. Mass picketing was organized, attempts were made to spread the strike to other units, and community support was sought. They were opposed by Chief Caesar Scavrada of the Flint police department. A measure of his regard for the law may be taken from his later testimony before a congressional committee about the arrest of protest marchers without bringing criminal charges. Said his questioner, Representative John Nelson, "You just arrested them?" "That is all," came the reply. Representative Carl Backman then asked, helpfully, "Why, you arrest them for disorderly conduct, do you not?" "Well," said Chief Scavrada, "possibly that would be a good excuse." Following an honored tradition, he argued that in stopping communism, violation of the law was not too high a price to pay. In the Fisher Body strike he quickly jailed eighteen people, including several Detroit Communists, without any semblance of a charge. In several days he and his mounted police had brought the rest of the strike in tow.

The eighteen were still locked up, held five days now without charge. Upon Sugar's recommendation, a young liberal attorney, Nichol Olds, was dispatched by the International Labor Defense to apply for writs of habeas corpus. He appeared before Judge Edward D. Black. There is no right in English law more sacred than the automatic granting of the writ of habeas corpus. Furthermore, a Michigan statute added that denial of such a writ left the officer of the court liable for one thousand dollars in damages. Judge Black, however, like Scavrada, apparently thought that Genessee County lay outside the jurisdiction of Magna Carta and the Constitution, for he informed Olds that he thought the police department was not holding these men in jail "unreasonably" and concluded, "therefore I do not want to issue the writs of habeas corpus." Although Olds had some trouble masking his shock, he persevered. To quote the official transcript,

> Mr. Olds: My understanding of the statute is that a writ of *habeas corpus* is a writ of right and not one of discretion and that the court has no right to refuse it when a proper application is made.

Judge Black: I don't like these fellows who come out from Detroit and start to create trouble in Flint. They have no right to come here.

Mr. Olds: They have just as much right to travel the highways as you or I have.

Judge Black: Well, if that is the way you feel about it, I again refuse to issue the writs.

Mr. Olds: We should not look upon the prisoners as criminals but should consider them no different from any one prisoner who is held in jail charged with murder or holdup or robbery.

Judge Black: I do not consider them the equal of any other criminal and so far as I am concerned they can rot in jail.

Mr. Olds: Can't you see that your attitude towards these men makes them hate us that much more because we refuse to give them their constitutional rights?

Judge Black: I don't care if they do hate us more.

Mr. Olds: I understand that these are the very rights that James Otis and our other revolutionary fathers fought for in the revolution.

Judge Black: (No answer).

Mr. Olds: Judge, you know what the statute provides as a penalty for your refusal to issue a writ of this kind.

Judge Black: You can pursue your remedy.

Mr. Olds: We ought to be fair about this matter.

Judge Black: I always try to be fair and it seems that only people from Detroit can come up here and tell me I am not fair, and if you don't get out of this office, I will kick your ass out of here.

The story did not end there. Later on, Sugar, Walter Nelson, and Patrick H. O'Brien represented the eighteen in an American Civil Liberties Union (ACLU)–initiated suit against Judge Black. It would seem that they had an open-and-shut case. Nothing was further from the truth. It turned out that Olds never actually "filed" the suit, that is, legally placed it before the court. Sugar and the others contended that he had been dismissed before he had a chance and, besides, that presentation was tantamount to filing. The case was heard in the same circuit court of Genessee County wherein Judge Black practiced his magic. Black was represented by General Motors' main law firm and won the case on the technicality. The appeal to the Supreme Court lost as well—on the same grounds—although one justice later confessed to Sugar that they thought that old Judge Black had had enough of a scare to be "good from now on." As we shall see, he was not, but Sugar would have the last laugh.[12]

This incident gives an idea of the arrogance of public authorities in the fiefdoms of the industrial giants. Black and Scavrada were tools of General Motors and willingly operated beyond the law that they were supposed to uphold. But nowhere was such industrial authoritarianism more pervasive than in the barony seventy-five miles to the south, in the land of the man who kept a picture of Adolph Hitler on his wall and feared that he would die at the hands of a Jewish assassin sent by the mythical Elders of Zion.

The Ford Hunger March

The assassins of 1932, however, came not from the shadow world of racist fantasy. Instead they were Henry Ford's own hired guns, either from his praetorian guard (otherwise known as the service department) or from the Dearborn police then under the authority of Henry's cousin Clyde, the mayor of that city. Sugar's education in the interrelationships between law and the class struggle reached a peak in the Ford Massacre of March 7, 1932. No incident summarizes the issue more clearly and no incident played a greater role in crystallizing Sugar's thinking about it. Moreover, his role as the main attorney defending the interests of the marchers in the legal aftermath of the march marked him as one of the key figures in Detroit Left and labor circles, a position increasingly carrying with it national prominence as well.

The roots of the Ford Hunger March go back to the brutal winter of 1929–30. The lightning-fast impact of the stock-market crash on employment took almost everyone by surprise. Governmental agencies were incapable of responding to the flood of requests for assistance and most political groups found it difficult to formulate coherent programs. The reigning opinion among economists, businessmen, politicians, civic leaders, and even important churchmen (the "best brains of the Depression," Sugar called them) was that the "skid" was a passing phenomenon. For his part, Henry Ford thought that the crash, in punishing foolish speculation, was a good thing. The thirty thousand Ford employees who had been laid off by Christmas 1929 tended to disagree. And things only got worse.

In the atmosphere of double-talk and paralysis, the position taken by the Trade Union Unity League (TUUL), the newly formed union arm of the Communist party under the leadership of William Z. Foster, offered a forthright alternative to mindless hope and to flophouse despair. The international Communist movement already had broad experience in work with the unemployed (we often forget that in much of Europe unemployment rates never got much below 10 percent all during the twenties), and throughout 1929, Communists in the United States were expecting the bottom to fall out. Thus, when the TUUL proposed the development of "unemployed councils" in the major industrial centers of the nation, response by party members and sympathizers was immediate. Coordinated by Herbert Benjamin, the unemployed-council movement sponsored a series of marches and demonstrations during the winter of 1929–30 organized around such slogans as "Don't Starve, Fight!" and "Work or Wages!"—the latter referring to their principal demand of unemployment insurance financed by employers and the government and administered by worker committees.

The quick response by the unemployed surprised even the Communists. A nationwide demonstration on March 6, 1930 drew hundreds of thousands of people onto the streets to protest the economic cataclysm besetting the country. In July, thirteen hundred delegates met in Chicago to form a solid national body.

Sugar, who attended the meeting, recalled the atmosphere: "To the press and to big business this was Moscow in diabolical action. To the unemployed it was loyal Americans in patriotic protest demonstration. I shall not forget the chill that swept through the gathering when word came that the Governor had dispatched the state militia to break up the meeting. The business was hurriedly consummated and the organization was firmly established." While coordinated by the Communist party, participation in the unemployed councils went well beyond it. They represented the first significant movement against the Depression and made a profound impression on U.S. working (or, rather, non-working) people. Perhaps their most important activity as time went by was the struggle against evictions. If Detroiters today remember anything about the work of the Communists in those days, it is usually about how the squads from the unemployed-council office would return furniture back to a house after the sheriff had moved it out.[13]

The Detroit Unemployed Council, under the leadership of Alfred Goetz, was regarded as one of the most effective in the country. The March 6, 1930 rally brought out eighty thousand people and resulted in unprovoked police violence that injured several marchers. Earl Browder praised the practicality of the Detroit council in an article published in the *Communist* and chastised his wordier comrades elsewhere, urging "fewer high-falutin' phrases, more simple every-day deeds." Jane and Maurice Sugar were deeply involved in the local effort, preparing and distributing leaflets, speaking at rallies, organizing endless meetings, defending demonstrators in court. She remembered it as one of the busiest times of their life. Cadillac Square and Campus Martius, the two largest squares in Detroit, became permanent forums for speaking to and organizing the unemployed. At any time of the day (and often through the night) clusters of people would be found gathered around speakers at various places on the squares. Although the subject was grim, many people still recall an atmosphere charged with real hope and excitement.[14] Folks talked, danced, and sang.

One of the songs they sang—and that hungry people across the nation increasingly sang—was Maurice Sugar's "Soup Song." Very few songs of the Depression enjoyed such wide currency. Its easy rhythms (sung to the tune of "My Bonnie Lies over the Ocean") and biting ironies encompassed both the despair and the dark humor that marked the workers' outlook in those years. And just beneath the surface, in both the song and in U.S. social reality, lay the explosive potential of protest. Sugar remembered that he wrote it late one night after giving a talk at a barren "lodge" for the homeless and destitute set up by the city. There were only bunks, a few chairs, and tables. "The room was packed with men, both white and black, native born and foreign born of many national origins." His talk, on poverty in the midst of plenty and the need for social reform, met with overwhelming approval. The men cheered and cheered. They then gave Sugar a "simple wooden cane that only cost a few cents." They apologized. Sugar wept. About 2:00 A.M. on that cold Febraury morning, the "Soup Song" was born:

117

I'm spending my night at the flop house
I'm spending my days on the street
I'm looking for work and I find none
I wish I had something to eat.

Chorus
Sooo-oup, sooo-oup, they give me a bowl of soo-oup
Sooo-oup, sooo-oup, they give me a bowl of soup.

I spent twenty years in the factory
I did everything I was told
They said I was loyal and faithful
Now, even before I get old.

I saved fifteen bucks with my banker
To buy me a car and a yacht
I went down to draw out my fortune
And this is the answer I got.

I fought in the war for my country
I went out to bleed and to die
I thought that my country would help me
But this was my country's reply.

I went on my knees to my maker
I prayed every night to the Lord
I vowed I'd be meek and submissive
And now I've received my reward.[15]

The spirit of rallies, "eviction parties," and songfests that marked the Michigan unemployed-councils movement remained high despite vicious attacks on its Communist leadership. One attempt to "root out the reds" came in the form of an act passed by overwhelming margins by both the Michigan House and Senate on May 18, 1931 that would have required all aliens to register with the state to prove their legality and simultaneously forced any Michigan resident to produce upon demand proof of his or her citizenship or "registered" status. Moreover, employers would be required to demonstrate that none of their employees were "illegal." The practical effects of this would be to give police and employers license to harass "undesirable" elements at will and make "suspects" out of anyone with "foreign-sounding" names or a trace of an accent.

The bill was sponsored by the Union League of Michigan, a "civic" organization whose list of officers read like a Who's Who of Michigan businessmen. Currently Jacob Spolansky, a native of Russia, Justice Department spy, and professional anti-Communist, was the head of its Subversive Activities Committee and lobbied it through the legislature. Republican Governor Wilbur Brucker, a member of the league, gave it his full support. A storm of protest arose from all ethnic groups and their organizations, whatever their politics. The liberal establishment of the state, spurred on by the Detroit branch of the ACLU, voiced its outrage and attacked the act as unconstitutional. The labor movement, however, was deeply split on the issue with the conservative forces in the local AFL, led by the Detroit federation's Frank Martel, actually supporting the act in the hope that it would reduce labor-market competition.

The "Spolansky Act," as Sugar dubbed it in a *Nation* article, backfired in its effect. Business interests had sponsored it specifically to thwart the growing Communist influence in Michigan, but it obviously threatened every person with an accent or who "looked" foreign. The lessons were clear and made for effective propaganda. Sugar recalled,

> I spoke at many meetings. In my talks I explained the provisions of the law and presented graphic illustrations of its application. But my emphasis was upon the role being played by persons in public office who reflected the will and carried out the designs of the industrialists and big business; and how these elements met the crisis of unemployment. My conclusion was that the ultimate solution of our economic and social problems could come only through the launching of a political party of the workers—a Labor Party.

The ACLU immediately challenged the law and on December 9, 1931 a three-judge federal court unanimously held it unconstitutional. A year later Brucker was smashed in his bid for reelection (running far behind Hoover) by a colorless Democrat named Comstock.[16]

In the course of 1930 and 1931 then, Sugar had become immersed in the efforts of the unemployed councils. He also became active in the John Reed Club, which, in Detroit, as elsewhere, brought leftists and intellectuals together to discuss critical issues in politics and art. In January 1932, they launched a literary magazine called the *New Force, a Monthly Proletarian Magazine of Art, Literature, and Current Events*. Among its editors and writers were friends of Sugar's such as Bud Reynolds, Paula Golden, Ben Bavly, and Carl Manela.

Sugar contributed a number of pieces—book reviews, essays, vignettes. The most interesting, which appeared in January 1932, was a review of *Our Lawless Police* (Viking Press) by Ernest Jerome Hopkins, a liberal who had done the research for the federal Wickersham Commission on Lawlessness in Law Enforcement. Sugar began with a standard Marxist analysis of how business runs the government and manages to maintain the "illusion of democracy" through its domination of "the agencies of information and education." But ultimately, the preservation of the state, especially the capitalist state in time of crisis, depends on the use of force. The military is the final line of defense, but "the form which this force takes, closest to us, is the policeman." Sugar then detailed a series of incidents that occurred in a few short months in Detroit during late 1930—direct brutality resulting in death or severe injury of local citizens, all of which went without penalty. Then there was the "loop," by which prisoners were sent from one station to another to elude habeas corpus writs and lawyers; during their short stays in each, prisoners would be stuffed into cells without proper facilities, would not be fed, and would hardly be allowed to sleep. The purpose was to encourage "bums" to leave Detroit (the capital of U.S. unemployment) and accused felons to confess. The special treatment of "reds" at the hands of the police was also noted. But, said Sugar, police brutality ultimately stems from "the system in which we live [which] in itself is the essence of brutality and cruelty. . . . It grows out of the institution of private property under which one class in society lives in luxury at the expense of the great mass of workers who are compelled to live in a state of poverty, wretchedness, and despair in order that the privileged group may remain undisturbed in its possessions." The real problem, at base, was not in the violation of the law by the police. Instead "it lies in the violation, by our economic and political system, of the right of workers to live."[17]

The events of March 7, 1932 and the days that followed seemed to illustrate every facet of Sugar's analysis. Workers demanding the right to live by working; murderous police, the front-line agents of the state, acting at the almost unmediated behest of big business; and a cover-up carried out by democratically elected officials—such was the stuff of the Ford Massacre.

As a part of a nationwide effort to dramatize the plight of the jobless, the Unemployed Council of Detroit and the Auto Workers Union organized a march of some three to five thousand people who were to walk from a point in Detroit down Miller Road into Dearborn and on to the employment office of Ford's vast River Rouge complex. Backed by this mass, a committee would then present a list of demands that included rehiring laid-off workers, half-rate pay for unemployed, a shortened day for lower pay, slowing down the breakneck pace of work, fifteen-minute rest periods, no discrimination against black people, and a number of immediate relief proposals for both working and nonworking Ford employees.

Bitten by an icy wind, but cheered by the sun, the marchers moved toward Dearborn. They were allowed to march in Detroit (though without an official permit) by the city's new mayor, Frank Murphy, who overruled his police chief, Heinrich Pickert. But Dearborn was another matter. The procession was halted at the border by a small army of city police. Responding to the command to identify their leaders with the cry, "We are all leaders!" the crowd pressed forward and caught its first dose of tear gas and possibly a few bullets. It dispersed toward an open field, many gathered stones, and a shower of missiles descended on the cops. The crowd pushed on down the road, the Dearborn police retreating before it. After reconnoitering with firemen who were attempting to hook up hoses, the police tried to set up a new tear gas screen, but the wind carried most of it away, and the marchers put all the uniformed men in renewed flight. Finally, at the gates of the plant another half mile down the road, a new, fresh mass of police from Detroit (why they were there became a major

120

issue later on) and a battalion of Ford service men reinforced Dearborn police and firemen. As the latter successfully attached their hoses and began to spray, the police opened fire. Three marchers, Joe York, Coleman Leny, and Joe De-Blasio, died on the spot and fifty others were felled with a variety of wounds.

Many of the marchers now fled in panic, although a leader got many to regroup in order to retreat in regular formation. At this point, Service Department Chief Harry Bennett appeared in a car coming out of Gate 3. His car was pelted with rocks and he was injured; he poured shots into the crowd until his guns ran out of bullets; he then grabbed a policeman's gun and emptied it before collapsing. The Gate 3 assembly of lawmen now exploded in a final fusillade, gunning down demonstrators from behind. Joe Bussel, a muscular sixteen-year-old Young Communist Leaguer, was killed by a bullet in the back, and scores of others were hit. As far as could be determined, none of the demonstrators were armed with anything more sophisticated than sticks and stones. At least, none of the injured "law-enforcement officers" suffered gunshot wounds. Forty-eight people were arrested, many of them wounded and in the hospital.

Sugar was called in immediately and witnessed some of the pandemonium at Detroit City Hospital, where families of dead and wounded frantically searched for news, while many of the latter were chained in their beds, lying in their own blood and sweat. Meanwhile a Detroit dragnet went out and hundreds of "suspects" were rounded up. The afternoon and morning press blared out the word: "Communists Inflamed by Foster Hurl Stones and Clubs in Prearranged Outbreak," said the *Free Press*. The tone of the immediate press reaction varied little, stressing provocation by outside Communist agitators. The American Legion and the Detroit Employers Association did their best to keep alive the visions of the Moscow menace and Harry Bennett heroism, but it quickly became apparent, as many journalists on the scene began to describe what they actually saw, that the real story was one of massive overreaction by the police. By March 9 the Hearst-owned *Detroit Times* was talking about "blunders:" the "Dearborn police evidently changed an orderly demonstration into a riot, with death and bloodshed as its toll." The *News* followed suit. Only the *Free Press* retained a hard line against the marchers.

Then came what might be called the legal massacre. At Ford, hundreds of workers were fired indiscriminately on the suspicion of participation or even of sympathy for the marchers. Anyone who gave money for the funerals of the slain marchers was subject to discharge. Ridiculous extremes were reached. Sugar wrote: "One Italian worker was 'suspected.' All the workers who lived on [his] block, all Italian workers, were discharged." Ford service men violated virtually every civil right employees possessed, searching lunch boxes and coats for any indication of workers' connection with the Communist party or the AWU. Throughout Detroit and the adjacent "Ford" suburbs, Communists were arrested in wholesale fashion. It seemed that the days of A. Mitchell Palmer were returning. The police deemed warrants unnecessary and did not worry about making formal charges against arrestees. The general scenario—and the position, Sugar discovered, of the Detroit Employers Association—was to focus on the Communists while feigning deep sympathy for the "real" unemployed.

It was left to Prosecutor Harry Toy to develop the key refinements of the legal massacre. The first was his "ringing statement" to the press of March 9 in which he pronounced the marchers guilty of "criminal syndicalism"—the use of violence and terrorism to obtain industrial or political reform—and called for a grand-jury investigation to ferret out the "outside agitators" responsible for inciting to riot. Sugar was aghast at the ethics of such a public pretrial of people against whom no indictments had been lodged. Secondly, Toy would not allow the routine courtesy, requested by Sugar, of having a physician representing the interests of the families of the dead men present at their autopsies. Sugar's suspicions were confirmed when the report was returned indicating that none of them had been shot in the back. Bussel came the closest, "shot," according to the report, "in the side of the body." Moreover, Toy allowed the murder bullets to be returned to the Dearborn police. The cover-up was underway.

Sugar decided to respond to this situation publicly. If the prosecutor would go to the press so, too, would he. In a long letter, he cited the various indiscretions of Prosecutor Toy and made the novel request to have himself appointed as a special assistant prosecutor assigned to the grand-jury investigation. Unfortunately, there was little public attention given to this letter, nor did Toy respond to it directly, although he remarked to the press that Sugar's request was impossible to fulfill "because the prosecutor is elected to represent the people, whereas Mr. Sugar represents one side of the controversy." The unintended irony of this remark was not lost on many workers. Despite the initial public sense that there was definitely some form of wrongdoing on the other side, the government, by focusing on no one but the marchers (only *they* were to be investigated by the grand jury), sought to convince the world that they alone bore responsibility. And in the end, double-talk and a captive press thoroughly diluted the initial hints of outrage against the oppressive power of the police in the Detroit metropolitan area.

The high point of disgust was reached early on. A great mass funeral march—wisely allowed by Murphy and free of police surveillance, thanks to the advice of his secretary, Josephine Gomon—drew up to seventy thousand participants on March 11. The majority were non-Communists, some perhaps influenced by the Party's work with the unemployed, but most just plain workers. The Party itself had no more than fifteen hundred members in the Detroit area at the time.

As time went by, however, concern waned. Even the positive efforts of the American Civil Liberties Union, whose chief, Roger Baldwin, came to town and spent long hours with Sugar in examining the mountains of evidence in the case, came to little. The focus of the grand-jury investigation kept the hunger marchers constantly on the defensive. Sugar acted as attorney for all those who appeared for the "defense" before the grand jury and pursued the line of presenting as many of the facts as possible because he knew that there was a great deal the prosecution wished to hide. Such an approach was successful in the most fundamental sense that no indictments were returned. But it was also clear that the police of Dearborn and Detroit, as well as the private army of Ford, were going to get away unscathed.

The final report, issued in late June, read, in fact, as if it had been written by the Detroit Employers Association: nameless outside agitators took advantage of Depression-wracked Detroiters to whip up a riot; the forces of law and order then did what they had to do. One juror dissented publicly from this view and accused the prosecutor of rigging the whole proceedings, but her charges (made July 3, 1932) were quickly forgotten. After all, said the press, she had been a member of the mayor's Unemployment Committee. Even the ACLU cooled toward the issue. Sugar's correspondence with Roger Baldwin indicates an unwillingness on the latter's part to commit the organization to a fight against the lawmen who killed or those who covered up their actions. This was not the first, nor the last, police riot to go unpunished. Meanwhile, with the great smokestacks of the Rouge looming in the distance, four of the martyrs to the workers' struggle lay silently in unmarked graves. A fifth victim, a black man named Curtis Williams had just died—racial segregation prevented him from being buried beside his comrades.

Overall, the Hunger March and its aftermath brought Sugar to the very heart of the struggle. It also made him understand how lonely it was. The Communists had been absolutely right, he felt, in sponsoring the march and in the general strategy that they had followed leading up to it. Yet in the end, they, not those who shot the guns, had been assigned the official blame for the deaths. And few voices really dissented. Frank Murphy, Sugar's friend, had clearly erred in allowing Detroit police to be in Dearborn on the day of the march, and they participated fully in the dragnet thereafter. Murphy wisely authorized the funeral march, but later remained silent as justice was repeatedly violated through the grand-jury fiasco.

More shocking, especially for Sugar, was the response of the rest of the Left. The Proletarian party, which had survived over the years as a small, largely educational organization, at first repudiated the march and condemned the Communists for organizing it. Then, seeing that there was some public sympathy for the fate of the demonstrators, they attempted to wangle their way into an official place in the funeral procession. As far as Sugar was concerned, this was the last straw. For them, he wrote, "the class struggle was only a conception. One engaged in it only by reading and discussing the works of Marx, Engels, and Dietzgen. But to engage in such activities as a hunger march to Ford's—that is unthinkable!" The Michigan Socialist party's resolution on the matter stressed the need for an impartial investigation and pledged to protest "efforts to hold any demonstrator responsible for any act committed in self-defense." As Sugar noted, "A carefully worded protest this." The Socialist Labor party took the position that the Communists' hyperactivism had no impact save to cause radicals to be fired from Ford's and to "discredit" the labor movement. Sugar wrote,

> I thought to myself: what does it matter that scores of thousands of unemployed workers were hungry? Better that they and their wives and children starve, meek and unprotesting, than that a few "radicals" lose their jobs at Ford. [As if] Ford needed an opportunity to discharge radicals! The "radicals" who did nothing and who counselled others to do nothing for fear of losing their jobs—these were the good radicals. They didn't "throw discredit on the labor movement"! With such "radicalism," the "excruciating exploitation of capitalism" that the radical criticizes could endure forever.

For Sugar, then, the Ford Hunger March marked the point at which he decided that among political groupings, the Communists were the best friends of the workers.[18]

Sugar's mother, Mary.

Sugar's father, Kalman.

*Brimley, with Bay Mills in the background.
(Photo courtesy of the* Soo Evening News,
Sault Sainte Marie, MI.)

Trestle to Bay Mills. (Photo courtesy of the
Soo Evening News, *Sault Sainte Marie,
MI.)*

Brimley school (all classes), 1900. Maurice is twelfth from the right in the first row. (Photo courtesy of McIver Photo.)

The company store, Scribner's (across the tracks from "K. Sugar"). (Photo courtesy of McIver Photo.)

*Maurice Sugar, football player, is standing
first on the left.*

*The Intercollegiate Socialist Society branch at
the University of Michigan, 1912. Sugar and
Jane Mayer are in front; Otto Marckwardt is
in the second row, far left.*

Sugar and Jane Mayer on a stroll.

Henry Sweet (left), *Clarence Darrow* (right),
*and attorneys Perry and Chawke pose during
the Henry Sweet trial.*

The unemployed on the streets of Detroit,
1932.

Tear gas barrage opens the attack on the
Hunger Marchers, March 7, 1932.

5 ❖ The Left Community and the Labor Movement, 1932–35

For the next three years, Sugar immersed himself in the workers' struggle in Detroit. He became one of the key figures in the Left community in the city. The work of this community—where workers and middle-class people mixed together in fraternal organizations, clubs, discussion groups, and institutions such as the ILD—in developing public sympathy for industrial unionism has received little attention. Sugar's activity, particularly his candidacy for public office in 1935, provides an excellent vehicle for exploring it.

Visting the USSR

After the legal battles in the wake of the Hunger March, Sugar and his wife took a trip to the Soviet Union. In his capacity as a member of the ILD, Sugar hit upon the idea of making "official" contact with the Soviet organization of public defenders to allow them to stay longer than the normal five-day tour. Following a chilling visit to Berlin, awash with Nazi rallies and parades, they entered the Soviet Union by train from Finland in mid-August 1932. Their first experience was disconcerting, for a rifle that Sugar had carted along in hopes of going deer hunting in Russia was held at the border, and the dozen books in English found in their luggage caused their admission to the country to be delayed for an hour until it was determined that their content was acceptable. Once on their way, however, the Sugars' impressions were almost wholly favorable.

Perhaps the most striking contrast with the United States was the fact that most Russians, including the majority of women, were employed. Nowhere was the destitution so common in Detroit in evidence. The social-insurance program, providing free medical service, sick pay, and pensions, was also now in force. Retirement was fixed at age sixty for men, fifty-five for women in most occupations. Paid two-month maternity leave, paid vacations, child-care centers, and dozens of other benefits that were mere dreams for most U.S. workers in 1932 were built into the system. Both Sugars were impressed by what they saw in the schools they visited, especially the children's sophisticated knowledge of world affairs. A list of questions asked Sugar by young teenagers in a summer "health school" ranged from "Tell us about Foster and Ford" (the Communist candidates for president in 1932) to "What is the attitude of the American people in relation to the Sino-Japanese situation and in relation to the Philippines?"

The Sugars also visited the Gorky auto plant then being built with the aid of Ford Motor Company engineers. Some production had begun and U.S. mechanics, many of them leftists whom Sugar knew, were working and teaching in the plant. The task was often difficult. Teaching peasants who had never even seen a machine how to work one through interpreters who had no Russian words for many of the parts provided quite a challenge. Sugar asked one of the Detroiters there if the trainees did any damage. "Damage! Why I've seen them, on misunderstanding some bit of instruction, proceed not only to destroy the part they are working on, but do thousands of dollars worth of damage to the machines themselves. I tell you it is heartbreaking." Sugar asked if an inept apprentice might be fired. "Hell no," he said with a grin. "You can't fire him. He owns the machine. He owns the whole damn plant."

This underlines one of Sugar's sharpest impressions of the Soviet Union, namely, that Russian workers really did feel they owned the means of production. Clearly, he visited no problem areas, such as the Ukraine, and clearly—as in China today—even the sympathetic tourist was not allowed free rein, but still the feeling was there. The children, especially, seemed to have a sense of the place of their class in the system and felt genuinely sorry for the poor workers of the United States.

But it was in the courts that Sugar felt he saw the deepest meaning of the workers' revolution. The comrades' courts—a unique feature of the system, copied later by most Communist societies—were factory tribunals. In Sugar's words, "matters which might be described as those of labor discipline, insults, slanders, 'uncomradely conduct,' minor assaults, petty thefts, lack of cooperation, absence from work, tardiness, and drunkenness" were tried in these courts by judges elected from among workers with some seniority. But all workers were asked to attend the sessions, held after work. Sugar reported,

> Procedure was informal but orderly, the testimony was unrestricted in scope, and the inquiry was thorough. Everyone present had the right to participate in the discussion, which was often spirited. The atmosphere was free, comradely, yet intensely serious. Where guilt was found the judgement [*sic*] of the workers' court would take any one of many forms. Frequently it was a comradely admonition to behave. It might be a public censure, a caricature of the offender posted in the

factory with appropriate words, a fine of up to 10 rubles, the money to go to some workers' organization.

Rarely would a worker be dismissed, although it was possible. In particularly serious cases, assistance to the accused would be rendered by MOPR, the lawyers' group that Sugar saw as the counterpart to the ILD. The judgement of these courts "had the sanction of law . . . and could not be ignored." The courts' purpose was to help workers adjust to the rigors of factory life, while engendering their belief in the concepts of social ownership of production and the value of working for the good of Soviet society as a whole. Finally, managers and workers were equally subject to trial. While the comrades' courts might later be used by Party officials merely to stimulate productivity, this innovative mechanism for dealing with one of the thorniest problems of the industrial transition seemed at the moment to be working.

Sugar also observed the operation of a misdemeanor court—the peoples court in Rostov-on-Don—and an appellate court in Moscow. The first, presided over by a three-person panel—one trained judge and two citizens—operated on a structured but informal basis. Sugar gave the example of a young truck driver who had lost control of his vehicle and hit a policeman, whose leg was broken. The story of the accident scene was out of kilter with all U.S. experience. The policeman had a prisoner in tow, a man who had been in a fight. After the accident he and a witness to the fight took the injured policeman to a doctor. The truck driver pleaded guilty. His sentence was to have his pay docked by a quarter for three months to cover the medical expenses of the policeman. Individual responsibility for one's acts was thus recognized by the system: in effect he repaid society (for medicine was fully socialized) for his mistake. As for the policeman, he admitted to Sugar that he was upset. "Of course," said Sugar, "you have a broken leg." But that was not the point—rather it was the time lost in the hospital during which a factory worker had to take over his job, and since every worker possible was needed in the factories, it was "really a serious injury to the country."

The case in the appellate court involved a woman who had lost her Moscow apartment to another. She was married to a man living in the South and after taking her vacation with him, had stayed on, without pay, for several more months. After a while, the other woman, who had children, was allowed to move into the vacant apartment. The first was now taking legal action to regain possession of "her" apartment. Both were represented by attorneys. The court ruled that justice—both individual and social—was on the side of the defendant. The plaintiff had overstayed her vacation in a flagrant manner and in so doing had put her personal interests above those of society both in terms of wasting living space in a very tight housing situation and in not working.

Sugar was not alone in being impressed with what he saw in the Soviet Union. Walter and Victor Reuther, for example, two young, searching, Socialist idealists, would make the trip the following year, work at the Gorky plant, tour much of the nation, and come away thoroughly impressed. In a letter to Sugar from Samarkand in central Asia of June 20, 1935, the Reuther brothers wrote of their impressions:

> In the 1½ years here, we have seen the Russian workers master technique and advance a long way on the road toward a cultured life. The shop life here, with the Red corner and the multiplicity of social and cultural activities, the atmosphere of freedom and security, shop meetings with their proletarian industrial democracy; all these things make an inspiring contrast to what we knew as Ford Wage-Slaves in Detroit. What we have experienced here has re-educated us along new and more practical lines.

Signing the letter "comradly [*sic*] yours," they expressed the hope, at that point, that "the changes which have come about in the international arena will have disillusioned enough of our American comrades and direct the movement along more militant lines." Many others shared their starry-eyed appreciation of the Soviet Union.

Sugar's and the Reuthers' reactions are in a way more valuable than those of the many Party members who made the voyage, for the latter were so closely tied to official circles that their views were almost necessarily positive. Steve Nelson, for example, was brought over under Party auspices, went through an intensive education program, and became a courier for the Comintern, carrying out some fairly tense, if not breathtaking, missions, all of which he found exhilarating. Eugene and Peggy Dennis were fully absorbed into Soviet life and made the ultimate sacrifice to the glory of the Socialist mission by leaving their son behind when they returned to make the revolution at home. The view of the Sugars, who went over as ordinary tourists, thus provides a somewhat more detached sense of Soviet life toward the end of the First Five-Year Plan.[1]

Upon his return, Sugar became the favorite speaker of the Friends of the Soviet Union, a group made up largely of non-Communist intellectuals. Apparently he was effective, because in December 1932 the Detroit School Board voted to prohibit him from using the city-college auditorium. The board, which passed on authorizations in normally pro forma proceedings, now refused because, it said, a "red group" had allegedly torn down a U.S. flag and replaced it with a red one at an earlier gathering. The prohibition in fact violated state law. Sugar then went to work and rallied a prestigious group of liberal professionals and AFL labor leaders to the defense of free speech. The board was taken to court, its patently illegal position there for all eyes to see. Before Judge Toms made a ruling, the board changed its mind and finally granted authorization. This little incident underlines the importance of a figure like Sugar: again and again he would go far beyond the usual confines of the Left to gather support on behalf of leftists' constitutional rights, thus keeping the door to the Popular Front ajar.

134

What kinds of things was Sugar saying in his talks? Besides his impressions of the Soviet Union, he also revealed uncharacteristic levels of revolutionary rhetoric. The following excerpt from a speech Sugar gave on April 30, 1933 at a Free Tom Mooney Conference gives an idea of his outlook at the time.

> Tom Mooney in prison personified the undying fervor of the militant worker. The militant worker cannot be subdued. The masters may starve and enslave him, their police may torture and beat him, their prosecutors may railroad and frame him, their jailers may mistreat and shackle him, but conquer him? Never! Like Tom Mooney, the worker strikes back in all these arenas of struggle. And then this great movement, like an all-engulfing flood, sweeps across the land, overwhelming, irresistible, and wipes all of the starvation and all of the slavery and all of the torture and all of the injustice—wipes it all off the face of the earth.

Sugar had gone on a nationwide tour for the Friends of the Soviet Union, visiting thirty-three cities and speaking to over ten thousand people altogether. The talks ended in California, where he met with Tom Mooney in St. Quentin. The experience—sitting down with an innocent man whose life had been sacrificed to the gods of greed and force—was almost as powerful as the visit to the Soviet Union. No individual represented the wrongs done to labor and its defenders more graphically. Sugar remarked that he had never felt such outrage toward the capitalist system.[2]

The Auto Revolt Begins

Workers were also beginning to express their outrage as well. Although the great boom in organizing came only after the mid-June passage of the National Industrial Recovery Act with its famous section 7(a), explicitly guaranteeing the right to organize "free from employer interference" in Michigan and elsewhere, strikes, mostly reacting against wage cuts that occurred despite a mild revival of the economy after November 1932, reminded the new administration of the powder keg it was sitting on.

Leftists were deeply involved in these job actions, especially in Detroit, and Sugar, as an ILD lawyer, made an important contribution. As the year 1933 dawned, the Auto Workers Union was the only active organization in the auto industry and Phil Raymond had proved to be a capable leader. The Ford Hunger March and its aftermath had made workers more sympathetic toward the AWU, and the unemployed councils continued to grow, probably peaking in the winter of 1932–33 at around thirty thousand members.

The months of January and February saw five important strikes in the city: Briggs Waterloo, Motor Products, Murray Body, Hudson, and the great Briggs

Strike that affected all four Detroit installations of the company, the largest auto supplier in the country. Walter Briggs, who also owned the Detroit Tigers, was now supplying almost half the bodies for Ford. Of these strikes, only the last failed, although it, too, contributed to the mobilization of the auto labor movement. At the same time, it brought the role of the AWU as an important force in auto organizing to an end. These circumstances had an important effect on Sugar's life and activity.

The main problem was that in the second Briggs strike, Communist leaders violated their own established principles. They normally followed a four-step procedure for union organizing: (1) a small "concentration group," working in targeted plants in key industries would propagandize to create a shop group; (2) this group would then set out a program of minimum demands and form a broader grievance committee; (3) then came an action, usually a strike in which the demands with a reasonable chance of winning would be pressed by a large strike committee drawing in many non-Communist members; and (4) once limited demands were met, the local, whether "recognized" or not, would move to solidify its gains and recruit more members. This careful, partial-victory approach was also to be accompanied by a clear avowal of Communist affiliation. Strikes should be well planned, short, limited, and democratic, and their participants organized in advance.[3]

Auto Workers Union action in the first Briggs-Waterloo strike of January 11–14, as in the other three undramatic and successful strikes, followed these guidelines. Beginning in November 1932, the AWU, invited by several pattern makers at this plant, built the shop group with care. By early January, when it became clear that another wage cut was coming, AWU people in the plant circulated leaflets calling for resistance and developed alternative plans for walkouts depending on management tactics. On January 11, the process unfolded like clockwork and the six hundred–worker plant was shut down. At a subsequent meeting, following a lively debate between the more cautious Communists and the fiery Wobbly, Frank Cedervall, demands were set. They included rescinding the wage cut, a 10-percent raise, a 50-cent minimum wage, an eight-hour day, a six-day week with no overtime, no reprisals, and recognition of shop committees. Calling upon the other Briggs shops for support and using unemployed autoworkers as well as strikers on the picket line, in three days they got a response from Briggs: the cuts would be rescinded in all four Briggs plants and all strikers would be hired back. After some debate, strikers took the offer and the following week elected officers for their new well-entrenched AWU local. The victory was modest, but it was a victory.

In the much grander strike that unfolded after January 23, things were quite different. At least, in the Briggs Highland Park plant, where it began, the AWU had no foothold at all. In the main plants of Briggs, Highland Park, and Mack Avenue, where bodies were actually made, skilled men—especially metal finishers whose job control was under constant attack—and semiskilled people rubbed shoulders under working conditions that were among the worst in the entire nation. As the local adage put it, "If poison doesn't work, try Briggs." On January 22, fed-up metal finishers at Highland Park simply walked out. They contacted the AWU and were advised to return to work and organize for a full-scale strike at a later time. But the following day, "the plant emptied and the Briggs strike was on, but with none of the preparation the AWU had urged." Still, the union responded enthusiastically, but now ran into ideological rivals who condemned it as Communist.

Here, the mistakes of the AWU began. The strike committee wanted Raymond's leadership but not his Party label. The local Party agreed to this, an error because it made it appear as if there *were* something wrong with being a Communist. (This form of "tactical" self-effacement would plague the Party again and again.) Nevertheless, under Raymond's expert guidance, the strike was effective. Henry Ford, to put pressure on both sides of the dispute, then closed his plants on January 26, putting some 150 thousand people out of work. Ford urged Briggs to make an offer, which Briggs did: "Hourly base rates dropped in October would be reinstated, dead-time would be eliminated, and all former employees would be given preference in hiring until noon on Monday, January 30." The elimination of minimum hourly rates for pieceworkers and in-plant layoffs (dead time) were the two key grievances of the strikers. But in the disorganized meetings that followed the offer, a new demand materialized—recognition. And the leadership, including Raymond, got caught up in the enthusiasm, rejected the deadline, and on Monday put on a mass picketing exhibition the likes of which Detroit had never seen.

The rejection of this offer turned out to be the critical error. The police now began harrassing strikers and breaking up meetings. Above all, they arrested Phil Raymond in Highland Park on Tuesday and held him without charge. Sugar, the strikers' lawyer, frantically tried to get a writ of habeas corpus processed. Late Wednesday afternoon Circuit Judge Richter finally demanded the charge (criminal syndicalism) and had to reject it. But the arrest, coupled with the rumor that the strike was the first step in a nationwide Communist plot, got Raymond fired as strike chairman.

The Communist response to this turn of events was mistake number three. They suddenly claimed all the credit for the strike, urged a hypermilitant stance, and put on a big rally at Danceland Hall to communicate both points to the two thousand strikers who showed up. This only further angered the other elements in the strike leadership, Wobblies, Socialists, and the increasingly powerful group of antiideologues under the leadership of George Cornell, an exforeman of politically conservative inclinations. Leadership of the strike became hopelessly divided, although everybody else now agreed to attack the Communists. Briggs put up his back, cheered on by the local press—especially *Detroit Saturday Night,* which depicted Raymond in cartoon as a bomb-wielding puppet of Moscow—and the other auto firms. Hunger began to take its toll, strikers began to drift back to work, and scabs were less forcefully resisted. Even though the strike dribbled on until May, it was generally downhill after the second week.

The consequences, while by no means negative for the auto labor movement as a whole, were disastrous for the fortunes of the local Party, the AWU, and Phil Raymond personally. Membership in both organizations fell precipitously in later 1933 and Raymond became a virtual pariah. Raymond himself remembered that after that time "a lot of people thought that if I took a back seat, it would be easier to force recognition of the union on the part of the employers."[4] This did not mean, of course, that the Communists ceased to play a role in auto organizing—far from it. It is true, however, that the main impact of AWU activity occurred elsewhere—in Chester, Pennsylvania or in Kenosha, Wisconsin or in Cleveland. Detroit had become the headquarters of the AFL organizing drive that unfolded in the wake of the National Industrial Recovery Act (NIRA).

President Green, who moved only at the persistent urging of John L. Lewis, appointed a flaccid, spiritless fellow named William Collins to head the organization of autoworkers in Detroit and throughout the land. The AFL, with the help of the Detroit federation, would issue charters to special, "federal" union locals (usually on a plant-by-plant basis) that would not be affiliated with existing AFL craft unions. The general unit was to be called the United Automobile Workers of America. The concept was a good one, but when Collins arrived in June, proudly noting that he had never voted for a strike in his life, activist autoworkers shook their heads in disbelief. Collins also declared that Communists were not welcome in the AFL, which was not such a bad thing, since it made their policies seem like a militant alternative to the AFL's exclusive reliance on the National Recovery Administration's compliance board. On the other hand, the Party retained its dual-union position and the weakening AWU remained their only approved avenue in auto.[5]

This straitjacket was being rejected in Detroit even as the position was being reiterated at the extraordinary Party conference in New York on July 7, 1933. A new labor union called the Mechanics Educational Society of America (MESA) had been founded in mid-February 1933. By summer it had attracted the support of a number of pro-Soviet tool-and-die makers in southeastern Michigan—and the interest of Maurice Sugar. The creator of MESA was Matthew Smith, a fascinating, mercurial Englishman who had been a leader in the rank-and-file revolt against the munitions manufacturers during World War I known as the Shop Stewards' movement. He had emigrated after the General Strike of 1926. Smith had also been a draft resister, finally going to jail rather than applying for deferment, which he might easily have obtained as a skilled metalworker. This was an important bond between him and Sugar. Smith's politics were Independent Labour party in Britain and left-wing Socialist party in the United States, but above all there remained a strong syndicalist edge to his talk and action, a spirit derived from the Shop Steward days and retained through World War II, when his union would not take the no-strike pledge. Smith encouraged full rank-and-file participation and responded well to spontaneous action from below.[6]

138

Sugar's association with Smith and MESA was important in solidifying his own perspective on the emerging auto-union movement. Above all, it convinced him that united-front principles—the rejection of dual unionism—must be the foundation of trade-union organizing activities. With General Motors turning a profit of eighty-one million dollars in the first three quarters of 1933, a new law inviting workers to organize, the old AFL beginning to shake out of its long slumber, and new unions like MESA, the minority-oriented, tenacious, keep-the-movement-alive role of a red union like the AWU made less and less sense. The AWU—with the blessing of district organizer John Shmies—quickly came to the support of striking MESA members in September and specifically called for a "united front" of "every rank-and-file member" of the AWU, the IWW, the AFL, and the unorganized against the bosses and company unions behind MESA. Sugar's place in the burgeoning trade-union movement in Detroit was important. For the first time in his career, he found himself in a position where he no longer simply reflected the historical evolution of the interplay among the law, the Left, and the labor movement but, in fact, significantly influenced developments.

The "National Run-Around"

Sugar became the attorney for MESA in the midst of their strike that began on September 21, 1933 in Flint. The organization had been founded by disgruntled members of the International Association of Machinists (IAM) as an "educational group" seeking to improve the training of tool-and-die makers. Quickly the potential for a union was recognized by men like Smith, Frank McCracken, and John Anderson. Like so many other early leaders of the automobile labor movement, these Britons had been active in the trade union and political struggles in Great Britain and now translated their experience into U.S. terms.

After the NIRA, MESA leaders put on an organizing drive that brought in a membership by mid-July of around five thousand in Detroit, Pontiac, and Flint. This response was rooted in a four-year history of skill dilution, wage cuts, and, perhaps above all, the pernicious practice, popular especially with the smaller jobbing firms, of contracting work to individuals on a competitive-bid basis. Moreover, the automobile code of the National Recovery Administration (NRA), in stipulating cuts in maximum hours of work to provide more jobs, had failed to increase wage minimums. Sugar estimated that a man lucky enough to make fifty dollars a week before now found himself making thirty dollars. And because of less drastic model changes and general employment circumstances, the months per year of relatively sure work in the trade had dropped to four by 1933.[7]

The tool-and-die workers' strike of September–November 1933 was a milestone in the struggle for an industrial union in the automobile industry and its outlines are well known. It began in Flint on September 21 after William Knudson, the GM-Chevrolet director, broke off negotiations. The MESA then called upon members in Pontiac and Detroit, whether working for automobile firms or jobbers, to join the stoppage, which they did after a close strike vote on September 26. Various approaches to the conciliation machinery of the National Recovery Administration got them nowhere, so on October 30, militant workers took matters into their own hands, carrying out a dramatic "riotcade" in which strikers drove from plant to plant smashing windows and inflicting other physical damage. This violence forced settlements during the next two weeks and brought modest gains to the men in most of the tool-and-die shops.

Sugar's role in the strike was to help MESA leaders understand how useless the conciliation mechanisms of the NRA actually were. Matt Smith contacted him a few days after the strike began in Detroit. The original attorney, Lewis F. Brady, possessed only a sketchy knowledge of the NIRA and its implications. Sugar knew it backwards and forwards. The Automobile Code of Fair Competition—basic NRA guidelines that appeared to limit management's powers—was gutted, in so far as labor relations were concerned, by the "merit clause," which read, "Employers in this industry may exercise their right to select, retain, or advance employees on the basis of individual merit, without regard to their membership or nonmembership in any organization." Under such a rule, what real meaning could collective bargaining have? Even more fundamentally, while the NRA set up machinery for bringing labor and management together (the National Labor Board [NLB], regional boards, and specific code-compliance boards for various industries, as well as roving conciliators), their rulings did not have the force of law. If a company did not choose to cooperate, it could not be coerced. The AFL had already wedded itself to the NRA (Green was on the NLB), and the relatively harmless federal-union movement was the consequence.

While the AWU simply scoffed at the code, the leaders of MESA took it more seriously. Sugar showed them and many other Detroit workers why a more appropriate meaning for *NRA* was "National Run-around." His perspective, drawn from his reminiscences, the press, and labor-board hearings, provides important insight into one of the key phenomena of 1933–34: the growth of a working-class consciousness rooted in what was felt to be deception by the Roosevelt administration. It was a consciousness of the need for greater worker self-reliance as the emptiness of the NRA was exposed.

Sugar compared the tool-and-die strike to a prizefight, but one in which "the referee"—the federal government—"was fixed." The early rounds of the fight took place in Detroit. The strikers duly appeared before Abner Larned's local compliance board only to discover that the auto companies (twelve major plants) and the 107 jobbers who were struck refused to meet with them. The grounds: section 7(a) only required that employers bargain collectively with employees, and since the strikers were on strike, they were no longer employees! Then came John Carmody, future New Deal satrap, to act as the National Labor Board's conciliator in the dispute. He interviewed both sides and made it clear to the press that the bosses were obstructionists. So what, he was asked, would he do about it? Nothing for now, was the answer: "The situation needs just a little more time to ferment."[8]

Sugar and Smith then issued a memorandum on the strike, which they sent to NLB chairman, Senator Robert Wagner, and released to the press on October 9. It accused the bosses of noncompliance and Carmody of "giving aid and comfort to the employers in their effort to evade the provisions of the law." In the meantime strikebreakers were beginning to have an effect, especially since "the employers [were] providing [them] firearms." The statement also pointed out that most of the smaller jobbing shops were willing to settle but were held back by the major companies. It then accused the manufacturers of encouraging the police departments of the cities involved to take the side of the employers, a fact amply demonstrated in action. The following day, Carmody called upon the national board to hear the case.

On Friday the thirteenth, things came to a head. The board agreed to hear the case on October 18, and Smith responded enthusiastically, "It is just what we have been working for." He also claimed that the board's ruling, made at the same time, that strikers were indeed "employees" was a "major victory." He thus retained the belief that the NRA could do workers some good.

Many of the strikers were less convinced. That evening a mass rally was held in Arena Gardens. The meeting was chaired by John Anderson and full opportunity to speak was given to AWU representatives, who stressed the need for a broad strategy of confrontation that would serve to back up the efforts being made through the NRA. Phil Raymond and David Jones of the AWU called for a general strike and a march on the Ford Motor Company, the only major manufacturer in Detroit that refused to recognize the NIRA at all. Judging from the reception they got from the audience, these ideas were not viewed as absurd. Raymond even received a rousing cheer when he said he was a Communist and "proud of it."

Matt Smith attended the meeting but did not speak. Two days before, in fact, the AWU had circulated leaflets calling him a "false leader," condemning his timidity and reliance on the board. That Anderson, Raymond's ally, chaired the meeting was a significant indicator that Smith's power was by no means secure. On the other hand, the radical demands were deflected and nothing came of them. This conflict in the heart of MESA found Maurice Sugar in the middle. He genuinely liked and respected Smith but was friendly with his opponents. He was also receiving a fee (though not much of one) for his work as a lawyer, and therefore could not very well take an active role in supporting one side or the other in a factional conflict. This circumstantial neutrality turned out to be very important not only in MESA but in a variety of other contexts, because Sugar could serve to resolve differences that might otherwise have splintered the movement.

That same evening, another lawyer, liberal Recorders' Court Judge Edward J. Jeffries, was telling a crowd in Flint that this strike had "put President Roosevelt on the spot." "He must go through with what he has started," continued Jeffries, "or it will be too bad for him. If he turns back now we'll know he either has cold feet or he didn't mean what he said when he started this NRA." Workers in the automobile industry, Jeffries said, "are at the crossroads. Just where you are going depends upon you. You have made a start and you should hang on to what you have and go on." Jeffries was right, for the tool-and-die strike was a crucial step in exposing the hypocrisy of the president and making autoworkers realize that they would have to carry on their own fight.

The Washington meeting of October 18 was an object lesson. The union representatives were Smith, McCracken, Harry Harrison, Harry Spencer, and Sugar. The board invited Alvin Macauley, chairman of the National Automobile Chamber of Commerce and president of Packard; Knudson; and C. L. Richards, president of the Automotive Tool and Die Manufacturers Association, as representatives of the other side. The first thing that the unionists discovered when they walked in the room was that only Richards had shown up. And he let it be known immediately that he was not empowered by his association to negotiate, but was there "as a matter of courtesy." Knudsen and Macauley had telegraphed their regrets, hardly bothering with an explanation. Two other well-known faces were there, however, "to advise," said Sugar, "Mr. Richards in the technique of the courtesy he was to employ": Chester M. Culver and John L. Lovett, the salaried spokesmen, respectively, of the Employers Association of Detroit and the Michigan Manufacturers Association. The first question then became whether to continue the charade at all. Smith was ready to walk out, but Wagner—red-faced at the casual defiance of the employers—convinced him to go on by assuring the strikers that the board would respond to the dispute: "We will either adjust it, if we can, or render a decision in the matter, one or the other." Asked Smith, "Do I understand a decision will be binding on the other two parties in this dispute representing the employers?" Replied the Senator from New York: "If we decide to make a decision, yes, but why engage in so many technicalities?"

This became a joke as the meeting proceeded. The union naturally wanted to discuss the particulars of its six-point indictment of the employers: that they violated the NIRA by refusing to bargain collectively, firing people for labor-union activities, hiring strikebreakers, paying them more than the demands of the strikers, intimidating and threatening tool-and-die makers to quit MESA (including the use of yellow-dog contracts), and compelling employees to work eleven to twelve hours a day "for reasons not covered by exemptions in the Code." These voluminously documented complaints were all but ignored as Gerard Swope, president of General Electric and an employer board member, took over and oriented the discussion toward the issue of why the Detroit and Pontiac strikers did not ask for negotiations. Labor representatives President Green and Major George L. Berry, president of the pressman's union (AFL), decided that was a good subject, too. They went on for an hour over the question of whether the presentation of a precise list of demands should have been made before the strike began (they *had* been negotiating with GM) and especially the "crucial" issue of whether the presentation of such a list, made later, constituted a request to the companies for a conference. Swope, seconded at every turn by Berry and Green, said that "technically" they had not requested a conference, and therefore the companies were not obliged to reply. A few lines from the hearing record will illustrate how Matt Smith's education progressed that day.

> Major Berry: You certainly must have a record of having sent a notice to them.
> Mr. Smith: Oh yes, we have copies of that.
> Mr. Swope: I think that ought to be done before a strike and not after.
> Mr. Sugar: But it has been done since the strike. Do you want us to do it again?
> Mr. Swope: Yes.
> Mr. Sugar: Why not ask the employers who have received our request, now, at this belated period, to meet with us?
> Mr. Swope: We will ask the employers to act in accordance with 7(a), which they have to do under the law, and any request from employees for a meeting to discuss collective bargaining, I am sure they will accede to.
> Mr. Sugar: But they have it already.
> Mr. Swope: You will have to do it again so far as this Board is concerned.
> Mr. Sugar: We have obeyed the law, because we have approached every employer. And we have been ignored. And you are asking us, not them, to reconsider their ignoring of us.
> Mr. Swope: No, because you did that after the strike.
> Mr. Sugar: But we would be doing it now after the strike; why should we do it twice?

Berry then returned to the "record" question—Why didn't they have anything in writing indicating that they had contacted the companies? "There is the record of our statements," said Sugar. "That is a matter of record, and it is not denied." Then, after some further "analysis," they went back to whether they really asked for a conference. Again to quote the verbatim record:

> Mr. Smith: We have sent a statement of our demands to each individual employer, and they understand that that is equivalent to asking for a conference.
> Mr. Swope: Do not make it "equivalent," just as Major Berry has said—
> Mr. Smith: It seems to me the Labor Board is trying to get rid of a shabby problem so they are throwing us back to Detroit.

143

Major Berry: We are in hopes there will be a basis on which we can act, but today there is no basis. That is a fact, and you can take it as you like it.

This little slice of NLB life,[9] where the labor member takes his cue from the management member, was ample evidence that *NRA* stood for more than one thing. The union men did bring the "shabby problem" back to Detroit and duly issued requests for negotiating meetings in proper legalese. Also, the board had promised to support MESA's demand that GM act as a single unit. Back in Detroit, the company refused. The board did not even respond to Sugar's telegram asking them to pressure GM. But finally, MESA and various GM representatives were assembled by Abner Larned. As Sugar remembered it,

> In the morning we had a "conference" with Fisher Body (General Motors). We sat around a huge table. Mr. Edward A. Fisher presided. At his right hand sat Mr. Archer of Ternstedt's (General Motors). Mr. Fisher stood up and took over. Holding in his hand the sheet containing the Union's 4 demands, he read the first one: increased wages. "Gentlemen, the answer to that is No." He read the second: no change in hours without negotiations. "The answer to that is No." He read the third: no victimization. He hesitated, "I don't know just what that means—but—but—the answer to that is No." He read the last: recognition of the Union. "The answer to that is No." Then he sat down.
> When a Union representative suggested that General Motors could absorb the entire increase in wages demanded by adding two and a half cents to the selling price of each car, Mr. Fisher snarled: "Nobody is going to tell us what price we shall charge for our cars."[10]

In an excellent analysis of these sessions, which were held on October 26, the *Detroit News*—hardly sympathetic to the strikers' position—made it clear how far they had come to try to reach a settlement. The original twenty-five-cents-per-hour demand had been reduced to five cents, thus putting GM on a par, for a pittance, with smaller plants that had already agreed to union demands. Sugar, who had presented the demands at the meeting, stressed that both parties should make concessions "in the interest of the community as a whole."

The strike now reached its climax. Funds and nerves were wearing thin. The Left had continued to barrage Smith and, especially, Jay J. Griffin, chairman of the strike committee (who, it was later revealed, had gangland connections), with accusations of timidity, despite Smith's response to the Washington seminar in double-talk. Specifically, the Communists were pushing for a drive to organize production workers through MESA. That Smith remained tepid towards this push reflected a weakness that had consistently dogged machinists, whether in Britain or the United States. Communists looked to the ordinary factory worker as the main agent of social transformation and therefore posed the question of skilled-unskilled unity as a matter of course, just as they condemned racial, ethnic, and sexual barriers to working-class solidarity. It is probable that Communist consistency on this score was the key factor putting them in so prominent a position in the development of industrial unionism under the banner of the CIO.

But nobody ever denied that toolmakers could be militant, which they proved in abundance on Sunday, October 30. Whether Communists or Smithites were responsible (both denied it at the time and claimed credit later), the motorcade of destruction that struck throughout Detroit in a last gasp of pent-up anger assured the strike a place in the annals of worker protest as much because of its cleverness as its toll. An estimated two thousand men were involved. "The strikers," wrote Harry Dahlheimer, "travelling with the precision and speed of a motorized force, sped from one plant to another, aided by a series of misleading phone calls to the police." Windows and blueprints were the main casualties, the latter hitting the companies where it hurt. Postmortems determined that the absurdities of the Washington meeting, and its aftermath, provided the principal motivation for this outburst. This daring exploit thus established the NRA as an object of ridicule in the minds of many Detroit workers.

After October 30, a combination of small-employer weariness and worker deprivation brought about a series of unsatisfying settlements. Ainsworth Manufacturing of Detroit provided the framework with a five-cents-across-the-board increase, an eighty-five-cents-per-hour minimum, and union recognition. It was agreed verbally that the contract system would be abolished. While the strike could not be called an unqualified victory, it was hardly a disaster (as some of the Communists would claim). If the material gains were minimal, recognition obviously was important. But above all, these events demonstrated the limitations of the NRA and the automobile code. Workers in Detroit were learning not to place too much trust in the law and not to expect much from the AFL. Sugar had helped move this process of education along.

Another aspect of this strike was highly successful and augured well for the future. MESA had virtually no strike fund (dues were only twenty-five cents per month), so the task immediately fell upon support networks to produce. A women's auxiliary was organized largely by veterans of the unemployed-council activities. They began the flow of free food to Schiller Hall, the old House of the Masses, which served as strike headquarters. Sam's Department Store contributed tobacco that volunteer workers rolled into cigarettes for the strikers or sold on the streets. Another important activity was the organization of demonstrations and support activities, such as providing courtroom audiences for the various cases against some two hundred strikers whom Sugar defended during the stoppage. Professional people and businessmen already enlisted in past causes contributed money. Sugar had also helped to coordinate these support groups through an institution called the Buck Dinner, which originated in 1929 when he asked a number of friends to join him for a venison feast in return for their contributions in favor of the unemployed. By the midthirties, attendance provided a means by which people who had little time, but some money, could give financial support to various left-wing causes. More important, the lists of labor-movement sympathizers could then be used in other circumstances—such

145

as meeting the immediate needs of tool-and-die strikers. What was forming, then, was a reliable group of several hundred progressive professionals and intellectuals whose services would become increasingly important in the development of the labor movement.[11]

A Left Leader Emerges

Before turning to the full examination of how this Left community, with Sugar in the lead, contributed to the early auto labor movement, let us set the stage by looking at the two key areas of Sugar's activity in 1934: his role as a persistent critic of the Automobile Labor Board (ALB) under Leo Wolman and of AFL leaders for their continuing support of it; and his work as a lawyer on behalf of black defendants. Both activities carried Sugar to a level of prominence locally that made him the most attractive political leader on the Left.

After the strike of 1933, MESA settled into organizational activity. The union held its first convention in January 1934. The membership elected Matt Smith general secretary and his slate swept the national offices. Detroit Local Number 7 under John Anderson and Number 9 under John Mack, were Communist strongholds. By that time, according to Elizabeth McCracken, "most of the Communists in Detroit were in the MESA," which, considering the fact that there were 632 Party members altogether in auto, is probably true. Smith, having been treated badly by the NRA, apparently thought he might do something about the way it operated and agreed to become the labor member of the regional labor board in February. He failed, and only won the ridicule of his union opponents. They also attacked him for dividing the union into two sections, one for skilled men and one for production workers. Finally, at the second convention in May, equal voting rights for all members was introduced and the assembly given total authority over union affairs. Sugar helped to draft this constitution, which served as a model for the UAW constitution of 1939.

If Matt Smith still hoped that labor might influence conciliation boards with the proper people on them, the AFL remained fixed in the assumption that the right people already *were* on them. If only, its leaders thought, they could find the right mechanisms, particularly for the automobile industry, all would go well.

Several federal locals in Michigan mounted a campaign early in 1934 that threatened a strike if a range of issues were not seriously addressed by the companies. William Collins immediately moved to deflect their anger into a national labor-board conference, the "most important," he pronounced, ever held. Instances of company antiunion discrimination were copiously documented at the Washington meetings of March 14 and 15. The companies thumbed their noses at the charges. Collins twice set general strike dates only to have them postponed. Finally, President Roosevelt intervened and proposed a settlement that, if anything, put the companies in a better position than they had occupied before: the only substantive change in the law was that "proportional representation" within single plants was openly encouraged, so that company unions were virtually invited to compete with real unions and the closed shop became an impossibility. Beyond this, all grievances would be taken to yet another body, a newly created Automobile Labor Board. Collins proclaimed that this was "the biggest victory [autoworkers] have ever won." Sugar, on the other hand, expressed the attitude of MESA people and militants in general toward the settlement in his telegram to Frank Martel: "I would like to let you know exactly what I think of it, but profanity is prohibited in telegrams."[12]

The new Auto Labor Board chairman, Leo Wolman, was hardly a person to inspire worker confidence, believing that the auto companies were so powerful that governmental coercion was unlikely to have any effect on them. Collective bargaining would have to be "edged in." Sidney Fine sums it up: "Wolman and [Nicholas] Kelley [Chrysler Corporation counsel and employers' representative on the board] were in basic agreement regarding the policies and role of the ALB and there is no indication that they differed on any matters, major or minor, [that] the board was called upon to decide." The labor representative, Richard Byrd, a federal local offical from Pontiac whose main claim to fame was a silver medal in the discus in the 1912 Olympic Games, belied his reputation as an effective speaker by saying little at board meetings. When he did talk, he was generally incomprehensible.[13]

These were the people dealing with the labor conflicts that unfolded after the "strike threat." MESA had made demands along with the AFL in March, but did not withdraw them after the "settlement." Instead, they called a strike for April 12. It caused a great deal of confusion, for different factions took different positions, and at no time did it have the full support of the ranks. The strike failed. Smith attempted to lay the blame on the Communists and tried to expel John Anderson and John Mack. They counterattacked, accusing Smith of turning the MESA into a "kite tail" of the AFL. Anderson's Local Number 7 reinstated him and Smith backed down at the convention that began on May 24. Sugar attempted, with some success, to mediate the dispute.

At the same time, Smith quit the NRA regional board, commenting that "even one-horse employers treat Board recommendations with derision." More important, the Wolman board, now taking all cases involving the auto and parts industries, gave Smith a dose of their justice in the Burroughs case. A MESA shop-committee chairman there was fired and the local immediately struck, claiming antiunion discrimination. The strike fell apart when the production workers failed to go out. The reason they did not was because the board, although it promised to withhold its decision until the company and union had met, rendered an immediate decision. Such incidents thus made Sugar's condemnation of the "referee" look better and better. Increasingly, as he concluded a speech given before a MESA audience that summer, workers are coming to understand that they would have to "go into the ring relying upon their own strength and skill. They could not win the bout on points. It would have to be a knock-out." Even AFL people were disgusted with treatment at the hands of the auto board. During the summer, board rulings so overwhelmingly favored management that any semblance of impartiality disappeared. Collins saw what was happening and applied for a transfer. In August he was replaced by another AFL hack, Francis Dillon.

By fall of 1934, labor, whatever its affiliation, had become mistrustful of the Roosevelt administration. To attempt to generate some good will in the automobile industry, FDR called upon the research arm of the NRA "to inquire into the possibilities of regularizing employment and otherwise improving the conditions of labor" in the industry. The first part of this statement was a specific response to the mounting use of short-term layoffs during 1934, but the second seemed open-ended. Leon Henderson headed the investigation and his committee came to Detroit for hearings on December 15. In "fairness" to the companies and under strict orders from Labor Secretary Frances Perkins, discussion of collective bargaining and section 7(a) was forbidden, as if they had nothing to do with "conditions of labor." This actually proved to be a boon to those who testified, for they could score the administration for kowtowing to the employers once again.

One of the highlights of the hearings was the testimony of Maurice Sugar. He was the official representative of MESA. His most important contribution and the one that got the longest applause was his condemnation of the Roosevelt adminstration for throttling discussion of the NRA: "In my opinion, this hearing, with the exclusion of this matter, is merely staging a show for some purpose other than the remedy of evils that plague labor generally." He nevertheless took the opportunity to educate the committee about grievances that his expertise as an investigative lawyer in discrimination cases before the labor boards brought to light. He spoke of the blacklist and the special significance of the telephone in keeping it out of print. To the hundreds of workers who had come to him for legal redress he had to say, "No American worker has any rights in this respect at all." There was the spy system, practiced to perfection at Ford, but practiced everywhere else as well. Sugar also introduced in evidence a letter, intercepted by a MESA member from a detective agency to all of the major employers. Its significance was that the agency (Corporations Auxilliary Company) had *already* been spying on MESA without pay and had prepared a report on them in the hope of getting the employers' business. In reference to code violations, Sugar had a perfectly logical, if unsettling, recommendation: "that organized labor be given the right to initiate and control criminal prosecution under the codes." The vision of Sloan or Ford or Chrysler being packed off to jail drew gleeful applause. Sugar finally addressed the question of layoffs. "Regularizing" employment, under current wage levels, would be no more than "spreading the misery." Thus only massive wage increases would combat the general problem. And there was plenty of money around—profit levels were demonstrably high. Finally, Sugar called for government-operated, employer-financed unemployment insurance. This insurance, combined with decent wages, would clearly go a long way toward "regularizing employment."

The Henderson hearing was an important moment for Sugar. Representatives of the entire labor movement in Detroit were there. He was saying the sort of thing that all militant workers believed. When he talked of "industrial peonage" or the end of profits, few in that room—the vast majority of whom were non-Communists—would disagree. Detroit was now into year six of the Depression and had suffered more than any city in the nation. Automobile workers had experienced almost two years of the Roosevelt administration's bumbling efforts to solve their problems. More and more believed, indeed, that it was all no more than a run-around and that they would have to go it alone.[14]

But there was one section of the Detroit working class that was not much in evidence at the Henderson hearings—black people, the most hard-hit of all Detroit workers. They were not regularly included in labor battles and, traditionally, were perceived to be antiunion. The local Urban League, the organization most concerned about the situation of black workers, actually discouraged black union involvement during the twenties and early thirties. The reason was simple enough: the fortunes of the black migrants to Detroit had become linked to the good will of several auto, parts, and steel companies. Black union involvement threatened to sever established ties.

The Ford Motor Company, motivated by Henry Ford's racist paternalism, was far and away the leader in the placement of blacks in the auto industry. In the early twenties Ford established a policy of hiring substantial numbers of blacks (never allowing the figure to exceed 10 percent of the work force, however) in large measure because he felt they were superior workers to European immigrants. A believer in Madison Grant's theories regarding the racial threat posed by eastern and southern Europeans and reserving his particular venom for the "wily Jew," Ford apparently viewed blacks, although deemed racially inferior to "Anglo-Saxons and Celts," as potentially solid citizens. They should, he thought, remain segregated residentially, and interracial marriage was a special taboo, but with good jobs and hard work, blacks could occupy a respectable, if lower, niche in U.S. society. Jobs were the key to racial peace. As Ford wrote in the *Dearborn Independent* in 1922, "When there are enough jobs to go around in this country, when every man shall have the opportunity to go forth in the morning to perform the work he is best fitted to do, and to receive a wage which means a secure family life, there will be no race question."

The work that "the colored" were best fitted to do in the Ford scheme of things involved the heaviest, most uncomfortable, and most dangerous jobs in the industry: foundry, rolling mill, and paint shop. Still, sprinkled throughout the Ford organization were handfuls of black skilled workers, foremen, and white-collar workers. Executive levels were closed to them except in the crucial personnel department.

Here Donald J. Marshall oversaw the Ford system of black recruitment based on intricate ties with the black churches, their ministers, and their middle-class lay leaders. No black person got a job at Ford's if he was not recommended as a "high-type fellow." This had a number of meanings, but one of them was an absence of radical or pro-trade-union opinions. Certainly, lots of people entered the industry by this route (the city's black population, lured to Detroit in large measure by the reputation of "Mr. Ford's place," increased from 41 thousand in 1920 to 120 thousand in 1930 out of a total of 1.5 million people). But the system created a conservative stranglehold on Detroit's black community. Even the Depression, which saw black unemployment outstrip white by substantial margins, did little initially to diminish Ford's reputation. Moreover, it must be remembered that black people in general thought of trade unions as racially exclusive enclaves of white skilled workers whose picket lines bashed the heads of black job seekers. (*Scab* has a moral meaning only to those for whom a union might have a practical meaning.)

How this image was broken is a complex problem. August Meier and Elliott Rudwick's path-breaking book, *Black Detroit and the Rise of the UAW,* takes us a long way toward understanding it. It was a difficult task to cement a strong relationship between blacks and the union, one not realized until after World War II and even then with ambivalence on both sides. The book does not give sufficient attention, however, to the important role of Detroit's Left community in cracking the Republican, deferential, church-bound, pro-Ford, and antiunion outlook of Detroit's black population. More specifically, the authors ignore the role of civil-rights activists before 1936 in shifting black opinion leftward, a shift carrying with it a more positive attitude toward the labor movement.[15]

There was much to be done in Detroit. The levels of discrimination and overt racism in the city were high. Black housing became rigidly segregated in the course of the 1920s, with restrictive covenants popping up everywhere. This was why the Sweet case had been a critical test. Historian Norman McRae estimates that by the midthirties 85 percent of the city's housing was off-limits to blacks. Their densely populated areas included the narrow east-side strip of "Paradise Valley," bounded by Woodward and Russell/Chene and moving north block by block as time went by, a smaller enclave in the west side, and some land hastily turned over to wartime black housing out on Eight Mile Road. Suburban Inkster completed the picture. Recreational facilities were virtually nonexistent in black areas of Detroit, and black youth was not welcome outside these areas (as the world would come to know in 1943). Substandard housing was the rule. "The correlations between inferior housing, over-crowding, lack of recreational opportunities, and social pathologies," writes McRae, "are too well known to require restatement." If auto jobs could be had (Dodge Main, Bohn Aluminum, Midland Steel, Briggs Mack, and Packard were the main places besides Ford Rouge), discrimination was the rule in all other occupations (domestic and laundry work for black women excepted, of course). Snow Grigsby, a postal worker who watchdogged the black-employment situation, found in early 1935 in the City of Detroit no blacks at all in the fire and water Departments, 35 blacks among 3,700 police officers, 59 among 4,579 employees in the street-railway department, 4 among 362 visiting nurses, and none, including doctors on staff, at Detroit Receiving. Public displays of racism, from the universal refusal to serve blacks in restaurants to regular beatings in the plants and the torching of homes where restrictive covenants did not do the job, accompanied its institutional forms.[16]

A particularly bitter experience for Detroit's black citizens was their treatment at the hands of the law. Police brutality was rampant, but more troubling still was the shabby record of the courts, particularly when urged on by the overtly racist Detroit dailies, which delighted in convicting Negro "criminals" before they were tried. It was in this arena that Sugar first came to the attention of black Detroit.

Although he had been involved in a number of minor cases defending blacks in the past and had gained something of a reputation, Sugar's most important case came in June of 1934. James Victory, a car washer in a gas station, was accused of "slashing" a white woman in an alley and stealing her purse. While Hearst's *Detroit Times,* in particular, spread visions of dozens of slashers and rapists roaming the streets of Detroit, Sugar took Victory's defense before an all-white jury and, fortunately, Judge Edward L. Jefferies. He focused on three things: the way the identification was made, Victory's alibi, and his character.

Unbelievably, the victim of the nighttime attack had been asked by the police to identify Victory by himself; only the following day was he placed in a lineup. Moreover, the police changed the description put out over the wire after they picked Victory up: the original one made no mention of long hair, which Victory had. Victory's alibi was solid—he had been with someone and had stopped several places far from the scene of the crime during the hour of the attack. The only problem was that all his main witnesses were black, and the prosecutor wove a fantasy-ridden story of a conspiracy among a half dozen blacks all protecting "their own." Sugar took both these issues on directly, arguing that the police had framed Victory and that the prosecution developed a blatantly racist argument in dealing with his alibis. Finally, Sugar asked the jury to assess Victory's character. Although he brought in an impressive group of character witnesses, black and white, the most important thing was Sugar's focus on Victory's life as a working man. He had no criminal record and, except for his time as a soldier in World War l and nine months in an army hospital later, had worked steadily since he was thirteen, no mean task for a poorly educated black man, especially after 1929.

In general, Sugar's approach was low-key, important because in all three areas he stressed points that might be somewhat hard for the white, middle-class jurors to assimilate without prejudice. He concluded his summation with a frank statement on the condition of blacks in the United States: "The Negro is doubly exploited. He is exploited as a worker and he is further exploited as a colored worker. He is denied his rights as a worker and then is further oppressed as a

151

colored worker. He is discriminated against on every side. His social rights are flouted. His political and economic rights are trampled upon. And his claim of equality under American traditions is met with derision and brutality." Victory was not asking for sympathy. A black worker "never gets sympathy by asking for it, any more than a white worker. He never gets anything at any time except by standing firmly on his two feet and fighting for it." And Victory was there fighting for his most elementary right—his freedom. Sugar's approach, honest, direct, and unapologetically radical, was effective: the jury returned a verdict of *not guilty.*

This trial catapulted Sugar to a place of prominence in the eyes of many black Detroiters. Its extensive coverage in the daily press and in the conservative black weekly, the *Detroit Tribune Independent,* gave him exposure as never before, a fact that would soon take on political significance.[17]

A Popular Front before the Popular Front

On December 19, 1934 a meeting of the Detroit and Wayne County federations of labor passed a resolution, warmly supported by Frank X. Martel, to urge Maurice Sugar to run for judge of the recorder's court, Detroit's criminal court. He would be "labor's candidate," not just a "friend of labor." The *Detroit Labor News* noted his long record as labor's attorney and praised his "yeoman service" to all unions. On the 28th, after a meeting of his friends for the purpose of "drafting" him, Sugar accepted. Two days later, the first campaign committee meeting occurred. Four months of intensive political activity followed. Before it was over the cause of organized labor was preached in virtually every fraternal hall and political club in the city and, more impressively, in black churches where the very word "union" had been traditionally uttered in low whispers, if at all.

Rich documentation covering the recorder's-court campaign allows us to view the process by which the network of Sugar's Left-community connections served to bring the message of industrial unionism to thousands of Detroiters.

A broad array of forces and personalities mixed in the Sugar campaign. On the Left, only the Socialist party would not endorse him, although individual members participated. Sugar had recently won a case gaining left-wing Socialist Walter Bergman the right to speak in a Detroit public-school auditorium, and several of his friends worked in the campaign. The entire organized labor movement, down to the most conservative locals of the craft unions, was involved. The network of liberal professionals that Sugar had previously established worked tirelessly. In looking over the list of precinct workers, it becomes obvious that women—wives of professionals and trade unionists, but above all teachers—played an especially important role in the grass-roots operation.

The organizational meeting of December 30 gathered fifteen key people to outline the structure and thrust of the recorder's-court campaign. It reflected the same popular front orientation. William Weinstone, recently appointed Communist party district organizer, assured his organization's formal support. The black community was represented by Reverend A. C. Williams, the pastor of the Metropolitan Baptist Church, and Crawford Nelson, an employee of the Detroit Board of Education who had been a character witness for James Victory. The rest of the assembled group were friends and associates of Sugar, mostly lawyers, whose politics varied from pro-Soviet to social democratic. Apparently, well before Popular Front, all got along just fine. The approach to the campaign was laid out in a professional manner. Sugar would set policy, but the political manager was his close friend, Sam Keene. They broke down the campaign operations—beyond labor groups—into ethnic and occupational groupings.[18]

An "Outline of Policy and Organization of the Campaign for Maurice Sugar" was agreed upon at that meeting. Five key positions would be stressed: (1) affirmation of the right of workers to organize and to picket and attack company unions; (2) an attack on the factory spy system, blacklisting, antilabor injunctions, and the use of police in labor struggles; (3) support for "improved standards for the workers" (especially in attacking speedup), "unemployment relief, wage increases, shorter workweek, and unemployment insurance in accordance with the Lundeen Bill"; (4) a strong stand "against fascism and the danger of imperialist war" and against anti-Semitism and Negro and foreign-born discrimination; (5) work "for the unity of labor in the struggle for all these issues," especially by campaigning for the removal of the Auto Labor Board.

The general strategy of the campaign was to carry it out as a fight against the "auto trust" and to "stigmatize" most judges as the creatures of big business. Sugar as battler for the rights of the oppressed would be the heart of it. They also specified the struggle for the rights of black people as a central aspect of campaign activity. Operating on a projected budget of ten thousand dollars, they would tap labor and all other sympathetic organizations while also holding fundraisers and passing the hat at mass meetings. All campaign workers were volunteers, and the money was thus to go for leaflets, brochures, flyers, and posters. They put out Sugar's summation to the jury in the Victory case and his speech before the Detroit automobile hearing as special brochures. All specific plans, dates, programs, groups to be contacted, and so on, were set out carefully in advance.[19]

This program was fulfilled almost to the letter. The elaborate infrastructure of Left organizations carried much of the initial burden. The International Labor Defense had between four hundred and five hundred members. Many were not lawyers but citizens concerned about legal injustices and activists in a variety of liberal causes. The International Workers Order (IWO) in Detroit had about twenty-six hundred participants in its mutual-benefit program. While one did be an activist in order to take out insurance with the IWO, it was only natural that leftists predominated, since personal contact was the main avenue of recruitment. The IWO was organized along ethnic lines and its various branches tried to meet on a regular basis for business, socializing, and political discussion. In Detroit there were Jewish, Polish, Hungarian, Russian, Ukrainian, Finnish, Rumanian, Armenian, South Slav, Lithuanian, Bulgarian, and English sections, and a total of forty-two branches altogether. A good number of them had their own meeting halls, financed from the mutual funds. The IWO was one of Sugar's key sources of support in his campaigns. It also had youth sections that could be counted on for vigorous political work, such as mailings, canvasing, demonstrations, and so on. Another group was the Housewives League to Fight against the High Cost of Living, which grew out of the Hamtramck unemployed councils. Beyond its stated purpose, this 350-member group was also instrumental in getting Mary Zuk, its leader and a leftist, elected to the Hamtramck City Council in the fall and gave all-out support to Sugar as well.

Finally, several organizations focused on educational, intellectual, and cultural pursuits. Besides several educational circles, there were the John Reed Club and its offshoot, the Detroit New Union Theatre, later renamed the Contemporary Theatre. The Reed Club continued its functions of bringing in famous figures from the world of art, music, and literature to speak or perform and of providing a forum for local talent as well. After *The New Force* failed in 1933, the new focus for the energies of the culturally inclined became the theater. They put on plays with left-wing messages ranging from famous dramas like Odets's *Waiting for Lefty* and Harberg's musical, *Pins and Needles,* to more obscure dramatizations of contemporary events such as *F.O.B. Detroit,* about the Ford Massacre, or *They Shall Not Die,* which concerned the struggle to free the Scottsboro boys. They would be used to entertain strikers or cap off demonstrations or to raise money for various causes. During Sugar's campaigns several plays were presented, and Sugar would speak afterwards.

Many community-organization leaders were also trade-union activists. Mary Zuk and Wilma Kowalski of the Housewives League were attempting to organize cigar workers. John Anderson of the IWO, Tony Gerlach, then Jack Mahoney of the ILD, and George Kristalsky of the Hamtramck Workers Alliance were all indefatigable trade unionists in the auto industry. Such leaders thus formed human links between community activities and the labor movement.[20]

In the Sugar campaigns of 1935, they mobilized their organizations for political action. Through these campaigns the Detroit population at large was presented with a specific platform and a general perspective on society that made the organizing of labor the central goal. And the people of the city responded. Coming from nowhere, with a political name, if known at all, that had been attacked in the popular press, Sugar finished thirteenth in the recorder's-court race with 63 thousand votes in its April 2 final vote. (The ninth and last electee and the only nonincumbent, Frank Murphy's brother George, got 104 thousand votes.) Sugar's message of support for industrial unionism in the auto industry thus reached a wide and diverse audience.

The early months of 1935 was a time when a radical perspective, challenging mainstream politics and its assumptions, could get a sympathetic hearing from many working people. The key moment for Detroit came on January 31, 1935 when Roosevelt extended the automobile code, with its merit clause, and retained the Wolman auto board. This brought about reverberations throughout the labor movement, with John L. Lewis speaking of "plots" and "betrayals" and even William Green declaring that the AFL could no longer cooperate with the NRA. There was little question in anyone's mind that the White House had "broken with labor," as the *Nation* put it. In Detroit, the AFL *Labor News* sounded a good deal more like Lewis than Green, and a MESA statement written by Smith and Sugar put it bluntly: "Not a single demand of the automobile workers has been met—even partially." Thus, they continued, "the lesson for the workers is plain. They must organize. It is the only way."[21]

This anger fueled Sugar's campaign. Workers should not be fooled by their so-called friends, whether in the White House or recorder's court. An opportunity to develop this thesis occurred when Francis Biddle, then head of the National Labor Relations Board (as it was now called), came to Detroit for a dinner "attended by more than 200 leaders in labor, industry, social work and the bar." As reported by the *Labor News,* Sugar tore into Biddle's smug defense of the administration's labor policy. It gives us a rare glimpse of his campaign speeches, none of which, if they ever were written down, have survived.

He began his attack by rebutting Biddle's assertion that collective-bargaining elections were "free." Sugar told the audience, "It is ridiculous to talk of labor's free choice of representatives for collective bargaining when you have in the automobile industry the most vicious spy system and black list which exist any place in the country. . . . The whole psychological set-up of the industrial system makes it absolutely impossible for the worker to have any freedom of choice. He is completely dominated by the employer." Biddle had wrung his hands over the uncompromising attitude of both labor and business, as if each were equally responsible for problems, and asserted that the government might have to impose more rigid control over economic life. Reflecting the fears of organized labor at the time, Sugar remarked, "This suggestion, although it does not contain the words 'compulsory arbitration,' actually constitutes a threat to effect such a result. This means that Labor is to be denied its most effective weapon, the strike. And this constitutes fascism."

But Sugar's main point was that the actual function of the various government labor boards was to pacify the worker without producing concrete benefits. Biddle had made the mistake of saying that when a worker gets a hearing, even though he might lose, the hearing itself "has a very beneficial psychological effect." Sugar responded,

155

This certainly has a psychological effect upon the worker. It tends to create . . . the illusion that his government is interested in protecting his rights at the very moment that his government is denying those rights to him. . . . The NRA did not come into existence because of any desire on the part of the administration to do justice to the workers. . . . Only the power of workers' organizations, and not the magnanimous attitude on the part of anyone, will bring about such changes as will give the American worker a decent standard of living.

Finally, there was the miserable record of the Justice Department in prosecuting employers. Biddle had admitted that they were "not very effective; juries wouldn't convict." Sugar replied,

Unfortunately we do not know whether juries will convict. Nobody has ever been able to get the Department of Justice to institute any criminal proceedings against an employer—certainly not an employer of any consequence. I have tried. I have tried to get the Department of Justice to prosecute one of the largest automobile manufacturers in this city on the basis of a clear violation of the Federal law. The Department of Justice declined to prosecute. It may have been too busy getting after some little tailor who had pressed a pair of pants on overtime.

This final dig, reported the *Labor News*, "drew tremendous applause."[22]

To have spoken of fascism, as Sugar did that night, was not simply to speak the words of a "red." By early 1935 the structure of the Nazi regime was clear, and Mussolini's Italy was in full flower, preparing for the invasion of Ethiopia. France had narrowly averted a fascist coup d'état in February 1934, the Nazi net was descending over Austria, and dictators reigned throughout eastern Europe. The only rays of hope were found in Scandinavia and in Spain, although the beleaguered republic there was showing signs of strain. Fear of "fascism"— generally defined as a brand of mass-based authoritarianism rooted in parades and plebiscites—was strong. Liberal journalism openly pondered the question of a fascist drift in U.S. life. (So did liberal novelists: Sinclair Lewis's *It Can't Happen Here* was published in 1935.) In February, on the heels of the auto-code extension, the Senate vetoed U.S. participation in the World Court. But as the *Nation* put it, the calamity was not so much *that* it was turned down as *how* it was turned down; Father Coughlin, Detroit's own anti-Semitic, "populist" priest and radio phenomenon, had, in "an hour's torture of the truth," caused the Senate to be flooded with two hundred thousand telegrams signed by over a million people opposed to adherence. Why, the editorial asked, did Roosevelt not "go on the air" in favor? "The President is no longer leading the country. He is leaving the field to the demagogues." This, combined with FDR's trying "to thrust [the automobile board] down the throat of labor," signified an ominous change, "the working of an insidious transformation in our national life which if unchecked must end in fascism."[23] Sugar's campaign thus developed in an atmosphere in which civil-libertarian fear of the Right intertwined with prolabor ideals.

·His main theme, however, remained labor versus capital. As one of his most effective campaign cards put it,

THIS MAN IS A DANGEROUS CHARACTER!
If you are a big stockholder of General Motors or Chrysler, don't vote for him!
If you are on the board of directors of the National Bank of Detroit, don't vote for him!
If you live in a swell house in Grosse Pointe and your daughter is about to make her debut "in society," don't vote for him!
If you are a stoolpigeon in the Ford plant, for God's sake don't vote for him!

Then at the bottom,

ALL LABOR UNITES TO ELECT A FIGHTER.

A fundamental element in labor's struggle was the battle against discrimination. Page 2 of *It's About Time!,* the tabloid put out in the recorder's-court campaign, carried the headline: "Sugar Fights for Rights of All Oppressed People." On one side was a story about his action against the Michigan alien-registration law of 1931 and on the other, along with a line drawing of James Victory, appeared a story about his defense of blacks in court.

Sugar's personal appointment book for the campaign has survived, and we can see how the campaign developed. His first speeches were largely in friendly surroundings—at meetings of left-wing unions such as the fur workers, the restaurant workers, and MESA. With the Detroit Federation of Labor (DFL) paving the way, however, he quickly spread out, making appearances at eighty-four union functions in two months. The only unusual aspect of it was the rather late appearance of the AFL auto-union locals on his list. He had only campaigned at the Chrysler and Cadillac locals, where the Left was strong, until a mass meeting of "all auto locals" on Sunday, March 10, broke the ice. There was possibly some resistance from UAW boss Dillon, particularly because of Sugar's association with MESA, a rival auto union. In the end, however, Sugar was invited to speak by more than a dozen federal locals.

The main goal of the campaign, however, was to reach the unorganized, the mass of Detroit workers who through fear, ignorance, or ideology kept trade unionism at a distance. Through his campaign, Sugar carried the union message to a wide, new audience. In order to reach them, the campaign was organized almost exclusively along ethnic lines. Communist-sponsored organizations provided the initial contact points. On Sunday, February 3, the first day of intensive campaigning, the International Workers Order held a fund-raising banquet to which all the branch leaders were invited, followed by an "IWO election rally" on Wednesday night. These meetings provided the basis for subsequent appearances before IWO branch gatherings, which in turn led to appearances before gatherings of the same ethnic group that were not necessarily left-wing.

For example, starting with *Freiheit* (a Jewish leftist club), he moved on to less radical Jewish organizations and congregations, speaking before eighteen groups by the end of the campaign. Contact with the Italian community began with a meeting on Sunday, February 17, with Italian IWO convention delegates, followed by a speaking appearance at an Italian IWO dance the next Saturday. Cross Misheff initiated Sugar's campaign ties with the sizable Bulgarian and Macedonian communities, while Joseph and Wilma Kowalski served as the key link to the huge Polish population of the city. Dom Polski, the big meeting hall on Warren, was the scene of several Sugar appearances and he received good coverage in the Polish left-wing weekly, the *Trybuna robotnicza* (Workers' Tribune).

Sugar had at least one meeting each with eighteen different nationality groups, from such Left groups as the Greek Workers Club or the Slovak Democratic Club to such politically neutral or varied organizations as the German Sport Club, the Slovenian National Group, or the Scandinavian Society. One of the important features of the campaign was Sugar's eventual contact with ethnic groups where the Left had little support. Detroit had a large Flemish-Belgian population that was politically moderate. Sugar wangled an invitation to speak before a "Flemish" group at Rosewood Gardens at Mack and Philips in the heart of their far east-side neighborhood on Wednesday, February 27. His appointment-book entry on this is accompanied with a star and "Be there!" Apparently he was a success, for he was invited back to a Belgian dance at the nearby Knights of Columbus Hall that Saturday. Thereafter he addressed a luncheon of "Belgian businessmen" and made an appearance at the Belgian-American Democratic Club Dance and Card Party on the last Sunday of the campaign.

Through this activity among Detroit nationality groups (he made fifty-three appearances in all), Sugar undoubtedly carried the ideals of industrial unionism to many new listeners. But at least he was not dealing, for the most part, with people who were actively hostile to trade unionism. With the black community it was another matter. While a few younger men, such as Christopher Alston, Joseph Billups, and Walter Hardin, had been active in the unemployed councils and the AWU attempts to organize, there was virtually no sympathy for the labor movement in the older, well-established black community. Recent migrants tended to view the Left and union organizers with suspicion—as people endangering their fragile security by arousing the anger of their protector, Henry Ford.

Sugar, however, was not viewed as a leftist, but as a defender of black people before the law. Chris Alston recalls that Sugar was not regarded as a "Marxist radical" in the black community. LeBron Simmons remembered that his reputation "was excellent, a friend of black folks, good lawyer, pro-union." Sugar's "bridge" function is clear. More important, he was willing to take his campaign directly into the central institution of black life, the churches. He had no ideological problem with doing so, which was not normally the case with the

Marxist Left. As Chicago sociologist Horace Cayton remarked to Studs Terkel, "One of the reasons the Communists flopped [here] is because they didn't know how to deal with the Negro Church. The church was the first Negro institution, preceding even the family in stability. . . . The Communists came in flat-footed with this vulgar Marxist thing."[24]

It is probable that Sugar's entrée into the black-church world was Rev. John H. Bollens, the white pastor of the Messiah Evangelical Church, secretary of the local chapter of the ACLU, and Sugar's close associate in the Friends of the Soviet Union. Through him he came to know Rev. William H. Peck of the Bethel African Methodist Episcopal (AME) Church, the second oldest and second largest black church in the city. Although Peck played the Ford recruiting game and was decidedly bourgeois, he had been impressed with John L. Lewis's nondiscriminatory policies in the United Mine Workers, and encouraged debate over public issues. A group of thirty-five to forty young people met every Sunday night in the Allen Christian Endeavor League, named after the socially conscious founder of the African Methodist Episcopal Church. LeBron Simmons, a lawyer and one of the future leaders in Detroit civil-rights battles, was a member. Unionism and social justice for blacks were the key issues discussed. Opinion on the former was divided. The membership, Simmons remembers, was almost a microcosm of the city, with manual workers in a majority. Sugar spoke to them several times. This was how he established his tie with Simmons and his father, who "was a real supporter of Sugar." In the campaign, LeBron Simmons was "in charge of his church" and served as one of Sugar's battery of speakers. On February 12, Sugar addressed a Tuesday night gathering at the church. Rev. Mr. Peck's endorsement came soon thereafter, a major breakthrough for the cause of labor and the Left vis-à-vis the black community.

Sugar's reputation, already strong because of the Victory case and an earlier extradition trial where he prevented Jesse Crawford from being returned to a Georgia chain gang, was much enhanced in January and February 1935 by new cases. The first was the reversal of a conviction of two young black men, Monroe Brown and Charles Lee, by Judge John V. Brennan for "vagrancy." They had been brought before his court on January 8 by the arresting officer, who said they had "no job, no home, no visible means of support," and, after a one-minute trial, were sentenced to ninety days in the house of correction. Even had the officer's "charge" been true, which it was not, it would only have put them in the company of several million other men in 1935. They wrote to Sugar, whom they had heard about from the Victory case, and he appealed the case to another recorder's-court judge, Henry Sweeney, who overturned "vicious" Brennan's decision.

Sugar fought a more bizarre case in February. The Roseland Cemetery in Royal Oak (across the street from Father Coughlin's Church of the Little Flower) had an unwritten policy that black customers could not use the main gate. Their argument, offered with a straight face, was that the newer sections of the cemetery, where most black plots were located, were closer to the back gate. Sugar was asked to file a civil suit by an outraged family who had been turned away from the front gate and in short order won a declaration from the Cemetery Association prohibiting the discriminatory practice.

Another incident also influenced the campaign. The management of the Hoffman Building, where the ILD had its office, informed Anthony Gerlach, the secretary, that "as it is against the rules of the building, we must ask you either to discharge your colored help or move from the building." The integrated office staff was of recent date and of great pride to the ILD people. Sugar officially informed the company that they would not vacate and that was that. For the next month the two sides jockeyed back and forth, but, amid wide publicity, the ILD won and the Hoffman Building was forced to eliminate its covenant. This turned out to be an important breakthrough, because several black organizations and professionals were later able to utilize its excellent facilities.

All three of these victories were followed closely by the *Tribune Independent*. (The liberal weekly *Chronicle* had not yet been established.) By mid-March it had endorsed Sugar's candidacy. His name and reputation as a defender of civil rights thus made its way into the main bastions of black conservatism.[25]

In the end, Sugar gained the support of virtually the entire network of churches in black Detroit, including most of those known as Ford strongholds. The three cases had an impact here as well. Only Rev. Mr. Peck was lined up by the end of February. Marian McGill, president of the Detroit Civic Pride Club, and a Rev. Mr. Wade had been helpful in getting Sugar early engagements before black groups; but through Saturday, March 9, he had spoken at only nineteen of them, whereas afterwards (in twenty-one days), there were thirty-three meetings, rallies, and pulpit spots. March 10 was the big day, as he preached first to Reverend S. D. Ross's Greater Shiloh Baptist congregation, and then at 11:30 in A. C. Williams's Metropolitan Baptist church. The following Tuesday morning he met with the Negro Baptist Ministerial Conference, representing the fifty-nine black Baptist churches in the city, spoke on the subject, "The Negro at the Bar of Justice," and won their endorsement. The following Sunday he addressed the congregation of Rev. Mr. Askew's First Mt. Olive Baptist, but March 24 was the final triumph. Maurice Sugar, whose life had been dedicated to the trade-union movement, whose condemnation of Ford slavery was well known, took the pulpit at the Second Baptist Church, Detroit's oldest and largest black church. Robert Bradby, its minister, had originated the Ford connection with Detroit black churches and the Second Baptist remained the main recruiting ground in the city. Sugar emphasized civil-rights issues, but could not help but associate these questions with the emancipation of all labor through trade unionism. Bradby endorsed him that day. Sugar also won the endorsement (on March 19) of the Negro Methodist Ministerial Alliance, thus giving him the vast majority of black churches in Detroit. Only Father Daniel's St. Matthew's Protestant Episcopal, which counted Donald Marshall among its members, held out. Sugar also gained the endorsement of one of the main black Republican organizations in the city, the East Side Progressive League.[26]

While it is always easy to talk about "critical turning points," there can be little question that something significant happened in the relationship between Left-oriented labor and the black community during this campaign. Bradby and many others would continue to shy away from support for unions out of fear of losing work at Ford and elsewhere for their people; but his former assistant, Charles Hill (who had just taken the pulpit at the Hartford Avenue Baptist Church), Peck, and several others broke with the companies. Only Hill's church would be available for actual union meetings, but a new atmosphere was emerging. In April, Simmons, Bollens, and several others organized the interracial Conference for the Protection of Civil Rights. It stood as an explicitly Left and prolabor alternative to the NAACP and would link up the following year with the National Negro Congress, an effective civil-rights organization headed by the dynamic black Marxist, John P. Davis. Overall, it can be argued that Sugar's recorder's-court campaign served as a catalyst in the emergence of black-community acceptance of unions and in opening a window to the Left.

If Sugar drew strong support from organized labor, ethnic Detroit, and blacks, he fared poorly with all elements of the local establishment and with the native-born, white Protestant population in general. The number of the latter had swollen recently by the arrival of as many as thirty thousand recruits gathered by auto-company agents from Appalachia. Louis Adamic perceptively examined their impact on the atmosphere in the city: largely young men, they were seen as job stealers and union busters. They were easy prey for the antiblack and anti-foreign propaganda of hate groups, especially the Black Legion, a secret society of vigilantes with members in the police departments of Detroit, Highland Park, and Dearborn. It is questionable how many of the new arrivals actually voted, but policemen, foremen, and legionnaires encouraged them to do so. More to the point, their presence created tensions that brought racist, antiunion, and anti-Left sentiment more to the surface among better established WASP citizens.

Sugar's campaign was at first greeted with a stoney silence from the daily press. The court cases and the Hoffman Building affair got some attention, but only in the aftermath of the Sweeney decision did recorder's-court issues get raised, and then it was to condemn the insult to Judge Brennan. The Detroit Citizens League, controlled by the automobile companies, was in the business of making political endorsements. It sent Sugar its usual form, but he returned a long letter challenging their objectivity while also discussing his qualifications. On February 7, its secretary, W. P. Lovett, responded by asking Sugar three questions that reflected establishment opinion of him: Will you interpret laws as you find them? Should changes be secured by ballots or bullets? Will you cooperate with other judges? Sugar decided to publish his answers in the *Labor News*. In so doing, he presented a serious conceptualization of what a labor judge should be.

To the first question, Sugar said that he would do what every judge does—interpret the laws in accordance with "my own intellectual background, my own conception of justice." But in his case, that would mean a democratic interpretation, "since my views are a reflection of the views of the great mass of the people, the workers and the oppressed sections of the middle class" and are not burdened with "the dead weight of the outgrown and rejected past." His sentencing policies would be influenced by his understanding of the causes of the crime: "I think I could be expected to inject some humanity into the administration of the criminal law." To the second, Sugar simply replied, "I have always opposed the use of bullets." It was a matter of record that workers have been regularly murdered by "the military, the police and private thugs." He cited the Ford Massacre and the fact that fifty-seven striking workers were killed in 1934. "That is what you mean by using bullets, is it not?" Finally, Sugar said that of course he would cooperate with other judges, although not to the extent, as in the Brown and Lee case, of supporting a fellow judge in "such illegal and brutal disposition of cases." The Citizens League, much to the approval of Alvan Macauley, Citizens League executive-board member and president of the American Automobile Chamber of Commerce, rated Maurice Sugar "unacceptable."

He was no more popular with the Detroit Bar Association. In a questionnaire sent out to its members, Sugar was the top negative vote getter, with 432, in a rating of candidates' ability and integrity. But he also got 120 *yes* votes, higher than all but one of the nonincumbents. Only a handful of members did not know who he was. Lest one think that this might have been measuring something other than the political outlook of Detroit lawyers, let us note that the two liberal-to-radical incumbents, Jeffries and Sweeney, followed Sugar in *no* votes with 397 and 350, respectively.

The Detroit Board of Education had a special ax to grind with Sugar. They now had the actual right to deny the use of the schools and, after his supporters tried several subterfuges, went so far as to declare publicly "that it would not grant a school building for a talk by Maurice Sugar at any time." MESA even had a meeting denied after it had cancelled a scheduled appearance by Sugar. After repeated requests by pro-Sugar unions and fraternal organizations, the board panicked and passed a resolution on March 12 banning all political candidates from using the schools. This set off a storm of protest. Sugar filed a brief and secured a writ of mandamus from Circuit Judge Toms reversing the ban. The final Sugar rally thus took place at Northern High on March 30.[27]

With nearly all establishment avenues of publicity closed to them, Sugar loyalists resorted to a variety of tactics. In light of the "conspiracy of silence" in the daily press, paid advertisements were necessary. The foreign-language press and radio provided some coverage. But the key was Sugar's army of campaigners, recruited from Left and labor circles. A whirlwind of meetings, door-to-door canvasing by precinct workers, and widespread distribution of literature (including the effective campaign paper, *It's About Time*) added more and more steam to the campaign. Sugar also had two sources of "mainstream" support. Clarence Darrow sent Sugar a praiseworthy telegram and it was widely publicized. More important, George Murphy, also a candidate for recorder's court and Frank's brother, campaigned jointly with Sugar. He said on March 6, "If Maurice

Sugar is not elected, I don't want to be. I'd feel all alone without him. We will battle away together and we'll take politics out of the court."

As the black and ethnic endorsements were added to those of organized labor, Sugar began to be seen as a serious threat. The last days of the campaign were thus marked by a new frenzy—the negative response from his enemies. *Detroit Saturday Night* ran its usual attack on Sugar as a bomb-throwing red, while the *Free Press* and the *Times* put him on their short list of who not to vote for. But the most ominous reaction occurred in the Northern High rally. Scattered on the floor after the rally was over, Sugar's aides—and a *Detroit Times* reporter—found a poorly printed flyer. Signed "The Communist Party of America," it read as follows:

> COMRADS: Rise against the capitalistic form of government. Throw out the Bosses and kill the agressors [*sic*] of the common People. Are YOU going to remain in the gutter and be trampled upon by the capitalists until you are dead? Get them first or they will get you.
>
> Negroes, rise against your white oppressors. We are ALL equal and you should have an equal chance with all whites. We offer you that chance. Do your part to bring this about by electing Comrad [*sic*] Maurice Sugar to the Recorders court. We will then have a chance to work from within and tear down this damnable form of Government.

While it had little bearing on the campaign itself—the *Times* did not print its story about it until the day after the election—the leaflet was troubling, especially in light of the fact that buildings at the Communist Workers Camp on Twelve-Mile Road had been set afire that night as well. Any Communist knew it was a forgery: not only was the language ridiculous but "comrade" was misspelled (and Communists never used it as a general form of address anyway) and the title of the Party was wrong (Communist Party *of the United States* of America would have been correct). Weinstone immediately wrote a letter to the *Times* pointing out these facts. Who was responsible? No one knew at the time, but this was the beginning of Sugar's long, bizarre, and, in the end, frightening persecution by the Black Legion.[28]

The campaign was capped off Sunday with a great motorcade that began at the four corners of the city and ended at Arena Gardens, on Woodward. It was a glorious day and all the campaign workers knew that they had done everything possible. That it was not quite enough was only a mild disappointment. Sugar finished thirteenth and did extremely well in black precincts. And George Murphy, at least, was elected. The postelection mood was one of elation. The *Detroit Labor News* wrote, "While Maurice Sugar failed in the election, the 64,000 votes cast for him by Detroiters, in spite of the silence campaign by the daily newspapers, was a splendid tribute to his outstanding qualities both as an attorney and as a man. . . . The forces of reaction will not brag about the defeat of Maurice Sugar." Sugar himself made up his mind immediately to stand for election in the council campaign in the fall and had the assurance from his mainstays, most of the political Left and Martel's federation, of their full support.[29] As it turned out, the game was not played that way. Sugar soon found himself squarely in the center of the great conflict that would split the labor movement in two. His common-council campaign would be an interesting preview of the struggle within the AFL.

6 ✣ Sugar and the Rise of the UAW

Three events occurred during the summer of 1935 that fundamentally transformed the U.S. labor movement and Left politics: the passage of the National Labor Relations Act in June/July, the declaration of the Popular Front strategy at the Seventh Congress of the Communist International in August, and the first convention of the International Union, United Automobile Workers, later that month.

The Wagner Act, introduced by the New York Senator in February shortly after the highly critical Henderson Report (based on the auto hearings) was released and in the midst of deep worker disillusionment with the president, passed the Senate and House with overwhelming majorities despite vociferous opposition from big business. Roosevelt had remained cool toward the bill during the hearings and signed it into law on July 5, 1935 without enthusiasm. Its significance was enormous. As McColloch and Bornstein, historians of the NLRB, remark, the act constituted perhaps the most important turning point in the history of U.S. democracy "since the Emancipation Proclamation." In guaranteeing workers the right of self-organization, the right to engage in collective bargaining through freely chosen representatives, and the right to engage in "concerted activities" (that is, to strike), it did amount to labor's Bill of Rights. Above all, its clauses provided five specific prohibitions and sanctions against management, legally punishable "unfair labor practices": (1) a general provision forbidding management from interfering with these rights (espionage and intimidation fell under this concept); (2) the prohibition of company unions; (3) a strong clause forbidding discrimination against an employee for union activities; (4) no discrimination for testifying under the act; and (5) the controversial stricture that management bargain "in good faith." The act also wiped out once and for all Roosevelt's proportional representation principle, awarding instead exclusive bargaining rights for the entire unit to the union gaining a simple majority in a board-certified election. The NLRB would define the unit—a

165

burdensome and controversial responsibility. Section 9 also defined the scope of bargaining rights, limiting the subject matter to wages, hours, and working conditions. This was a profoundly important point because it legally restricted the demands labor might make. Indeed, while a tremendous advance for labor had occurred, the entire act served the purpose of defining labor's place *within* the capitalist system. It was for this reason that the Communist party, for example, initially opposed the Wagner Act as a "deception."

It did in fact place the U.S. labor movement in a unique position in the capitalist world. As McCulloch and Bornstein put it, "Congress chose to shape labor relations . . . according to legal standards. By contrast, in other industrialized Western nations, notably the Scandinavian countries and Great Britain, collective bargaining had come by voluntary acceptance, rather than by force of law. From 1935 forward, there has been no turning back from the statutory approach to collective bargaining, and ours has become an industrial-relations system regulated in large measure by legal prescription." The Act was thus a force both liberating and containing the American labor movement.[1]

The address by Georgi Dimitroff outlining the Popular Front did a good deal to ease the immediate ideological pressures imposed by the Wagner Act, for in promoting cooperation with bourgeois democracy against the threat of fascism, it oriented Communists toward the path of compromise. The Wagner Act's positive benefits and the apparent shift of the New Deal to the side of labor could now more easily be viewed with equanimity. The fact was that U.S. Communists, particularly those in Detroit, had already been emphasizing cooperation—if not with Roosevelt, at least with those elements they regarded as prolabor—for a long time. For non-Communists like Sugar, Popular Front realized a goal long harbored: a stress on unity of the Left and an end to ideological nitpicking.

It was in the ranks of the automobile workers' movement that Sugar's legal skills and political acumen found their full expression. The International Union of the United Automobile Workers, the first industrial union chartered by the AFL, held its opening convention in Detroit, August 25–29, 1935. It was not exactly what the delegates expected it to be. Dillon's lackluster and cautious leadership was resented by most of them, and they assumed that they would be electing their own officers. They also assumed that *industrial* union meant "industrywide" union and that all AFL affiliates, such as the IAM in auto and the metal polishers, would be absorbed into it. Neither turned out to be the case. Green crammed Dillon back down the throats of the union and chose moderates Homer Martin and Ed Hall as the other officers. He also vetoed attempts to give the UAW jurisdiction over traditional craft-union domains, a circumstance prompting Wyndham Mortimer's famous line that "the craft form of organization fits the automobile industry like a square peg in a round hole." The left-wing rank-and-filers almost bolted the convention, but were restrained by Mortimer and Henry Kraus from Cleveland, who said that was exactly what Green wanted.

166

The aftermath is well known. A committee of seven that included such future leaders of the UAW left as Mortimer, Carl Shipley from South Bend Bendix, and (the then more moderate) George Addes of Toledo Auto-Lite went to the AFL executive council to protest, but were rebuffed amid accusations of Communist influence. At the AFL convention in Atlantic City in October, again with the rafters ringing with anti-Communist resolutions (Green had called them "slime"), the industrial-union issue came to a head; and John L. Lewis, with one punch to the chin of Big Bill Hutcheson of the carpenters, announced the crucial turning point in the history of U.S. trade unionism. The following month Lewis formed the Committee for Industrial Organization (CIO) and resigned as vice president of the AFL.[2]

The Federation Schism in Politics: The Council Race

Sugar had little to do directly with these dramatic events. But his political fortunes in the summer and fall of 1935 were affected by the deepening split in the labor movement, as was his long friendship with Frank X. Martel. The unity of the recorder's-court campaign could not be maintained in the common-council campaign. After April 1935, AFL national leadership and their lackeys like Dillon saw Communists under every toadstool. Martel, who had never red-baited, got caught in the middle and was forced to side with his bosses or lose his place in the local labor hierarchy.

Immediately after the recorder's-court election, Sugar and his key lieutenants in the unions and the community were determined to keep the political presence of labor alive. They decided that Sugar would run for election in the fall and formed an association called the United Labor Conference for Political Action. Its members were those who worked hardest in Sugar's campaign and tended to be overrepresented by the pro-Soviet Left. But others, such as Matt Smith and Socialist Fay O'Camb, were also part of it. Sugar looked upon the group as the nucleus for a united Labor party. Martel was not a member, but the statement that he issued on the eve of the recorder's-court election left no doubt about his personal regard for Sugar:

His more than 20 years of service in the labor movement has won for Maurice Sugar that recognition and esteem which only comes to those whose lives are bound up with the cause of labor. Not only as a practicing attorney, but in hundreds of other public appearances, he has been a consistent and courageous champion of labor's rights. The campaign to elect Maurice Sugar as judge of Recorder's Court is a challenge to the open shop automobile manufacturers who are trying to control the political, as well as the economic, life of our city. His election would place on the bench a public servant of outstanding qualifications, a true representative of hundreds of thousands of working men and women of the city of Detroit.

Immediately after the election, Sugar was invited to speak at the DFL-sponsored Labor Forum. On April 29, the federation held a special conference at which the proponents of a Labor party calling themselves "progressives" won a majority in favor of the abandonment of the "reward your friend, punish your enemies" approach to politics. Sugar's friends and others (and presumably Martel) favored this.

The following Monday, Martel, Sugar, and John Bollens went to Lansing to testify against the Dunckel-Baldwin Bill, currently being promoted by the Liberty League and Hearst publications, which sought to regulate strike activity by statute. They went as "delegates" from the local ACLU, which Bollens headed. On May 15 Sugar again spoke at the Labor Forum, this time on organizing in the auto plants. He emphasized the need for labor to act on its own and not rely on the government. Specifically, Sugar argued that workers did not have to wait until they had 100-percent organization in a plant—"when you're ready to strike, strike."

This was reported favorably in the *Detroit Labor News* and could be taken as a slap-in-the-face to Green and Dillon. All during the late winter there had been agitation among the federal local ranks for a "united general strike" and votes overwhelmingly authorized the AFL president to call for a strike. But Green—and he was proud of it—failed to bow to their pressure. Toledo Chevrolet workers did not wait and walked out without Dillon's authorization on April 22. Dillon did everything he could to keep the radicals at bay and to end the strike as quickly as possible. Two days before Sugar's talk, a weak settlement had been accepted after Dillon (1) advised Flint Buick workers not to go out, too, and (2) threatened James Roland with termination as a union organizer. Tempers were running high, and Sugar's pointed remarks undoubtedly reached Dillon. Still, as of May 15, Sugar remained in the good graces of Martel and the leadership of the DFL.

But then things began to go sour. A meeting later in the month, which was supposed to specify DFL policy on independent-labor political action, broke up in confusion. A motion in favor of independent politics lost, "because," according to the *Progressive Trade Unionist Bulletin,* "of a lack of cooperation between the progressive forces who were opposed to the old policy." The conflict among the "progressives" (a term used in 1935 to designate those AFL members opposed to Green) specifically concerned the Sugar-sponsored United Labor Conference of Political Action. A mimeographed sheet signed by the name "Progressive Trade Unionist" group was put out before the second meeting. It said, in part, "What is needed is a definite political policy which may be pursued over a period of years. The matter of endorsing candidates or selecting a labor ticket for any election in the immediate future may well be deferred until such policy is determined upon by *accredited* representatives of the unions and approved by the local union membership. The United [Labor] Conference for Political Action is not an agency decided upon by the unions themselves, thru the procedures of their organizations." No slate of theirs, therefore, was a "genuine labor slate."

The latter had to be generated by the federation; otherwise candidates were still "friends of labor." Thus Sugar was a "labor candidate" before but would not be now.

Who, precisely, constituted the "Progressive Trade Unionists" is not clear. But they *did* support Sugar in the council campaign in the end, while continuing to complain about the United Labor Conference "working outside regular trade union channels." They were probably in the building trades and some of the federal locals who came only slowly to Sugar's support and were influenced by Left Socialists, Proletarian-party people, and Musteites.

But more important, Martel was cooling toward Sugar in late May. Sugar was never invited to speak to the Labor Forum again. And Martel blocked his endorsement for city council, both in the primary and in the general election. The latter was the kiss of death because Sugar had every chance of winning, missing, even so, by only one place. Obviously Martel had initially taken advantage of the split in the "progressive" ranks to defeat their motion in late May. But why, after such ardent support of Sugar, after such favor shown toward him immediately after the election, did he turn his back on him, and on the progressives in general?

Although local AFL papers are available, Martel never tells us. In a response (after the campaign) to the irate pattern makers who broke with him to support Sugar, he feigned innocence of exerting any personal influence. In fact, he did not attend the meeting considering endorsement for the final election, but he offers this: "It is this writer's observation that there was a good deal of resentment against the Sugar campaign on the part of many of the delegates because of the efforts of those in charge of the Sugar campaign to dominate the political policies of the Central Body." In other words, that which upset the "progressives," incensed the conservatives and moderates (like Martel) even more.

But the accusation that the United Labor Conference "pretended to speak for labor" was somewhat of a smokescreen. On a deeper level, two interconnected developments seem critical, and Martel had to be sensitive to them.

Despite their outrage after the auto-code extension, the AFL leadership still looked to the government for help, and as the Wagner Act moved toward passage, they became reabsorbed by the hope that the government would pave the way for them. More generally, the fox in the White House, the greatest politician in U.S. history, was sniffing the wind. If a Martel (and many of his counterparts elsewhere) were thinking about a Labor party, perhaps he, Roosevelt, was in trouble. He would not move too fast, but he would move. And by May–June, especially after the stunning 63–12 Senate vote in favor of the Wagner Bill on May 16, he thought it best to extend his hand to labor. The AFL accepted it. Hence the hesitancy on the part of Martel, who realized the power of Democratic-party politics in Detroit, to announce to the world that he would support a Labor party candidate. Whether Green had specifically threatened Martel, we do not know, but late May was the moment of his change of heart toward Sugar.

The other side of the coin was the shrill anticommunism emanating from the AFL and the general polarization going on in U.S. society. Restrictive anti-"subversive" and antilabor laws were introduced in many states. While the AFL condemned such legislation, it also tried to avoid any taint of communism. Their national office and conventions had for years taken a general stand against communism, but in 1934, as noted earlier, it was specified that no officer or representative of an AFL local might be a Communist. The Detroit federation had participated in the purge, specifically with the expulsion of Billy Allan from the federation council in December 1934. Still, the local AFL worked with the CP in the Sugar campaign. Exactly what happened on the local scene therefore is, again, not clear, but the AFL nationally was certainly tightening the screws. The Atlantic City convention of October 1935 took the final step by ordaining that no organization "officered or controlled by Communists . . . shall be allowed representation or recognition in this Federation, or in any central body, state federation of labor, national or international union connected with the AF of L under the penalty of the suspension of the body violating this section."[3]

The situation in 1935 in Detroit was particularly ticklish because of the presence of a strong populist, even fascist, Right. Father Charles Coughlin's influence was at its apogee. Presenting himself as a friend of the working man, the radio priest railed against "Jewish" bankers while condemning all forms of radicalism, but specifically "Bolshevism," which he saw as somehow "Jewish" as well. On the other hand, Coughlin had not originally been antiunion. He attacked the "class bigotry" of the AFL and had stimulated the growth of an independent industrial union under Richard Frankensteen called the Automotive Industrial Workers Association. As 1935 progressed, however, he abandoned his prounionism and took his final step toward the authoritarian Right when he condemned the Motor Products strike. Coughlin's popularity among Catholic workers contributed to the anti-Left tenor in the city and no doubt was a factor in Martel's and the AFL moderates' growing caution vis-à-vis Sugar, who willingly accepted Communist and any other Left support he could get.

There was a direr presence in the metropolitan area, although its dimensions were little known at the time. This was the avowedly fascist and racist secret society, the Black Legion. The legion was an organization dedicated to the phsycial extermination of those elements in society who threatened "American womanhood" and the flag. This meant generally anyone who was not white and Protestant. Several random murders had been attributed to them, and it was reported that these gun-loving fanatics were now recruiting by force. In the course of the spring and summer of 1935 the "Communist nigger lover" Maurice Sugar was receiving death threats from them on a regular basis. He finally took heed and moved his desk away from his office window after noticing that he was being watched from the office across the street. He also applied for and obtained, after some difficulty due to his prison record, a license to carry a hand gun. Worst of all, Dayton Dean, a legion hit man, moved into his apartment building on Third Avenue, intending to bomb Sugar's dwelling. The only reason he did not do it, Dean later testified, was because he did not want to kill any "innocent" people. While much can be said for historian Peter Amann's thesis that "invisible, unsuspected power is powerless," people knew enough about the legion to hesitate to support known leftists, their chief targets.[4]

A polarized city, a paranoid AFL, and a prolabor shift in Democratic party politics thus seem best to explain the split in Detroit's labor movement over backing Sugar. He ran anyway, of course, trying to present in the primary a "labor ticket" that crossed political and trade-unionist lines without compromising with AFL leadership's rightward shift.

Sugar and his allies chose as "running mates" two long-time trade-union activists, William McKie and Fay O'Camb. McKie, a veteran of British labor struggles born in Carlisle, England in 1879, had immigrated to the United States after the 1926 General Strike. Identified with the British CP, he became active in the Auto Workers' Union and achieved fame as a fearless combatant against the Ford Motor Company. A skilled metalworker, McKie was now president of the Ford local of the International UAW. He was a vigorous critic of Dillon and Green and had fought side-by-side with Mortimer at the recent convention.

O'Camb, a less well known personality, nevertheless represented a significant new variable in Detroit Left politics. He was a member of the Socialist party and an activist in the Metal Polishers International, a craft union in the AFL. He was born in Erie, Pennsylvania in 1876 of old-line "French and English parentage." He had been an officer of a Cleveland local of his union. In Detroit his politics kept him out of office, although he was several times a delegate to national conventions and served as an organizer throughout the region. O'Camb thus came from the "old" AFL and, above all, was a Socialist. The Socialist party had been experiencing internal tremors for some time, as the Old Guard, formerly all-powerful Social Democrats under the leadership or Morris Hillquit, began to fade. Young radicals flocked to the Socialists, and the tone of party declarations increasingly sounded again like old-fashioned Marxism. With the fading of the Old Guard faded the most vociferous of its anti-Communist pronouncements, although men such as New York labor lawyer Louis Waldman and the ILGU's David Dubinsky, still bleeding from earlier battles with the CP, kept it up. The shift—which Norman Thomas managed to ride out as a middle-ground figure—produced a type of Socialist willing to cooperate with Communists, especially after the Dimitroff declaration. Fay O'Camb was one of this number, as was Professor Walter Bergman, also active in industrial-union organizing. Unfortunately for O'Camb and the Sugar campaign, Old Guardists remained the majority in Michigan, and they expelled him from the party.[5]

The three men represented a broad range of Left and trade-union opinion, with Sugar bringing along MESA and a variety of AFL locals loyal to him personally. The approach taken by the United Labor Conference for Political Action (ULCPA) recognized the new political realities. They brought out a

171

leaflet called "Labor Holds the Key" that was passed out at the UAW convention in late August. Sugar was the principal author, although other key figures in the ULCPA such as Keene, Simmons, Weinstone, Matt Smith, McKie, O'Camb, and Mary Zuk no doubt gave their approval.

First and foremost, they emphasized that "the Conference does not presume to dictate to the Trades Unions the course which they must follow. The Conference seeks to include all unions and all active forces of the Labor movement and thereby make of the Conference a truly all-embracing body of labor groups. . . . Labor must take the offensive. IT MUST FIGHT WITH BOTH FISTS—its economic fist—the union—and its political fist—a Labor Party." In other words, it invited all unions to participate—as long as they favored an independent third party. But by the summer of 1935, with Roosevelt bending to the Left, this was not as appealing an idea as it had been a few months before.

The leaflet nevertheless made a strong argument, stressing local and state politics more than national. It noted the sad record of "friends of labor" of both parties, who, once in office in Detroit, "turned out to be willing tools in the hands of the employers and their powerful union-busting agencies." "Labor has been thrown a few crumbs," it declared "while the bosses have retained the whole loaf." Above all, labor leaders can take unanimous stands on issues, but their lack of political clout condemns their efforts to failure. The leaflet cited the recent examples, on the state level, of the passage of Dunckel-Baldwin, the defeat of an antiinjunction bill, and the failure of the legislature to expand the Workmen's Compensation Law to cover industrial poisoning. Detroit's common council did nothing to protest police brutality against pickets and labor demonstrators or to condemn the board of education. It also tried "to railroad through an anti-leaflet ordinance" (similar to the quite effective one in Dearborn) pushed by the auto manufacturers. Only labor's quick action to arouse public opinion stopped it. And this occurred in the context of a labor movement politicized by the recorder's-court campaign.

Sugar's leaflet then emphasized the great significance of that battle, which proved that labor was mature enough to run its own political operations. But the leaflet also showed the strain of Martel's reticence and the whispering campaign against the conference: "It may be said that this [independent labor candidacies] is a 'red idea.' The answer is that every idea advanced by labor in its own interests is today stamped as 'red' by the employers and their agents. . . . Shall we take our line from them?" The concluding rhetoric was effective: "The door of the political arena has been locked against labor. Up to this time it has contented itself with peeping through the cracks. All the time labor had held the key to that door in its pocket. Let labor use that key to open the door and enter the political arena. What a licking it can give the employers!"

The big question for many AFL leaders, however, was by what blueprint was that key, labor unity, to be built? There existed a concern that the Communist party had played too strong a role in Sugar's earlier campaign. Now the campaign committee, the ULCPA, was seeking to act as the agency effecting labor unity in the city. Moreover, many labor activists were far from certain that the goal of Sugar's group, a Labor party, was now what they wanted. Still, it is important that out of 126 local AFL unions (not including the federal UAW locals) who had explicitly endorsed Sugar in the recorders-court campaign, 35 braved the wrath of Martel to come to ULCPA meetings in the summer.

As the campaign got under way in September, the ULCPA headlined *It's About Time!* (now the "official organ" of the conference) with "Labor Names Own Ticket for Council." This was debatable. MESA, "twenty AFL locals," and "other" independent unions endorsed the three candidates, but a large majority of the AFL stayed away. The specifics of the "Labor platform" were similar to those of the recorder's-court campaign. Newly added was a focus on the high cost of living, reflecting the work of the Housewives League (Sugar had been their lawyer when leaders were arrested for picketing during the summer meat boycott), and a condemnation of the recently implemented state sales tax. Also, unlike the recorder's-court fight, campaign literature explicitly touted a Labor party.

This campaign was as elaborately organized as the one for recorder's court. The precinct canvasing was thorough, with virtually every neighborhood in all but the wealthiest parts of Detroit covered. More showmanship was added, with public demonstrations, plays, concerts, and a preprimary auto parade. They even had a campaign song for which Sugar wrote both words and music. One can imagine a big rally at Arena Gardens concluding with "We're Moving to the City Hall."

> They think that they can cut our pay
> And do just as they like;
> Their coppers slug our pickets
> Every time we go on strike.
>
> *Chorus*
> So we're moving to the City Hall
> Moving to the City Hall
> There's a job we've got to do
> And we're going to do it, too
> So we're moving to the City Hall.
>
> When we get wise and organize
> To battle for our rights
> They set their sneaking stools and spies
> To get the guy that fights.
>
> And when we get upon relief
> And want more bread and meat
> They tell us to be thankful we've
> Got anything to eat.
>
> They tell us when we're forty we're
> Too old to stand the pace

173

We answer we are young enough
To go and take *their* place.

They tax the poor and leave the rich
To fatten on their gains
They brand as un-American
The fighter who complains.

If fascist Willie Hearst believes
That with his dirty lies
He's fooling us Americans
He'll get a big surprise.

Our pioneers of early years
Knew how to place their kicks
We're fighting with the spirit
Of the boys of seventy-six.

And Jefferson and Lincoln too
Would help our fight along
They'd back the labor ticket
And they'd join us in this song.

With O'Camb, McKie and Sugar
We will get a worker's deal
We'll put them in the Council
And we'll make the bosses squeal.

The special concern for the problems of older workers reflected an issue that had always been around, but took on special meaning with men the age of McKie and O'Camb running in this campaign. Seniority rights were rare in most plants (especially at Ford) and the most persistent Depression victims were the older workers. Just as interesting was the song's appeal to U.S. democratic traditions. This reflected the new Popular Front perspective and is a very early example of it. The pioneers, Jefferson, and Lincoln, those great U.S. representatives of individual freedom and social justice, would increasingly be installed in the left-wing pantheon. Sugar, as a real pioneer with a Lincolnesque image, was an "American" personality perfectly suited in this regard as well for Popular Front politics.[6]

Sugar finished tenth, with 18,367 votes, in the October 10 primary. He was the leading nonincumbent except for club woman Laura Osborn. O'Camb and McKie ran well, getting 7,000 and 8,500 votes respectively, but were not among the eighteen nominees. Chances for Sugar's election were excellent. Many areas of Sugar support in the recorder's-court campaign had low turnouts for the primary and could only improve in the final election.

Voting in the black community was particularly light and renewed attention was given to it. Sugar retained the same ministerial and professional support that he had in the recorder's-court campaign. He was also involved in another case involving injustice toward a black, a young man named William Turner, who was beaten by firemen and policemen at Firehouse Number 30 in the heart of the black community on Rivard. It was a classic case of police brutality. A fireman with nothing better to do threw water on Turner and shot a racial epithet at him, and a fight began. Turner was then dragged into the firehouse and pummeled by firemen. Police arrived, arrested Turner, took him inside again, and beat him to a pulp. In the meantime a large crowd gathered, yelling for the thrashing to stop. As Turner was finally hauled off to jail, police, ordered out by Mayor Couzens, cordoned off the area and, according to one report, "instituted a reign of terror in the neighborhood." A group of black citizens demanded an investigation of the incident from Mayor Couzens, who not only turned them down flat but called their leader a "damned liar." Sugar's defense of Turner then became the focal point, but on October 4, despite a parade of witnesses to the beatings, an all-white jury convicted Turner of assault and he got thirty days in jail. Fortunately, Sugar was able to win a new trial amidst what the *North Detroit Herald* (a new black paper) reported was "a wide movement to fight the Turner case to the finish, as it is considered a serious blow at the civil rights of all people, Negro and White." Turner was again convicted, however, and no disciplinary action was ever taken against his attackers.

The research of Snow Grigsby and the Detroit Civic Rights Committee on the tiny percentage of blacks in municipal jobs (there were none in the fire department) became highly relevant at this point. Grigsby sent an open letter to all common-council candidates (as well as the mayor, who was up for reelection) asking what they intended to do about the deplorable record of the city in hiring blacks. Only Sugar responded with anything more than an acknowledgement of its receipt, declaring that he would work hard to reverse the situation and to enforce "existing state law": he had been involved in unearthing a long-ignored post–Civil War law prohibiting discrimination in any form against blacks. Overall, Sugar's standing among Detroit's blacks remained high. His flawless civil-rights record was still the main source of his appeal, but this campaign put even more emphasis on labor organizing. Unquestionably, more black people were listening.[7]

In the last days of the campaign a variety of dramatic events put Sugar in the public eye as never before. The most exciting was a debate with Upton Sinclair, who had founded in California a grass-roots organization called End Poverty and recently contended for the Democratic-party nomination for governor. He did well and was currently promoting the idea that radicals work to capture the Democratic party. He had declared his support for FDR. In the debate, which took place at the Armory before six thousand people two days prior to the election, Sugar presented the Labor party position. With the partisan crowd cheering him on, he warned Sinclair that the latter had been "seduced by the demagogy of the New Deal and by Roosevelt, a demagog whose demagogy had not been matched in decades." The debate became acrimonious toward the end. Sinclair was nonplussed, and the crowd impolite about it, so

Sinclair lashed out at the Communists, who, he said, "supported Hitler to defeat the Social-Democrats" in Germany. The bitterness was not as serious as either the *Detroit News* or the *Daily Worker* painted it, for Sinclair would later ask Sugar to read the manuscript of his novel about Henry Ford, *The Flivver King,* and they would correspond with obvious cordiality.

Another important boost for the campaign came from labor. The Detroit Building Trades Council, representing thirty-five AFL unions, bolted from Martel's control and endorsed Sugar. This opened a minor floodgate, and in the end Sugar had the support of thirty other AFL unions, including "several" locals of the UAW.

The coverage that the Sinclair debate received in the "capitalist press" was a measure of Sugar's growing prominence. Shortly after the primary, the voice of local conservatism, *Detroit Saturday Night,* had warned "those complacent individuals who dismiss the red menace with a superior smile" they had better open their eyes: "Tenth on the list is Maurice Sugar, as outspoken a radical as has appeared as a serious contender in Detroit's arena of ballots in modern times." Sugar's campaign for the final election was no longer greeted with silence but by attacks in the daily press. Even the sedate *Free Press* went out of its way to condemn Sugar. More serious, in what appeared to be a coordinated operation, the Black Legion planted yet another, even more inflammatory leaflet at the Sinclair debate (it attacked the church and said that Sugar would "fight for [Negroes'] right to marry white women"); and the following day the CP office in Detroit was raided and Weinstone and two others arrested. The raid certainly seemed aimed at disrupting the campaign, because mountains of real Sugar literature were seized and key campaign coordinators taken briefly out of circulation. Whether the alleged connection between the Black Legion and Heinrich Pickert, chief of the Detroit police, had anything to do with the operation can only be conjecture, but this new leaflet forgery had its desired effect.

The extent to which these last-minute efforts to undermine the campaign influenced the outcome is impossible to determine. But Sugar lost, finishing tenth with 55,574 votes. Robert Ewald, who got the endorsement of the Detroit Federation of Labor instead of Sugar, received 69,000. For the *Free Press,* 14,000 votes "was an uncomfortably narrow margin of safety." Sugar had become a major, and disturbing, political presence in the city. His name and his cause—organizing the unorganized—were much better known than they had been a year before.[8]

But now, the lines were clear. The established AFL leadership, especially Martel and Dillon, had rejected one of the major forces attempting to shake Detroit workers out of their fear and caution. The ULCPA was considerably more than a "Communist front," but even if it were, it had made industrial unionism an important political issue and caused the open-shoppers to tremble a bit. Sugar and his campaign had used the "political fist" to strengthen the "economic fist."

Auto Organizing: The Community Front

Events over the next three months sealed the fate of the conservative AFL leadership and opened the way toward the triumph of industrial unionism in the automobile industry. Sugar had little influence on the process directly, although, as lawyer for MESA, he had plenty of work to do. But the raising of Detroit workers' union consciousness throughout 1935 now began to show its effects. It was also a time when job security had increased due to further advances in auto production. Semiskilled workers, the great mass of the unorganized, were beginning to respond to UAW appeals as well as those of the independents— MESA, Frankensteen's Automotive Industrial Workers Association (AIWA), and Arthur Greer's Associated Automobile Workers of America (AAWA).

The key event dislodging Francis Dillon and, with him, the last vestiges of the craft-union mentality from the UAW was the Motor Products strike. It began on November 15, 1935, after negotiations with the AIWA (which was the main force in the east-side supplier's plant) broke down. Militant AIWA workers overrode leaders' pleas for a delay and voted an immediate strike. MESA went along, somewhat reluctantly, and both were joined by workers in the small AFL metal-polishers and the larger UAW local. The plant was closed down 100 percent the following day. Apparently, Loren Hauser, the local president, had not informed Dillon, and Dillon complained immediately about not having been consulted. This puckish attitude flared into outright opposition five days later. Dillon thus began a wildly inconsistent relationship to the strike that discredited his leadership.

He ordered UAW members to cross the other unions' picket lines with police escorts on November 25. The atmosphere of violence was heavy. On the day before, the metal polishers' union hall had been bombed, and that night (in retaliation, it was thought) an AIWA member's home was bombed. Two days later Carl Swanson, a MESA picket, was shot in the back by a scab. On December 3, strikers, provoked by the police, besieged the plant. Twenty-two were injured, along with five policemen. The following day, the police attacked strike headquarters, leaving many more injured workers, and on December 5 the mayor prohibited picketing. Deluged with protests, Couzens reauthorized picketing after Sugar argued law with him. Dillon now said he would cooperate with the strike, and Hauser got authorization from his local to fix a date for their renewed participation. The Dillon pendulum then swung the other way and back again from December 10th to the 16th (Swanson had died in the meantime). The UAW finally called an on-the-job work stoppage on December 17. Reports as to its effectiveness are contradictory, but in any case, the company rejected all the union's demands—and that was that. Thereafter, despite an attempt to breathe life back into it, the strike was doomed. Dillon's incompetence was the source of the failure. It was a good time to strike and with any kind of sensible policy from the UAW president, something might have been accomplished.

Perhaps Dillon was angered by the fact that the three independents had been discussing merger and had even planned a convention on December 21. Perhaps he also was under orders from Green to avoid strike action. More important, his seemingly distracted state of mind may have simply been a result of disinterest: he had told Homer Martin even before the strike that he was "sick of auto organizing."

Whatever the case, Dillon had dug his grave. Martin and Hall turned fully against him. Early in January, Martin went to Cleveland to consult with Mortimer, who had opposed Dillon from the beginning. Martin had already touched base in Toledo and pledged to leadership there his support in granting a charter to the large prospective Local Number 12. Dillon had told them to break up into what amounted to craft locals, and they, led by George Addes, had refused. Mortimer was already planning a mass rally in Cleveland featuring John L. Lewis. Martin, although leery of Mortimer's politics, saw no other way to go. On January 7, 1936 he wrote Green, "I say in all loyalty, respect, and sympathy for him that in my opinion [Dillon] can never gain the support of the great majority of the auto workers." Hall, typically, was more direct. He told a South Bend audience on January 15 that Dillon was "a dirty rat."

Martin, Hall, and Mortimer went to Miami to urge Green to call for new elections at an early date, which he and the AFL board authorized for April 27. Martin and Hall then came to Detroit and simply moved in, physically taking charge of the office and shunting Dillon aside on February 12. The first thing Martin did was to issue the Toledo charter. Dillon's protests were ignored. Martin and Hall mended fences with the beleaguered independents and formed a Motor Products strike-relief committee. Over the next two months, they prepared for the South Bend convention, which would give the UAW independent status. Martin, reportedly a Socialist at the time, remained friendly with Mortimer, giving license to the full exercise of "progressive" power within the union. The result was a delegation farther to the left than that going to any subsequent convention, with the possible exception of 1939 in Cleveland. The Left had been central in Dillon's overthrow and Martin happily condemned red-baiting, while gathering in the support of the radical factions across the union.[9]

Many idealistic young workers with left-wing sympathies sought to join the UAW organizing cadres now. It was a time of great enthusiasm, a time when a giant bottleneck seemed to have opened. Sugar, because of his varied connections on the Left and in the labor movement, helped to "place" activists in the plants around Detroit.

A good example of the process was his assistance to Walter Reuther. He and his brother Victor, it will be recalled, were enthusiastic about their experience in the Soviet Union, and they returned to Detroit in the fall of 1935 wishing "to take up the work once more—this time we hope with a more definite understanding of our goal and methods of attaining it." Shortly after their arrival, the Reuthers came to see Sugar about finding a useful outlet for their energies. He suggested that they go see Weinstone, whose knowledge of existing shop units was considerably better than his. Sugar assumed from their correspondence and discussions with him that they were close to a Communist perspective, although they were members of the Socialist party.

Through Weinstone (and no doubt after talking to Sugar about his experience on the circuit) they first undertook a lecture tour arranged by the Friends of the Soviet Union. Both were blacklisted among Detroit employers and could not find jobs in the auto industry despite their considerable skills and experience. While lecturing, Victor was induced by brother Roy and Tucker Smith to work with Brookwood College, the labor education institution in Katonak, New York. Walter returned to Detroit, however, determined to join the auto labor movement—and perhaps also because May Wolf, whom he would marry, lived there. What happened thereafter remains a matter of debate. Weinstone claims that Sugar brought Reuther to a weekly district meeting, and shortly thereafter the DO asked the young militant to join the Party. Although it is entirely unlikely that Sugar would go to a regular Party meeting, that he might have served as a go-between seems plausible enough. Whether the offer was accepted is another matter. Nat Ganley, the future CP whip in the UAW, later said that he accepted dues payments from Reuther. Weinstone insists that he joined. Sugar did not say, but when he wrote—in the 1960s—he would not avow that anyone was a Party member. The best evidence that Walter became very close to the Party was that he obtained his union membership in the Ternstedt Local 86 (and hence also his position as an alternate to the South Bend convention) thanks to the good offices of the Party unit chief in that GM plant. Reuther was lucky enough to be elevated to the status of delegate at the convention (though his credentials were challenged, since there was no proof that he actually *worked* at Ternstedt), voted with the Progressives, and was elected to the UAW executive board. Many assumed that he was with the CP caucus, although the Socialist paper, the *Call*, claimed him as one of theirs in their story on the convention (May 9, 1936).

Far too much has been made of all this. Whether or not Reuther or anyone else was a member of the Communist party then is largely immaterial. It is obvious that he had great sympathy for it, worked with it, and benefited from his association with it. That he later shifted more clearly back to the Socialist party was not unusual. But it did leave a bad taste in the mouths of many Communists and their friends, and Reuther with a reputation of being opportunistic.[10]

The Reuthers' experience was typical of many militants in 1936. The possibilities opened up by the Wagner Act, the upswing in automobile sales, the emergence of the Committee for Industrial Organization under John L. Lewis and the growing worldwide significance of the Popular Front made specific political affiliation considerably less important than it had been previously. There was a job to be done, and the time was ripe. If a suspicious expreacher like Homer Martin or a political conservative like Lewis encouraged Communist participation and if Communists were bending over backwards to cooperate with other groups, then to join the Party (or refuse to) was not a terribly important decision in 1936. Leftists worked together. The tiny Proletarian party saw Stanley Nowak, the inveterate organizer of Polish autoworkers, migrate to the Communist milieu and stay there, while Emil Mazey retained his connection; but both worked feverishly and with full cooperation. Socialist John Brophy and pro-Soviet Wyndham Mortimer worked in harmony on the broad problems of auto organizing. Victor, Walter, and Roy Reuther were again clearly identified with the Socialists by the end of 1936, but this did little to disrupt their cooperation with Communists in Flint and Detroit during the Great Sit-down. If being a Communist in 1936 was not quite as "American" as apple pie, it had lost much of its fearsome and mysterious aura.

May Day of 1936 provided the best proof of the new atmosphere. The *Front Populaire* was fully operative in France as Socialists and Communists worked together for their great electoral victory two days later. Spain's people's front had already triumphed and a full scale one-day general strike showed the strength of labor united. In the United States, Socialists, Communists, and even Jay Lovestone's Communist Party Opposition (which gathered the losers of the power struggle over Third Period policy in the U.S.) marched arm-in-arm in a massive New York parade estimated at 175 thousand people. The *Call* reported on Detroit: "A joint May Day celebration packed the Deutsches Haus here with 2,500 workers who gave tremendous ovations to Albert Goldman, speaking for the Socialist Party, Al Renner of the Proletarian Party, and William Weinstone of the Communist Party." The U.S. Left had never been more united. The significance of this for the triumphs of industrial-union organizing that followed, for the emergence of a working-class movement the likes of which the United States had never seen before and would not see again, should not be under-estimated.[11]

Neither, in the case of Detroit at any rate, should the work of the Left in exposing the radical Right and, more generally, in revealing the layer upon layer of repressive instruments, legal and illegal, that had hamstrung the labor movement in the city for so long. This would be Maurice Sugar's most important work from 1936 to 1941. Detroit and southeast Michigan remained the least-organized area in the automobile industry. Dillon's heavy hand and the inertia at the center had something to do with it. But more important, Detroit, Pontiac, and Flint were towns dominated by the barons of the industry who had, over the decades, created mechanisms of control that extended from their obvious police state in the plants through the media and on to local government and the police. The hegemonic apparatus also included civic groups, fraternal organizations, many churches (we have seen it at work in the black community), and the schools, where values of rugged individualism and belief in social mobility were mixed with images of the "natural" capacity of male WASPs to lead. There was also the more subtle promotion of "American" middle-class mores—eagerly embraced—among the merchant and professional leaders of Detroit's ethnic

180

groups. And beyond all this was the seamy world of spies, finks, and stool pigeons in the direct employ of the auto magnates, and the self-appointed vigilantes of the capitalist system, such as the Black Legion.

This is the world that Sugar would engage in battle as the United Auto Workers took wing. He was never an organizer or a strike leader (although his advice was often sought), and only in 1939 would he become an official of the union. His work was nevertheless critical. Along with dozens of other non-manual workers on the now-cooperating Left, he fought to expose the companies' modes of domination at all levels. Through the law he took on the multiple abuses in the plants and the variety of restrictions on labor outside them. Through public appearances either as a spokesman for the union or as a politician, he exposed the broader networks of control, both real and psychological, wielded by Detroit's automobile establishment. The auto labor movement constituted a two-front war, one the direct confrontation in the plants and on the streets against the companies and their agents, the other the struggle to break the power of the corporations over Detroit life in general. The two had to operate simultaneously and with coordination. It can be argued that no one played a greater role in making that linkage work than Sugar.

The main event of 1936 on the community front was the exposure of the Black Legion. Sugar and many others in the labor movement had long complained not only about company spies, blacklists, arsenals, private police, and strikebearer recruitment networks (which the LaFollette Committee would soon start to investigate), but also about groups that needed no pay from the companies to do their dirty work. The Black Legion was the largest of several fascistic organizations dedicated to upholding the "American way of life." Amann estimates its peak membership at around a hundred thousand spread throughout the Midwest but especially along an axis of towns from Bucyrus, Ohio, to Bay City, Michigan, manufacturing centers for the most part, whose populations included large numbers of midwestern farmer immigrants and people who had taken Route 23 north from the hills of Appalachia. Legion members were especially concentrated in the Detroit area, the city itself housing five thousand. While the Legion's membership reflected an occupational cross section of the area (especially after a recruitment drive to bring in politically ambitious Republican professionals), its base was among poorly educated Protestant workers, salesmen, and clerks from rural backgrounds.

The legion was modeled on the Ku Klux Klan, particularly in its intricate rituals, atmosphere of internal intimidation, and dedication to night riding. Like the Klan, it penetrated "regular" politics and was probably more successful, at least in its peak years from 1934 to 1936. It was estimated that at the 1935 Wayne County Republican Convention, one hundred of seven hundred delegates were directly controlled by the legion. Eighty percent of the adult male voters of Lima, Ohio and its county were legion members. The legion controlled city hall in several smaller Ohio and Michigan cities, such as Lima, Ecorse, and Highland Park and, as noted, made deep inroads into police departments everywhere. While it would be inaccurate to call it a fundamental threat to U.S. democracy, Amann argues plausibly that it was the most important paramilitary fascist group in the United States in the 1930s.

In many respects, however, its exposure was more significant than its influence. Amidst blaring headlines, sixteen members of the Black Legion were arrested in May 1936 for participating in the murder of Charles A. Poole. Executioner Dayton Dean and three others were the perpetrators of the crime, which was carried out after Poole had been picked up in Detroit and taken into the country by a small caravan of cars. The killers said Poole had beaten his wife, and the legion was against that sort of thing, "defenders of American womanhood" that they were. In reality it was because Poole, a Catholic who swore he was a Protestant in joining the organization, later made fun of it in the presence of his brother-in-law, who unfortunately was a most serious member.

The Poole murder arrests opened up a massive investigation of the Black Legion that dominated the media throughout the summer. Before it was over, a dozen murders, including two random "thrill killings" of blacks, were officially traced to the terrorist organization. Bizarre plots were uncovered. One of the most chilling was the plan of State Commander Arthur Lupp, an inspector for the milk division of the Detroit Department of Health, and Charles McCutcheon, a department bacteriologist, "to inject typhoid germs into milk and dairy products distributed through Jewish markets."

Public officials everywhere in southeastern Michigan were proved to be initiated members. They included Oakland County Prosecutor Pence and all his staff, the police chiefs of Pontiac and Royal Oak, a state representative, a variety of drain commissioners, city treasurers, and other lesser officials. Sheriff's deputies, police, and firemen were removed by the dozen from Detroit, Wayne County, and suburban departments. Most shocking, although it had been known for some time that Wayne County Prosecutor Duncan C. McCrea had previously signed a membership card "by accident," on October 21, 1936, a deposition was made by a legion member that McCrea had actually been initiated and attended several legion "secret" meetings. Finally, it was alleged and widely believed (but never proved) that Detroit's police chief, Heinrich Pickert, was a member. It was certain that he, as well as McCrea, had not energetically pursued investigations of violent acts and threats occurring in the years before the Poole murder that were later shown to be the work of the legion.

This was why, immediately upon the Poole murder revelations, the leaders of the Conference for the Protection of Civil Rights (CPCR), Rev. John Bollens, Marie Hempel, and Sugar (joined, on this occasion, by Frank Martel) got a hearing before the mayor and city council to consider the impeachment of Pickert. The move was rejected, but favorably reported by the *News* and the *Free Press*. (Hearst's *Times* was conspicuously low-key on the Black Legion question throughout the year.)

Thus began a rare era of harmony between the Left/labor forces in Detroit and the molders of public opinion. Much of the so-called "ranting" of the Left about the power of "fascism" in U.S. society now seemed to have some substance. More specifically, mysterious occurrences undermining the labor movement in the city, including unsolved murders and bombings, were now discovered to be Black Legion operations. The public imagination became caught up in the daily revelations. It was impossible to doubt their veracity since Mayor Couzens, his police chief, and the prosecutor were hardly antifascist alarmists. It was a perfect situation for putting the wrongs done to labor before the public eye. Sugar's organizations, the CPCR and the ILD, naturally dedicated themselves full time to the investigation and won grateful recognition for their work.

Almost immediately, with Dayton Dean confessing right and left and his exwife telling the press of his activities to prod him further, it came out that two murdered Communist labor organizers, George Marchuk of the AWU and John Bielak of the Hudson Motor Local of the AFL, were victims of the Black Legion. The series of bombings that accompanied the Motor Products strike was not the result of AFL-AIWA antagonism, as was widely thought to the discredit of both, but the work of legionnaires. Then there were the fake leaflets and their impact on Sugar's campaigns, the torching of the Communist labor camp, the flogging of three AWU organizers in Pontiac in 1931, the bombing of CP headquarters and a left-wing bookstore—and on and on.

The Black Legion worked with company spies. On June 4, Homer Martin, using information gathered together by Sugar from his interviews with Motor Products strikers, revealed at a press conference that some members of the Dawn Patrol, a notorious detective agency whose agents "riddled" the ranks of the strikers, were also in the Black Legion. One anti-Communist striker was prepared to testify that he had joined the Black Legion and that "after the unmasking [following his initiation] he noticed that the leaders, including the men who had admnistered the oath, were some of the union members he had been told were Dawn Patrol operatives."

More conclusive was the exposure of legionnaire Frank Rice, one of the dozens arrested for criminal activity in 1936. His story was never fully revealed in the daily press. Sugar, however, interrogated Rice and was able to extract a fantastic history, which he laid out in his unpublished "Memorandum on the Black Legion." Rice was listed in company records as the bodyguard of Harry Weiss, a Packard executive, and as an "investigator" for the personnel department. What he did, however, was to spy. "Rice," wrote Sugar, "was a member of organizations, including the MESA, the Socialist Party, the Communist Party, and the AAWA." Packard (whose hard-line president, Alvan Macauley, used his power in many ways) supplied Rice with employee lists and lists of job applicants. His job was to compare those lists with membership rolls of the various labor and left-wing organizations of which he was a member. He organized the operation through the Black Legion:

> The department of the Black Legion which undertook this work was called the Intelligence Department. Rice would [also] meet from time to time with persons

183

in similar employment from other automobile establishments, usually in Rice's home, and check with them on persons engaged in labor activity, reporting back to their respective employers. Thus the Black Legion was used by the automobile manufacturers for the purpose of weeding active laborites out of their plants and preventing them from obtaining employment.

The same department also functioned as a kind of house of call for Black Legion members to get jobs in the auto industry. The grateful men were then easy recruits for the spy operations. Moreover, they knew what awaited them if they failed to cooperate.

The most dramatic charge made during this summer of revelations was that an entire local of the AAWA, Arthur Greer's Hudson Local Number 2, was dominated by the Black Legion and that Richard Byrd, of ALB fame, was also a member. Sugar had gathered the information on the question and elicited a sworn affidavit from Tice Woody, president of the AAWA Local Number 3, GM Truck, in Pontiac. In 1934 Woody had briefly joined the "Bullet Club," as the Oakland County branch of the Black Legion was called, "to learn what the organization's attitude is towards labor, as several members of the union . . . approached me with the idea that labor may benefit by linking up with such outfit." Woody discovered in a few days "its dangerous character" and that the aim of urging him to join was "to tie labor to the Black Legion's kite." Woody quit and discouraged membership in the organization, but apparently did not bar union men from belonging to it.

Woody then made the following deposition:

> I further want to cite that I was surprised to find that several outstanding officers of my union were already enrolled into the Black Legion before me. They are notably Arthur Greer and several of his associates in the union. Also Richard Byrd, who[m] President Roosevelt appointed as "labor representative" on the Automobile Labor Board. The fact that Richard Byrd had in place of serving labor practically served the manufacturers is a good indication of the program of the Black Legion in unions—it is to break them.

Woody's disclosure was corroborated by other Black Legionnaires.

Besides explaining the ineffectiveness of Byrd, it made Greer's checkered career in automobile unionism more understandable. At Hudson in 1933–34, he had transformed a company union into one of the largest AFL federal locals in the industry with little company resistance. Then, after the June conference of 1934 failed to declare for an independent International, Greer dramatically bolted with 24 delegates from Hudson, GM Truck, and Oldsmobile and two months later formed the rival AAWA. At the time this was regarded as a militant act, but it is significant that Mortimer and the left-wing caucus, who also criticized Green and Collins mercilessly, realized that to quit the AFL would rob their movement of legitimacy. More to the point, Greer's local, while generally

184

talking a tough game, hesitated to press demands and found the paternalistic Hudson management amenable to moderate wage increases but not to anything altering its power in the shops. At the Henderson hearings, Greer had actually called for Justice Department officers to enter the plants to administer the auto code "fairly," a position that Sugar blasted the following day.

Then, in the fall of 1935, it was Greer and Byrd who had pushed the hardest for a merger of the AAWA, AIWA, and MESA in order to rival the UAW. The AFL had little to be proud of at that point, but clear heads among the anti-Dillon forces were just as worried as Frank Martel's *Labor News,* which had written on October 4,

> Arthur E. Greer, once chairman of something or other at the Hudson Motor Plant, is . . . seeking to preserve his spot in the picture. Back of the scene is Richard Byrd, better known to auto workers as "Dickie Byrd," former member of the ALB. Byrd, and his every-busy little wife, are the ones that are pulling the strings to create the new union in the automobile industry. It is rumored that Byrd is to be president of the new merger, which all makes strange bedfellows. However, we will leave it to Matt Smith to explain to his people.

The merger fell through, due to Smith's last-minute withdrawal. It should be remembered that both Marchuk and Bielak, the Communist organizers murdered by the Black Legion, were in the Hudson plant. Had Greer set them up?

By mid-July, 1936, when his Black Legion connections were revealed, Greer had already brought the AAWA into the UAW. His reputation was obviously tarnished by the whole affair, but his denials left the question up in the air. Later that year, after functioning for a while as an international representative for the UAW, new sets of charges were developed against him—including good evidence that he was a Pinkerton agent—and he left the labor movement.

Finally, of course, there was the plot to murder Sugar. On June 19, Dean told McCrea, under questioning, that Lupp and another leader, Leslie Black, had instructed him to take the apartment beneath Sugar's and to bomb the place. He gave up on that idea and laid out a variety of other plans, none of which proved efficacious. It is some measure of McCrea's and Pickert's less-than-enthusiastic pursuit of the legion that this information had been known to the police since Dean's arrest, because he was carrying clippings about Sugar in his pocket. George Morris of the *Daily Worker* found out about this (he does not say how) and pressed McCrea for an answer. On June 19, Sugar was allowed to interrogate Dean in McCrea's presence and the confession was made. Sugar also elicited the full information on the fake leaflet question and on the burning of the Workers Camp.

Overall, the exposure of the Black Legion made it clear that labor's cause (and not just the Left in the labor movement) had been hurt by an obviously evil force. It gave reality to the charges that organizers and labor's public defenders, like Sugar, had been making all along. Without question, the Black Legion did a

185

good deal more for the Left and the labor movement in its demise than it ever did against them while it was active. The revelations helped a skeptical public to believe that there were dark, mysterious, and, above all, unfair forces working against labor. While actual company ties with the Black Legion were rare, it was now much easier to talk about Harry Bennett's service department or the massive sums spent by General Motors on spies. To suggest that public officials or newspapers were "owned" by corporate interests was hardly foolishness after it was known that a crackpot hate group could own them. In short, the Black Legion affair was an important element in the cracking of the corporate image in Detroit.[12]

Sugar, whose personal stake in the matter was obvious, worked nonstop on the Black Legion, making many of the most important breakthroughs during the summer of 1936. He also developed an increasingly acute appreciation of the vast networks of control and repression that the companies operated within the plants. One of his main activities in the fall was work with the UAW (largely free of charge) investigating and taking depositions about spying, strikebreaking, and other company abuses. He transmitted the information to the LaFollette Civil Liberties Committee. This Senate subcommittee, formed in June 1936 under the chairmanship of Robert M. LaFollette, Jr., grew from NLRB hearings revealing violations of basic civil rights and of the Wagner Act by the major corporations. The committee limited its inquiry strictly to company abuses and thus shied away from other organized forms of civil-rights violations, such as the workings of the Black Legion. But their main charge gave them plenty to do.

A good example was a spy case against an auto supplier. In a letter on January 29, 1937 Robert Wohlforth, the secretary of the committee, thanked Sugar for sending along the sworn affidavit of Arthur Dobrzynski, an organizer at National Automotive Fibers, an upholstery plant of some fifteen hundred workers in Detroit, regarding the activities of one Francis Arthur Roszel. The plant, which had a large minority of Polish-American workers, was one of many in the charge of Stanley Nowak, assigned by the UAW as its organizer among Poles. Roszel was hired on November 21, 1936 at a point when organizing activities were moving along well. He joined the union immediately. In a week he was made assistant foreman. While there were only six actual members of the UAW in the plant at that point, large numbers were interested, and the nucleus held a meeting of some 150 men, which Dobrzynski's brother Zygmund chaired. Zygmund was fired a few days later. Still, recruiting went on, and "many new members were taken into the union." On December 13 a closed union meeting elected six men to formulate demands to the management. Arthur Dobrzynski was one of them, Roszel was not. Three days later all six, whose names were supposedly not known to management, were fired, although Dobrzynski got out of the plant before notice was served on him.

Despite Nowak's words of caution, a strike was called for the following Monday. Participation was total. On the picket line, Roszel, who had previously urged non-Polish union members to reject Nowak's and Dobrzynski's leadership because they were "foreigners," now sought to get the men to go back in. His position was that "the strike had been called by a handful of men," and "that the members of the union had not been consulted." It was to no avail, and at 4:00 P.M. on Wednesday, the company capitulated, signing a temporary agreement to rehire the men and give pay increases. It was followed by permanent agreements on a variety of issues, including official recognition of the UAW.

Through some subsequent spying of their own and with the assistance of Ben Allen, an investigator for the LaFollette Committee who proved to be of immense value to Sugar in building his cases, the union men discovered that Roszel was a hired detective from a local agency that transmitted information to the company president in California, who then authorized the dismissals. They analyzed the handwriting of a spy report Allen had intercepted and compared it with that of Roszel on union documents. He was confronted with the accusation of *stool pigeon* by Zygmund Dobrzynski just before the end of his shift on January 7. After parading him around the plant "so that the men could get a good look at him," union leaders took him to the manager's office, at which point he talked for the first time, asking for police protection. After another most unpleasant trip through the plant, "police took him away." The plant manager never identified him as a spy, but did acknowledge that "he knew the company utilized some kind of 'service' in the plant."

Sugar operated a kind of clearing house for such information and developed an armory of facts that he would later use in his many cases against the auto companies, especially Ford. Some elementary idea of the scope of espionage activity can be gained from the raw figures of money paid to private detective agencies for their services by General Motors. The LaFollette Committee found that the company had spent close to one million dollars in the eighteen months after January 1, 1935. Some two hundred spies were currently at work in GM plants. The system had become so complex that spies were being used to keep an eye on spies. General Motors was Pinkerton's largest customer, and the other auto companies (save Ford, which had its own "service" department) were not far behind.[13]

Busy as he was in exposing the underside of capitalism's defenses, Sugar also entered yet another political campaign in 1936. This time he stood as a candidate for the House of Representatives from Detroit's thirteenth district on the Farmer-Labor ticket. The common-council campaign had already stressed the need for independent labor representation. The concept of a Farmer-Labor party had been around for years, and in both Minnesota and Wisconsin such political groupings were dominant forces in the state, electing senators, representatives, and governors. In Michigan the traditional parties were solidly entrenched, but the power of labor politics was beginning to be felt, at least in Detroit. The state's farm population had also suffered, and the Left's work on behalf of evicted farmers left positive memories. (Sugar himself had been a lawyer in some of these battles, notably the White Cloud case of 1933.) The idea of a united Farmer-Labor party was not ridiculous. The Communist party had

187

committed itself to the concept almost immediately after the declaration of Popular Front. The Socialist party, though still badly split, increasingly moved in that direction as the Militants (as the leftists were called) took over the party.

The earliest record of a Farmer-Labor party organization in Michigan was a banquet held on January 15, 1936, to which a wide spectrum of Detroit's Left and labor leadership was invited to hear Representative Thomas A. Amlie, a Wisconsin Progressive pushing a nationwide third-party movement. Sugar chaired the meeting. The theme was sounded by Walter Nelson, at that time the attorney for the milk farmers' union and an independent radical close to Sugar, who asked, "Are we going to have a united front or not?" and went on to use France as the example of how "fascism can be stopped." The Socialist Militants turned out in force led by Walter Bergman, Weinstone was there for the Communists, Matt Smith came, several UAW people and state labor officials participated, and even Larry Davidow, steadfastly right-wing Socialist, showed up. The Detroit Federation of Labor leadership was conspicuous in its absence. Amlie's speech was uninspiring, but Sugar was encouraged, telling the *Daily Worker*, after the meeting, "With the forces represented at this meeting and the tremendous organizational backing of the United Labor Conference we could, in my mind, make outstanding progress in the next campaign."

Judge Jeffries and Dr. I. W. Ruskin, a physician who headed the Motor Products–strike citizens committee, were drawn in and a series of organizational meetings launched the party. The *Detroit Labor News* immediately attacked Jeffries for not securing the reappointment of AFL favorite James Darr as clerk of recorder's court. The reality of the matter was stated by Jeffries in a rebuttal: Martel was incensed because Jeffries had joined the cause of "independent political action." Typical hard work followed during the next few months, although the energies of many were drained by the Black Legion investigations and the politics surrounding them, and by September the Farmer-Labor party could boast of twenty-six candidates for state and national office from Wayne County alone and several dozen more across the state.

Its base, however, had narrowed considerably. As the year had passed, the political appeal of FDR had grown immensely. The Socialists, in particular, had been torn apart. Sidney Hillman declared for FDR and David Dubinsky had quit the party in order to join the American Labor party, a New York outfit founded by Louis Waldman for the express purpose of supporting FDR while running local and state candidates holding clear prolabor and Socialist views. The SP ran rival candidates and ended up with little. In Michigan, the large moderate element in the Socialists pulled away from the Farmer-Labor party, which would not declare for Roosevelt, leaving everyone the weaker. Hence, by September, the Wayne County branch of the Farmer-Labor party was dominated by Communists and their allies, with three interesting exceptions. Walter Reuther, who was one of four vice chairs; Fay O'Camb, secretary; and James Murdoch, a MESA official, treasurer.

As the election neared, even Communist-party enthusiasm for the Farmer-Labor concept had cooled because the decision had been made, despite Browder's candidacy for president, to support Roosevelt in a broadened united front against fascism. This did not need to mean that Farmer-Labor candidates should suffer. In New York, the ALP, with strong Communist support, worked for Roosevelt while doing quite well for congressional and local candidates. Vito Marcantonio was first elected to Congress on the American Labor Party (ALP) ticket in 1936. But in Detroit, the network generated through Sugar's earlier campaigns worked less ardently for his candidacy than for FDR's. Sugar bravely pushed on, wrote one of his less inspiring songs called "We've Got a Baby All Our Own" (the Farmer-Labor party), and sought labor support as in the past.

In this effort he failed rather dismally. Martel again blocked any meaningful consideration of Sugar's candidacy. More important, perhaps, the DFL president failed to act when it was revealed that the fake leaflets of the campaigns of 1935 had been printed by union men—members of Frank Martel's own local. Sugar sought an apology and did not receive one. This situation thus further hardened the relationship between the two men, both of them remarkable in their own ways, whose careers had begun side-by-side in the struggle for labor's emancipation.

On the eve of the election, Sugar made a fifteen-minute radio speech over WJR, Detroit's most-listened-to station, that gives us a glimpse of the issues of the Farmer-Labor campaign. It was entitled "The Swing to the Farmer-Labor Party." Most important, he was quite clear on his opposition to the Roosevelt administration. He began by attacking the new Social Security Act, saying that it was "too little, too long from now." That it provided a modicum of security to the aged was good, but the Farmer-Labor party also wanted "security now"—in the form of sickness, accident, childbirth, and unemployment benefits. Roosevelt had said that the United States had now moved from "stormy seas to fair weather." Sugar asked, for whom? General Motors' profits had soared under the Roosevelt administration, reaching a staggering $175 million in the first three quarters of 1936. Meat packers were in great shape too, "partly due to the policy of the administration of killing off the little pigs of the country in the interest of the big pigs of the country." And there were still twelve million unemployed and twenty million on paltry relief.

Sugar then reviewed tendencies toward "fascism," including company labor espionage, the recent Teachers Oath Law of Michigan (a loyalty and "antisubversive" teaching vow), the Dearborn Handbill Law (by which the Dearborn city clerk would "determine the truth" of the handbill before allowing its circulation), and the general red-baiting policies of the Hearst newspapers. The Black Legion naturally took pride of place. Sugar pointed out its multiple connections with the Republican party of Michigan and the fact that Wilbur Brucker, running for governor again against Frank Murphy, was officially endorsed by it.

He concluded with a checklist of the Farmer-Labor positions: real social security, union-scale wages in the Works Progress Administration projects, op-position to the sales tax, tax exemption for homes valued at four thousand dollars or less and on income up to the same level, heavy taxes on "corporate surpluses," rent controls, and a meaningful tenure law for teachers. The last point was in reference to further layoffs of married women and teachers whose political views were suspect in the eyes of the board of education. Sugar's strongest support in this campaign had been from the American Federation of Teachers, whose mem-bers in Detroit were under siege from all sides. In general, the language of the Farmer-Labor party was sharply anticapitalist and antiauthoritarian, but its eco-nomic proposals were moderate and constructive.

It is clear from surviving documents that this campaign was the least vig-orously pursued of any Sugar engaged in during the thirties. Moreover, Con-gress was not really Sugar's cup of tea. His interests were local. His focus was on the class struggle in Detroit. How mortified he would have been had he actually won: to have been shut up in the Capitol while the greatest events in the history of the U.S. working-class movement unfolded back home! Fortunately, that would not be a problem: Sugar finished a dismal third.[14]

Sugar could nevertheless look back on several years of fruitful activity in politics and community action. He had made an essential contribution to the raising of working-class consciousness in Detroit. The payoff was soon to come.

7 ❖ Sit Down, You've Got 'Em Beat

Throughout 1936, industrial unionism was on the march. The CIO parted ways with the AFL and, under John L. Lewis's resolute direction, opened a new era in the history of the U.S. labor movement. In January the Akron rubber workers struck against the big three manufacturers. Using the "stay-in" tactic that rank-and-filers at Firestone initiated, they won important gains. The sit-down strike, as it soon would be called, had an honorable history. Under the name of "factory occupation," this tactic was widely used in the great North Italian movement in 1919–20 and had been employed by the Wobblies in the United States. More recently, it was the chief tactic employed in the great strike wave in France during the summer of 1936. It was a close relative of the British-designed "work-to-rule" strategy, a slowdown strike in which every work regulation was followed to the letter, destroying normal operations without actually walking off the job.

The advantages of the sit-down were immediately recognized. As later enumerated by UAW leaders for the *Christian Science Monitor,* they included:

> 1. Effectiveness—when workers stay in a factory they hinder the company from attempting to operate with new men, minimize strike-breaking, and shut off production most efficiently.
> 2. Peacefulness—violence is reduced by strikers being inside, instead of massed in picket lines without, and liable to clash with police.
> 3. Best for union morale—strikers sticking together in a factory can keep up their enthusiasm better than going their separate ways outside, subject to disintegrating influence and rumor.

In late 1936 automobile workers used the sit-down in several stoppages in the Detroit area, notably at Midland Steel Products and Kelsey-Hayes Wheel.[1]

The essential goal of sit-downs and other job actions during this period was union recognition. The UAW, well supplied with cash and good advice from the CIO hierarchy, had generated a tremendous organizing drive during the summer and fall. The most effective way to demonstrate a union's power (especially in a context where slower means could be dissipated by company espionage and intimidation) was the strike. Organizers like Stanley Nowak, Roy Reuther, or Robert Travis understood this well, but late 1936 presented a special problem. Auto production was booming and many workers were shedding their old fears. The chief difficulty was knowing when the appropriate moment to act had arrived. Even the most militant leaders found themselves being outstripped by the ranks. Nowak, for instance, thought the Automotive-Fibers strike was premature.

As it turned out, in contrast to some of the disastrous strikes of yesteryear, spontaneity generally bore positive fruit. A class-conscious sense of destiny seemed to grip the workers of southeastern Michigan. The frustrations bottled up for years exploded into unified action without historical parallel. The recriminations and political backbiting that plagued strikes in the past all but disappeared. For five months the region became the focal point of the world labor movement.

Like all such great moments in the past, the surge came from below. But it would not be accurate to argue, as does Jeremy Brecher, that the success of the great CIO organizational drive came *despite* leadership. Indeed the sit-downs are a textbook case for studying the ways that leadership interacted with militant workers, how each nurtured the other.[2]

Flint

The dramatic story of the Flint sit-down against General Motors has been told many times, although often from a self-interested perspective. As time passes, however, the endless conflicts about whose roles—political groups' or individuals'—were more important than others becomes less and less interesting. What can be said for certain is that it was, as Frank Murphy remarked at its conclusion, "the greatest industrial conflict of our time" and the catalyst for the rise of the CIO. It also witnessed such an extraordinary degree of unity among leaders of various political persuasions that distinguishing one "role" or another often becomes meaningless. That many associated with the Communist faction in the union were prominent in the strategic direction of the strike or gave a particular cohesion to the "sit-down community" in Fisher Body Number 1, as recently stressed by Roger Keeran, is unquestionably true. That Socialists John Brophy and Powers Hapgood of the CIO or Roy and Victor Reuther and Genora and Kermit Johnson of the UAW were key figures is also unquestionably true. But that they all—and hundreds of others—*cooperated,* in part because of the peculiar political circumstances of the era and in part because of the awesome responsibilities that they bore in an event understood at the time to be of earth-shattering significance, is the truth that really matters.

People thus fit in a whole variety of ways into the web of events, intertwined with each other and with the general flow of the forty-four-day strike. One of them was Maurice Sugar. His place in the overall picture lets us look at the Flint sit-down from an angle that is not much discussed in the literature, although it was one of those pieces without which the entire structure might have collapsed. His main role, naturally, was in the legal struggle. But it was also political, particularly his ability to assess the outlook of his old friend, Michigan's brand-new governor, Frank Murphy.

Sugar almost was not involved at all. When the night-shift workers in Chevrolet (Fisher Body) Number 1 decided to sit down after their 10:00 P.M. lunch break, Sugar was not the UAW's lawyer. Constitutionally, legal work was contracted by the union president and Homer Martin's man was Larry Davidow. Martin and Davidow shared a moderate Socialist perspective and a mistrust of Wyndham Mortimer. Sugar had come to know Mortimer quite well and was identified with his camp in the union. Both mistrusted Martin more than he mistrusted them.

The Martin-Mortimer differences ran deep. Martin had given Mortimer the responsibility of attempting to organize Flint, where forty-seven thousand workers toiled in Chevrolet, Fisher Body, Buick, and accessory plants. He did so in the hope that his enemy would fail. Flint was a classic company town. Every aspect of life, from reading the GM-run *Flint Journal* in the morning to hearing the sirens of GM-dominated police in the night, was somehow connected to the world's largest corporation. Any union organizer was unwelcome, much less one with a "red" reputation. The UAW had had a substantial federal local membership, but those incredible sums GM spent for spies paid off. What was left was a tiny group, many of whom were members of the Black Legion. Mortimer nevertheless made progress consolidating the federal locals into a single new local (Number 156), while using his numerous left-wing contacts in the city to sign up less-suspect members.

In late September 1936, just when his policies were beginning to pay off, a bizarre thing happened. Martin called a meeting of everybody concerned with Flint—himself, Vice President Ed Hall, Secretary-Treasurer George Addes, Bob Travis and Fred Pieper, who had made reports on the Flint situation for Martin, and the executive board of Local 156—except Mortimer. It was obviously an attempt to remove him. Travis called him up and he headed for Detroit. In the meantime, Hall and Addes raged at Martin, with the normally mild-mannered secretary-treasurer "roused," according to Henry Kraus, "to utter his most extravagant cuss word: 'Son-of-a-pup! You've got a lot of guts . . . asking us to move Mort out when he's actually doing the job up there.'" In the end, to keep peace, Mortimer resigned the assignment, only to be replaced, at Addes's suggestion, by Travis, who saw eye to eye with Mortimer on most issues. Mortimer himself was happy enough to have made a good start in Flint and went back to organize in Cleveland. Travis, for his part, pushed the Flint drive forward, especially with the help of Kraus, who moved from Cleveland to edit the *Flint Auto Worker*.

Mortimer, Travis, Kraus: this was Sugar's circle. But Martin chose the lawyer. Davidow, while he had some experience in the area, had never exclusively focused on labor law. He was politically ambitious, having headed the Detroit office in the 1924 LaFollette campaign, run for office as a "liberal Republican," been city attorney for the down-river suburb of Lincoln Park, and remained active on the right fringes of the Socialist party. "Fighting Bob," the elder LaFollette, was his idol, and he one day hoped to spearhead the revival of progressivism in Michigan. Unfortunately, not having been involved in the major auto strikes of the 1933–36 period, he had little sense of the methods of dealing with the companies that Sugar and others had already perfected. Almost immediately after the strike began, it became clear that the job was more than Davidow could handle.[3]

On January 2, GM decided to go to court for an injunction and hit upon the right judge, Edward D. Black. This was the man, it will be recalled, who did not recognize such legal trivialities as habeas corpus and who swore at attorneys. He gave the company everything it wanted—a sweeping injunction that not only demanded that the struck plants (Fisher Body Numbers 1 and 2) be cleared, but that would prevent picketing. The injunction was read out by the sheriff to the strikers that evening. Davidow was of the opinion that that was that. He told Travis, "There's nothing you can do. You'll have to obey the order." Martin echoed him the next morning, saying, "We can't fight the law."

In the meantime, Travis had sent a deputation of strikers to Detroit to ask Sugar if he would "come to Flint and do the legal work." As Sugar related it, he said that he had to have official word from Martin or Davidow. The next morning (January 3) he got a call from the latter. "He merely said that he had become overwhelmed with the legal work in Flint, particularly with respect to the accumulation of minor cases, misdemeanors and the like, which were constantly arising between union and anti-union workers," and wondered whether Sugar could handle them. Sugar graciously accepted the offer, realizing what had happened. Davidow himself recalled that Mortimer and Addes had prevailed upon Martin to bring Sugar in.[4]

January 3 was the first critical day in a strike that would have a good number of them, for it appeared as if the workers faced compliance with the injunction or a pitched battle with the forces of order. The ball was in the lawyers' court. Lee Pressman, a young Harvard lawyer trained in New Deal politics (like many other radical lawyers) by a stint in the Agricultural Adjustment Administration, had been tapped by Lewis as the CIO's principal attorney. He was dispatched to

Michigan, arriving in Detroit, it appears, on January 3. According to Davidow's recollection, the three of them met that day in his Detroit office, with Pressman greeting Sugar "like a novitiate greeting a master"—quite a compliment for Sugar, especially since it was reported by Davidow, whose relations with Sugar deteriorated totally in later years. Pressman knew Sugar as a great labor lawyer and as the man who originated the drive to create the National Lawyers Guild, just then beginning to materialize. The three of them apparently discussed the situation, without resolution, and then Sugar and Pressman took off for Flint.

Precisely how it happened is not clear, but sometime that afternoon or evening the idea came about that Judge Black might have some "unclean hands" of his own. Could he be a GM stockholder? Sugar suggests a plausible explanation—that it arose out of conversation within the strike committee at the Pengally Building in Flint. He did not recall who first suggested it—himself, Pressman, one of the committee members ("after all," he wrote, "good ideas do not all come from lawyers")—but given Black's track record, which Sugar knew in detail, his own contribution had to have been substantial. Sugar also knew that under Michigan statute, "No judge in any court shall sit as such in any case or proceeding in which he is a party or in which he is interested."

Pressman returned to Detroit and met with union leadership in Davidow's office (at least that is Davidow's recollection), and further discussed the idea. A phone call from Flint (probably from Sugar) let them know they were on the right track and Pressman called his partner in New York who checked further. The following morning, hands shaking with excitement, Pressman went through the shareholders list at the GM building in Detroit. There it was: Black owned 3,365 shares worth $219,900.

The authorship of the idea is a matter of some controversy—political controversy. Historian Sidney Fine, using Adolph Germer's diary of the strike, awards the honor to Germer. Henry Kraus, in his book on the sit-down, *The Many and the Few,* gives it to Pressman in dialogue with Sugar. Was Germer Sugar's committee member? Quite possibly, but it is not clear whether he was in Flint on January 3 or whether he floated the thought at the meeting in Detroit and Pressman agreed that it was a good idea. At the time, we can be sure that nobody worried much about whose idea it originally was, but the passage of a decade of conflict between Socialists and Communists within the union had something to do with the specification of credit by later writers. Sugar's concept of a collective process seems closer to the reality, political and otherwise, of the moment. It is worth noting also that Davidow, violent anti-Communist that he had become, claimed no credit and thought of it as a joint decision made in Flint.[5]

In any case, on the morning of January 5, a UAW press conference told the world that Judge Black was breaking the law again. His responses varied from chattering about "Communist talk" to comparing his payment of county taxes and judging cases involving the county to the current situation, but it was clear that the GM injunction had no future. Jubilation spread. Flint workers had turned an important corner. This created the basis, however, for GM's next, much more direct, step: a police riot.

With the sweet revenge against Judge Black carried out, the strike moved into high gear. While the sit-downers organized their lives and developed their communications systems with the outside, George Boyson, former mayor, Buick paymaster, and now a GM supplier, organized the Flint Alliance, which attempted to bring Flint "citizens" together with GM workers who opposed the strike. Tensions mounted as the alliance threatened violence and was answered by tough talk from the union. On January 11, at the insecurely held Fisher Number 2 an armed conflict began when an attempt by plant guards—who occupied the ground floor—to oust the sit-downers erupted into a pitched battle with the Flint police. Dubbed the "Battle of Bulls Run," it ended in a rout, as the union held its ground. Victor Reuther leapt to fame in the fight, giving battle orders and generally sustaining morale from a sound truck. Fourteen workers were hospitalized with injuries and promptly arrested. The field leaders, including Travis, Reuther and his brother Roy, and Henry Kraus, were accused as well. Sugar and Davidow rushed to Flint to carry out the necessary legal work.

Sugar would not go home for a while. He had been made a member of the strike committee that included Pressman, Davidow, Addes, Germer, Len De-Caux, CIO publicity director, Leo Krzycki of the Amalgamated Clothing Workers, and Allan Haywood of the rubber workers. They were to work with Travis in the field at Flint and with general-strategy directors Martin, Mortimer, and John L. Lewis's personal representative, John Brophy.

Governor Murphy called out the National Guard after this first explosion of violence and immediately invited the principals in the strike to Lansing in order to negotiate a truce. Murphy had been in daily contact with the strike situation, but this marked the beginning of his direct involvement. Probably no event in his illustrious career, which ended on the bench of the United States Supreme Court, tested him so severely or gave him more satisfaction in its outcome than the Flint sit-down. Murphy was an enigma for many people, especially those on the Left. While he had a certain reputation as a liberal—he skyrocketed to fame as the judge in the Sweet case—he bore the scars of the inconsistent stance he held during and after the Ford Hunger March and of having accepted the governor-generalship of the Philippines, a U.S. colony. The *Daily Worker* tended to treat him as a New Deal hack whose ambitions knew few bounds, and Left-liberal magazines like the *Nation* were not always kind to him. He had been swept into office by the Roosevelt landslide. His checkered record made some strike leaders apprehensive about how he might respond. He was, after all, the chief law officer in the state and bound by statute to execute the law.

Sugar, however, knew some things about Murphy of which few others were aware. First, there was his unyielding dedication to fundamental principles of justice. Sugar was acutely aware of it by virtue of his own experience: Murphy's decision to assist in his reinstatement simply because it was right. They were hardly close friends at the time. On more than one occasion they had been opponents in labor cases. Sugar knew already what I. F. Stone would say in 1949 in his moving obituary for Murphy: "He was a man of warm heart and saintly spirit who cared deeply about justice and about liberty."

More pertinent—and virtually unknown—were Murphy's own radical roots and his continuing interest in radical ideas. As Sugar put it, "Murphy had a personal and family history so close to the conflict in Ireland that resort to state violence against workers seeking only their rights, as were the Irish workers, was . . . virtually impossible." Murphy maintained his boyhood admiration for the great heroes of the Irish revolution (which extended to radical émigrés like James Larkin) and studied Irish history in detail. He had a strong sense of identity with freedom fighters of all sorts and would never trample on their right to protest. He also read Marxist literature or at least purchased it. Stanley Nowak sold Marxist classics and contemporary analyses for the Kerr Publishing Company during the early thirties and vividly recalls that Josephine Gomon, Murphy's secretary, used to buy materials regularly "for the mayor." Sugar's closeness to both Gomon and Nowak make it certain that he was aware of this.

Sugar's role in the strike thereafter was to serve on the strategy committee certainly as legal advisor but also as chief Murphy-watcher for the union. Henry Kraus recalled recently that the latter role was very important, since Sugar, a trusted figure among the left-wing autoworkers, acted to allay their doubts and fears about Murphy, unquestionably helping to keep things from flying apart at crucial moments.[6]

Murphy's first significant contribution was to arrange a truce on January 14 by which the company agreed to negotiate and not shift production or reopen the twenty struck plants across the nation if the sit-downers would evacuate the plants. Travis was upset with this settlement and made no move to leave Fisher 1 and 2. Elsewhere, in Detroit (Cadillac and Fleetwood Fisher Body), Janesville, Cleveland, Norwood, and Atlanta, preparations were made to leave. In Anderson, Indiana, where GM-owned Guide Lamp had had a particularly bitter fight already, the White Motor UAW brass band was scheduled to lead the strikers out. This and several other evacuations occurred over the weekend. But then, fortunately (from Travis's point of view), the company began to violate the truce. Above all, only two days after its signing, GM "agreed to negotiate" with the Flint Alliance, which purported to be a union of "loyal workers." Then, as soon as the Guide Lamp strikers evacuated, police tore down picket shacks and forbade picketing, peaceful or not. The following Monday, GM called back workers to the struck Cadillac plant in Detroit. Thus, the main body of strikers, in Flint, "sat tight."

Joseph R. Joseph, county prosecutor in Flint, spurned Murphy's plea "to drop all charges" against the Bulls Run accused by declaring the seven leaders would receive warrants. Meanwhile Sugar filed charges against Joseph in Lansing because he, too, owned GM stock. In the end, Sugar also had to advise Kraus, Travis, and Roy and Victor Reuther to show up for their arraignment.

197

They were booked, with mug shots and fingerprints, said Kraus, "like common criminals."

After GM President Sloan refused to meet with Secretary of Labor Perkins (thus violating the statutory charge accorded to the secretary when the office was created in 1913), all bets were off. General Motors had declared war, and Lewis, who had agreed to the parley, was livid and resolved to fight to the finish. For his part, Sloan had pointedly announced on January 25 that GM was ready to act on its own.

Anderson exploded that same day. A miniature Flint in terms of GM influence, it had the added ingredients of rock-ribbed Indiana conservatism and a Ku Klux Klan tradition that made it a welcome environment for southern white immigrants. A majority of the town's forty thousand people (including many who worked in the Guide Lamp and Delco-Remy plants) assumed unionism and anti-Americanism were synonymous. After a few days of tension following GM's reopening of Delco-Remy, "the most violent night ever experienced in Anderson" occurred on January 25 as a mob, urged on by Delco-Remy foremen and given courage by liquor provided by GM, sacked union headquarters and moved on to chase off the pickets who had persisted at Guide Lamp. Many unionists were injured. The Anderson police blotter did not even show that anything out of the ordinary happened that night. United Auto Workers organizer Hugh Thompson returned to Detroit to report and was replaced the next day by Victor Reuther, who had to set up shop in nearby Alexandria. At about the same time, Detroit police took a more active role in assisting the company at the Cadillac plant in Detroit, although the picket lines, under the direction of Walter Reuther and with the help of the original "flying squadron" from Dodge Main, held. And in Saginaw, union organizers were physically attacked, then given a police escort back toward Flint—only to have their taxi run off the road by a "grey sedan," seriously injuring all four occupants. The police did not bother to chase the other automobile.

Ed Hall and Sugar were assigned to go to Anderson to investigate the situation. When their train reached Union City, on the Indiana-Ohio border, in the early hours of January 27, a contingent of Anderson UAW men boarded and informed them that a mob of "loyal" Delco-Remy employees with guns and clubs awaited them at the Anderson station. They got off in Muncie and contacted the governor of the state, M. Clifford Townsend, with whom they met later in the day. While he was no Murphy, the Indiana governor authorized the deputization of peace-keeping forces acceptable to Reuther. Sugar had encouraged Townsend both by showing that regular police in Anderson were simply company agents and by putting Murphy up as a model. This was the turning point for the establishment of the union in Anderson, though the history of the two locals was far from peaceful thereafter.[7]

The situation in Flint was reaching critical proportions in late January. A back-to-work drive, sponsored by the Flint Alliance, was under way. Demoralization increased with the news that GM was reopening nonstriking plants it had earlier shut down and "thousands" were returning to work. On January 28, Sloan released a statement to all employees reiterating GM's refusal to negotiate "with a group that holds our plants for ransom." Negotiations would begin only after the "trespassers" were removed. The *Detroit News* obligingly editorialized that same day that the sit-down "infringes on a right so elementary and fundamental that, whatever the equities involved, it can not be fitted into our legal system." The Hearst-owned *Times* called for compulsory arbitration. At the same moment, GM, having allowed the dust to settle after the Judge Black fiasco, went to a new court, that of Judge Paul V. Gadola, for another injunction.

Throughout the strike, morale had always been a problem. To enhance it, elaborate routines for keeping the strikers busy, visiting rights for children (but not wives or sweethearts), and various entertainments were arranged. The latter included performances by the Contemporary Theater group from Detroit, whose function in the class struggle had never been clearer. Bands played outside and music groups were organized within. Because of the backgrounds of many of the strikers, country and western music was particularly popular. One of the favorites was a song to the tune of "The Martins and the Coys," written at the beginning of the strike, that related the story of the takeover:

> Now this strike it started one bright Wednesday evening,
> When they loaded up a boxcar full of dies.
> When the union boys they stopped them
> And the railroad workers backed them,
> The officials in the office were surprised.
>
> Now they really started out to strike in earnest,
> They took possession of the gates and building too,
> They placed a guard in either clockhouse
> Just to keep the non-union men out.
> And they took the keys and locked the gates up too.

Sugar also wrote a little ditty that was sung regularly. In waltz time, it captured the air of relaxed superiority that the sit-down tactic inspired. The tune had an old-fashioned lilt that the farm boys must have appreciated:

> Bring me my robe and slippers, James,
> Pull up my easy chair.
> Bring my pipe and cushions, James,
> I'm not going anywhere.
> Let me have peace and quiet, James,
> Free from the noise and din,
> And send my regrets to Mister Sloan,
> Just tell him I'm staying in.

A cartoon by William Sanderson accompanying a Carl Haessler article in the *New Masses* exhibited the same mood: a huge worker, legs crossed and with his

199

chin in his hand, sits back astride the GM complex gazing serenely at bosses, guardsmen, scabs, and FDR scrambling around below, unable to touch him.[8]

It should perhaps have also depicted a judge coming up from behind. The injunction move was acted upon by Gadola on January 29. He wisely decided not to issue a ruling ex parte, as Black had, and hearings were scheduled for the following Monday, February 1. Pressman, Davidow, and Sugar were all to be involved and huddled over the weekend to outline their approach.

There was some huddling going on among the strikers as well. Recognizing that morale was slipping, especially at Fisher Number 2, and that if the injunction was to be resisted, a highly motivated group of strikers would be necessary, Travis needed an inspiring event that would also produce more man-power. Another occupation would do it. Top leadership concocted a plan that, when executed on the afternoon of February 1, immediately took its place as one of the most brilliant maneuvers in the history of industrial warfare. Only Roy Reuther, Henry Kraus, and three strikers, Kermit Johnson, Howard Foster, and Ed Kronk, were in on the specifics, although Mortimer and the CIO brass knew the general outline. The point was to feign the capture of Chevy Number 9, get all the company guards massed there, and then take the giant motor shop, Number 4. The details need not detain us; but chief of operations Arnold Lenz, a man who still openly praised the "efficiency" of Hitler's Germany, was totally fooled. His spies (who had been included in a "secret" meeting) had told him Chevy Number 9 was the objective, the security forces were dispatched there, and a battle royal—complete with the women's brigade under Genora Johnson banging out windows—ensued. Meanwhile Chevy Number 4 sat-down en masse (with some less than courteous encouragement to slackers) and the plant was invested with union troops.

While this was going on, Sugar, Davidow, and Pressman, though unaware of the real plan, were doing their job: delaying the injunction as long as possible. For Sugar, this was old hat; he knew every trick in the trade. They had already gained a postponement from the morning of February 1 to 2:00 P.M. Whatever the excuse, the main reason was so Sugar could go over to Lansing to see Murphy. There he extracted not a request from the governor to delay (as Murphy claimed when running for reelection in 1938) but, as Sugar reminded him in a letter of October 25, 1938, authorization "to inform the judge of [Murphy's] belief that a settlement was near." When they arrived in court at 2:30 (one half hour gained), all attorneys went immediately into the judge's chambers. There had already been some excitement: four hundred workers had come for the one hundred seats in the courtroom (another old Sugar tactic) and the press of bodies had broken down one of the courtroom doors. In the chambers, Sugar "scrupulously" adhered to Murphy's wishes: in consideration of Murphy's belief, Sugar said that he (Sugar) "felt the hearing should be delayed a few days to permit [Murphy] to effect a settlement without the added complications of the legal controversy." Gadola's responded, "To hell with Governor Murphy." (A recall campaign against Murphy was already under way.)

The hearing began at 2:40 and Pressman formally requested a delay on the grounds that they had not had time to prepare. Roy Brownell, GM attorney, said: "You've had since January 2," a not inaccurate statement. Thereafter, a lawyer's version of a sit-down (or at least of work-to-rule) unfolded as Pressman, Davidow, and Sugar took as long as they could. As the exasperated *Flint Journal* headlined its article on the hearing the following day: "Counsel Offer Four Hours of Argument, Defense Attorneys Taking Most of Time." At one point Pressman pulled out a nineteen-page affidavit and proceeded to read it. On page four of the anti-GM document, oposing counsel objected, saying "we are not holding a union meeting." Pressman then launched into a tirade. "After much argument"—no doubt taking as much time as if Pressman *had* read it—Gadola told him to give the "gist of it." Both Davidow and Sugar followed with similarly slothful behavior.

While delay was the main objective, there were serious arguments involved. Both sides avoided debating the sit-down's legality. The company claimed that it was a simple criminal case: a "conspiracy to commit criminal extortion." Its property had been taken and it wanted it back. The union's position was that GM did not have a right to be in court at all. A claimant in an injunction case comes before an "equity court." Normal law courts are transformed into equity courts for the purpose of "doing equity," a concept that developed quite early in the English legal system for handling "litigation where money damages would not be suitable, where 'remedy at law would be inadequate.'" This means, usually, restraining someone from doing something. In an equity court, a litigant must come into court with "clean hands," that is, have no record of illegal activity in regard to the other litigant. If it can be proved that such is not the case, that he has "unclean hands," the proceedings may be terminated. Sugar had pioneered the use of this concept in the twenties, having done the research for it while still disbarred and working for Beckenstein. The main work was done for a 1920 case involving Bernard Schwartz Cigar Company and its union, the Cigar Workers International.

Such an approach, while normally ignored by judges (although it certainly would not be by the NLRB, as we shall see), also served the purpose, if one could get an injunction hearing at all, of introducing pounds of data on the company's transgressions, thus slowing things down. And this is what the three lawyers did throughout the afternoon. About the only excitement came when Pressman interrupted Sugar's catalog of company offenses in Anderson (including buying the police department) with the announcement that seven workers had been killed on Chevrolet Avenue in the riot currently going on. (The riot was certainly in progress, but no one died.) The courtroom buzzed. Sugar concluded and requested that court not reconvene until the following afternoon since the lawyers had to return to Detroit that evening. It was granted.

The capture of Chevy Number 4 changed the entire character of the strike: violent confrontation had been met by violent confrontation. But the imaginativeness of the action and the massive change in personnel sitting down had an electrifying effect on the union. It also apparently stimulated Gadola as well. He wrote one of the longest decisions in an injunction case ever handed down. The essence of his argument on the unclean-hands question was simple enough. "The court yesterday asked the defense counsel if they were of the opinion that one wrong could be righted by another wrong. The falsity of that position is apparent by merely the stating of the position. The courts are open to the defendants, if they are wronged, and they may have redress if they seek the assistance of the courts." This last amounted to an open invitation to bring to court the hundreds of illegal acts by the companies now being exposed by the LaFollette Commission. Gadola set the evacuation time for 3:00 P.M. on Wednesday, February 3, and a fine of fifteen million dollars against the union if it failed to comply. The injunction also forbade picketing. In general, it was a poor ruling, especially since it relied heavily on a case from the World War I era that declared striking workers to be no longer employed, a concept now widely rejected by the courts. Sheriff Woolcott, a Democrat and melancholy over his role, read out the injunction in a "mouselike" voice amid jeers and boos from strikers in the plants.[9]

The night before, John L. Lewis had headed for Detroit. Roosevelt and Murphy had also conferred, and the following day, the governor moved into action again, arranging a meeting between Lewis and GM's chief negotiator and executive vice president, William S. Knudsen. ("Knuts to Knudsen" was a favorite sit-down cheer.) It began on Wednesday morning in Judge George Murphy's Detroit office.

The night of February 2 had been filled with tension. No one knew whether force would be employed or who would employ it. Governor Murphy was angered by the Chevy Number 4 operation, and there was speculation that he would beef up the guard and use it. (Sugar recalled that a man in one of the plants had heard from his brother, a guardsman, that they were on alert.) The strike strategy committee mulled over alternatives. The lawyers informed it that despite Judge Gadola's claim that he could personally order the guards into action, Murphy could overrule him. Moreover, GM had to obtain a writ of attachment for the removal process to be implemented. The strike leaders, especially Travis, argued for firm, active resistance in the event of forcible removal. The men in the plants were ready to fight, if necessary.

Clearly, if Murphy could be convinced that force must be avoided, it would be, barring sheer vigilante action. They resolved to send wires from the men in the plants, but prepared by the committee, to the governor. The tone, it was felt, was crucial.

Davidow initially prepared a draft that Sugar criticized as too pleading, an appeal to Murphy's "good graces." Murphy might well interpret it as a lack of resolve and assume that a bluff of force might do the trick. Everyone knew that the men in the plants would fight. Phone calls were going out all over the Midwest for union reinforcements. If force were used, the UAW would meet it with force.

Based upon his feeling about the governor's outlook, Sugar argued that the more strident the tone the better: it would not anger him, but on the contrary remind him of his own history and his commitment to workers. And to allow a situation to develop whereby a violent explosion might occur would be a disaster for all, but above all for the governor. The committee therefore instructed Sugar to "retire and produce a draft of [his] own." It read, in part, as follows:

> We feel it proper to recall to you the assurances that you have given many times publicly that you would not permit force or violence to be used in ousting us from the plants. . . . The police of the City of Flint belong to General Motors. The sheriff of Genesee County belongs to General Motors. The judges of Genesee County belong to General Motors. It remains to be seen whether the Governor of the State also belongs to General Motors. Governor, we have decided to stay in the plant. We have no illusions about the sacrifices which this will entail. We fully expect that if a violent effort is made to oust us, many of us will be killed, and we take this means of making it known to our wives, to our children, to the people of the state of Michigan and the country, that if this result follows from the attempt to eject us, you are the one who must be held responsible for our deaths.

The way out obviously was for Murphy to prevail upon GM not to apply for a writ of attachment (and to make sure Gadola did not try anything stupid, for he was rapidly becoming something of a megalomaniac).

Unquestionably this is the first thing Murphy discussed with Knudsen when they met in Detroit the next morning. The latter was an engineer dedicated above all to building good cars, not a tyrant bent on crushing workers. The writ of attachment was not requested, although it clearly remained GM's trump card. The people in Flint, however, had no way of knowing what would happen when the deadline came. The UAW built a massive picket line around the two plants (Chevy Number 4 was not under the injunction), equalled only by the great eleven-mile line around Goodyear a year before. The brothers and sisters poured in from everywhere. The streets belonged to the union. The Women's Emergency Brigade was out in force. And everyone sang. *Detroit Times* correspondent, Herbert Brean, was moved as he wrote about it. While they sang "Solidarity Forever" and other songs, "Flint's big hit of the week" was the "Soup Song:" "Thousands of voices roar the words. . . . The crowd particularly relishes the whip-like effect of the 'sou-oops.'" The frightening moments of the late afternoon passed. Nothing happened, and tens of thousands heaved a sigh of relief. Brean went on:

> As night falls fires are lighted in metal barrels around the little picket shanty and the men in the plants throw out boxes to be used as fuel.
> The crowd thins out to a couple of hundred and gradually the picket line shortens until only three are left. Then these gather around the fire. It's getting

203

cold. Their voices sound high and thin in the empty street:
"Sou-oop! Sou-oop . . . Give me a bowl of soup! [sic]"[10]

While the tension remained in Flint, the focus now shifted to Judge Murphy's office in Detroit. For eight days and nights Frank Murphy shuttled back and forth between Lewis, Pressman, and the UAW representatives on the one hand and Knudsen and his men on the other. Homer Martin began the negotiations, but simply went berserk after several days and was replaced by Mortimer. Lewis sent him out on a speaking tour that Martin was assured was more important than working in the "stalemated" negotiations in Detroit. Ed Hall went along to look after the UAW's unstable president.

The negotiations were going badly. On February 5, GM had obtained the writ of attachment, thus placing the entire task of preventing violence in Governor Murphy's hands. The latter felt betrayed. The GM people retained an imperious posture that further infuriated Murphy. But Lewis simply reminded them daily that Chrysler and Ford were putting out over twenty-five thousand units a week, while GM, the giant, barely managed fifteen hundred. The critical issue was sole recognition of the UAW in the struck plants. The situation in Flint remained dangerous, as the Flint Alliance recruited vigilantes and strikers' families got hungrier. Finally, on February 9, Murphy decided to do something to try to break the stalemate. He summoned the union negotiators and the strategy committee to his suite in the Statler. Sugar was at the very heart of the drama that ensued.

Murphy had now carried the burden of not enforcing the law—the writ of attachment—for four days. Public pressure was becoming intense. General Motors had bent to a degree. They had spoken about a three-month period of sole recognition without actually putting it in so many words, but Lewis rejected it. Murphy now decided to squeeze the union. He began with Lewis, presenting him with a strong letter emphasizing the necessity that he uphold the law, that is, to use force to evacuate the plants if it came to that. He had spoken to Roosevelt, who approved, and he planned to make the letter public the following morning. Lewis's actual reply has been the subject of controversy (Lewis claiming that he told him that he would be inside the plant with the men when the troops arrived; Murphy, that Lewis withered under the blow and in fact did not take to bed with the flu but was "knocked out by the Murphy ultimatum"); but, as Sidney Fine points out, whatever happened, Lewis did not change his position one iota. That Murphy did not issue the letter the next day may or may not have been influenced by Lewis's alleged threat, but it was certainly influenced by the sequence of events at the meeting with the committee, which Lewis, indisposed, did not attend.[11]

There is no reason to doubt Henry Kraus's account of it, especially given what we know of the rather special relationship between Murphy and Sugar.

Murphy began by outlining the difficulty of his situation. As the chief law officer of the state, he had to uphold the law at some point. (Sheriffs often delayed delivery of writs of attachment out of humanitarian considerations, especially in foreclosures.) He had bent over backwards on behalf of the union, but the time had arrived for the union to make the sacrifice and break things open by voluntarily leaving the plants. Kraus goes on:

> The governor's plea was ardent and eloquently worded. He felt that he had made an impression on the union men and putting his hand on his former classmate Maurice Sugar's knee, he asked confidently:
> "Morrie,* what do you think about it?"
> The union's legal adviser felt that the situation was more than delicate since all the arguments of propriety bade him not to take the lead. Yet his conscience would not permit him to evade a grave responsibility on a mere personal scruple. He started with apparent hesitation: "It's hard for me to say, Frank, being a lawyer, but. . . ." Then he outlined the situation in perhaps unlegalistic but highly humanistic terms, his argument summing up to the point that he thought the men ought to stay come hell or high water.
> "Who is General Motors anyway that they should dictate to you or to these thousands of workers?" he demanded.
> Murphy was pained [he had no doubt hoped to get support from another lawyer] and tried to brush Sugar's opinion aside as being dictated by "principle" rather than by legal necessity.
> "Well, I'd like to ask you a question, Frank," Sugar persisted. "What exactly to you propose to do if the men don't come out?"

Then came the bombshell, an idea which may have been precipitated by this meeting and, indeed, by Sugar's hard line.

> The governor proceeded to give a long, circuitous answer which led up to this: he would go into the plants personally and ask the men to leave voluntarily!
> "And I would expect you boys to help me," he concluded.
> It was a simple answer quietly given but it contained the possible destiny of the strike, as the sudden silence of the union leaders upon hearing it indicated.

What he had done, of course, was to find a way around the violence that Sugar had been sure all along he would not use. There is a good chance that Sugar was playing that card again in his response, but Murphy found a way to trump it. Murphy's personal popularity with the strikers was known to all, and there was little question that he could pull it off. At the same time he had "temporized," as Kraus termed it, since his meeting with Lewis.

If this situation had softened the union up a bit, the realities of capitalist competition softened the company. Chrysler Corporation, scrambling to avoid the same fate as GM, had decided upon a 10-percent raise for all employees, and

---

*The diminutive of Sugar's name (Murphy always spelled it *Maury* in letters) was only used by friends who knew him well years before; Jane called him both, although she shifted more and more to *Maurice* (pronounced *Morris*) as time passed.

205

GM negotiators had no doubt known about it. They knew also that pressure was on the union and that they could now move without losing face.

What they finally ended up with was a six-month agreement that the UAW would be sole bargaining agent in the seventeen struck plants; that there would be no discrimination against strikers; that elsewhere the union was recognized for its members only; that direct solicitation of members on company property was forbidden but "discussions" were acceptable; and that collective bargaining would begin on February 16. The company added a 5-percent increase across the board to sweeten the pot. It was not very much on paper, but the world's largest corporation had just been brought to a sitting position, if not to its knees. In Flint, pandemonium broke loose as the strikers filed out of the plants at 5:00 P.M. on February 11. A great hand-painted sign. "Victory is Ours," floated from the roof of Fisher Number 1.[12]

Detroit

Sugar was hardly able to catch his breath, for the phone had been ringing off the hook from Detroit unions asking for legal advice after they began *their* sit-downs. Flint had started an avalanche of sit-down strikes across the nation, but what happened in Detroit itself was probably the most significant consequence. In February, and especially in March, strikes occurred throughout the auto industry. Just as important, AFL locals and unrepresented workers sat down in droves. The latest estimate puts the number of sit-downs in Detroit alone at over one hundred, with the direct involvement of over thirty-five thousand workers and with twice that number on picket lines.[13]

Despite his preoccupation with UAW affairs, Sugar still served as the lawyer for MESA. There had been a major sit-down going since February 2 in the Nash-Kelvinator plants in Detroit. The day after the Flint settlement, as he read the morning paper about renewed antiunion violence in Anderson, Sugar was called by Matt Smith to join him at the negotiating table against Kelvinator management. 'Round the clock bargaining produced a settlement at noon on February 16.

The strike was typical of the middle-level sit-downs that occurred during the next eight weeks. The two thousand workers in the plants were already organized. The strike began when the company failed to act on grievances arising from "misunderstandings" at the Plymouth Road and Fort Street facilities. The union immediately added wage demands. On February 9, while great events were in the offing at the Statler, MESA picketers captured the office building as well, saying that "the company harbored strike breakers in the office." This touch of Smithian audacity was answered by a petition for an injunction by company lawyers two days later. The show-cause hearing set by Judge Henry Nicol (a liberal) scheduled for February 16 thus set a convenient deadline. Alex Groesbeck, the company's attorney and chief negotiator, may have been a little intimidated at the thought of facing one of the Flint heroes in court. In any case, the negotiations ended with solid 65–75 cent minima for men, depending on class, and 60–65 cent minima for women, plus general wage increases of 5–7½ cents per hour. Further negotiations would deal with other matters, including the original grievances. "Judge Nicol," wrote the *Free Press,* "congratulated Groesbeck and Sugar on the adjustment" and dropped the injunction. Smith called it a "clean fight," the workers overwhelmingly ratified, and a big parade took place that afternoon on the near west side. Newspaper photographs of Sugar the following day showed him surprisingly bright-eyed.[14]

In fact, life had never been more exhilarating. The moment he had been waiting for after twenty-five years of struggle had arrived. United States workers were on the march. From the paragon of the open shop, Detroit was becoming a union town. *Time* magazine might speculate about the "revolution" (as indeed might some of Sugar's friends), but for the ever practical Sugar, first things would have to come first. The groundwork lay in a viable labor movement. Its time had come.

On the day the Kelvinator strike was settled, five other stoppages or threats were terminated, from a laundry to Detrola Radio and Television Corporation. Thirteen others were still in progress, while Ferry-Morse Seed had just sat down and Timken Axle—with Walter Reuther, president of the West Side (Number 174) local, in the lead—had staged a forty-minute sit-down to revive stalled negotiations.

It was heartening to see AFL shops or workers logically in the AFL orbit prominent in the Detroit movement. The national leadership of the AFL had taken a purely factional position on Flint, almost siding with GM during the strike and then saying how terrible the settlement was. John Frey, president of the Metal Trades Association of the AFL, had pronounced the sit-down illegal and would be joined by Green in this opinion by the end of March. But Frank Martel publicly disagreed with the national AFL position, pledging to Lewis his "full support" on March 3. He was invited to join the UAW strategy board. This long history, checkered though it was, of local AFL openness toward industrial unionism should not be underestimated, nor should the constant efforts of people like Sugar to maintain labor unity in the city despite rebuffs. It was obviously paying off in the great awakening of late winter 1937.[15]

One example was the cigar-workers strike, which commenced on February 16. The Cigar Workers International, AFL, led a moribund existence in the six Detroit plants of the hard-pressed industry, which employed mostly low-paid women workers. Bernard Schwartz (makers of R. G. Dunn) had invited their workers to form a grievance committee and then fired all twenty-five of them on January 6. Outrage seethed throughout the cigar district, but only on February 16 was action taken. The women of Webster-Eisenlohr sat down and a coalition of workers from various plants went to the headquarters of "that wonderful Flint union," the UAW. George Addes was the only officer around. He told them they had come to the wrong union and, besides, that all his organizers were busy. The group thereupon threatened to sit down in his office. Addes decided that he had better do something and told them that he would assign Stanley Nowak to them. With this sign of support, the other five shops, including the thousand-worker Schwartz factory, struck in quick succession.

Sugar's relationship to the strike was largely in his function of legal advisor, but in a certain way he and his left-wing friends, active in politics and community-action programs, had laid the groundwork for it. It is worthwhile pausing for a minute to examine the cigar-workers' strike and its background, for it provides a fine example of how working-class consciousness was forged in the midthirties.

The Detroit cigar industry was a shadow of its former self, having lost out increasingly to New York and Tampa. Typical of declining industries, wages were low, hours long, conditions of health and safety grim, and terms of employment exploitative. In the midthirties, the semiskilled workers were normally paid one mill per piece, and faulty cigars went uncompensated despite the fact that they were sold as seconds. Curiously, in slump times or if workers should complain, the numbers of rejects shot up dramatically. If a woman cleared twelve dollars for a six-day week, she was lucky. The average autoworker made more than twice that. Because of the need to retain constant high levels of humidity (as in textile factories), there was little ventilation of the foul air in the factories. A ten-minute lunch would be gobbled down amid the stench.

Why would such conditions be tolerated? Where was their union? Women workers were traditionally the last to be organized. If they were in an industry scratching to survive, their bargaining power was bound to be low. For these specific women, however, other factors entered in, weaknesses that in the long run would be turned to strengths when their great moment came in February and March 1937.

A large majority were Polish-Americans who lived in Detroit's "Poletown" and Hamtramck. The Poles were among the last immigrants to the city. As people of largely peasant background with few urban, industrial skills, they were heavily concentrated in semiskilled and unskilled jobs. They shared with blacks, although not as much, the curse of "last hired, first fired." This meant that their male population was riddled with unemployment even during the twenties, a situation that turned to total disaster with the Depression. Polish women, like black women, thus filled an important gap. And the cigar industry was one place that welcomed them, hiring both single and married women, with the latter in the majority. In the early Depression years, many of their husbands were out of work. By 1937 a more likely situation was that of Eva Briskey. She was a forty-one-year-old cigar maker with eleven children ranging from two to eighteen. Her oldest daughter worked in the storeroom of her plant. Her husband was a night watchman in a grocery warehouse, making about the same as she, but he was also available to share child-care duties with the older children. Women's work was thus crucial to the survival of the family. They seemed to have no choice but to take ill-paying, exploitative work and not cause any trouble.

The cooperative nature of Polish-American families contributed to the willingness of the women to work within a family economy where pooled incomes were normal. Low wages were therefore more acceptable. Unions, moreover, had little sanction in their culture. The women were almost universally devout Roman Catholics, whose parish served as their moral universe. The priest's influence was great, and rare was the Polish priest who did not condemn trade-unionism as tantamount to Godless Communism. Such opinions reflected the attitudes of the elites of the Polish community and reinforced the deference that they demanded and generally received from their poor and ill-educated compatriots.

Things turned around rapidly with the sit-downs, as the very factors that seemed to hold the "cigar girls" in thrall now tended to operate to their advantage.

In 1935 and 1936, this part of Detroit and especially Hamtramck had gone through a period of rapid politicization. In the first place, the Depression spawned idealistic young priests with deep sympathy for the plight of poor working people, and they began to find their way into pulpits. Moreover, while many Catholics agreed with Father Coughlin and his Polish counterpart, Father Justyn, many others were shaken from their apathy by these demagogues and began to articulate their opposition to them. On the positive side, in 1935 an active organization had tried to do something about the squeeze on the family budget. Many Polish women in this area worked with the Housewive's League against the High Cost of Living. Many others, and their menfolk, worked to elect Mary Zuk to Hamtramck's city council and worked for Sugar's efforts in Detroit. The Polish IWO hall and the Yeman Street headquarters of the Polish and Russian "fractions" of the Communist party were popular centers for political discussion.

The heart of this discussion was much less "politics" per se than the need for strong unions. In 1936 the UAW drive in the Polish community was commanded by Zuk's and Sugar's ally, Stanley Nowak. Not only did he head many organizational efforts—such as Automotive Fibres—but he found time to edit the left-wing Polish-language weekly, *Glos ludowy,* and to present perspectives on politics, economic life, and union activities in a weekly radio show, also in Polish. He thus brought an anticompany, socially progressive point of view to Detroit Polish-American workers that had been much less visible before.[16]

The cigar-plant sit-downs, while coming from the bottom up, did not occur in a vacuum. An organizational and ideological foundation had been laid. This was obvious as the strike—to be Detroit's longest sit-down—unfolded. Everywhere, instant mobilization developed as blankets and cots were provided, soup kitchens set up at nearby Polish clubs, and committees of all sorts created. Quickly, neighborhood and wider Polish community support began to materialize. A mass meeting at Dom Polski, held on February 19 to publicize the strike and to raise funds, was followed by a parade around the neighborhood that stopped at each struck shop. Popular Polish radio humorist Waclaw Golan-

209

ski announced strike meetings, kept his listening audience abreast of developments, and told rhymed stories about the strike in the voice of his comic character, Antek Cwaniak ("the joker"). Councilwoman Zuk joined Nowak in making the rounds of the plants. On Saturday, February 20, the two of them became martyrs as hired thugs invaded the General Cigar Company, rushed them as they spoke to the sit-downers in the shop, and forced them to jump out a second-storey window. Zuk had the good fortune to land on a policeman, but Nowak broke a bone in his foot. This incident became an instant legend, and to this day more people remember Nowak's leap than any other event in his illustrious career.[17]

As the strike settled into a protracted struggle, the women in the plants set up elaborate systems of maintenance and supply. General became the "Hôtel de General Cigar Corp." and was organized like a hotel with clerks, bellhops, chambermaids, and house detectives. There was even a beauty salon. The Schwartz Company had a kitchen from which the 350 women who occupied the plant over the next month fed themselves. The families of the strikers were looked after by husbands, grandparents, and neighbors. Some of the men grumbled, but the remarkable cohesiveness of the Polish family now came fully into play, bolstering the determination of the women to stay out on strike as their men took on often unaccustomed roles. One they could not perform was nursing babies, so in a few instances they developed regular schedules for bringing unweaned infants into the shops for their mothers to feed.

Strike leaders like Helen Nowak and Cecilia Chroniecki organized regular provisioning expeditions to the stores and food manufacturers throughout Detroit's Poletown and southern Hamtramck, and their owners responded generously. Little by little the old elites of the community, many of them quite conservative, began to see this as a fight between exploited Polish women (who had previously been looked down upon because they had to work) and an outside, WASP establishment. Beginning on February 25, a series of hearings before a committee of prominent figures in the community was held in the court of Judge Nicholas S. Gronkowski to investigate working conditions in the cigar industry. The shocking findings further cemented the support of the larger community. Perhaps trade-unionism *was* something more than communism. As the secular leaders of the community softened in their attitudes, so did individual parish priests, who gave vocal support to the strikers, while encouraging religious observances in the struck plants themselves. Support from these quarters was never universal, but it turned out that the very ethnic and religious relationships that had previously fostered docility and deference in the cigar workers now served to bring them support well beyond the confines of the working class. The four smaller companies settled in early March in part because of this mounting pressure, but General and Schwartz, national outfits, fought on.

At this point, the cigar workers' struggle can no longer be discussed in isolation. While sit-downs were being settled regularly—Sugar had helped to negotiate the Ferro Stamping Company strike, a particularly long and bitter affair, late in February—new ones popped up all the time. The atmosphere, although occasionally punctuated by humor and fun, as in the famous Woolworth saleswomen's strike of February 27 or the Webster Hotel stoppage (in the middle of dinner) on March 7, became more and more forbidding. When Chrysler negotiations broke down and the massive sit-down at Dodge Main (up the street from the cigar area) began, patience and good will were hard to find.

The question of the legality of the sit-downs now burst into public view. It had been slow in coming. While the companies assumed from the beginning that there was no way to construe the occupation of their property as legal, little public debate had taken place over it. The issue was generally skirted in court fights because it was a problem in equity, not law. It was a question of trespass on someone else's property and the remedy sought was removal—without criminal charges being filed unless damage was done. Nevertheless, it was generally assumed that sit-downs were illegal, as the *News* had written. Even Sugar, in his first recorded interview on the question (in the *Christian Science Monitor* on February 8) only argued the worker's moral right to a job, the proprietary content of that job, and therefore his right to stay in the plant. Implicitly, he recognized that sit-downs lay outside the law when he noted that first unions themselves, then picketing, had been deemed illegal only to be legalized; now "it is logical to look for a development in the law reflecting the conviction that labor has a right to stay in the plant."

At the same time, it seemed that in February the news had been dominated by violence and illegal acts against workers by vigilantes and law officers. The case of Anderson, Indiana, which exploded again after the GM settlement, was widely reported. Victor Reuther and his men were battered so regularly, with encouragement from the police, that Anderson became synonymous with antiunion terror. Simultaneously, February was the month that the LaFollette Committee hearings began to reveal wave after wave of shocking information about company spies, professional strikebreaking, company purchases of gas and armaments, and all the other abuses of the law Sugar and the labor movement had been screaming about for decades.

But the counteroffensive had been mounting, even in February, as all three Detroit newspapers editorialized about property rights as "the very foundation of our nation." More practically, the *News* developed an interesting new form of reportage: checking out labor organizers for police records. When they found one, they then printed his picture—front view, side view—from the police mug shot! In the case of Sam Cooper, the first to be so honored, they published a long article in which (if one went beyond the headline and photograph) it was discovered that while he was arrested seven times, he was never convicted. The following day he was arrested again, this time charged with "peddling literature without a license" in Highland Park. The incriminating brochure was entitled, "The Great Sit-down Strike."

On March 2, a bill was introduced by Republican State Senator D. Hale Blake to make it a felony for employers to negotiate with sit-down strikers. This

211

proposal was one of several nationwide that were floated by conservatives "to enforce the speedy recognition of property rights." Bombs (tear gas, stench, and otherwise) were placed in various union headquarters in early March. No one was hurt, although on March 11 the Hoffman building, where many unions were located, was shut down by tear gas.

By that time, the key event of the Detroit phase of sit-down fever was under way. The Chrysler strike grew out of the failure of management to grant sole recognition to the UAW, despite the facts that sixty thousand out of Chrysler's sixty-five thousand employees supported the union and the company union had been dissolved. Although all Chrysler plants in the metropolitan area were on strike, it was the dramatic capture of the gigantic Dodge Main in Hamtramck that caught the public imagination. The plant, which employed a total of twenty-five thousand persons, was initially occupied by an astounding ten thousand sitters. By March 10, the *News* headlines declared, "Highland Park Area under Union Rule. Streets are Seized by Strikers," meaning that the UAW had prevented executives and white-collar workers from entering the company's headquarters. The Chrysler strike brought Frank Murphy's Florida vacation to an end, and he reluctantly bade farewell to host Joseph P. Kennedy and his large family in their house at Palm Beach. Upon his arrival in Detroit, he declared a hands-off policy toward the strike and gave signs that his patience was running thin. That same day (March 10), Chrysler sought an injunction against the strikers, and Sugar swung back into action.

He had been busy, however, at the piano. Hudson Motor Company also went out on March 8—ten thousand were idle and three hundred sitting in the main plant. A newspaper reported that "small picket groups headed by a banjo-strumming union leader move back and forth between the Hudson plants and the Chrysler factory." And what were they singing?

When they tie the can
To a union man
Sit down! Sit down!
When they give him the sack,
They'll take him back.
Sit down! Sit down!

Chorus
Sit down, just take a seat.
Sit down, and rest your feet.
Sit down, you've got 'em beat.
Sit down! Sit down!

When they smile and say,
"No raise in pay,"
Sit down! Sit down!
When you want the boss

To come across,
Sit down! Sit down!

When the speed-up comes
Just twiddle your thumbs,
Sit down! Sit down!
When you want 'em to know
They'd better go slow,
Sit down! Sit down!

When the boss won't talk,
Don't take a walk.
Sit down! Sit down!
When the boss sees that
He'll want a little chat.
Sit down! Sit down!

Sugar's most famous song was written at the height of the sit-down mania in Detroit and instantly became the war cry of the movement. If it had any rival, judging from newspaper accounts, it was the ubiquitous "Soup Song."

The Chrysler injunction hearing was scheduled for 9:00 A.M., Saturday, March 13 before Judge Allan Campbell in circuit court. Detroit's ancient county courthouse swarmed with UAW people, wearing their Sunday best and sporting the union's black and yellow buttons. Sugar made his way up the steps and through the crowded corridors, men yelling encouragement and flashbulbs popping. Corporation attorneys, "bristling with brief cases," slogged their way through the crowd. The courtroom, packed with more workers, quieted as Sugar rose to speak: he began with the traditional motion for a continuance until Monday. "Motion denied," said the court. Then, as reported by the *Detroit Times*, "Sugar dug deep into his brief case for more papers. Outside . . . hundreds of unionists paraded with picket-line placards, a band, and cheers. At police headquarters, four blocks away, reserve officers were held in readiness for the first hint of trouble." Sugar began in time-honored fashion with affidavits demonstrating Chrysler's unclean hands. Summarizing the list of the usual offenses, he declared, "The corporation has presumed to set itself above the law of the country. . . . It intends to precipitate a labor war. . . . Its hands are not only unclean but reek with illegality." Moreover, Sugar continued, Chrysler deemed the Wagner Act unconstitutional and therefore would not grant officially what it admitted to be true, namely, that the UAW had the vast majority of corporation workers in its ranks, thus giving it sole bargaining rights under the act.

Sugar took the whole morning and was surprised when Campbell failed to recess for lunch: "How long does your honor intend to run? As long as I do?" "Longer," said the judge. The *Times* article continued,

On Sugar went, now into a new idea. He argued ingeniously that a temporary injunction would permanently terminate the issue (remove the strikers) and settle

213

the litigation without a final hearing. Sugar said he had [Michigan] Supreme Court precedent that such a double-dealing temporary injunction might be ignored by the defendant.

Judge Campbell leaned across the bench with interest.

"Would you advise your clients to that effect?" he asked.

Sugar, seeing the trap he was laying, responded,

"I could, but I will tell the Court that I would not. If the Supreme Court found the injunction wrongfully issued I'd be all right. But if I were wrong I could go to jail for contempt and be disbarred."

He then quoted *Sanford v. Newell* (1918):

"An injunction action by preliminary hearing cannot turn even a wrong-doer out of possession. The court (in the case referred to in the decision) here has issued an interlocutory order on a preliminary inquiry which no one need respect or obey."

He looked up with a half smile.

"I hope your honor doesn't find the Supreme Court guilty of contempt," he said.

The corporation lawyer Thomas Chawke did not tangle with that argument (it was for the judge and the public anyway), but intoned the well-worn position:

The maxim of 'unclean hands' does not apply to this situation as the matter in controversy here is our right to possess and enjoy our own property. A malicious trespass has occurred and whether we have been guilty of unfair practice is a far relation [*sic*] to this investigation.

The judge issued the injunction the following Monday. The union refused to budge.

In the meantime, Frank Murphy had moved into action, this time veering toward the bosses. He organized a committee of prominent citizens to act as an unofficial arbitration panel. United Auto Workers officers Martin and Dick Frankensteen, the leader of the Chrysler strike, were asked to join, but refused. Simultaneously, the papers wrote about the need for compulsory arbitration. Murphy issued a statement emphasizing respect for the law: "It is elementary and undebatable that whatever differences may exist between employers and employees, public order must be preserved and public authority must be respected." On Monday. March 15, the day the Chrysler injunction was served, Murphy, speaking before public prosecutors from industrial areas, was more pointed still: "There must be no willful disobedience of court orders or defiance of public order." On March 16 Chief Heinrich Pickert put all police on twelve-hour shifts. The deadline for evacuation of Chrysler plants was 9:00 A.M., March 17. It came and went with no movement. A picket sign read, "Refuse to Move:

We'll Die Before We Do." Twenty-five other plants, including the cigar shops, were tied up and injunctions were being sought right and left.

That afternoon, speaking before the first meeting of his new commission at the Statler Hotel, Murphy issued a statement that minced no words—the law must be respected: "We have the means to enforce respect for public authority and we propose to use them with proper vigor if need be." His "law-and-order" speech won the instant approval of the media. The *Free Press* said, "It is a statement the people of Michigan have long been waiting for." And it opened the floodgates. Despite concern that the police force of Detroit and Sheriff's deputies combined did not have nearly the manpower to clear the plants, plans moved forward to begin to act on writs of attachment. On March 18 Murphy gave further ammunition to reaction by condemning mini-sit-downs aided by outsiders. They were, he said "raids, a modified form of banditry."

The following morning came this simple announcement from the six thousand sitters in the Chrysler plants: "We don't intend to leave these plants without a satisfactory settlement." While Chief Pickert, Sheriff Wilcox, Prosecutor Mc-Crea, and Mayor Couzens decided to delay action against the Chrysler workers that weekend, they hit upon a remarkable expedient: they would attack the women strikers at Bernard Schwartz! And they did so without a court order, arguing that they had a right since they had reports that nonstrikers were in the plant and that "there was danger that the boilers might blow up."

Thus on Saturday, March 20, mounted and foot police invaded Milwaukee Street and battled some 500 strikers and sympathizers outside before attacking the building. Inside, some 150 women fought the police step by step up four floors to the roof. Only clubs and fists subdued them, and they were dragged by hair and clothing out of the building. The most shocking incident, however, was the manhandling of a pregnant neighbor, Anna Rzembowska, who, after shouting at the police to stop beating a man lying on the pavement in front of her house, was clubbed in the head and pushed through the railing of her porch by a policeman. She and the unborn child survived, but she came perilously close to a fractured skull and a miscarriage.

In response to this "police terror," the entire labor movement of the Detroit area mobilized the grandest demonstration the city had ever seen. On Tuesday, March 23, as many as 150 thousand workers gathered in Cadillac Square to hear speakers from all walks of life—and now including important figures from Detroit's Catholic hierarchy—who condemned the antilabor actions of the city administration and promised to extend the sit-down movement.

This event, preceded by a vow from Martin that the UAW would call a general strike if the police attacks continued, was the catalyst that broke the Chrysler deadlock and in fact opened the way toward settlement of most of the strikes then going on, including the cigar workers. Murphy was again at the heart of it as his mediation produced recognition of the UAW as the bargaining agent for its members throughout Chrysler Corporation, while the company agreed not to negotiate with any other group. Hudson, Reo, and Packard followed. Many smaller companies saw both AFL and CIO locals established and contracts drawn up. Finally, after a conference with the governor on April 22, elections were held between the AFL and the CIO for representation in the cigar industry. The women's choice was clear: the cigar workers of Detroit became Cigar workers Local Number 24 of the CIO, with sit-down heroine Sophie Myszka its first chairwoman.[18]

The Law

Although the victories were monumental, the question of the legality of the sit-down strike had now become a burning national issue. It fell to Sugar, above all others, to defend it.

His first act had been to send a scathing letter to Murphy, condemning his law-and-order speech. It was most effective, reiterating a variety of points the governor was clearly aware of, beginning each paragraph with "Don't you know . . . ?" He reminded Murphy of the long lists of employers' illegal acts, the recent bombings, police arrests, the newspaper smears, all aimed at workers and all of which Murphy had ignored. He concluded, "Governor, your words have inspired unbounded jubilation by every Liberty Leaguer in the country. Most jubilant of all is the unspeakable Hearst. Do you not see that your words have provoked violent physical attacks—illegal attacks, led by the Mayor and Police Commissioner of Detroit, upon the workers—upon even girls and women, whose miserable starvation pittance of 12 dollars a week have driven them to sit-down—to passively protest their destitution and the wretchedness and suffering of their children?" Murphy, usually scrupulous in his correspondence, did not reply. But these words unquestionably remained with him as he mediated between bosses and workers over the next six weeks.

Writing in the *New York Times Magazine* on Sunday, April 4, Russell B. Porter spoke the truth when he said that "the sit-down is unquestionably the easiest and most effective method organized labor has ever devised to stop production and force business and industry to meet its demands or at least negotiate. Against the background [of recent ferment], it stands out as the most important development, for good or evil, in the social history of industrial civilization." It had become the "critical issue" of the day, "as shown by the debates in Congress, the press and public meetings throughout the land and by continued sit-downs even in plants where they have been barred by agreement." While the historical importance of the sit-down was obvious, virtually no one defended them on legal grounds. Leon Green of the Chicago Law School, came closest, arguing that if a company refused to negotiate, thereby violating the Wagner Act, there was some legal ground to argue on. Lawyers' written opinions, in law journals or more popular forums, were universally negative. Even the ACLU found it impossible to defend them.

Still, there was a body of legal opinion that could justify, in the best sense of that word, the sit-down strike, if not argue for its strict legality. Sugar took the lead in developing this perspective. In April and May he spoke in many cities where the auto battles were going on and utilized the developing network of a new organization, the National Lawyers Guild, to spread the ideas to sympathetic lawyers.

On April 14, 1937 Sugar was invited by the Cuyahoga County Bar Association to speak on the "Legality and Ethics of the Sitdown Strike" at the Cleveland Hotel. It was broadcast simultaneously over WGAR, one of the city's principal radio stations. The text of this speech survives and is quite similar to that of his article appearing in the *New Masses* on May 4, so we can assume this was the position he developed in his many other appearances. He began with the ethical question, Is it just for an employer, such as Ford, who breaks the law and who creates public law for its own purposes (the Dearborn antileafleting law) to make a claim against workers who are ostensibly breaking the law by sitting in? It was the old clean-hands doctrine—which Sugar later notes is being regularly rejected by judges—but put as a moral imperative.

Sugar was also willing to argue the essential constitutionality of the sit-down strike. He began by claiming that every worker had "a right in his job." Was there a logical basis for such a claim? "We start by asserting that every worker in America has the right to live in decency and as a free man." Sugar said this was an axiom. Everything flowed from this axiom. To live in decency one had to have a job—the worker had a right to it: "Indeed, the right to work has been expressly recognized as a property right by our highest courts." And to live decently, the worker had a right to decent wages, hours, and working conditions. Moreover, under the existing complex and tenuous economy, where "it [was] impossible to move freely from one job to another," he had a right to his *particular* job, or at least to work for his particular employer, if he did the work adequately. It follows that the employer had to use his property so that the worker might enjoy his right.

And here, continued Sugar, is where the conflict lay—between the employer asserting his property rights, the worker his right to live. "Rights" did not exist in a political or economic vacuum. And the history of legislation reflected that. Recently, especially with the Wagner Act, "the people [had] been . . . taking a position on the conflict—with the right of the worker in his job in the ascendancy." He continued, "Now, when the worker engages in a sit-down strike, he sits down on his job. Is this an encroachment upon the property rights of the employer? Of course it is. But encroachment upon property rights is not *ipso facto* illegal. The law books abound with adjudications which justify encroachments upon property rights. This is what we lawyers call *damnum absque injuria*." Sugar then went on to point out that virtually all acts by employees in concert against employers had involved encroachment of the latter's property rights. Strikes and picketing troubled an employer's property, even though the activity took place outside the plant. But the law had largely recognized these

217

encroachments. The social and economic conditions of the time dictated that the sit-down was just a further extension of the law under a living Constitution. And from a certain point of view, the sit-down was better for property rights *and* the right to live, because it was much less violent than outside strikes.

But Sugar's ultimate argument went beyond even the written Constitution to the very legal foundations of any society and, with his gift for irony, he quoted Edmund Burke on his behalf. What had in fact happened in the winter of 1936–37 was that U.S. workers were "breaking their chains" on their own, and with them the "chain law" fell, too. "The sit-down strike" declared Sugar, "is legal to millions of workers. It will remain legal to them, and to millions more as time goes on. And who dare say that millions of American workers have suddenly become criminals. Edmund Burke once said, 'I do not know of the method of drawing up an indictment against a whole people.' May I presume to add that he who would indict a whole people is himself a criminal?"

Beneath the constitutionality of the sit-down, then, Sugar concluded, lay the deeper truth of democratic principle. Burke said, "People crushed by the law have no hopes but from power. If laws are their enemies they will be enemies to the laws." The simple point—unless the arbiters of the law wished to invite solutions "from power"—was that labor had already caused the law to be changed: "Now we await only the acceptance by the courts of the change which has already been made."[19]

Sugar thus presented a cogent perspective. He did not give an inch on his Marxist principles, yet simultaneously remained firmly in the Anglo-American legal tradition. It was a comfortable position to be in. In time, however, as the law seemed to bend progressively to the workers' will, as the NLRB ruled in unions' favor, as Left, labor, and New Deal legislation seemed to mesh remarkably well, reliance on the physical struggle tended to decline. As labor became more and more protected by the law, it became more and more enmeshed in it. And Sugar—and many of his friends on the Left—found themselves caught in a dilemma, one that in the end would be resolved against them, as first the War Labor Board restrictions, then Taft-Hartley, strangled the labor movement. But for now, despite the fact that Sugar's argument was never validated by the Supreme Court, the sky seemed to be the limit. Armed with the Wagner Act and a continuingly militant working-class movement, the marriage of labor and the law appeared to be a happy one.

8 ❈ HOMER AND HENRY:
THE TWO-FRONT WAR, 1937–41

Oh, old Hank Ford, he ain't what he used to be,
Ain't what he used to be, ain't what he used to be,
Old Hank Ford, he ain't what he used to be,
   Since the CIO.
                                        —Maurice Sugar

As usual, Ed Hall put it succinctly: "The international union is going to organize Ford despite his damned thugs." With that, at 3:00 P.M. on April 14, 1937, Hall took to the air. Not on the radio, but in an airplane equipped with loud speakers, he let Ford workers at the giant Rouge complex know that Henry Ford was no longer in a position "to break the law." The Supreme Court had just ruled the Wagner Act constitutional and Ford had run out of excuses. The Ford drive was on, although the union had not yet developed a comprehensive plan.

Henry Ford first offered an intriguing reason why his employees would be "foolish to join a union." Unions, he said, were just what "Wall Street" wanted "to stabilize" the industrial system. Wall Street bankers promoted "management" as opposed to entrepreneurship to capture the side of capital and now were pushing unions to control labor. Ford intimated that he would pay more than anyone else and simply price the union out of business. Before long, however, it became clear that the Ford Motor Company would use less subtle means of fighting unionization than the old man's version of finance capitalism. He had not hired thousands (the UAW put the figure at ten thousand) of "service" men for nothing. Violence was soon to become the hallmark of the Ford organizing drive.

It was compounded by duplicity and conflict in the UAW that almost destroyed it from within. Homer Martin, in league with the AFL and ultimately with the Ford Motor Company itself, sought to create a personal dictatorship and organized his campaign largely upon the basis of anticommunism. He did so with what may be described as "professional" help from Jay Lovestone and his followers, ex-Communists still claiming left-wing allegiance but actually serving little purpose in life other than attacking their former comrades. Thus, from the very moment of triumph in the sit-downs, which had seen so little red-baiting and factional conflict, grave problems arose. The struggle with Homer would

219

last until 1939 and that with Henry until 1941. Both monopolized Sugar's energies.

The Martin and Ford problems emerged in an atmosphere of growing intolerance of the sit-down concept by public authorities, the media, and, finally, public opinion. In Detroit, the Yale and Towne Lock Company strike illustrated the hardening mood. Sugar was the strikers' lawyer. The sit-down at this five hundred–employee west-side plant began on March 8, mainly involving women. Male employees ran food supplies, communications, and picket lines. The UAW organizer assigned to Yale and Towne was George Edwards, who later became a prominent judge. He learned a fair amount of law in this situation.

Circuit Judge Arthur Webster turned out to be Detroit's version of Judge Black. On April 10 he compared the 150 "girl strikers" to "kidnappers who claim their crime is justified because the kidnapped child's parents refused to enter into preliminary negotiations" and gave them until Monday, April 12, to evacuate the plant. He was responding to Sugar's usual argument that since the company would not negotiate, the strikers had a right to occupy. They did not budge and were finally evicted the following Wednesday. The battle inside the plant was mild, but clashes with police outside resulted in a number of injuries on both sides. Several union officials, including Walter and Victor Reuther, who were operating a sound truck, were arrested and held without charge along with those who had sat in or fought.

Amid widespread reports of police brutality and bad judgment (Walter Reuther was picked up for allegedly saying, "Get that _____ Pickert" when he actually said about the plant, "Get that _____ picketed"), Sugar had to defend 120 indicted strikers. At the arraignment, they sang "Solidarity Forever" despite deputies' attempts to silence them. On April 27, the mass trial took place. Sugar argued that the injunction had been improperly served, not having been heard by the strikers, and sought a dismissal. Judge Webster was not so inclined. All defendants were found guilty of contempt and four, including strike leader Edwards, received short jail terms. Their pictures, smiling and arm-in-arm behind bars, made all the papers. As the first sit-downers jailed for contempt, they became heroes.

The outcome of the Yale and Towne strike was one of many indications that the courts were not going to accept the worker-imposed changes in the law that Sugar had hoped for. The local press increasingly emphasized the "irresponsibility" of the UAW. The *Free Press* was especially indignant over the brief power outage caused by UAW strikers against Consumers Power Company in the Saginaw area, calling it an "outrageous strike." Sugar, Mortimer, and the strike leaders met with Frank Murphy, who again helped negotiate a settlement but rebuked the union for the threat posed to public security. More indicative still was the Michigan Industrial Relations Bill, which Murphy sponsored in the legislature. While officially sanctioning collective bargaining in Michigan, it ruled out picketing that would block the public roadway or entrance or egress from the employer's property. In a New York speech Murphy said, simply: "The state must retain its police power."[1]

As the conservative backlash mounted, communications among lawyers fighting the trend was improving with the growth of the National Lawyers Guild. While motives for joining the Guild were diverse (only opposition to the American Bar Association united its members), a Left-liberal tenor existed throughout the organization, and the vast majority supported the CIO.

The origins of the lawyers guild are usually traced to Morris Ernst of the liberal New York firm and several of his pro–New Deal, anti–corporate law friends who met in the City Club early in December 1936. But Sugar—who was not only a charter member but on the guild's first executive board—claimed credit for the idea. When he made his lecture tour in 1933, it occurred to him how isolated liberal lawyers were. "By the time I had returned to Detroit, I had worked up an outline for a national bar association of liberal lawyers." He felt New York was the place to start and sent the plan to "some New York lawyers of my acquaintance." They "doubted that the time was opportune." He wrote again in 1935 "and in the winter of that year . . . met with a group of attorneys" there who indicated they were for the plan but would need time to launch it.

Morris Ernst was one of them. They met with other liberals in the city and finally initiated the organization in December of 1936. Ernst wrote Sugar, "I fully believe that this is the start of the very thing that you had in mind when you were here last winter," and asked him to organize a Detroit chapter. By midsummer close to three thousand lawyers had enrolled nationwide. Its prime objective, said its first permanent national president, Judge Devaney, was to convince "the ordinary citizen that all the members of the bar are not working to defeat the legitimate demands and aims of the great masses of the people for a better and fuller life." A network of "people's lawyers" thus rapidly emerged. Almost immediately, however, it was labeled a "Communist front."[2]

Anticommunism had been in the air for some time. If anything, Popular Front had increased the fears of the conservatives because it seemed to bring Communists into the mainstream of world politics. The 1936 presidential campaign was marked by red-baiting attacks on Roosevelt by the Liberty League and the Hearst publications. The landslide victory over Landon and the "economic royalists," however, silenced such talk for a while. The postelection liberal euphoria itself was a factor in the success of the sit-down movement. But in following the press carefully in the spring of 1937, one can see a creeping revival of the "red question" as the sit-downs were increasingly condemned by the establishment. Just as important, red-baiting also became an instrument in the attacks of Green and the AFL on Lewis and the CIO. In late March, Green had explicitly condemned the sit-down tactic, calling it "illegal" and "Communist inspired." By late May, the AFL's executive council declared all-out war on the CIO and told central bodies to expel "all CIO locals." Frank Martel, who had strongly supported the auto drive, was forced again to back away. John Frey also

221

hit the Communist issue again, but International Typographical Union president Charles Howard tried to set a more moderate tone.[3]

More disturbing was the fact that anticommunism was becoming a factor in UAW politics. Flint local elections pitted Travis, Roy Reuther, and their allies against people who declared their loyalty to Martin. Many of the latter had been associated with the pre-sit-down leadership of Local 156 and were decidedly right-wing. Martin had already demoted Henry Kraus from the general editorship of the *United Auto Worker,* replacing him with William Munger, a man later proved to be a dedicated Lovestonite anti-Communist. Martin was making moves against Travis and branding him a Communist every chance he got. Moreover. he did not deny a *New York Times* report accusing the Communists of fomenting a recent rash of wildcat sit-downs in Flint that actually arose from a failure on both the company's and union's part to handle grievances in a timely fashion. Martin had even intimated that the slowness of Chrysler workers to evacuate the plants in Detroit after the sit-down truce had been work of the reds.

The Flint election pointed up clearly Martin's main motives—to consolidate the union's power where it stood and centralize his authority. The main issues dividing the Travis and Martin slates concerned the latter's desire to subdivide the local and curb membership drives in order to benefit the current members. Facing defeat, Martin found a majority at an open meeting on April 18 willing to "cancel" primary elections. Shortly thereafter, Travis was demoted to plain "organizer," and Roy Reuther reassigned. In Detroit, Kraus was removed entirely from the paper, Mortimer assigned to St. Louis, and Victor Reuther to Adrian, Michigan. The only prominent anti-Martinite who survived the onslaught was Walter Reuther, who reorganized his eighteen thousand–member west-side local (Number 174) along the lines of Toledo, creating an assembly representing its thirty-six plants—one delegate for every five hundred members—that would govern the local. Officers would still be elected by the entire membership. This democratization, which also maintained an important power bloc on the local level, was warmly applauded by Mortimer, who swore in the new officers. It was a plan that could work in Flint, but Martin successfully opposed its adoption there.

At the long Washington, DC executive-board meeting that concluded on May 9, Martin's decisions regarding staffers were ratified, and the way was paved for his reelection. Opponents recognized that his frequent flights around the country to address meetings in his impressive preacher style (he was dubbed the Peter Pan of the labor movement) still made him the most popular figure in the union. Moreover, the Communists, under instructions from Browder himself, backed away from direct confrontation, feeling that unity at this point was too important. This was not a position universally shared by their allies, including Mortimer, Travis, and other Left Flint leaders and the Reuther brothers. None of them supported wildcat strikes and outright rank-and-file insurgency, for the union was too fragile to sustain much of that, but they were experienced Martin observers and knew that he had to be opposed openly.[4]

Another decision of the April-May 1937 executive board meeting was to forge ahead with the Ford organizing drive. In the midst of the meetings, Martin had publicly announced a plan to take Ford to the NLRB for unfair labor practices. He did so without getting any clearance from the board at all, a practice he would soon make a habit of. This was all Martin wanted to do, for he wanted to go slow in organizing Ford, concerned as he was about the consolidation and centralization of the union. There is even a possibility that he had already been in touch with Ford executives, a point to which we shall return. In any case, the board endorsed a full organizing effort and gave Richard Frankensteen the job of leading it. Walter Reuther, as head of the west-side local, was the other key figure in the fight.

More and more Ford workers had been taking cards since the court decision and retaliation was not yet fully underway. Bill McKie, Shelton Tappes, and all those who had labored in the shadows to open Ford up could now begin to see some daylight. The law was on their side, and indeed Sugar, Davidow, and Sugar's associate, Jack Tucker, were in the process of amassing evidence of Ford's brutality and espionage.

Then, on May 16, 1937, came the counterattack. Little cards bearing "Fordisms," pearls of wisdom from the king of Dearborn, were distributed to the company's 150 thousand employees. The message was direct: "Our men ought to consider whether it is necessary to pay some outsider every month for the privilege of working at Ford's." Moreover, "corporate control and labor control . . . are two ends of the same rope. A little group of those who control both capital and labor will sit down in New York and settle prices, dividends, and wages." All one needed to add was the word "Jewish" to the conspiracy, and it would be Adolph Hitler speaking. Moreover, physical force had already been used, as Ford service men beat up three UAW organizers in Chicago the week before.

The UAW began its push against Ford in earnest on May 25, opening two offices in Detroit just across the Dearborn boundary. The Rouge plant was the target. With ninety thousand workers, it was the largest automobile factory in the world. Huge banners on the union offices boldly proclaimed, "Unionism, Not Fordism" and "Yesterday General Motors, Tomorrow Ford." Walter Reuther noted in a *Daily Worker* interview that solid groundwork had been laid: "For the past eight months, while all on the surface was quiet, we have been holding these small group meetings throughout the plant with the aim of developing leaders in the shop who can carry through the campaign."

They also planned a direct propaganda effort. With a carefully worded leaflet cleared by Sugar, the organizing committee managed, after some difficulty, to cajole the Dearborn city clerk to authorize distribution. On May 27, several dozen young women from the 174 Auxilliary and Emergency Brigade were to distribute the leaflets at the five main plant gates. Reuther, Frankensteen, Robert Kanter, and J. J. Kennedy were to direct the operation. They mounted the walkway over Miller Road at Gate 4 in order to survey the placement of the distributors. In seconds the most famous beating in the history of auto organizing began. Reuther and Frankensteen were singled out and pummeled by a dozen Ford service-department thugs. They were kicked in the face, ribs, stomach, and groin and knocked senseless before being bounced down the iron steps. Below, other union men and many women were attacked, brutally beaten, and leaflets thrown to the wind. Although Henry Bennett, Ford's "personnel" director, denied participation by his company goons, it was obvious that the Battle of the Overpass was a calculated operation intended to frighten the union off.

It had the reverse effect. As the union stated, "Today the world has seen the true character of the Ford Motor Co. We don't intend that it shall forget it." It gave tangible proof of the reign of terror operating at Ford. It certainly "destroy[ed] the Ford myth of benevolence and philanthrophy." In many respects, despite the pain of the victims (neither Reuther nor Frankensteen, the most viciously attacked, sustained lasting injuries), the beatings were potentially a gold mine for the UAW.

Immediately, at Sugar's instigation, a one-man grand jury formed for another purpose was converted into a preliminary hearing on the attacks. The court (Judge Liddy) recommended further investigation by the NLRB, and hearings before the board, based on a long and detailed complaint filed by Sugar, began on July 6. The complaint listed not only the incidents of May 27 but a variety of other Ford violations of the Wagner Act, including general antiunion propaganda, a loyalty pledge ("vote-of-confidence" cards) issued on June 1, attempts to get employees to join an ill-disguised company union, and thirty-seven documented cases of firings, layoffs, transfers, or demotions due to union activity. It is noteworthy that the daily press reprinted the complaint in full. One of the reasons (and perhaps Bennett's men's biggest mistake) was also found in the complaint: "respondent [the company], by its officers, agents, employees and representatives, sought to and did willfully and forcibly interfere with, threaten, and intimidate representatives of the public press by seeking to seize and by seizing, their cameras, films, notes and memoranda, by pursuing them on the public highways, and by other acts of force, violence and intimidation."

Thus when the hearing began before trial examiner John T. Lindsay, press coverage was extensive and sympathetic. The *Free Press* pictured Sugar, pipe in hand, Lindsay, and Ford attorney Louis J. Columbo overseeing measurements being taken at the scene of the beatings. The *News* applauded Lindsay for stifling Columbo's attempt to show that the UAW was "lawless." The shoe seemed to be, however fleetingly, on the other foot. The *Times* reported other aspects of the situation, including the developing criminal proceedings against several of the service men arising from Judge Liddy's grand-jury investigation. All gave voluminous details on the hearings, of which the entire story was first told by Reuther on July 7. The *News* also included Columbo's artless red-baiting of Reuther in cross-examination and accompanied the story with his photo, looking relaxed and confident on the witness stand. Over the next two weeks, parades of witnesses followed, and Ford's dirty linen was on display. The deep history of spying, intimidation, firings, blacklistings, and all the rest were entered into the record and the press followed it closely. The word "crimes" was often used by newspapers to describe Ford acts. Sugar even had the opportunity to pry out of foreman Harry Reynolds the story that he had once been fired for shaking hands with him. Unionism also gained sympathetic coverage in the Monroe, Michigan confrontation between the Newton Steel Company and the Steel Workers Organizing Committee (SWOC), which ended in another brutal police riot on June 10. The UAW rallied to SWOC's support, and Sugar filed suits totaling a hundred thousand dollars on behalf of injured picketers against "the mayor, police chief, sheriff, and vigilantes."[5]

During this early summer glow of sympathy, Sugar and the Ford organizers devised another publicity operation in Dearborn. They hit upon a plan to use the technicalities of the law to their advantage. Sugar pointed out that while Dearborn Ordinance Number 67 banned unauthorized distribution of "circulars and handbills," it said nothing about newspapers. And Ordinance Number 36 required newspaper *sales*people to be licensed, but said nothing about giving newspapers away. Thus they planned a free distribution of the *United Auto Worker,* a recognized and legitimate paper, for July 7.

Sugar wrote Frank Murphy a long letter recalling the violence of May 26 and asking the governor for state police protection; this was based upon the assumption that local authorities would not do their job. He also pointed out that the Dearborn leaflet ordinance was unconstitutional in any case. After getting the opinion of his attorney general, who thought it presumptuous of the UAW to ask for protection of "*their* constitutional rights . . . when they have constantly flouted the law and the rights of others," Murphy responded, "I must assume that the local authorities will comply with the law" and added that if they "fail[ed] to do so, legal remedies [were] available." In other words, no state police would be provided. The UAW therefore canceled its first effort, which would have coincided with the opening of the NLRB hearings.

On July 23, the plan was renewed, as Sugar sent letters to Murphy and Dearborn police chief Carl Brooks. To the first he made the same request as before. He informed Brooks that the distribution would occur on August 11 and asked for "adequate precautions for the protection of the persons engaged in the distribution." The reply from Dearborn corporation counsel, James E. Greene, not made until August 6, took the amazing position that since he was unable to find the UAW listed among the firms and corporations of Michigan, it was therefore a "legal nonentity." Hence "we . . . are at a loss as to whom the city shall offer or afford the police protection you demand."

Sugar replied on August 9 with one of the great letters of his career. After documenting that Carl Brooks had been placed in the Dearborn Police Department by Harry Bennett in 1923, he launched a measured invective worthy of Voltaire: "It is to be regretted, Mr. Greene, that your knowledge of the law is not as great as your devotion to the Ford Motor Company. The International Union, United Automobile Workers of America is not a corporation and it is not a partnership, but if you will turn to page one of any appropriate treatise on the subject you will no doubt be startled to note that the Union is an unincorporated, voluntary association, falling in exactly the same category as thousands of other groups—unions, lodges, clubs and societies." Sugar then pointed out that the Knights of Dearborn, a Ford-sponsored, 100-percent "American," "fraternal" association, must be a nonentity too. To verify the fact, Greene might get in touch with its current president, Sam Taylor, in care of the Ford service department. Failing that, "you should be able to make contact with him when he appears for trial next month on the charge of felonious assault upon members of the nonentity, the UAWA."

Sugar continued, "In the event that you desire to make further study of the problem, perhaps we can be of help to you." At the recent NLRB hearings, this nonentity had brought charges and been recognized by the federal government. Indeed "there appeared at the hearing one James E. Greene, . . . who requested permission to intervene in the hearing to 'protect the interests of the City of Dearborn.' We are certain that a lawyer of Mr. Greene's standing would never have asked . . . to intervene in a hearing instituted by a nonentity." He then pointed out that the UAW newspaper had been granted mailing privileges by the federal government and that legally recognized contracts existed between the nonentity and hundreds of employers. Moreover, "if it is not an imposition, we suggest that you examine the statutes of this State. You will be astounded to learn that since the year 1897, these statutes expressly provide for the status of such associations as legal entities."

But in any case, Sugar continued, the UAW did not seek protection for an abstract "entity": "You can't gang up on an entity or a nonentity and pound it into insensibility or fracture its skull or break its back. What we really want is protection for people, real, live American men and women." In conclusion, Sugar said, "Your letter must be considered more than an impertinence. It must be considered as a direct incitement to violence on the part of those interested in depriving the members of the Union of their constitutional rights." It "constitutes a sanction of criminal conduct on their part."

Sugar's letter was made public and written up by the press. Murphy decided to send state police "to observe." Representatives from the NLRB, the sheriff's and prosecutor's offices, the LaFollette Committee, and the Conference for the Protection of Civil Rights showed up as well. Even Cornelia Bryce Pinchot, the prominent humanitarian, was on hand. On the appointed day one thousand UAW members carried out the distribution. They did so without incident as the world looked on.[6]

Such marvellous publicity, however, went to waste because the Ford drive soon became mired in the great factional conflict that plagued the union for the next year and a half. The fight between Homer Martin and his so-called Progressive caucus (he preempted the traditional Leftist terminology) and the Unity caucus would become an all-absorbing struggle that severely affected the union's capacity to operate. It coincided with a major slump in automobile sales in

1937–38. Layoffs and disgust with union leadership combined to reduce drastically the paid-up membership in the UAW. In the end, as Martin and his opponents fought it out in late 1938 and early 1939, it was not at all clear to whom one should pay dues.

While not so obvious at the time, historical consensus exists on one point: Homer Martin was an unstable charlatan. Moreover, as one wit put it, "he gave megalomania a bad name." But worst of all, perhaps, was his embarrassing lack of knowledge about facts and concepts essential to the union's health. The other officers covered for him on many occasions. These various traits combined to make him a positive danger in and of himself. But the problem did not stop there. Beginning in March 1937, Martin made a definitive commitment to Jay Lovestone and his circle of self-proclaimed Communist anti-Communists by appointing Munger as editor of the *United Auto Worker,* Francis Hensen as administrative assistant to the president, Eve Stone as head of the Women's Auxilliary, and Irving Brown as an International organizer. George F. Miles (alias Alex Bail), Stone's husband, served as Lovestone's chief correspondent. And sometime in early 1938, Martin began secret personal discussions with Harry Bennett and met with Henry Ford himself.

What this all meant was simple enough: Martin had to be dealt with. How to do it and under what circumstances was another matter. He got it into his head—undoubtedly assisted by Munger and company—that the chief threat to his power came from the Communists and their purported allies. The only problem was that during the summer, fall, and winter of 1937–38, as noted, the Communist position was not to fight, just to deny, accusations regarding their "disruptive" activities, especially the troubling problem of continuing unauthorized strikes. The Unity caucus was a rather fragile grouping that included the Communist contingent in the union, their friends and allies, most of the Socialists and their friends, and Left-liberal or unpolitical trade-unionists of the stripe of George Addes or Ed Hall. At the beginning, Martin's key ally was Frankensteen, although he switched sides in May 1938 as he came to understand Martin's motives. Among names of note, only R. J. Thomas, the hero of the Chrysler-Jefferson strike and president of that local, stayed by Martin until the late stages of the fight in early 1939. Martin's only significant allies on the Left were Trotskyists.

Neither of the factions was stable. Certain Socialists vacillated in tune with the international situation, while opportunists of all sorts abandoned the Martin ship as the wind blew against him. Just about the only "principle" uniting the Progressive caucus was anti-Communism (or *anti-Stalinism,* to be precise), while the Unity caucus was united only in self-defense against Martin.

The long and tangled history of the Martin fight need not be repeated here. But Sugar did play a critical role in it and the perspective provided by his collection of materials on it allows us to view it from a unique vantage point. That the battle was central in making the UAW what it was goes without saying.[7]

It first seemed as if things might be patched up. The late August convention of the UAW in Milwaukee took place in the midst of factional strife, but CIO officials—finally including Lewis himself—attempted to introduce some harmony by balancing the officers. Martin was unstoppable for president, as was Addes, who had done a marvellous job overseeing union finances and business affairs, for secretary-treasurer. Lewis proposed five vice presidents: Mortimer, Hall, Walter Wells (the incumbents), Frankensteen, and Thomas. This made a place for most of the union's major figures and tipped the balance slightly to Martin, for Wells was with him and Addes had not yet committed himself. The executive-board elections of nonofficers, given Martin's power at the convention, gave the Progressives a 14 to 8 edge. Walter Reuther and Mortimer pled for and got Unity-caucus acquiescence. Lewis held his breath and hoped he had made peace. Unfortunately, a thick residue of bitterness remained after Milwaukee.

Another event, little discussed in standard UAW histories, that might have acted as a force for harmony was the Common Council election that fall. While Martinites babbled about the "red menace" in local union halls, a renewed effort at independent labor political representation developed. This time it was firmly CIO, whose state and local councils had been set up recently after the AFL expelled all CIO unions. Frank Martel did not support the labor slate, but that made much less difference now. The candidates were Sugar, Walter Reuther, Frankensteen, R. J. Thomas, and Tracy Doll, an anti-Greer activist and Socialist from the Hudson local. It was a good slate, balancing Martin and anti-Martin people and giving representation to left-wing opinions as well as mainstream politics. A complicating factor was the candidacy of Democrat Patrick O'Brien for mayor. O'Brien, a former Upper Peninsula judge, state attorney general, and staunch defender of Left and liberal causes, entered the race without consultation with the CIO. After he surprised everyone by finishing second in the primary to Richard Reading, a Republican and inveterate red-baiter with KKK connections, the labor slate had no choice but to link up with him. He probably had a negative effect on the chances of the UAW candidates. As Campaign Chairman Alan Strachan remarked, "Judge O'Brien lacked the color and glamour to inspire the auto workers to really get behind him. Again, at his age, he can hardly be expected to be the representative of a young, militant, vigorous organization such as the UAW."

With the full force of the UAW behind it (and Martin stymied, at least when it came to red-baiting Sugar or Reuther), this labor candidacy did quite well, with all five candidates making it through the primary and Sugar finishing an impressive seventh. He seemed a shoo-in for a spot on the council, and Frankensteen had finished ninth. Even Doll and Reuther, who were thirteenth and fourteenth seemed to have a chance. But when the final vote was in, they finished in the same order but were slotted at tenth (Sugar seemed jinxed), eleventh, thirteenth, fourteenth, and fifteenth with Thomas moving up well.

What had happened? Strachan wrote an excellent postelection analysis that may serve as a guide. It pointed up a number of important problems. The difficulty was not the candidates. "Of the candidates," wrote Strachan, "one cannot speak too highly. Maurice Sugar closed his law practice and devoted himself full time to the campaign. Through his previous political experience he was a tremendous asset to the Political Action Committee." Strachan then assessed the key problems. It was a class-conscious campaign. Detroiters were asked to "vote labor" and the whole structure of the political process created a "labor-versus-capital" complexion. They frightened the "middle class, particularly the small businessman, who was led to believe that industry would move out of the city and taxes would increase" if the labor candidates were elected. One of their opponents even talked about a "dictatorship of the proletariat." On the other hand, it was possible that the resolve of working men and women was increased by such an emphasis, creating a solid "150,000 votes [Sugar got 145,342] that all the propaganda and vilification of the reactionaries cannot shake." Strachan felt that if pro-UAW voters had "plunked" for council (voting only for the five labor candidates), they might well have outdistanced the last three "establishment" winners. Most failed to do so out of fear of spoiling their ballots.

Two other problems were important, both heartbreaking for Sugar. The first was the black vote. The campaign was frank in its appeal: "Don't Fear the CIO" said a headline in their little newspaper published explicitly for the black community:

> In all the shops, the CIO organizes Black and White Workers together without discrimination. Moreover, in all the shops with CIO control will be found Negro stewards and members of shop committees and officials enjoying all the privileges of union members.
>
> In other words, the CIO comes to the unskilled Negro Worker as a Godsend because he is for the first time recognized as being of organizational worth and placed in equality with his white brother.

The networks that Sugar had developed were reactivated—though among the churchmen, only the liberals like Charles Hill would now risk support—and his record of defense of black people was reiterated. The removal of Heinrich Pickert was one of the main planks in the platform, an attractive point for blacks, who had tasted police brutality more regularly even than UAW militants. The labor slate also supported Snow Grigsby's struggle for jobs for blacks in municipal departments. And indeed, in the primary, the UAW candidates, led far and away by Sugar, did well in black wards.

Then came disaster. Strachan described it clearly:

> The one fatal blow was the holding of a dance by Local No. 235 [DeSoto] at the Book Cadillac Hotel at which Negroes were barred. This barring is in itself bad

229

enough, but to make matters worse, the Local refused to fight for the rights of its colored members to attend this dance. Following this, the Negro press carried a streamer headline, "Jim Crowism in the UAW." The reaction of the Negro people to this was natural and did a great deal to destroy the prestige of the UAW as a union and to have a serious effect on the political campaign.

Although Sugar wrote a "refreshing" letter, sent out to the locals over Homer Martin's name, about the incident, the damage was done. While Sugar still ran well in black neighborhoods, O'Brien lost badly to Reading and the other labor candidates fared far worse in the final election.

The second problem was internal. While the campaign, by uniting members of the opposing factions on the same slate, seemed to serve the cause of reconciliation, factionalism may have undermined it, particularly because Martin chose October to mount his verbal barrage against the enemy. Some campaign workers and boosters actually worked only for their factional heroes, going to the point, earlier in the campaign, of painting out the names of factional opponents on campaign tire covers and posters. Strachan felt they were lucky that the daily press did not make more of the matter than it did. Overall, however, "it must be recognized that the internal situation in the UAW did not help the campaign."[8]

Sugar's preoccupation with the campaign, followed by his annual pilgrimage to the north, took him out of the factional nitty-gritty. In December, he returned to reality and was greeted by the resurrection of Larry Davidow. He had largely eclipsed Davidow as the union's attorney, handling almost all of the major cases, culminating in the NLRB hearings on Ford. But his associations placed him on the wrong side of Homer Martin. Though we lack the details of how it happened, Sugar was relieved of his duties on December 30 in a letter not from Martin himself but from hatchetman Fred Pieper, brought up from Atlanta to work on the problem of "staff reduction" occasioned by the recession in auto. In many respects, the Martin fight pitted the periphery (UAW locals in Missouri, Wisconsin, Indiana, Georgia, the West, and the East) against the center (southeast Michigan and northern Ohio). Martin himself had always been a kind of outsider and gathered the more distant, less sophisticated types like Pieper around him. Sugar wrote Martin for confirmation and got it: "I am in general agreement." He went on ("Dear Maurice" had been the opening),

It is my hope that you will turn over all material to Larry Davidow. . . .

In the future, we are trying to cut down expenses for legal work by coordinating all our work under one head. This does not imply that the cost of your services or the services of the other attorneys we used have been exorbitant, but the fact that we had no special plan resulted in an enormous total outlay for legal work.

I want you to know that I appreciate very much all the work you did for us in the past and hope that our personal friendship may continue.

Signing "Fraternally Yours," Martin had just closed another door behind him. The purges had by now removed dozens of people who had been central to the process of union building. Many, but by no means all, were associated with the Communists. Even the hero of Flint, Bob Travis, was forced out and was lucky to land a job with the mine workers in New Jersey.

The factional battles now became very involved and do not merit retelling. The simplest outline, however, shows Martin's red-baiting becoming increasingly shrill after the Communist party finally began to condemn him in January, Walter Reuther and other Socialists cooling toward the Unity caucus after debates with the Communists over collective security and the Spanish Civil War, the Communists' sudden switch from Vic Reuther to (then) Martinite Richard Leonard for vice president at the first state CIO convention in late April (thus incurring the Reuthers' enduring hatred of them), the CP's wooing and winning of Frankensteen away from Martin in May, and Homer's near apoplectic fit thereafter.

Then came the move to the center ring: Martin decided to suspend all the officers except Thomas. Sugar now reentered the picture. Martin's charges, written up by Davidow, were many and complex, but they boiled down to this: the officers had been conspiring all along to remove him from office illegally and had undermined the union in so doing. The immediate circumstance was a special board meeting on June 6, 1938 called to discuss a group insurance plan that Martin fancied. The meeting was turned into a censure vote against Martin when he and three of his followers were absent. This action was deemed both illegal and inappropriate in light of the "twenty-point program" of unified action adopted at the last (May 26) Board meeting. The fact was that with the defection of Frankensteen (which Keeran argues *was* the result of a meeting with Communist leaders Weinstone, Foster, and B. K. Gebert, as claimed by Martin and Davidow at the time), Martin realized that he was in trouble, pushed for reconciliation, and hoped for the best. The Unity caucus had smelled blood and tried to bring the situation to a head on June 6. Martin countered with the suspensions, which were to be followed by a trial before the executive board to expel the five men from the union altogether. This gathering finally took place from July 25 to August 6.

The opening briefs of Davidow and Sugar have survived and make interesting reading. The heart of the Martin argument was that the five tried to set up a counterunion (the term *dual* is used). As early as March 1938, Mortimer and Hall took a separate post-office-box number (Henson, in fact, had been opening their mail) to serve as their faction's address. After the suspension they went all out, attempting to stop all the union business by directing that a hold be put on the mails and on the union bank account. Sugar had sought a court order to that effect and consistently advised the five to make the break. Martin, whose authority was respected, for better or worse, by outside authorities, was able to block these moves, but included them in the charges. Davidow's brief also spent a good deal of time talking about people, like Travis, Mortimer, and Kraus. who were, he said, "by common reputation . . . communist." He also pictured Frankensteen as a "captive" of the Communists and in general red-baited at every opportunity. He called upon a former Communist stool pigeon named Jean Herbster to help out.

Sugar built his case around the famous "Lovestone correspondence," a bundle of letters "liberated" from Lovestone's New York apartment by persons unknown, but whom everyone assumed were Communists (Lovestone said they were Russian agents). They were very detailed and showed quite precisely that Munger and company had been manipulating Martin since March 1937. They thought him a fool, but hoped that by keeping the focus on the Communists (and getting rid of their very real influence), they could weaken the Unity caucus enough to allow them to run the union through Martin. On several occasions, they made it clear that they preferred disruption, whatever the cost to the union. Though totally shocked by Frankensteen's switch, they then nicknamed him the "peacemonger." In all, the letters revealed a thoroughly slimy crew. They were an embarrassment to many of their allies, especially Socialists who, like Alan Strachan, had flirted with Martin.

This last brings up a painful subject. Because of the growing feeling on the part of their Socialist allies in the Popular Front that the Communists were not acting in the interests of Loyalist victory in the Spanish Civil War and that they were pursuing a policy in their "collective-security-against-fascism" doctrine that might lead to war, pacifist Norman Thomas was encouraging a kind of "defraternization" with the Communists when the Communists had already attacked the Socialists by abandoning Victor Reuther in the state CIO election in April. Although William Weinstone, the Party district organizer, was demoted for this "mistake," the Reuthers did not forgive the "double cross." While a person like George Addes might legitimately ask what in the world these politics had to do with the union, this was obviously a period of growing disaffection between the ideologues of the two parties. Its consequences were monumental. These conflicts were the roots of the great chasm that would divide the union at a later time. Despite the Communists' attempts to heal the Unity caucus after Weinstone's dismissal, the great factional fight now became almost a three-way affair, with Walter Reuther seeking an independent line. Herein lay the belief among Sugar, Addes, Frankensteen, and their various allies that Reuther was an opportunist and Reuther's that these people were dupes of the Communists. Sugar's perspective adds new information to the controversy.

After the suspension of the officers, Reuther, while saying that they must be "immediately reinstated," nevertheless avoided specifically attacking Martin and, speaking as president of Local Number 174, tried to sound above it all:

> I want to make it clear that I believe the war in the UAW must be stopped immediately. No amount of name-calling among international officers will stop wage cuts or organize competitive plants or solve the problems of the workers,

unemployed or in the shops. The workers in the automobile industry will not tolerate a power struggle between Martin and Frankensteen or anyone else, at a time when the full strength of the union must be behind a constructive program for building the union. . . . Peace is impossible on the basis of the 20-point program.

While the Olympian tone was impressive, it seemed to cover a distinct political perspective, one which had to do with the Socialist-Communist split. Norman Thomas favored Martin because of his pacifism. Thomas's contact man in Detroit, Tucker Smith, had convinced Reuther at least to keep an open mind about Martin. The Socialists knew that Reuther's support for Martin was imperative if the latter were to have a chance. On July 29, he wrote that he thought Reuther might be wooing Martin away from "the reactionaries" and toward "healthy constructive union work." This was during the trial and is good evidence that Reuther was flirting with Martin.

Sugar was more explicit. In a memorandum prepared in 1946, he recalled to old Unity-caucus associates Walter Reuther's behavior in 1938. "It was discovered," Sugar wrote, "that Reuther, while playing along with the anti-Martin forces, had concocted a program of his own and, in the furtherance of his ambitions, had surreptitiously held conferences with Martin at the very height of the struggle—conferences kept secret even from his own colleagues." These were no doubt the meetings that encouraged Tucker Smith to believe that Reuther was urging Martin to abandon the "reactionaries" like Pieper and the Dillonite crowd in Flint. There is nothing inconsistent about all this: Reuther was trying to pull Martin to the Left (though the non-Communist Left) and get him to give up the factional battle.

But there was more. The five officers were in fact found guilty and expelled from the union by a narrow majority on the board. (None of them could vote, of course, since they were suspended.) Sugar's recollections, written in 1971, are critical to understanding the Left's feelings about Reuther. As the anti-Martin board members analyzed the vote at Ed Hall's flat after the trial, it was realized

that some Board members of the trial committee who were presumed to be definitely on "our side" and who were assumed by everyone present to have voted for acquittal must have voted for conviction. This narrowed down to two persons, one of whom was Walter Reuther. Confronted with that charge, Reuther admitted it. I shall not forget the reaction of Frankensteen. He was enraged, arose from his seat, burst out his anger in the threat to immediately leave the room and telephone the newspapers advising them of Reuther's "treachery."

But Sugar convinced Frankensteen that this might have disastrous results for the union. Sugar goes on to say that he then proposed that all the board members sign a pledge forswearing their desire to become president, which would then be passed along to John L. Lewis to prove that ambition was not a factor in the struggle against Martin. "It was signed by everyone present except Walter Reuther." Later, Lewis held a meeting with the anti-Martin board members, Reuther included, and asked him why "I don't see your name here." Reuther said he would explain later, but never did.

Charges regarding Reuther's opportunism abounded throughout the years of his rise to power and multiplied after he achieved it. The general response from the Reuther camp had been that actions appearing to be two-faced in fact were done in the hopes of eliminating factionalism, of reconciling differences. Furthermore, since Reuther never denied his ambition to lead the union, the rest of Sugar's story is easily explained. Such justification did not lessen the Unity caucus's suspicions of Reuther. The division that would widen into an abyss by the forties was formed in the Martin fight.[9]

Sugar achieved a new kind of prominence during the Martin affair. He became extremely close to George Addes, and together they came to represent for a large majority of the union's members the kind of honesty and integrity that they expected of leaders whose salary they paid with their dues. When Martin installed Delmont Garst of Kansas City as acting secretary-treasurer, letters to members from Addes, seconded by Sugar, held payment of the per capita tax to a minimum.

Sugar's integrity was challenged in a public statement by Martin claiming he had said that the "constitution was not worth the paper it is written on." Sugar prepared a written statement circulated to the membership detailing the circumstances: Addes's notification of his trial had come the day before the trial was to occur. The constitution specified that "reasonable time" should be allowed to develop a defense. Martin said a day was reasonable, to which Sugar replied that any constitution that could be so interpreted was not worth the paper it was written on. With typical irony, he concluded, "Both Martin and myself are well known to Union men throughout the country. Because of this I am confident that my version of this incident will be unhesitatingly believed." It obviously was in the end, and Sugar would be entrusted with the task of overseeing the writing of the constitution—passed at the Cleveland convention of March 1939—that would be the instrument guiding the union's affairs for the next decade.

A second incident was even more revealing. At the beginning of the trial itself, Sugar was accosted as he left the elevator on the eleventh floor of the Griswold Building (the union headquarters) by a group of black Martinites. There was some jostling and an exchange. Martin gave reporters the story that Sugar had insulted them. On July 28, Sugar wrote Martin:

> I have your letter in which you presume to speak for the 400,000 members of the UAWA in demanding a public apology from me for what you term my insults to the colored members of the union.
>
> It won't work, my boy, it won't work.
>
> Yesterday you had a group of colored workers stop me. You had the stage set for them to beat me up. One of your associates, Morris Fields, prodded them on. But your little scheme did not work. I talked to these colored workers. And when

our conversation concluded, they realized that no man who had fought for the colored people as I have could be guilty of the things which you had told them I had done and said.

Sugar then reiterated his record and again asked Martin whom he thought the workers of the UAW would believe. This exchange was published and sent to members as part of the fight.

The moral outrage expressed by Sugar was that of the entire anti-Martin force, which was rapidly growing. Local unions fought it out as the "expelled" officers moved into high gear. It was a difficult fight because they were off the payroll. Sugar was getting no money either. Sympathetic printers gave them addressograph plates and extended credit to them. The officers went deeply into debt. But the tide was turning all through the fall, especially after Lewis threw the full weight of the CIO leadership to their side.

Martin got desperate. His anticommunism suddenly became a mortal danger to the union and to the trade-union movement as a whole. Called to testify before the recently formed House Committee on Un-American Activities (which had already perverted the English language by turning such phrases as *fellow traveler* and *communist sympathizer* into frightening code words), Martin "wilted" under the interrogation of its chair, reactionary Democrat Martin Dies of Texas, and "admitted that virtually all strikes which have slowed production in the automobile industry in the last two years were inspired [another word captured by the Right] by Communists." Martin thus insulted the self-determination of U.S. workers, even though he was paying a backhanded (if untrue) compliment to the Communists. From the point of view of Dies and the reactionary trend he represented, of course, it implied—coming from the horse's mouth, after all—that "outside agitators" paid by a "foreign power" were responsible for all the turmoil.[10]

This probably turned the tide against Martin within the union. Things came to a head in early January as local after local declared against Martin. Physical battles between rival "flying squadrons" and shameless red-baiting ensued. The officers called themselves the legitimate power and suspended Martin. He thereupon suspended fifteen more board members. Sugar was kept busy trying to convince banks and suppliers and the post office, as well as members, that they were the real union leaders and Martin the renegade. Sugar also collected depositions from dozens of ex-Martinites about the president's transgressions. More importantly Sugar's investigations of Ford espionage turned up evidence of Martin's connections with Ford executives Harry Bennett and John Gillespie.

Everyone knew that Martin had private meetings with Bennett once the split occurred in January 1939, but Ralph Rimar and others asserted that such meetings went back "months and months" before, opening the possibility that Martin's acts were part of a Ford plot. While it was never proved that Martin was the highest-placed company stooge in history, his cordial relations with the

235

company after he joined up with the AFL in April 1939 led to such speculation. When Ford bought him a house in Dearborn in 1941, it seemed confirmed. Certainly as one looked back at the shambles of the Ford organizing drive of 1937–38, which had seemed so promising in the summer of 1937, it was clear something had gone wrong. Economic woes were significant, but Martin's disasterous course hardly helped.[11]

The cleanup after the Martin affair was protracted. Much of it fell into Sugar's lap as suit and countersuit were filed. The goal was to determine legally whether the UAW-CIO or the UAW-AFL was the real UAW. The fact was that the members had already voted with their feet, and overwhelmingly (although in many fewer total numbers than the union had in 1937), to stay with the CIO. Sugar nevertheless took the court fight quite seriously. In a brilliant move, he lined up Charles P. Taft of Cincinnati, son of the president and brother of "Mr. Republican," Robert Taft, as attorney for the case. This led to some amusing remarks about Taft and communism, but the fact was that the Taft connection reassured many of the union's more conservative members that they had made the right choice in staying with the CIO and quieted the Communist talk in the press and the Congress considerably. Photographs in May of Taft and Sugar consulting provided one of the better news stories of 1939. Taft later pulled out to run for office in Cincinnati, but the publicity value early on was the important thing. The case itself dragged on interminably, only reaching settlement in July 1941, after the Ford victory. While the UAW-AFL maintained the right to exist, that was about all. Homer was really finished as of March 1939.[12]

It was time to return to Henry, although the UAW first had to get things back into some semblance of order. Membership had declined precipitously from a high approaching a half million in mid-1937 to around 150 thousand in early 1939. Martin was able to shear off only a paltry number, and when his personal convention met in Detroit on March 4, snickers about the size of his following abounded. He did retain some real strength in Ford, however, and this would be one of the key problems for the UAW-CIO in organizing this last bastion of employer resistance. Martin could not merely be dismissed, and most people at the time assumed the key battle ahead remained the struggle between the rival unions. Sugar, in his legal report of March 21, 1939, emphasized that this was the central legal problem faced by the union, more important than NLRB work or assistance in negotiations. When the AFL threw its entire weight behind auto organizing in April, when companies seemed eager to sign up with it, and both red-baited the CIO during the summer and fall of 1939, its importance could not be denied. Only historical hindsight (since the CIO won so clearly) has minimized the ongoing battle.

The anti-Martin forces met in special convention in Cleveland on March 27. With the eyes of the trade-union world on them, the delegates faced a number of difficult problems, but the central one was the image of the union. Martin's maniacal red-baiting had taken its toll and the Dies Committee had hardly helped matters. Fear of war was rampant and the stand of the Communists denouncing Munich and appeasement made them doubly suspect. Top CIO leaders wanted to bind the wounds of the Martin fight and scotch all rumors of "Communist domination." Sidney Hillman and Philip Murray, Lewis's chief lieutenants in the CIO, were dispatched to Cleveland, as were key leaders in all the political groupings in the country, including the Communists. The CIO position emerged quickly: for the sake of unity and hopefully to woo more Martinites to the UAW-CIO, why not elect R. J. Thomas, a last-minute convert and a good, solid union man, to the presidency?

The other logical candidates were Wyndham Mortimer and George Addes. The former was probably too strongly identified with the Left to go down well with public opinion, but Addes seemed the perfect candidate. Born in Wisconsin of immigrant Lebanese parents, he was a good Catholic and staunch trade-unionist. He had experience in the shops of Detroit and Toledo and played a role in the great Auto-Lite strike of 1934. His schooling in accounting and his extraordinary ability to attend to administrative detail, as well as his impeccable record in handling union funds, gave him the bureaucratic skills and moral appeal requisite to the job. He was also the most popular man in the union and would have been overwhelmingly elected.

Hillman and Murray, however, were fixed in their purpose. More surprising, so was the top leadership of the Communist party. Party policy makers had been very concerned about the impact of red-baiting on the labor movement and had determined on a position of total support for Lewis and the established powers in the CIO. Anything that would build the industrial trade-union movement, whatever the consequences for the visible (or invisible) strength of the Party, should receive support. Such a policy was predicated, in the larger perspective, on the need to sustain the democratic struggle against fascism. It sometimes put the Communists in ridiculous positions—like voting for anti-Communist resolutions in union conventions—but it was deemed preferable to taking an ideological stand that might both hurt the labor movement and end toleration of Party activists within it altogether.

This was a worldwide policy, based loosely on the Popular Front position of the Third International. In the U.S. case, under the leadership of Browder, there was now, and would continue to be through the undulations of Soviet policy for the next six years, a tendency to exaggerate the "line." It might be said that national Party leadership took the position of the International and squared it. Such a tendency bore the potential not only of making the Party look foolish, but, much more seriously, of causing it to lose sight of its Marxist purpose, which was, after all, the creation of a Socialist United States.

But in a latter-day—and flawed—version of "one step backward, two steps forward," Browder, supported by Gebert, ordered the Communists in the union to support Thomas. While Party members like Anderson and Ganley did so—not without misgivings—those whose ties to the Party were looser, like Sam Sweet of Dodge Local 51, argued vehemently to the contrary. Support for Mortimer was no longer conceivable, and the scene now shifted to George

Addes's hotel room. Mortimer and Travis said in effect that they would not oppose Addes's nomination, but Sugar and Lee Pressman actively encouraged him to run. This was not an untypical position for Sugar to be in, for he regularly disagreed with Party positions. Left opinion since—including all the principals except Browder—is unanimous that support for Thomas was a mistake not only because it seriously reduced the influence of the Communist Left and presented more of an opening for Walter Reuther but also simply because it gave the UAW less competent leadership.

Addes, for his part, now concedes that he should have followed Sugar's advice and made the stand anyway. The Communists had already gained their political mileage out of their pledge of obeisance to Lewis (indeed they could even have voted for Thomas), and Addes would have won easily in a two-man race. But Murray and Hillman sat him down and cajoled and threatened and pled. Murray, a devout Catholic, leery, like Addes, of the recently formed anti-Communist Association of Catholic Trade Unionists, had long had a brotherly influence over Addes and now applied the pressure. Hillman stressed that Roosevelt wanted unity in the trade-union movement, especially in this time of national crisis with economic recession and war clouds in Europe combining to threaten the very fabric of U.S. democracy. Addes also remembered that the Russian-born Jewish leader of the Amalgamated Clothing Workers had emphasized that Addes's swarthy complexion gave him a "foreign" look that would not sit well with public opinion. "I then made the biggest mistake of my life," he said in 1979. He acquiesced. Thomas ran unopposed and Addes was returned by acclamation to his post as secretary-treasurer. He was now second man in the union, because all the vice presidencies were eliminated.

The Communists continued their weird dance of death and did not even bother to put Mortimer or Party whip Nat Ganley up for the executive board. Addes was now their key friend in high places, although he was bemused by their antics. While executive-board members like LeRoy Roberts from Indianapolis, Richard Reisinger and Paul Miley (both friends of Mortimer's from Ohio), and Leo LaMotte from Detroit remained trustworthy allies of the Left, the fact was that with the effacement of Mortimer, Sugar as general counsel found himself in the not always comfortable position of being the person most closely identified with the pro-Soviet Left in the high leadership of the union.[13]

Sugar's appointment by Thomas as general counsel was a foregone conclusion. His perception of his task and of his relationship to the trade-union movement as rendered in reports to Martin in 1937 and to Thomas in 1939 demonstrate the distance that separated him from a knee-jerk fellow traveler. But there also was an evolution from one report to the other showing that Sugar himself was beginning to feel the enormous pressures that also drove the Communists toward accommodation in 1939.

The earlier report, made August 9, 1937, provides a summary of Sugar's conception of the law and the labor lawyer in relationship to the working-class movement. The GM and Chrysler injunction cases, he wrote, "called for the presentation to the courts and simultaneously to the people of the country, of a new concept of property rights as applied to the employer-employee relationship. [They] also called for the use of the courts as an instrumentality in publicizing to the world the iniquitous practices of the corporations. . . . One of our principal objectives was to reflect on the legal field the offensive of labor on the industrial field. Thus militant unionism was brought to play on all fronts." While, technically speaking, the legal battles were lost, they contributed immensely to the overall victory. "Labor cannot win a strike in court; but labor may prevent a strike from being lost in court."

This was vintage Sugar. It was rooted in the historical reality, stressed from the dawn of his career, that the employer, upon a serious challenge from labor, "has turned to the machinery of the state for aid—and . . . has not turned in vain. This is as might be expected since the employer has in the past, with rare exceptions, completely dominated and controlled the state machinery." Sugar went on to catalog the ways the lawyers had helped to fight the combined forces of the bosses and the state in 1937—picketing rights, criminal cases (the police "shoot them, then prosecute them for being shot!"), collective bargaining, and the rest. But he left no doubt that the real power was not the law or lawyers "but the active and vigorous marshalling of all forces at the command of the union," that is, workers on the march.

Even in discussing the National Labor Relations Act, Sugar played down the idea of the law as a panacea, while emphasizing the "utmost importance" of "bringing the employers to account for their wholesale violations of the NLRA." But even here, lawyers remain less important than the setting up of "machinery in every local for handling the preliminaries in all cases where members are victimized by employers." Lawyers and the law should be servants of the workers.

Sugar certainly did not change this opinion, but circumstances over the next two years altered the situation dramatically. The law was becoming more and more crucial to the UAW and the labor movement generally. Sugar's report of April 24, 1939 to R. J. Thomas, in which he outlined the plan for the creation of a legal department under the full-time direction of a general counsel and using three other lawyers on a full-time basis, makes this abundantly clear. The Martin fight itself created hundreds of matters demanding legal attention and the struggle with the AFL would create hundreds more. Moreover "the normal legal work which goes with collective bargaining . . . is now greatly increased due to the employers' desire to take advantage of the difficulties created by the anti-CIO forces." National Labor Relations Board election cases, he noted, would increase as well.

But it was the opportunities afforded by the NLRB to which Sugar wished to give greatest emphasis.

> In addition to those matters which I have already mentioned, it is my opinion that the National Labor Relations Act offers the opportunity for the prosecution of a large number of cases against anti-union employers with real prospect of success. I

am of the view that a great many "good" cases go "by the boards" for want either of recognition on our part that action is warranted under the Act, or simply negligence in failing to present them. I think that too great stress cannot be laid upon the value of the prosecution of these cases. The organization of workers into our Union, and their retention, once organized, often depends upon action or lack of action under the Act. I am of the opinion that great value will follow upon diligent work in this field.

He noted that the work was important enough to warrant full-time work by an attorney on nothing else.

True as this may have been, we have an important indication here that even a radical labor lawyer like Sugar was most intrigued by the possibilities of the law working on labor's behalf. It is perhaps significant that neither this report nor the one submitted to the Cleveland convention said anything about the employers' "domination of the law," using the courts as forums, or statements about final victories coming "in the industrial field." Sugar had not changed his mind about such matters, but the tone of 1939 was both more "professional" and more optimistic about what the law might do. Workers had a friend in the NLRB. Why not exploit it to the hilt?

He spent most of the report outlining the structure of the legal department. While hardly a bureaucratic maze, its purpose was to regularize, coordinate, and make cost-effective the legal work of the union. Sugar would operate from his own facilities and use three lawyers of his own choosing for the full-time tasks involved. Regular processing of problems and cases, assigned by Sugar, would occur. A file of reliable and knowledgeable lawyers across the country would be created, and such people would be retained for local union work. Sugar calculated the total cost for his office and fees at a modest fifteen hundred dollars per month, which would leave him a fixed salary of five hundred dollars per month. He would also get 10 percent of the fees paid to his associates in the office.

Henceforth, the UAW-CIO would have efficient, cheap, and totally dedicated legal representation. Sugar insisted on the importance of commitment and reiterated in his report the need for lawyers with broad experience in the labor movement. As for himself, the record was known. But above all, Sugar was attempting to give a new kind of credibility to the union, a new legitimacy. It would work within the law and with the law. John Safran, a young radical lawyer associated with Sugar, was of the opinion that in 1939 the new general counsel "wanted to make the union as legitimate as possible, as well-accepted as possible." Moreover, Safran felt that Sugar himself "was more radical before the union came in, because after that he became concerned about conserving what they had won. This was natural enough."[14]

Almost as if to make himself appear more legitimate and to shed some of his radical image, Sugar undertook personal litigation in the summer of 1939 that many of his friends thought was a mistake. But he was thinking about the union and the red-baiting attacks it had endured; it was also the moment when Charles

Taft had begun to work for the union. He decided to take a Martin supporter named Raymond Tessmer to court for distributing the old "faked leaflet" at a meeting in February in order to discredit Sugar as a Communist. Sugar filed the charge of criminal libel on April 12 shortly after being attacked by Martin on radio station WJR as a member of the Communist party. This was followed by Martin's order to distribute copies of the leaflet all over the country. In a press release of April 4, Sugar had bluntly demanded retractions (which he did not get) and stated "I have never been and am not now a member of the Communist Party," those sad words that thousands would have to repeat in the future. He decided on the Tessmer action as a test case against the entire Martin red-baiting campaign. The trial date was July 25, 1939.

Larry Davidow, now the key lawyer for the Martin forces, took Tessmer's defense. Already used to calling people Communists from the trial of the five officers, Davidow now had a chance to let loose on Sugar, his former friend and semirelative. Something had happened to Davidow since 1937. The Martin influence was unquestionably important, but he had become caught up in the anti-Communist hysteria spawned by the Dies Committee and the daily press in a way that bordered on the pathological. He had already written a tract for a Catholic publication introduced by future McCarthy supporter Clarence Manion of Notre Dame entitled *The Genesis and Present-Day Methods of Communism* and would soon begin writing a column full of conspiracies for the reactionary local weekly, the *Redford Record*. As time went by, he would take nothing but company business as a lawyer in labor disputes and workmen's-compensation cases. In the late sixties he became the lawyer for the notorious radical-Right and racist organization in Detroit, Breakthrough.

Davidow bragged in his summary about "putting Sugar on trial." His manner was worthy of Dies or McCarthy. He hauled out professional ex-Communist witnesses Joseph Zach, William Nowell, and John Pace (also an exmember of the KKK), but elicited no testimony demonstrating Sugar's membership in the Party. He sent a secretary to New York at the UAW-AFL's expense to gather evidence. She came back with photostated copies of Sugar's 1919–20 articles and one from the *Soviet Union Today* on the Soviet legal system (1933), all available at the Detroit Public Library. Thus Davidow took the "Communistic beliefs" path and even got the judge to volunteer a question, "Do you subscribe to the Communist philosophy?" to which Sugar responded, "I never have"—an accurate answer. "What's the difference between a Communist and a Red?" persisted the judge. "Red," said Sugar, "is a word used to stigmatize anyone you don't like." Davidow went into the old articles in which Sugar did demonstrate, as we have seen, a strong Leninist perspective. But he made more points with the jury with lines of questioning such as the following: "How many times have you been to Russia?" "Once, in 1932," Sugar replied. "Did you visit the Kremlin?" "Yes I did." Davidow had also kept up with *Detroit Saturday Night,* catching Sugar at the Browder rally in 1936 *and* finding out that the assembled sang one of his songs. And so the idiotic questioning went.

Tessmer was hardly interrogated at all, and the assistant prosecutor, Ralph Garber, put on a rather weak exhibition. The all-white jury of eight men and four women found Tessmer not guilty. Sugar, though vowing to do the same every time that leaflet was circulated, had fallen prey to red-baiting. He would not make the same mistake twice.[15]

The verdict was rendered August 1. Twenty-three days later Nazi Germany and the Soviet Union signed their nonaggression pact. On September 1, Hitler invaded Poland, and France and Britain declared war on Germany. World War II had begun. W. H. Auden wrote for an entire generation,

> I sit in one of the dives
> On Fifty-Second Street
> Uncertain and afraid
> As clever hopes expire
> Of a low dishonest decade:
> Waves of anger and fear
> Circulate over the bright
> And darkened lands of the earth,
> Obsessing our private lives;
> The unmentionable odor of death
> Offends the September night.

So absorbed in the work of the union had Sugar been that the international situation had almost slipped away from him. The shock of that week was incredible. Communists were numbed. Spain had already collapsed. Now came this strange, unfathomable turn of events. Anti-Fascist meetings were canceled. Steve Nelson recalled that his comrades in California were totally disoriented. One had to weep for Poland, no matter what justifications might be made regarding the strategic necessity of the pact from the Russian point of view.[16]

Within the UAW, reaction to the pact among the leadership was unanimously negative. Only Frankensteen and Addes even hinted that the weakness of Soviet military forces provided some rationale for the move. Their Communist allies squirmed through convoluted arguments to justify Stalin's every act; had they not again taken a hypersupportive position, they might have more effectively taken advantage of the substantial antiwar sentiment among U.S. workers. In this situation, Walter Reuther made considerable political capital. He had already taken a pox-on-both-your-houses position in the spring. "In condemning the factional activities of both the Communist Party and the Lovestone Communists," Reuther said in a radio speech on March 3, "Local 174 has served notice that it will not tolerate the interference of any outside political group." In the summer he consolidated his power, using his GM division directorship as his lever, and tied himself closely with the Association of Catholic Trade Unionists (apparently not classified as an "outside political group"). This organization was rapidly becoming the key conservative element within the union. An offshoot of Dorothy Day's and Peter Maurin's Catholic-worker movement, the ACTU was formed in opposition to their alleged "softness" on communism (they were Tolstoyan anarchists, if anything). Its raison d'être from beginning to end was to fight communism in the trade-union movement. With the pact and then the Soviet "defensive" invasions of eastern Poland and Finland in the winter, Reuther's castigation of the Communists became easier and easier, and he won many supporters to his "moderate" caucus by chiding Addes and Frankensteen for their failure to condemn the Communists outright. Finally, at the convention in Saint Louis in August 1940, Reuther forced them to take a stand and they did so, supporting an anti-Soviet, anti-Communist resolution sponsored by the Reuther forces. Ganley and Anderson and some thirty other delegates who voted against it found themselves totally isolated. This vote provided a hit list for later demotions and electoral targets within the union.[17]

What did Maurice Sugar think about all this? Nowhere in the public record or in his papers do we have any indication. Interviews with close associates and family members reveal little. But Ernest Goodman remembers his own position well and is sure Sugar's was quite similar. Goodman emerged as Sugar's key assistant in 1939. He moved into Sugar's office that fall, having been given a series of referrals by Sugar from 1936 on. His work was heavily in the area of civil rights, particularly the defense of people whose rights were violated because of discrimination against their political outlook. His most important case to date involved five doctors "named" during the Dies Committee visit to Detroit in October of 1938. They had spearheaded both an industrial-illness campaign for the UAW and a tuberculosis-detection program for the city. They were reluctantly removed from the latter role by Health Commissioner Vaughan after Mayor Reading ordered their dismissal for "fraud." Amid wide national publicity, Goodman fought the case to a stalemated conclusion, but severely injured the political fortunes of Reading.

Goodman and Sugar were similar types in terms of background, interests, and political outlook. His recollections on the question of the pact are therefore invaluable.

> I moved into this office a few weeks after the pact was signed. Our concern was to fight against repression, fascism, and strengthen the labor movement. Our responsibility was to labor and black people and to anti-fascist, anti-conservative forces. We had very little problem doing that kind of work. We were not involved in intellectual debates. We were involved in doing work for these organizations. That hadn't changed one bit with the pact. We tried to avoid a split with those in these organizations. Did everything we could not to raise, but to avoid ideological issues that divided. In Detroit, relatively few people we were working with raised the Nazi-Soviet Pact as an issue. Those who did didn't get much support in matters we were working on together.

Goodman's personal response to the pact was "shock, very difficult to understand and to deal with. . . . Russia was a Socialist country moving in the right direction. [*pause*] So very difficult. It shook many organizations and individuals." He and Sugar both felt that the Western powers seemed to be pushing the Nazis to the east after Munich—thus "we could understand" the Soviet reaction "but were unhappy about the circumstances. When Hitler invaded in 1941, we breathed a sigh of relief—a remarkable release of tension."

Anticommunism again became virulent, especially when given licence by the government. Early in November 1939, Earl Browder was arrested. Protest meetings were organized around the country by Communists. On November 9 Detroit Communists held one at Finnish Hall on Fourteenth Street, their usual assembly place. That night a counterdemonstration was organized by the pastor of the all-white Southern Baptist Church (Temple), G. B. Vick, and UAW right-wing leader Pat McCartney. While police watched the action, over a thousand men, wearing American Legion caps and other patriotic insignia, broke out of their picket line and attacked the seven or eight hundred people coming out of the building after the rally was over. Several people were injured by clubs, fists, and brass knuckles. Cries of "kill the Russians" pierced the night air. Reflecting the tensions of the time within the UAW (for many of the "patriotic" demonstrators were union members), those burned in effigy by the crowd included not only Stalin, Hitler, and Browder, but Maurice Sugar as well. Despite his efforts to concentrate on business, Sugar remained a key target for the red-baiters.[18]

Sugar nevertheless kept his nose to the grindstone, focusing on union work and civil-rights activity. Typical of the latter was the case of thirteen students, members of the left-leaning American Student Union, who were not allowed to reregister in the fall of 1940 at the University of Michigan after having attempted the previous spring to integrate a well-known student hangout, the Pretzel Bowl. President Ruthven, a conservative, had signed the order blocking their reentry. A Michigan Committee for Academic Freedom, with Goodman as secretary, was created and dozens of prominent liberals, leftists, and trade-unionists, including Max Lerner, Paul Robeson, and R. J. Thomas were signed on as sponsors. After the university board of regents refused to hear a delegation from the committee on the case, an open hearing was scheduled for early November. It would "try" the case, and Sugar was to be the attorney. The Masonic Temple in Ann Arbor was booked, but at the last moment authorization for its use was revoked. Hence on November 9 in Island Park, as icy winds whipped through the crowd, "Examining Attorney" Sugar put the University of Michigan on trial, gloved finger pointing at the empty chairs of the regents and president who failed to honor their summons. The verdict of *guilty* was unanimous. The university in the end allowed a few of the "less guilty" back in, while others went elsewhere in disgust. The following spring Stanley Nowak, now a state senator, and young Charles Diggs introduced an academic-freedom bill in the state legislature.

The atmosphere of 1940–41 was thus unfavorable for liberal causes. Goodman, as the Sugar associate most involved in such matters, dealt with a number of similar cases, including the frightening nocturnal roundup of several professional people by the FBI. They had committed the "crime" of aiding in the recruitment of Spanish Civil War soldiers, thus violating the Enlistment in Foreign Services Act. It had been passed in 1818! After a long battle, they were pardoned, and Goodman blasted the FBI for its Nazi tactics.[19] But for all members of Sugar's team, which included long-time associate Jack Tucker, lawyers-guild activist Nedwin Smokler, and Goodman as the three-man UAW staff, the real business of 1940–41 was the Ford Motor Company. Nowhere were the combined inequities of civil-rights violations, worker oppression, union-busting activities, and outright fascist ideology as prominent as in the Ford fiefdom.

While noises about organizing Ford's Rouge plant—the great hole in the UAW organization charts—were heard, little of substance was done in 1939 or the first half of 1940. The condition of the company was substantially weakened by poor sales due to adverse publicity over Ford's pro-German politics, the government's hesitation to give him defense contracts, and declining quality and imaginativeness in production. Both the hard-won Chrysler and GM contracts of 1939 had brought substantial improvements to the workers and CIO organizing was going well everywhere. One after the other, the steel companies capitulated, although several of the Little Steel outfits, such as Great Lakes in Ecorse, had not yet seen the light. Ford's time was coming and the St. Louis convention declared open war in August 1940.

Again, the dramatic story of the final push to organize Ford need not be retold here. But it is likely that no other effort in previous labor history depended so much on the coordination of the struggle "on the legal field" with that "on the industrial field." The NLRB cases demonstrating Ford's multiple violations of the law led to further and further public disenchantment with the flivver king and finally to a decision on the part of the U.S. Army not to award new defense contracts of any sort to companies that refused to submit to the NLRB machinery. This decision, pushed by Hillman in the National Defense Advisory Board, finally came two days after Christmas in 1940 and probably was the turning point in the thinking of executives of the ailing company (if not of Ford himself).

A sympathetic labor board was crucial. Ford attorneys railed about the NLRB's prejudice, but Edward Barnard, lawyer for the UAW-AFL, had put it best in June 1939 when he remarked about supposedly neutral board attorney Harold Cranefield: "Every time Mr. Cranefield has spoken, it's been exactly as though Mr. Sugar were on his feet." Nathan Witt, a radical attorney, was executive secretary of board operations and hired most of the staff. Under Chairman William Madden and with the support of left-leaning Edwin S. Smith, Witt was safe, even after Roosevelt-appointed economist and mediator William Leiserson to the three-man board in April 1939. But things began to get tense when the president buckled under company and AFL pressure and announced in May 1940 that he would replace the retiring Madden with Harry Millis, another arbitrator, in August. This was one of John L. Lewis's reasons for not backing FDR for a third term. The NLRB's liberal tradition was not immediately damaged, given the slowness in personnel changes, but the move against Ford had come none too soon. The law could cut both ways, as the labor movement was increasingly to learn.[20]

But for now it was presentation, exposure, and victory. The first break-through had come back in August 1939 when the board ordered Ford to rein-state, with back pay, twenty-four Rouge workers, including Local 600 President Percy Llewellyn, on the grounds that they were fired for union activities. This battle had been going on for two years and was the original basis of Sugar's minute investigation of all aspects of Ford's discriminatory and intimidating activities. The company defied the order and was therefore taken to circuit court of appeals. Although Ford tried to rehire the men in October as if it were part of a normal recall of laid-off employees, their back pay would not be won for another fifteen months.

In the summer of 1940, Ford became the major target of the entire CIO apparatus. Michael Widman, a key CIO organizer, was sent to Detroit to head the drive. A major new legal issue, the firing of twenty Rouge pattern makers and a protest taken to the NLRB, advertised the cause in September. As campaigning picked up, AFL people began to drift over to the UAW-CIO.

In December the pace further intensified, spurred on again by a legal victo-ry, this time on the long-debated leafleting issue. On December 8 Judge Chenot of Wayne County Circuit Court upheld the brave decision made the previous month by Dearborn Judge Lila Neuenfelt that the Dearborn antileafleting ordi-nance was unconstitutional. The following day intensive leafleting of the Rouge began. Widman, Thomas, and Sugar hailed the victory as one of "national importance." Sugar's battle with Dearborn authorities was beginning to swing his way. This was the first actual *court* decision against Ford.

As the *Daily Worker* put it, Henry Ford had a "horrible week" thereafter—his plant was inundated with placards, leaflets, and all the other paraphernalia of propaganda. Union buttons were seen everywhere, inside and outside the plant. Mass meetings were called and people came. Fear began to dissipate. But Ford struck back and on December 19 fired many people, had service men rip buttons from unionists' shirts, and generally renewed the old strong-arm tactics. Widman immediately telegraphed Roosevelt that Bennett was trying to provoke a strike. The organizer called for the rehiring of the workers and for NLRB elections. This then set the stage for the army decision to deny Ford further orders until it held an election.

In January 1941 came controversies over rehiring these people, with Ford first promising, then reneging. On January 19 the news broke that the union's legal staff had won another NLRB case—this time the order was to rehire with back pay a staggering 1,021 people dismissed from the Kansas City plant in October 1937. The rulings now came fast and furiously. The original Rouge back-pay case was won when the Supreme Court refused to hear Ford's appeal of the negative circuit-court decision. Three other appeals to the courts were pending. A total of seven rulings had been made by the board against Ford as of late February and four more were in process. Moreover, dozens of lesser cases before state agencies arose. Sugar and his men, especially Goodman, who was rapidly becoming an expert on the intestines of the Ford Motor Company, were working nonstop. Meanwhile Ford Rouge workers signed up in droves.

A typical example of the kinds of cases handled during this period was that of a Rouge assembly-line worker, John Gallo, who was fired on November 14, 1940 and whose appeal was heard before Michigan Unemployment Compensation Commission referee Charles Rubinoff on February 7, 1941. Goodman handled the hearing. Gallo, a member in good standing of the UAW since October 1937 and a model worker, stood accused of laughing on the job. The general foreman, Henry May, dismissed him. May's questioning by the referee went as follows:

Q What did he do that attracted your attention?
A When I walk around through the department, that is my job, if I notice anything unusual, I can't help but see it.
Q I understand that, but what was it that was unusual about his conduct?
A He was standing around talking and laughing with the other fellows.
Q Were the other fellows laughing also?
A Not so much as he was.
Q In other words, there was some laughter. He was the most boisterous. Did you find out whether his general disposition was that of a lively, vivacious, exuberant person? Maybe he liked his work and was enjoying it.
A I don't know what was the cause of it, no.
Q Well, I mean was it the expression on his face that attracted your attention or his general demeanor?
A Well, the expression on his face, and the fact that he would look around at one man and then the other talking.
Q The other fellows were laughing, too, around there?
A No.
Q They were solemn?
A They weren't laughing, no.
Q He was the only one that was laughing?
A Yes.
. . . .
Q Do you mean to testify that the line actually stopped?
A Yes.
Q For how long?
A Oh, maybe a half minute.

Mr. May testified that the above episode occurred about 2:30 P.M.; that he warned the claimant to quit "fooling around"; and that when he caught him in the same spirit of comicality an hour later, though the line "did not stop," he ordered his discharge. The examination continued,

Q Would you say talking on the job was against the rules of the company?
A No.

Q In other words, they are permitted to talk?

A Sure.

Q But when they talk, they are not supposed to fool around and smile about it?

A They can smile, but they don't have to fool around. You can tell when a man is talking about the job and when he isn't.

Q In other words, when you watched the claimant's demeanor, you were led to believe that he wasn't talking about the job, either the first time or the second time, this was about quarter to four. The second time the line didn't stop, isn't it true, Mr. May?

A Yes.

Q The only thing you did see on the second time, while the line didn't stop, was that he was still smiling?

A Yes.

Q And then you decided to lay him off?

A Yes.

Rubinoff had little trouble finding for Gallo and ordered that his unemployment benefits be awarded retroactively. (Since Gallo did not wait around for the "final disposition" after complaining to the employment office about his "dirty deal," the company claimed that he "quit without good cause"!) The referee found that "laughter on the line is not misconduct under the Act." He added in a footnote, in reference to Ford's expectations, "If a worker on a production line had manifested such pious solemnity and rare virtuosity in screwing on a nut, he would be more a subject for a psychiatrist than a referee." Most cases of Ford firings were less amusing, but the UAW usually had the last laugh.[21]

Sugar allowed his name to be put up for recorders' court again in early January 1941. Billed as the "UAW candidate," he used the campaign to advertise the cause of unionism and rekindled his old alliances, especially with the black community. The conservative churches were now again receptive and in general his efforts likely softened continued black resistance to the union at a critical point in time. One of the key aspects of the UAW Ford drive was to pay special attention to the needs and concerns of the large group of black employees. Horace Sheffield, Shelton Tappes, Chris Alston, and many other black organizers poured their efforts into the drive and coordinated with Sugar's campaign. In the primary, he finished first among the nonincumbents with strong labor support everywhere. As usual, he would lose in the runoff.

But by then, it hardly made any difference. On April 1, 1941, Ford fired eight committeemen and spontaneous stoppages occurred throughout the Rouge. That night, at 12:15 A.M., following hectic meetings and legal briefings from Sugar, the union declared that workers in the world's largest auto plant were on strike. The final phase of auto organizing in Detroit was under way.

The following day, thousands of pickets massed around the complex clashed with "loyal" workers, largely AFL people urged on by Homer Martin and a sizable number of black workers. Harry Bennett screamed about a Communist conspiracy. The week before, Ford attorney Capizzi had argued that the NLRB hearings be suspended because the CIO was dominated by Communists, and listed people from Phillip Murray (now CIO president) to Earl Browder. Sugar (who was on the list side by side with Walter Reuther) responded, "We feel that you ought also to add the names of President Roosevelt and Robert Wagner, both of whom sponsored the NLRB and are responsible for the position in which the Ford Motor Company finds itself today."

Despite Ford's desperate tactics, only thirty-five hundred workers (out of eighty-five thousand), entered the plants on April 3. The critical difference was now the growing respect for the picket line from black workers. The years of work to convince black people that the union was on their side were finally paying off. Sugar could certainly take pride in his role in that process. A week later Ford capitulated and promised elections within forty-one days.[22]

Now came the last court battle of the Ford drive. The strike settlement included interim recognition of the UAW-CIO, reinstatement of all strikers and five of the eight fired key men (the status of the other three to be arbitrated), a promise to raise wage levels to competitive levels, and no interference by Ford in the election. The election of May 21 overwhelmingly voted the UAW-CIO in. Negotiations got under way between Ford and the UAW in early June. Simultaneously, Sugar put on a final fireworks show in NLRB hearings on unfair-labor-practices charges. Former Ford spies and service men paraded to the witness stand and confessed their sins. Ralph Rimar outlined the intricate interconnections between the company, police, spies under his command, and suspect activities by union men, especially Zygmund Dobrzynski, hero of the Automotive Fibers strike. The unclean hands were there, palms up. After two days of such revelations, Sugar and Capizzi agreed to call off the hearing in order to generate further good will at the bargaining table. Two weeks later the Ford contract was signed in Washington by Thomas, Bennett, and Murray. The terms were the most generous in the short history of the union. Besides a variety of wage and conditions improvements and a solid grievance procedure, the industrial world was shocked by the following: Ford would have a closed shop and a dues-checkoff plan (the first in the industry); the union label would go on every car; and (for many the greatest victory of all) the service department would be eliminated. Jubilation rang throughout Detroit: the citadel had been taken.[23]

It was symptomatic that even in the end, the legal front played a role in giving a push to negotiations. The luxury of NLRB support was slightly intoxicating. Sugar remained skeptical perhaps, but the sturdy legal structure protecting the union from the capitalists would weaken under the impact of war and the postwar reaction. Its shapeless form increasingly seemed to be a net.

Heroes of Bulls Run in court in January, 1937, with their lawyer: (left to right) Victor Reuther, Robert Travis, Roy Reuther, Sugar, and Henry Kraus.

Sugar, Lee Pressman, and Larry Davidow in Judge Gadola's court, February 1, 1937.

The great Cadillac Square rally in Detroit,
March 23, 1937.

The UAW "Labor Slate": 1937 City Council
candidate Sugar, R. J. Thomas, Richard
Frankensteen, Walter Reuther, Tracy Doll,
and Sugar's campaign manager Alan
Strachan.

Campaign workers for one of Sugar's several candidacies for Recorders Court (1941 in this case).

Maurice and Jane Sugar share a joke with Richard Frankensteen in 1939.

A 1941 Ford strike demonstration.

Signing the Ford contract: Philip Murray joined by UAW officials Richard Leonard (third from left) *and Sugar, R. J. Thomas, and George Addes* (beginning third from right)

Ford pays off: back pay to the tune of seven
million dollars is awarded to Ford workers for
whom Sugar and his staff pled in court.
*Richard Leonard (*left*) presents the check as*
*Sugar and staffer Ernest Goodman (*fourth*
from left*) look on.*

Sugar speaks to UAW local 887 during World
War II.

*Sugar discusses law with activist Coleman
Young and attorney LeBron Simmons, leaders
of the Detroit branch of the National Negro
Congress, in 1942.*

*Sugar and Ernest and Freda Goodman
emerge from the 1946 UAW Convention in
Atlantic City.*

Maurice and Jane Sugar at Black Lake, 1962.

Sugar came south for the inauguration of George W. Crockett as Recorders Court judge in 1966. Shown here are other members of the law firm Sugar founded (from left): Dean Robb, Robert Millender, Sugar, Crockett, Ernest Goodman, and George Bedrosian.

9 ❖ DEMOCRACY, BUREAUCRACY, AND ANTICOMMUNISM, 1941–45

The recovery of the union had been remarkable. Generous estimates put the membership of the UAW-CIO at 150 thousand in May 1939, when Martin took his people into the AFL. But paid-up members were probably half that. The records were in a shambles, banks and suppliers distrustful. A moratorium on back dues was declared for people who suspended payment during the confusing months after the trial of the officers. The correspondence among Sugar, Addes, and lawyers hired by the union elsewhere reveal a dire situation. Legal fees were the principal expense in 1939 and Sugar did everything he could to get lawyers to reduce charges. Locals were urged to pay as much of their own expenses as possible. Sugar summed up the situation in a letter to Grover Johnson of the liberal Los Angeles firm of Gallagher, Wirin, and Johnson on June 15: "We regret very much that it will be impossible, certainly at this time, for the International Union to be of any help in the payment of the obligations of Local 230. Within recent months there have arisen so many serious emergency situations that the International Union has been fairly hard put to hold its own financially." Indeed, by August Addes and Sugar discussed the possibility of bankruptcy.

The turnaround was not immediate, but slowly, as more and more elections went the CIO's way (they swept GM in the fall) and as Addes applied his fiscal expertise to the problem, the union repaired its financial situation. By midsummer 1940, Thomas could report a 93-percent increase in membership since the Cleveland convention. A record 647 plants were covered by UAW contracts. In plants where representation elections had occurred, the UAW-CIO had won 110 of them, while the UAW-AFL won only 14, and AFL craft unions 13. By the time of the 1941 Buffalo convention in August, the UAW had reached, in Thomas's words, "the peak of its strength." After the Ford check-off began August 1, paid-up membership was 528 thousand, a quantum leap from the previous year. A total of 700 thousand workers in 982 plants were now covered by contracts and the union's income had doubled. Thomas singled out the legal

257

department for special praise, noting its central role in the Ford drive. George Addes went so far as to say, at a later time, that Sugar had been the "soul" of the final push against Ford.[1]

These happy reports about the union's power and Sugar's excellence were accompanied by troubling signs, one quite explicit, the other hidden but no less real: anticommunism and bureaucratization. These were the forces that would transform the union completely in the postwar period. But they were offset until then by another force that became the hallmark of the UAW: internal union democracy.

The constitution adopted in 1939, which Sugar helped to draft, called for annual conventions and the annual election of officers and executive-board members. The former were elected by a general vote of the delegates, the latter (other than the officers who sat on the board) by delegates from the region they represented. Local union officers were elected annually as well and delegates to the national convention were chosen in separate elections. While local officers usually were selected, there was nothing automatic about it (as in the Teamsters today, for example). The trial procedures for misconduct or other offenses were elaborately fair and the restrictions on the International's power over locals numerous. There was a large per capita tax paid to the International (40 percent of dues), but the benefits were enormous. International officers were among the lowest paid in the union world, and their expenses were watched closely, with specific limits built in. The convention was the highest authority in all matters, and the twenty-two man executive board served the same function between conventions, although its decisions could be appealed to the convention.

The constitution was a fine instrument, but the spirit in which it was administered became the key to union democracy in the UAW. And the men who made democracy tick within the union were, above all, George Addes and Maurice Sugar. Addes generally chaired the conventions during their working sessions. He was the man who recognized people on the floor and who made rulings on motions and all the other business at the gatherings. He was scrupulously fair in the manner he ran things and always sought ways to compromise and balance out. His key advisor on parliamentary issues was Sugar. Their popularity with the membership was immense.

Their work at the conventions was respected, but perhaps more important was their performance in dealing with constitutional questions that arose every day in the locals around the country. The voluminous files in both the Addes and Sugar collections reveal a record of conscientious, prudent, and judicious decisions. A good deal of time was taken up in soul-searching between the two over even such matters as suspension for nonpayment of dues. The men and women of the UAW knew this and deeply appreciated it.

Many local constitutional problems arose over election procedures or internal judicial action taken against members. These were often laden with factional politics. This was the arena where the Sugar-Addes reputation was truly won. Tempting as it might have been, they did not play politics with the constitutional

258

decisions they were required to make. They knew how quickly their credibility would dissolve if they did. This became an issue in 1947 when Emil Mazey, who replaced Addes then, would accuse them, particularly Sugar, of doing so. While both Addes and Sugar were identified with the "Left" faction in the union in opposition to the grouping that grew around Walter Reuther, they valued union democracy—"the will of the workers," as Sugar would put it—far too much to jeopardize it for factional gain.

Fair factional fights were the lifeblood of democracy. While some members would prefer to stifle the voices of both the Communists and the Association of Catholic Trade Unionists (as well as a variety of other political minorities), their right to speak guaranteed that same right to all rank-and-filers. For Sugar no belief was deeper than that the voice of the workers be heard, that the power of the workers be felt. Within the key instrument by which this was transmitted into social action, the trade union, to deny any worker his voice or his power would have been unthinkable. Sugar and Addes were the keepers of the seal, the chief protectors of democratic principle in the UAW.[2]

Democracy long held its ground against the threats of mindless red-baiting and the insidious growth of what might be termed *bureaucratic centralism*. But after the war the balance shifted, and a new kind of union (and union movement) emerged.

The Red Menace and the Rise of Walter Reuther

The first great round of anticommunism occurred in 1941 itself. The Ford Motor Company had attempted to bring the "red" herring into the organizing drive and the strike. By and large, it had little effect on public opinion, in part because the local press was by now tuned to an anti-Ford wavelength but, more important, because Ford was of such little importance in the defense industry. Roosevelt had, from June 1940 on, put the nation on a war-preparedness footing and the country's plants, particularly in steel, auto, and aircraft began churning out gigantic quantities of war materiel. Labor militance, especially in the union most directly concerned with all this, the UAW, came to be regarded by many as unpatriotic. It was difficult to mix such sentiment into the Ford situation, however, since the old man at least, was more antiwar than the most loyal Communist.

But in the aircraft industry and, indeed, in almost all the other companies with which the UAW dealt, strikes could easily be labelled *un-American*. What this meant in most people's minds was not "Fascist," but "Communist-inspired." Bert Cochran argued correctly that a majority of U.S. workers remained pacifistic even after the fall of France and during the Battle of Britain, despite Roosevelt's strong encouragement of an interventionist mentality. But the Communist party's flip-flop and its shrill denunciation of anyone who remotely suggested help for beseiged Britain as a warmonger did little to ingratiate it with

259

workers who might otherwise have been sympathetic. The Party did not have a very good name in 1940–41.

Thus the press, politicians, and big business declared open season on reds, suspected reds, and especially, as Sugar had put it so aptly, on "people whom they don't like." A random example was poor Joseph A. Rubin, a Democrat, who was appointed by Governor Murray Van Wagoner to the state labor-mediation board and whose confirmation was held up when a Republican state senator produced a photostat of a Communist-party membership card issued in 1938 to one J. Ruben. Senator Hittle added little to the Senate's reputation for literacy, but still got public accolades for his patriotic watchfulness. Rubin was nonetheless confirmed by the majority of the upper house who knew how to spell.

More serious, however, was the fact that because of the pact, it became easy to view Communists as potential traitors. While there had been plenty of talk about Communists subverting U.S. society because they were revolutionaries, and so on, for the first time since the Polish War of 1921, Russia was virtually a military enemy. Loyalty oaths became the rage among companies engaged in defense production. Aside from the potential civil-rights violations this implied, it was also a marvelous way to weed out rebellious workers, since they were precisely the types who might refuse to sign.

Sugar wrote a number of opinions on this question and had them distributed widely throughout the union. A typical pledge was that of the Modine Manufacturing Company in Racine, Wisconsin. The worker would swear not to be a member of any group advocating the overthrow of the government and specifically not a Communist or a member of any Fascist or Nazi Bund organization; neither would he "embrace the philosophy" or even "aid or assist" the same. The company also passed out copies of the sabotage and espionage acts as "requested" by the government. While workers themselves were just "requested" to sign, the whole structure of the process ("return them in a week" and so on) was to make it seem compulsory.

Sugar's opinions stressed that "there is no requirement of law which makes it mandatory either upon employers to require employees to answer such questions . . . or upon employees to give such information to an employer or any governmental agency." Besides, the practice of giving criminal statutes to workers and having them sign them is "a gratuitous insult." Ultimately, he said, such an affidavit of allegiance "violates that privacy and that security which has been characteristic of American institutions since our country was founded." While Sugar was correct (for now) that such pledges were unconstitutional if demanded by private employers, the civil service and the post office could and did require them. Moreover, Roosevelt had personally pushed J. Edgar Hoover into numerous "antisubversive" investigations in the last year.

The green light was on and the red-baiters responded enthusiastically. With far more important things to do in May 1941, Sugar had to assign the expensive time of William Henry Gallagher to the defense of the union, accused along with the Communist party (represented by Walter Nelson) of injuring two scabs during the Ford strike. Larry Davidow represented them and the case went before Federal Judge Frank Picard, who joined Davidow in wondering whether the Communists "control the CIO." Almost as if in response, the state CIO council went on record as opposed to "the election or appointment of Fascists, Nazis, or Communists to CIO offices." And so it went. The state legislature attempted to pass a law denying the Communist party a place on the ballot. It was narrowly defeated in the Senate after passing the House. Hearst's *Detroit Times* printed in bold letters the names of the five Detroit senators who voted against and wrote a hysterical editorial entitled "Reds Win in Michigan." U.S. Representative George Dondero of Michigan's seventeenth district raised the red flag on the House floor and also swiped at Walter Reuther on May 13 for threatening a strike in the GM situation. A week later, when an unauthorized strike did occur in Flint, Reuther then implied in an interview with Blair Moody that those responsible were Communists. Lee Pressman correctly assessed the scene in late May 1941 at a National Lawyers Guild convention where he and Sugar were featured speakers: the war hysteria and fears of subversion were provoking antilabor legislation all over the country that would "destroy the labor movement and guarantee monopoly profits."[3]

The big blowup, however, and one with profound reverberations within the union, came over the North American Aviation strike in Inglewood, California that occurred in June 1941. This plant had been recently established and was entirely devoted to defense work. Its workers were inexperienced, young, and unenthusiastic about getting killed in war. Union sentiment had been sorely tested by an election fight between a Communist-dominated UAW-CIO group and the red-baiting IAM. The former won a very close vote early in the year and faced negotiations in the spring. The company—rich and arrogant, but bristling with defense orders it wanted to fill in a hurry—tried to rush to a cheap contract. It was facing an array of old pros, however, including Wyndham Mortimer and Henry and Dorothy Kraus. Elmer Freitag, the local president, was a registered Communist voter and Lew Michener, the head of the West Coast Region, a Party member. Both were smart, tough negotiators.

On May 27, in response to a variety of international dangers, Roosevelt declared an unlimited national emergency. In this context the negotiations were transferred to Washington for hearings before the National Labor Mediation Board, set up in March and suspected by the labor movement of being a first step toward outlawing strikes and instituting compulsory arbitration. Workers in the North American local took a strike vote and overwhelmingly authorized their negotiating committee to call a strike if need be. On June 4, the decision to strike was taken and the following day pickets ringed the plant. Roosevelt was unable to contain his rage and his cabinet meeting rang with dire (and unconstitutional) threats against "labor agitators." It was a tense situation.

The strike was not authorized by the International. Richard Frankensteen headed the aircraft division of the union and had been actively involved in negotiations. In telephone conversations on the night of June 4, he told Mortimer and local leaders that he would not endorse the strike. He then flew to Los Angeles on Saturday, June 7, and proceeded to read the riot act to the union. He fired Mortimer and four International representatives on the spot. After appeals to heckling strikers (plus an array of left-leaning unionists from all over the area) failed, Frankensteen suspended the local officers and withdrew the charter. His entire rhetoric that weekend was punctuated with anticommunism. He was livid. On June 10, Roosevelt ordered regular army troops into the plant, the first time the army had been used against civilians since the Bonus Marchers were routed in 1932. They broke the strike. Elmer Freitag wired Roosevelt: "You can't build bombers with bayonets."

This is one of the most controversial incidents in the history of the UAW. It drew battle lines that were never erased. Communists were probably more reviled at that moment than any other until the depths of the McCarthy period. Roosevelt had full support from the press and a majority of "patriotic Americans." *Life* magazine began its extensive picture story with a fictional news item about a strike in Germany against its largest airplane maker. "Easily imagined," said the Luce publication, "is the thrill of joy and hope which would have surged through the democratic world if such a report had appeared last week. Exactly similar news . . . did come from Inglewood, Calif." Within the union, patriotism versus "un-Americanism" was not the issue. Frankensteen's principal concern was the fear that such a strike would unleash "a wave of repressive legislation" that would set the labor movement back years. The Roosevelt administration had been unfriendly toward labor since the national election and would soon replace Smith with yet another conservative on the NLRB. On the other hand, North American workers were at a militant peak and strike leaders felt that if mediation discussions dragged on, their enthusiasm would wane while hotheads would push for departmental wildcats. Besides, a short strike had worked at Vultee Aircraft the previous November. Communists and their friends were at the heart of the decision-making process at North American, of course, and it was natural that they were suspected of ulterior motives—of giving political aid to the Soviet Union and its allies by disrupting war production.

The sentiment of the rank-and-file at North American was taken into little account either by historians or critics at the time. Michigan CIO boss Gus Scholle spoke for Frankensteen's supporters in the UAW when he sent the latter a telegram arguing that North American workers were misled by the Communists. "Balked in their efforts to take over the labor movement, the Communist Party is now out to discredit and wreck the whole American Union structure." But anyone who takes the time to examine the situation carefully, as has historian James Prickett, will realize that rank-and-file feelings against the company were running very high. Its pay levels were ludicrously low (50 cents per hour on the average) and working conditions were chaotic. The strike authorization vote, after all, was 5,829 to 210.

But everyone ignores a fact that was foremost in Maurice Sugar's mind. The negotiations with the Ford Motor Company and the Ford NLRB hearings came to a head precisely on the day the West Coasters decided to strike. Imagine the fears of Thomas, Widman, Sugar, Addes, and the others directly involved with the Ford situation! Having just nudged the company toward meaningful discussions through the startling revelations that the hearings produced (Rimar's testimony was on June 4), an embarrassing strike ignoring the established legal structure (the mediation board) and without clearance from Detroit was declared in Los Angeles. The timing was disastrous. And this, according to George Addes, who consulted Sugar about support or nonsupport of Frankensteen, was one of the key factors influencing both of them to endorse sending Frankensteen to Los Angeles. "We agreed that he should be sent and try to settle things out, but we had no idea he was going to do it the way he did," said Addes in a later interview. Asked for a comment on June 10, Addes, unlike most other union spokesmen, had none, saying that he would wait for an "official report" on the facts.

Sugar himself has left no evidence concerning his position on the North American strike, but his preoccupation with Ford, the fact that June 4–5 was the crucial moment in the court battle with Capizzi, and his closeness to Addes make the latter's recollections seem valid. Moreover, when one considers that the Ford fight was the longest and most arduous of all the UAW battles and was just reaching its climax, an argument stressing the centrality of Ford in the high officers' decision to put the lid on North American simply makes good historical sense. Obviously, Sugar would never have wished the fate of Mortimer, Kraus, and the others on them, and he never forgave Frankensteen for what he did, but it would appear that he thought the strike was a mistake because it jeopardized the Ford settlement. Whether it could have been stopped in any case was questionable.[4]

The consequences of the North American strike were important for internal union politics, but they were overshadowed by two great events: the signing of the Ford contract on June 19 and the Nazi invasion of Russia on June 22. While Sugar, Goodman, and their friends "breathed easier" after that, the situation of the Communists in the union was little altered. Now they flopped the other way and, with typical hyperreaction, exploded, almost overnight, into a frenzy of support for Roosevelt's defense policies. This included condemning the handful of leftists, especially Trotskyists. who continued to take an antiwar stance. In the case of the Minneapolis Teamster leaders who were connected with the Socialist Workers party (SWP), the main voice of Trotskyism in the United States, their position bordered on treachery. The Minneapolis Teamsters were active, vigorous trade-unionists and stood opposed to the growing mob influence in the union. In early June they withdrew their locals from the AFL and joined the CIO. Urged on by political friend Dan Tobin of the AFL Teamsters, Roosevelt had the Justice Department raid the SWP headquarters on June 28 and, in effect, destroyed the new CIO affiliate while publicly condemning the latter for taking them in. They were tried and convicted under the new Alien Registration Act (Smith Act), with their antidefense position prominently displayed. The Communist party officially supported the government in a volte-face so glaring that it made all the accusations of caring about nothing save the Moscow line seem perfectly accurate.

The Communists in the union and without thus remained isolated, and attacks on them—as much for hypocrisy as anything else—continued. At the August convention in Buffalo, Walter Reuther wrote a program endorsed by Frankensteen and Richard Leonard, head of the Ford department, that was pointedly anti-Communist ("No one whose loyalty is first to a foreign government can be trusted to hold office or serve the best interest of our union") and spearheaded a drive, gleefully supported by the ACTU, to oust George Addes and replace him with Leonard. Addes was deemed to have been "soft" on the North American strike and had made clear his feeling that a great man like Mortimer should be reinstated. For that, he stood accused of "playing with the Communist Party."

In an atmosphere charged with anticommunism, Walter Reuther had his first big moment in union politics. He openly took the leadership of what the press described as the union's "right wing," whose best organized and most dedicated element was the ACTU. Using the North American situation, as well as the criticism that had been aimed at leftist Harold Christoffel of the Allis-Chalmers Local 248 in his handling of a long strike there, Reuther mounted an anti-Communist campaign of major proportions and found a following whose size "surprised everyone," as Edwin Lahey of the *Buffalo Evening News* wrote, "including itself." He lined up Leonard with the promise of support for the secretary-treasurer's job and Frankensteen, who disliked him intensely, on the basis of the latter's now virulent anticommunism.

As it turned out, Frankensteen did not stick with the coalition, ultimately siding with the resolution calling for the most lenient punishment of Michener and the North American leaders. He had backed Reuther on the Allis-Chalmers challenge (it was alleged that their election of delegates was illegal—operating in "the same manner as Stalin and Hitler" said the Reuther-backed report), but balked at the harsh punishment of North American. Frankensteen recognized that if he were to remain a key force in the union, he needed some independence from Reuther. Moreover, he could win one of the revived vice presidencies even without Reuther's active support and Allan Haywood of the CIO wanted Addes to stay on.

So all of Reuther's plans were not fulfilled. Addes, only feeling obliged to condemn *all* outside political groups (including the ACTU and the Socialist party), was reelected, with 56 percent of the vote. But Frankensteen honored his pledge to support a resolution barring Communists from union offices, which passed by a margin of two to one. Leaders closed the convention with a plea for unity, but the press heralded a Reuther victory: "Reuther's anti-Communist forces [this is the way they were always identified] . . . claimed that they had won control of the union despite the re-election of . . . Addes, following a harmony plea by CIO President Philip Murray," wrote William J. Coughlin of the *Free Press*.

For Sugar, the Buffalo convention was, at best, bittersweet. He was personally at the peak of his popularity in the union. He had won the admiration of R. J. Thomas. Even Reuther could not think of attacking him at this point. The Ford victory, the final settlement with the UAW-AFL, and all the other legal triumphs of the past year made him invaluable. But he was also watching his friends being assailed pitilessly. Reuther people pilloried Mortimer and ridiculed his plea for the "rank-and-file" position in the North American strike. John Anderson, at whose testimonial the previous December Sugar had been a featured speaker, rose as a voice in the wilderness against all forms of anti-Communist denunciation during that debate. Sugar must have smiled bitterly to see Reuther brush aside as "phony" a letter from the Soviet Union which he allegedly signed "Yours for a Soviet America," when he knew well of Reuther's past sympathy for the Soviet experience as written in a quite real letter to him. But he could hardly jump into the factional fight by releasing his letter. It was nevertheless perfectly clear to him now that Reuther would "stop at nothing," as Sugar later put it, to achieve the presidency of the UAW.[5]

While Reuther and his forces certainly remained strong, his goal would not be achieved for some time. One of the principal reasons was the rapid waning of anti-Communist sentiment in the United States after it entered the war. With the nation officially allied with Stalin's Russia, government and media opinion of pro-Soviet politics in the United States shifted radically. Images of Russia turned around with amazing speed. If, in 1939, moviegoers had roared with laughter at the ridiculous postures of Soviet officials in *Ninotchka,* they thrilled to the romance and high adventure of *Song of Russia* in 1943. Very rapidly U.S. Communists, under the slogan *Everything for Victory,* gained a kind of respectability that they had never had before. The Party's membership rolls swelled and expectations of revolutionary discipline subsided. While Reuther did not abandon his anti-Communist program, the new atmosphere made scapegoating the Communists increasingly difficult.[6]

What evolved in the war years was what George Addes has described as "the two-party system." It pitted Reuther and his forces against Addes and his, with Leonard and Frankensteen bouncing in and out of coalitions and Thomas trying to stay above it all. It was a system that kept the leaders on their toes, humble, and honest. Any hint of scandal or graft would have been grist in the propaganda mill of the other side. There was always some controversy to raise about something and while the press might rail about "factionalism" (actually the press loved it, for it was exciting and sold newspapers), it was democracy in the best sense of the word. Trotskyists like J. W. Anderson or Martin Glaberman would not have had a chance to make their voices heard, and Emil Mazey would have had little opportunity to test his ideas about ways around the no-strike pledge had it not been for the annual confrontations (and interim skirmishes) between the major parties.

Anticommunism versus toleration of communism remained at the heart of the differences between the two. Better put, it was anticommunism versus anti-Reutherism. And it was Reuther's anticommunism and the way he used it that provided the main foundation for the other side's attitudes toward Reuther. We have already traced aspects of Reuther's activities that developed the suspicions of the Addes caucus toward him. Clearly his relationship to the Martin fight in 1938 was the turning point.

But we have less of a sense of why Reuther made anticommunism the critical issue. It is easy enough to say it was sheer opportunism, but it is more complex than that. If Reuther was ambitious, so were those on the other side. Addes certainly was, but, like John L. Lewis, he came to view Communists as hardworking trade-unionists, useful to the cause and to his personal advancement. Unlike Lewis, however, he did not simply use them. Many Communists and their friends were people he liked—people whose ideals, feelings of justice, perspectives on racial and ethnic equality, and cultural values were generally similar to his own. They did not seem to be "tools of a foreign power," although, like them, Addes was intrigued by the evolution of the only Socialist state in the world. In short, Addes had an ideology, if not a clearly defined one, and there was an ideological dimension to his relationship with the pro-Soviet Left.[7]

The same may be said for Reuther, whose severing of ties with the Communist Left follows a clear ideological pattern. Only in mid-1938, when the debate over collective security and reported Communist outrages in Spain were brewing, did Reuther veer definitely away from them. The influence of Norman Thomas was strong and it led him to flirt briefly with the possibility of working with a "reformed" Homer Martin. He was also toying with such thoughts at a time when it looked as if Martin might just win. The critical moves in Reuther's career seemed always to come when ideology and personal opportunity coalesced. A "Communist" bent was both ideologically consistent and personally rewarding in 1935–36; a "Socialist" reorientation was so in 1938. In early 1939, with Martin discredited, but the Communist party exceedingly moderate in its outlook, Reuther could return to a "unity" perspective while rising above the Lovestonites or the Stalinists.

Still, Reuther had never been explicitly anti-Communist. Indeed, he was on record in staunch opposition to red-baiting. In the Ternstedt-unit newspaper of Local 174 during the flurry of management-sponsored anticommunism in the wake of the Detroit sit-downs, Reuther argued that the bosses, having played out the tactic of fomenting Catholic/Protestant, native-born/foreign-born, or interethnic antagonisms, "are raising a new scare: the red scare." He went on,

> They pay stools to go whispering around that so-and-so—usually a militant union leader—is a red. They think that will turn the other workers against him.

What the bosses really mean, however, is not that the leader is a red. They mean they don't like him because he is a loyal, dependable union man, a fighter who helps his union brothers and sisters and is not afraid of the boss.

So let's all be careful that we don't play the bosses' game by falling for their red scare. Let's stand by our union and our fellow unionists. No union worthy of the name will play the bosses' game. Some may do so through ignorance. But those who peddle the red scare and know what they are doing are dangerous enemies of the union.

This was a statement the Left did not let Reuther forget.

How, then, did he become the organizer and orchestrator of antired feeling in the UAW? Again ideology mixed with opportunism, but, as Sugar saw it, there was a definite turning point. At the state CIO convention in Grand Rapids in late June 1939, the Communist group in the UAW had indicated that it would back Victor Reuther for the presidency against Adolph Germer. But it abandoned him "in unity with Lewis." Inasmuch as this was the second time a Communist about-face had affected Victor's fortunes directly (the first was the previous year in the April state CIO convention when they withdrew their support of him as part of the Frankensteen deal), the latter felt it was the last straw.

Still, the Reuther brothers sought further discussions with the Communist leaders and asked if Sugar might serve as an intermediary. This he did, contacting Weinstone, and a meeting was held in his apartment. "My participation," wrote Sugar about this incident, which Walter Reuther would later use to brand Sugar a Communist, "consisted solely of bringing the parties together. . . . No agreement of any kind was reached . . . and what has stood out in my mind were the words uttered by Victor Reuther at its conclusion: 'I shall spend the rest of my life fighting the Communists.'" Since Victor was regarded as less staunchly opposed to the Communists in 1939 than his brother, one can imagine Walter's perspective after this perceived betrayal.

Sam Sweet, Education Director of Plymouth Local 51, recalled this incident in 1971 and, besides verifying Sugar's honest-broker role, made this interesting observation: "I for one honestly feel, that if at that 1939 convention all the progressive forces had supported Vic Reuther for the presidency against Germer and select[ed] a decent person for Sec'y Treasurer against Gibson, we could have [succeeded] as we had the delegates and the strength. I feel that we made a mistake by supporting Germer and Gibson." Sweet concluded his letter by capturing the mood that followed shortly thereafter: "From then on, people like Vic Reuther and other individuals who had worked with us before felt that the closer they were to us the less support they would expect." What Sweet was remembering was the larger framework of opprobrium that rained down on the Communists after the Nazi-Soviet pact in August.

Here was where Reuther's personal antagonism, ideology, and opportunism all came together. To the ill feelings against the local Communists was now added the last ideological straw and the tortured logic of the U.S. Party in defending it. Since Communists left the Party in droves over the pact, it is not surprising that the Reuthers, long since disillusioned, were now ready to attack openly a group whose position *did* seem attached to the foreign policy needs of Russia. Add to this the marvellous opportunity that the anti-Communist atmosphere in the nation and the union afforded for advancing his ambitions, and we can understand, if not justify, Walter Reuther's abandonment of his 1937 stand against red-baiting.[8]

Victory at What Cost?

With the war, as we have already noted, attacks on Communist "disruption" and "deception" were less profitable and indeed Reuther's fortunes faded significantly in 1942. The Chicago convention in August was a war-unity love feast with Reuther and Addes nominating each other for their offices and Communists and Reutherites voting together on most issues. Sugar's legal report to that convention reflected the mood: "We must win the war. All our problems are important, but the extent of their importance must be measured by one yardstick: How can we help to win the War? Defeated, we shall have no union. Victorious, it is true that we shall be obliged to tackle new and greater problems—but they will be problems for which we shall ourselves be permitted to find the solution." This put the dilemma of labor in World War II—the most "necessary" war in all U.S. history—in a nutshell. The problems were fast arising, and their numbers and magnitude would increase before it was over, but the UAW was unquestionably committed to the prosecution of this war: fascism was the quintessence of antiunionism. Sugar personally represented the difference between this war and the last one. He proudly registered for the draft, although overage, and spoke frankly about his earlier opposition.

Except for Trotskyists (and even they were not unanimous), the Left and the labor movement were thus behind the war effort. The Communist party, as usual, tended to expunge all nuances from its position. Earl Browder developed a line so totally committed to massive production for war, all-out mobilization on the home front, and bold action in the war zones that he lost sight of any dangers inherent in the process. Bert Cochran presents a remarkably persuasive, though most unflattering, picture of Browder's single-minded, almost monomaniacal, new patriotism. What delight the Kansas-born Communist, whose position in the Party was certainly not hurt by his multigeneration roots in United States soil, took in the happy circumstances where "Communists could be both Russian patriots and American patriots"! The Communists thus ended up representing the most extreme position within the labor movement in defense of national unity and, practically, of everything the Roosevelt administration did. As time went by, this meant a position in defense of greater and greater limitations on the hard-won rights of labor.[9]

And *this* meant that anti-Communism still had a healthy future: one could attack the Communists for being antilabor. This was a tricky business, for one might easily be branded in return pro-Fascist (as the antiwar Trotskyists certainly were). But there were serious violations of labor's rights going on and to speak for the needs of the rank-and-file, to emphasize that wildcat strikes (while they had to be condemned) did have real bases, and to oppose schemes to increase or control production that would undermine labor's recent gains were thoroughly defensible positions. This became Walter Reuther's new strategy. Union militance and anticommunism seemed complementary when viewed from that perspective. The Communists, or at least the Browderites (which until late in the war meant the vast majority of Communists), had largely themselves to blame.

The other aspect of Reuther's strategy was to assail Addes and Sugar because they were the men most intimately involved in carrying out the bureaucratic and legal work necessary in dealing with the multiple connections between the union and war mobilization. As Sugar put it in his official report in 1943, "During this period it may be said that all of our roads lead ultimately to Washington." They thus left their flanks exposed, and the Reuther faction nipped away at them.

The attack, by and large, was not legitimate. This is the point that histories of this period seem to miss. Addes, Sugar, and their caucus were hardly dupes of the Communists. Moreover, as Roger Keeran makes clear (without being explicit about it), Communists in the UAW were considerably less rabid in their victory fever than the *Daily Worker*. Sugar and his staff, arms-length friends of the Communists, and George Addes, who respected their opinions, took a position that avoided the stupidities of the Communist line and sought to retain the integrity of the labor movement while nonetheless remaining steadfast in support of the war effort. The key to their perspective, which rubbed off on R. J. Thomas, was a healthy disrespect for the Roosevelt administration.

At the same time they were also the bureaucrats responsible for administering the policies imposed by the government. In looking at their perspective, we are looking at the heart of the U.S. labor movement during World War II. Neither Julius Emspack's slavish dedication to incentive pay nor Matt Smith's dreams of reviving the Shop Stewards movement (and a third federation of labor), neither Mike Quill's violent denunciations of John L. Lewis as a Fascist nor Lewis's willingness to hamstring the coal industry while U.S. soldiers died at Anzio represented widespread opinion in the labor movement. Only a taste for extremes among contemporary journalists and some historians have made it seem that way. The essential reality of 1942–45 was not nearly so dramatic. It was instead the discordant interplay between the desire to seat the union firmly in a regular, respectable, inevitably law-bound and bureaucratic place in U.S. society and the will to resist the Roosevelt administration's apparent willingness to allow U.S. capitalism to reconsolidate its dominance under the smokescreen of war.

Within days after Pearl Harbor, labor—CIO, AFL, and most independents (including MESA at that point)—pledged not to strike "for the duration." The no-strike pledge became formalized through the War Labor Board, which was to adjudicate industrial relations during the war. While in the spring the CIO, spearheaded by the UAW, declared a policy of "equality of sacrifice," meaning profits should be rolled back and controlled, the fact was that labor had, in the parlance of the time, been *taken for a ride*.

Despite the war-support focus of the legal department report of 1942, even a casual reading of it reveals a recognition and denunciation of the bind. The aviation companies were using the situation to take advantage of the union, resorting "to every device, legal and illegal—usually illegal—that had been practiced by the automobile manufacturers in the early days of our union." Such resistance was much more difficult to meet because of the loss of the strike weapon, "a weapon which had been found absolutely indispensible in circumventing the legalistic maneuvers of the employers." Then comes the crux of the dilemma. In order to operate effectively under these conditions, the amount of legal work and contributions from experts on this or that intricacy of the War Labor Board regulations had multiplied geometrically. The report went on, "While the ingenuity of our legal department has been taxed to the utmost . . . , it may be reported with gratification that the successful disposition of our legal problems has contributed in substantial measure to the phenomenal progress which has been made by our union."

This dependency on the law was exacerbated by an increasingly hostile National Labor Relations Board. Roosevelt's appointment of Gerard D. Reilly in 1941 completed the conservative conquest of the board. In time, Harry Millis would be considered a liberal. R. J. Thomas had already rued this development late in 1941: "Numerous decisions handed down by the board of late show a distinct trend away from the enforcement of the Wagner Act in the interests of the workers for whose benefit it was enacted." The key problem here concerned the impediments placed on new organizing activity, which was stimulated by the growth of the defense industry.

Sugar was acutely aware of this trend, as he was, too, of the problems created by having the War Labor Board act as the final arbiter of the collective-bargaining process. In marked contrast with the Communist-party position, he was sharply critical of both, as he was of other failings of the Roosevelt administration. Even in 1942, the year of greatest rapport between the UAW and the administration, he fought the government on several fronts.

Aliens were being summarily discharged from defense work under orders from the army and the navy. Thoroughly familiar with the historic disabilities suffered by the foreign born, Sugar prepared an exhaustive memorandum on the issue, pointing out the abuses. This critique forced the service branches to crack down on "the discriminatory practices which had been employed by management with respect to alien workers."

Another problem had been the dismissal of "subversive" workers. This was especially delicate because subversion was certainly there, coming from pro-Nazis, but the ease with which management could transform its definition of subversion to include union activism or militant behavior was well known. Civil rights of U.S. citizens had already been trampled on in the case of the infamous Japanese "internment" policy, and union members had to keep on alert. Investigations of victimization of union members led to "the elimination of almost all these practices." There was concern about "fifth-column" activities, but it is significant that whereas the Communist party called for the ruthless rooting out of subversion, and vigorously attacked the ACLU for its defense of "Fascists," the legal department of the UAW remained fully aware of the inherent constitutional dangers of such a path.

Fingerprinting of defense workers was a related issue and the legal department took steps to assure that such records could not be "utilized by employers to destroy our union." Sugar also took up the problem of questionnaires and loyalty pledges. Approved army and navy forms were legitimate (and there was often quite sensitive defense work being done), but workers were instructed not to fill out and sign employer questionnaires if they had not been agreed to by the union through regular collective-bargaining procedures, for such matters related to "conditions of employment" covered under section 9(a) of the NLRA.

Sugar also moved immediately for the enforcement of "equal pay for equal work" for women war workers. In a test case in June 1942, Jack Tucker won back pay for twenty-nine women workers in the Lansing Oldsmobile plant under a new Michigan law. In states with similar laws, success was obtained as well, but equality in others would be more difficult to achieve and a "salutary political activity" would be to pursue them.

Sugar and his associates thus did not allow their enthusiasm for the prosecution of the war to run away with them and remained cognizant of the dangers to civil rights and union security that the national emergency presented.[10]

Such vigilance increased as time went by. A great deal has been made by those bent on attacking the UAW administration during the war (and by the Reuther caucus at the time) of the "incentive-pay" issue. The idea apparently originated in government circles, but was warmly embraced by the Communist party in late 1942. The concept amounted to a return to piecework, with output beyond a certain level of production being rewarded by extra pay. With wages, in effect, frozen by the "Little Steel formula" at mid-1942 levels, this was seen by both Addes and Frankensteen as an interim policy that would increase production and make up some of the inflation-eroded income losses experienced by their members. Addes remembered Sugar being skeptical of the plan from the beginning, not only because of traditional workers' mistrust of piecework (it was so easy to raise production "standards") but also because of the use to which

271

Reuther would put the issue for factional purposes. In general, however, it was not a question that preoccupied the legal department, because legal opinion about it was largely unnecessary. The issue itself became a dead letter as the membership solidly demonstrated itself opposed to it. But Reuther regained much lost ground vis-à-vis Addes because of the latter's initial support of it. At the October 1943 convention in Buffalo, Addes and Frankensteen were accused in verse of taking their orders from "Joe Staleen," and Leonard came within seventy votes of capturing the secretary-treasurer's office.

The actual preoccupations of the legal department during the war concerned governmental abridgments of trade union rights and the abuse of members' civil rights. The struggles showed the increasing conservatism of the courts, the Roosevelt administration, and legislatures as the war ground on, but the union managed to fight off the worst reactionary threats.

One of the most vexing issues concerned the taxation and social-security benefits of workers who were awarded back pay for time lost because of illegal layoffs (usually for union activity). Winning back pay had been the last triumph of the Ford battle, and Sugar, Goodman, Smokler, and Tucker had gained awards for several thousand workers worth millions of dollars. The problem was that the federal government taxed the full amount of pay awarded in the year the worker received it and at the tax rate (which had increased substantially due to the war) of that year. This meant, in effect, that the Internal Revenue Service was taking advantage of companies' past unfair labor practices. A related issue was the Social Security Board's refusal to recognize that back pay constituted "remuneration for services rendered" and thus refused workers the benefits under the act. Both issues took virtually the entire period of the war to settle. The federal government put up furious resistance.

On the tax issue, the union lost an appeal to the Treasury Department and in federal court in 1942 but sponsored a bill, introduced by Congressman John Dingell, a Democrat representing Dearborn and vicinity, to amend the tax law. As the 1946 legal report proudly states, "We succeeded [in 1944] in getting Congress to enact an amendment to the income tax law (the first success of labor in this field) under which the amounts received were taxed at the greatly lower rates in effect for the years covered by the award." The social-security benefit question took even longer: while they kept beating the government in court, the case was appealed all the way to the Supreme Court and only late in 1945 was it decided in the union's favor.

On the other hand, in a major test case in 1943, the Supreme Court had refused to hear the Chrysler unemployment-compensation case, in which the union demanded unemployment compensation for workers locked out of Dodge Main during the fall 1939 negotiations with Chrysler. The damage done here was made up in part by victories in the Supreme Courts of Michigan and Indiana, which awarded unemployment benefits to workers fired for wildcat strikes. In many other states, particularly in the West and South, however, antilabor legislation and judicial decisions were becoming a fact of life. Sugar summarized the frightening dimensions of these laws in 1943:

> Among the provisions appearing in the laws of one or more of these states are provisions which require that (1) labor unions must incorporate; (2) they are subject to state regulations in such matters as frequency of meeting, method of voting, and qualifications of members and officers; (3) complaints by a member against his union may be taken to a state commission rather than be determined by the union itself; (4) expulsion or discipline of members is prohibited without state approval; (5) no one may solicit another to join the union without first obtaining a license; (6) closed shop contracts are forbidden except upon a vote of ¾ of the employees; (7) non-citizens may not hold office in the union or solicit memberships; (8) peaceful picketing is prohibited unless the strike has first been called by a ¾ vote—and the number of pickets may be limited by the state; (9) each department in the plant may have a separate election to determine its bargaining agent; (10) unions engaged in prohibited acts may have their right to function forfeited for as long as a year, during which period they can conduct no activity as a labor union and shall have no right to employer recognition; and (11) penalties of fines and imprisonment are provided for violations.

Simply to enumerate these provisions is to understand the serious nature of the "sun-belt" reaction against labor, occurring at the very moment when states like Michigan and Indiana were being won over.

The Texas law became famous when, in September 1943, R. J. Thomas himself was sent by Sugar to test it. He gave a speech soliciting union membership without obtaining a permit. He was also under a restraining order from the state attorney general not to speak and thus was tried both as a criminal under the law and for contempt for violating the injunction. On the first charge, he was acquitted, but there was no test of the law's constitutionality. On the second he was convicted and sentenced to three days in jail and a hundred-dollar fine. An appeal to the state supreme court lost. Amid wide news coverage, it was appealed to the U.S. Supreme Court, and the case was won in January 1945, argued by Ernest Goodman. This opened the way for other appeals—especially of the Florida law, which in most particulars was ruled unconstitutional in 1945. Positive decisions on Colorado, Kansas, and Alabama laws followed.

Looking back on this experience in early 1946, Sugar wrote, "We cannot over-emphasize the importance of the battle centering around the anti-labor enactments of the various states. It is clear that our success over the past years in blocking such legislation in Congress has caused the anti-labor employers to divert their energies to the field of state legislation. . . . Our success has been exceptional [in blocking this attack]." He concluded, however, by noting that "the anti-labor interests are again reverting to the form of their original attacks." The congressional struggle would be protracted but eventually end in defeat with the passage of Taft-Hartley.[11]

The UAW's legal department also made important contributions in the area of civil rights. Two of Sugar's lieutenants were also prominent civil-liberties lawyers. Goodman had long been associated with the Civil Rights Federation (CRF), which grew out of the old Conference for the Protection of Civil Rights. During the war he acted as its principal legal advisor and spent many hours working on its projects. Ned Smokler was the executive secretary of the local branch of the National Lawyers Guild. In their functions, they were in a position to bring these organizations to the service of the UAW and—just as important—they engaged officers of the union like Addes and Thomas to lend their prestige to non-labor-movement issues important to the CRF and the guild.

Particularly significant in this relationship was the aid each gave to the other in the pursuit of racial equality. The CRF's first big battle after the war began concerned the Sojourner Truth Housing Project, undertaken to help ease the critical housing shortage in Detroit that had developed during the defense period. As the name indicates, it was originally slated by the federal government to be a black project. It was located in a predominantly lower-middle-class white neighborhood in northern Detroit and the congressman in whose district it fell, Rudolph G. Tenerowicz, lobbied to have it made a "white" development. After considerable vacillation and amid intense local controversy, the government reaffirmed black occupancy early in 1942.

Attempts to start moving in were met by a race riot fomented by white toughs, some of whom were associated with the KKK. The explosion led to red-baiting by Tenerowicz, who accused the "Communists" of the CRF of creating the crisis. The whole city stood in fear of a major racial upheaval. But liberal forces and the labor movement coalesced in March and April. The Wayne County CIO council, on a motion from UAW leaders, wired President Roosevelt, asking him that "the Negro people be assured by him that they would not be deprived of the homes built for them." While tensions remained high, this unity, effected above all by the multiple Left-labor connections of Sugar's legal office, was an important factor in the eventual occupation of the project in late April.

As war production moved into high gear in 1942, the influx of new workers was enormous. Housing rivalry was certainly important, but job competition between blacks and whites posed a greater threat. Since many of the new white arrivals were from the South, an atmosphere of open racial denunciation and display existed. A *Harpers'* article described a meeting of Packard Local 190 members during one of its wildcat "hate" strikes in which a white southerner delivered the following harangue: "I don't wanta work nex' to no nigger. They all got syphillis. If one of 'em touches you, you'll sure get it." Not withstanding the fact that he thereafter asked a black man for a cigarette, such talk was serious, and tensions were great.

There were some fifty-five thousand blacks out of roughly five hundred thousand UAW members in 1942. The proportion of blacks increased substantially during the war. Their greatest concentration, both in number and power, was in Rouge Local 600, where they comprised eighteen thousand out of ninety thousand members in 1942. The UAW leadership had taken a strong stand on racial equality throughout the organizing drive and had received consistent backing (and prodding) from Detroit's Left community. It was no accident that Local 600 was also a Left stronghold, for its black membership, led by Shelton Tappes, was left-leaning. (Horace Sheffield led a smaller element loyal to the Reuther faction.)

In 1942 and 1943, however, leadership confronted the most serious challenge to its commitment that the union would ever face. Traditionally, work in auto plants for blacks was limited to the most menial tasks. As transfer to defense work occurred, under the combined pressure of the federal Fair Employment Practices Commission (FEPC), the local citizens Committee for Jobs in War and Industry (organized by Rev. Charles Hill and the leftist Michigan division of the National Negro Congress [NNC], whose secretary was Coleman Young), and union FEPC committees, companies were encouraged to place blacks in all sorts of positions, including skilled work. In general, as historian Nelson Lichtenstein has pointed out, skills required for defense work were higher on the average than in automobile production because the products were often new, model changes frequent, and special handling necessary; this also meant that knowledge of production procedures developed with the job, giving the production-unit personnel greater job control than was normally the case in more routinized auto production. The "upgrading" of blacks and their entrance into such groups (usually they were a tiny minority in upgraded situations) provoked resentment among whites.

Whites' response was often to strike. Beginning with the Packard strike of April 1942, more than two score of these "hate strikes" occurred in Detroit and elsewhere. The union was hard-pressed to deal with them because it meant that leaders had to challenge the wishes of a majority of their members. But as Meier and Rudwick show in their excellent analysis, the combined forces of steady union pressure (and discipline), the public action of the citizens committee, and the research of the NNC and the CRF on conditions fomenting the white response progressively eliminated these confrontations. The CRF, under the vigorous leadership of Jack Raskin, put a special focus on the role of organized racist and fascist groups like the KKK and Gerald L. K. Smith's following. Goodman served as an effective link between the CRF and the UAW.

Finally, in the great Detroit race riot of June 1943, the UAW acquitted itself extremely well. "Flying squadrons" organized in the old days for picketing action or factional fighting, now served as peacekeeping units both in the plants and on the streets. That the rioting stayed out of the plants and main industrial areas in general was a tribute to the union. Thomas, Addes, and all the other leaders of the union spoke out vigorously against the white racism that ran rampant for days. On June 22 a black-white committee of civic leaders was formed and issued an appeal to Detroiters to end the conflict, arguing that the white attacks on blacks was significantly influenced by organized hatemongers of

275

the Right. Among the committee members were UAW leaders Thomas and Hodges Mason (in his capacity as vice president of the Wayne County CIO council). The entire CIO establishment was present. Both Jack Raskin and Ned Smokler played important roles in drafting the manifesto of the "white leaders."

The following day, Thomas, after consultation with Sugar and his staff, issued an eight-point program of investigation and recuperation. After complementing "our membership, white and colored," on "realiz[ing] their highest responsibilities and carry[ing] them out," the statement called for (1) a special grand-jury investigation that would include a "competent Negro attorney as an assistant prosecutor"; (2) construction and opening of more parks and recreation facilities (the riot started in Belle Isle Park); (3) more federal housing projects for "Negro slum dwellers"; (4) "insistence that plant managers as well as workers recognize the right of Negroes to jobs in line with their skill and seniority"; (5) the investigation of laxity by the police department in quelling the riot; (6) "special care by the courts" in dealing with arrestees, severe punishment of the guilty, and no racial discrimination in the proceedings; (7) a muncipal fund to make good property losses due to the riot; and (8) "a bi-racial committee of ten to make further recommendations looking toward elimination of racial differences and friction," especially in the high schools, where much of the conflict originated.

This proposal was followed on June 28 by a long release, edited by Smokler, presenting the National Lawyers Guild's call for action to eliminate the deeper cause of the riot, which, it said, "is the long-fostered prejudice of whites against Negroes, coupled with the known facts that Negroes have not been given their full rights and opportunities as citizens and qualified workers, and their resentment of this discrimination."

Both Thomas's plea and the guild's sociological perspective were largely ignored by the authorities. A grand-jury investigation was turned down by the city council and by the governor. Prosecutor William E. Dowling took the responsibility of investigating the events himself and issued a statement, followed by a long report to the governor, which took the outrageous position that blacks started the riot and inflicted the greater harm. Twice as many whites as blacks were injured, he said. The fact was, of course, that twenty-five of the thirty-four killed were black, twenty gunned down by the police. Dowling further accused the NAACP of fomenting the riot by all the "radical talk" at its early June convention in Detroit. The *Redford Record* followed this up with the amazing news that Walter White's gray-flannel organization was run by the Communists.

The black community gasped in disbelief that this was to be accepted as the official report on the riot. But, except for the *Detroit Free Press,* which editorialized that Dowling merely "shakes the trees instead of getting at the roots," white Detroit remained remarkably silent at the news of the prosecutor's literal "whitewash." Naturally, the largely white CRF and Lawyers Guild protested, the latter flabbergasted at the "incredible effrontery" of Dowling's committee in blaming the victim and lamenting that the report "clearly reflects a maligant prejudice against the Negro." Among the major voices of white opinion in Detroit, only the CIO forthrightly attacked the prosecutor. The CIO council issued a statement saying Dowling "completely disqualified himself" from any further association with the investigation and renewed the call for a grand jury. R. J. Thomas released a statement (ignored by the daily press) calling the report a "hysterical alibi" for the prosecutor's own ineffectiveness and compared the NAACP to the union: "It . . . is a trouble-making organization in the sense that unions are trouble-makers for unfair employers, and in the same sense that those who believe in liberty are trouble-makers for Hitler."

Meier and Rudwick quote this statement and go on to argue that the union had become the staunchest ally of black people in Detroit. Addes and Reuther agreed on this, if little else. The UAW had, in Addes's words of 1946, "the largest group of organized Negro workers in the country" and, while not perfect, it had "the best record in this field of human relations of any comparable organization in American life, including the churches." But these authors lose sight of the important fact that there was a large Left community in Detroit—represented by organizations like the National Negro Congress, Civil Rights Federation, and the Lawyers Guild—that had for years been instrumental in tying together the goals of unionism and the aspirations of black people.

White and black leftists in Detroit had been chipping away at black suspicions of unions and prejudice against blacks by stressing their common destiny as workers. And within the union, leftists remained the main proponents of full equality. Sugar had been and remained at the very heart of the process. In the past, going at least back to the recorder's-court campaign of 1935, he had hammered home the point that the emancipation of black people and the emancipation of labor were the same thing. Now, at the moment when the alliance reached its culmination, he and the lieutenants were central in the union's decision-making process on racial issues. Not only were the CRF's and Lawyers Guild's opinions respected (indeed often followed to the letter) within the UAW, but both Thomas and Addes always sought Sugar's personal opinion in civil-rights and racial-equality issues. Speeches and press releases made by both, but especially Addes, were regularly sent to Sugar for comment and, according to Addes, many of his own presentations were outlined by Sugar or developed out of conversations with him. Despite the horrible circumstances, 1943 was a moment of triumph for Sugar, the Left, and the union in their long battle to win the trust of black Detroiters.

This consistent position of the Left within the union also paid a political dividend in 1943. At the Buffalo convention, Reuther mounted a vigorous campaign that came within a hairbreadth of unseating George Addes. But prior to the convention, the Addes faction, at the suggestion of Shelton Tappes, had developed the idea of creating a minority-affairs department headed by a black executive-board member. This quickly gained wide support among black delegates and put the Reuther faction in a bind: since Tappes was leading the campaign, he was sure to be the choice of the UAW blacks. This meant that the evenly divided board just might swing decisively to Addes's side with Tappes's addition. Reuther therefore opposed the "Jim Crow" arrangement (others called it "racism in reverse"), although he supported the idea of a minority-affairs department.

When Addes beat Leonard by just seventy votes, it was clear that the black delegates put him over the top. But the closeness of the vote convinced the Addes strategists, black and white, that the resolution would have to be watered down to pass. So they decided upon the expedient of trying to woo a few of Reuther's followers who liked the idea of a black member of the board but feared factional losses because of it, by reducing the number of votes possessed by that board member to one (board members had a range of votes from ten to eighty-two, depending on the size of their constituency). This insulted a few black voters and Reuther loyalist Horace Sheffield made a great deal of it in taking his generally unpopular stand in support of the department but against the board member. As it turned out, both positions lost. The momentum did carry over to the following year, however, as FEPC lawyer George W. Crockett, Jr. was named to a newly created Fair Practices Committee, a subdepartment in the union.[12]

While the union took its stand for civil rights vis-à-vis black people, it was sorely tested again and again with regard to the rights of its own members, who continued to do what union people do: they struck. The war years saw a remarkable persistence of strike activity despite the fact that labor "took the pledge." John L. Lewis and his miners were the only important union to refuse to do so initially, but many independents later joined him. The major unions remained steadfast, however, and the vast majority of the wartime strikes, which caused the loss of thirty-nine million man-days, were wildcats. Unlike the hate strikes, which were rooted largely in social and cultural biases, most of these stoppages were caused by the chaotic conditions of work of the defense industry and the fact that through speedup, cheating on overtime, and a general will to violate the rules of the game, companies reaped profits as never before, while wages remained frozen. *Equality of sacrifice* was a joke.

This is not the place to review the complex and fascinating history of the wartime wildcats, which has received much attention recently. The work of Martin Glaberman and Nelson Lichtenstein is particularly important. There has been a tendency to castigate union leadership for its repressive policies toward striking members and to assume these "labor bureaucrats" blindly followed the dictates of Washington. Those in the Left caucus of the UAW, meaning above all Addes and Sugar, are deemed to have let the membership down. Unquestionably, the issue became central in Walter Reuther's attack on them, although he never veered very far from the straight and narrow on the issue either.

In 1944, when the matter came to a head at the Grand Rapids convention, Reuther took the position that the no-strike pledge should continue to receive support (which was the Addes/Thomas position) but that with the defeat of

Germany, the pledge should be lifted for plants engaged in nonmilitary production. A third, "rank-and-file" caucus, strongly influenced by Trotskyists, called for rescinding the pledge altogether. Its numbers at the convention were small, but support from the membership at large was significant. After the convention a referendum on the issue was held. Although the pledge was upheld, nonvoters outnumbered voters by three to one and wildcats continued. Glaberman estimates that more than half the members of the UAW participated, however briefly, in wildcats during the war. Overall, Reuther stayed in somewhat closer touch with this sentiment than the Addes forces and did not take a position on the referendum, thereby implying support for abstention.

That the Communist party blindly supported the no-strike pledge is well known. But it is unwarranted to translate this into the position of the entire Addes caucus. Viewing the question through the action and the recommendations of Sugar is certainly worthwhile, for it helps to clarify exactly what the policy was.

We have already seen that the legal department understood the bind that the no-strike pledge put labor in and looked at some of its efforts to fight off its reactionary implications. Sugar was hardly the "dupe" of the Roosevelt administration and hence of capitalism. (And never did he talk about "making capitalism work" to win the war, a regular feature of Communist rhetoric.)

An early indicator of his attitude arose over the related questions of the "swing shift" and overtime pay. To increase production in the fluid war conditions of 1942–early 1943, the government encouraged the development of the swing shift, a program of irregular working hours whereby a worker might be called in on short notice or work extra time, thus completely disrupting leisure and family time. The overtime-pay question had to do with remuneration for the extra work. Both were based on Executive Order 9240, which abolished the payment of overtime specifically for Saturday and Sunday work, but "permitted" payment of time and a half for any sixth day worked in a row and required double time for the seventh.

Sugar and Addes, who were the responsible union officials, received many complaints about the hardships of the swing shift, particularly the fact that weekends were eliminated. Time with children, church, and other weekend activities was torn asunder. It was also a cause of slowdowns and stoppages. While sympathetic, Sugar developed this simple argument in return: the sacrifice of regular activity among civilians was clearly less significant than the sacrifice of all control over one's time being experienced by millions of citizens in the military. This was the union's position, though it worked to minimize inconveniences for its members.

But on the overtime-pay question, Sugar was unequivocal. Secretary Perkins, through her interpretation of the law, was allowing the companies to get away with murder. She made a "complete perversion of the intent of the order" by her definition of the work week. She "originally ruled that double time must be paid for the seventh consecutive day worked regardless of whether the seven days fell within one or more work weeks." Later, without consultation with labor, she changed this to say that double time need be paid only in those instances where the seventh day falls within a "regularly scheduled work week." This amounted to a license for employers to manipulate the work week in such a way as to avoid paying overtime altogether: "Workers may be employed," Sugar pointed out, "for as many as 12 consecutive days in a two-week period without receiving double time." While Perkins did not bend on this issue amid an uproar from labor (except the Communist party), the legal department of the UAW "spent considerable time" revising local union contracts to protect the rights of UAW members in this regard.

These examples perfectly illustrate the position Sugar encouraged: reasonable sacrifice of individual comfort for the war effort without relinquishing the essential rights of labor.

How did Sugar advise Addes and Thomas to respond to worker protests that violated the no-strike pledge? The picture we have from Trotskyist writings (Art Preis, Cochran, Glaberman) is that UAW leaders, virtual tools in the hands of "the Stalinists," clamped down immediately and with severity on all wildcats. This is not true. Addes's own policy, which he said developed in consultation with Sugar, was to apply in the first place what might be called the "twenty-four hour rule"—let a stoppage go for a day and see what happens. Anything longer, one had to examine the type of plant and the nature of the grievance. Response to hate strikes was instantaneous and tough (although Addes had trouble making his power felt even in a local like Packard 190, where his influence was great), but on overtime-pay conflicts, health and safety problems, foreman confrontations over job procedures, all speedup questions, black worker walkouts over racial discrimination, stoppages over women's rights, and a host of other wildcats based on legitimate grievances, the response time would lag and the informal conciliatory work would be considerable. Public statements were often harsh and certainly Thomas and Addes got angry at defiant strikers (especially if they felt the strikes were promoted by "Trotzkyites" for political ends), but calm discussion and cajoling and real attention to grievances were the more normal course. The very bureaucratic procedures of the union meant that orders to return to work would often be delayed for days. Correspondence between Sugar and Addes reveals that Sugar often rendered legal advice that made speedy action to end a wildcat difficult while nevertheless keeping up the public show of condemnation.

Moreover, "there were hundreds of ways short of striking" to make the bosses feel the workers' power and these were encouraged by all save the most dedicated New Dealers or Browderites. The very fact that conversion gave workers greater on-the-job power meant that they could often restrain speedup attempts by the bosses without resorting to an actual stoppage. In going through Glaberman's magnificent list of wildcats and their causes between December 1, 1944 and February 28, 1945 (the height of wildcat fever), a full three-quarters relate to protest over management counteraction against such use of worker job control (transfers of workers out of job units, firings for "loafing," disciplining a committeeman for threatening a foreman, etc.). The act of punishing in-plant slowdowns and work-to-rule was the main cause of wildcats.

The point is that the story of wartime strikes is much more complicated than it is often presented and the tendency to emphasize extremes (in this case Trotskyists versus Communists) has done a great disservice to the historical record and the reputations of union officials not on the extremes. In the end, this kind of polarization worked to the advantage, as is always the case, of the "outs" (Reuther) more than the "ins."[13]

One of the clearest cases where the Addes caucus leadership explicitly condemned its own extreme was the union's response to Roosevelt's "National Service Act," or "labor conscription" (as it was called by its detractors), proposed on January 11, 1944. It was a response to a rash of wildcats and fulfilled the dire predictions of union leaders about the repressive legislation they would encourage. For Roosevelt it was also a timely political act, designed to intimidate established labor leadership, whose pressure for more stringent price controls and wage increases had recently been great. It would have officially outlawed strikes and put defense workers under military discipline. He artfully combined it with the call for a new "bill of social rights." The reaction of the Communist party was predictable: it was all for it. Within the UAW, however, response was immediate and fiercely opposed. Emil Mazey and Paul Silver, Socialist-party activists who had already started a third-party movement and were among the union's strongest non-Trotskyist opponents of the no-strike pledge, said this now assured the success of their Farmer-Labor party. Two weeks later Mazey, president of Briggs Local 212, was drafted. But somewhat more surprising, Thomas and Addes immediately blasted the proposal. Sugar was not called upon to make a public statement but Addes had consulted with him and was assured that Sugar thought it a danger "of the first order." Within the UAW, the only high official who publicly voiced support was Leo LaMotte, who was quickly throttled. The entire labor movement condemned the idea and toward the end of January, the CIO national council (including Harry Bridges, Joe Curran, and the rest of those identified with the CP) unanimously denounced the plan. It died a quiet death, but the Communist party again came away with egg on its face. Addes and Sugar did not, although guilt by association even in this matter would not be forgotten by the Reuther camp.[14]

Beyond the raging controversies that occupy the attention of historians of the International, quiet, efficient, routine work was being done to build the benefits union members received and to strengthen the union internally. The "maintenance of membership" provision that accompanied the no-strike pledge meant that erosion of past gains in members was minimal while new plants for defense brought in more and more people. By 1945, the UAW was the largest union in the nation with 1.25 million members. This, combined with George Addes's continued efficiency and the fact that no money was spent for strike benefits, meant that the union was in the best financial shape of its life. It had amassed a reserve fund of over two million dollars. Its bureaucratic routine was well established, and staff in its various departments were committed and active despite their modest salaries. The *United Auto Worker* was one of the best labor papers in the country, the union was moving into FM radio, the education and research departments were invaluable, and special departments for women and minority workers were established during the war. The busy Washington office handled the union's often delicate relations with the government.

Sugar was directly involved with several programs and developments that both stabilized the union and brought popular routine benefits to the workers. Because of their legal expertise, Sugar and his staff became the principal advisors to local unions on group insurance plans, which proliferated everywhere during the war. They also served as the key advisors to the Medical Research Institute (expanded in 1944 into a nonprofit corporation called the Health Institute), which studied health and safety conditions in the plants. On the basis of this close relationship, Sugar reported that the "legal department has utilized the experience of the Health Institute in its preparation of recommended legislative changes in workman's compensation laws."

The legal department was also responsible for the not always pleasant task of advising on trial procedures and other disciplinary activities carried out by the local unions. While the UAW made every effort to keep down reprisals against wildcat strikers, there remained a special concern regarding right-wing provocateurs, who in fact were plentiful enough, if not as ubiquitous as the *Daily Worker* imagined. One such case turned out to be of great significance in legitimizing the internal justice system of the union.

In March 1943, Arthur O'Brien, a committeeman, was charged with failure to represent workers in his department, berating members before supervisory personnel, and attempting to get black workers to strike against whites. He was tried and convicted by the trial board of Local 600, strongly implying that he was a right-wing provocateur, although the charge was "conduct unbecoming a member of the union." He then followed the constitutional appeal procedures, which took him through the local's general council (it reduced the sentence), the International executive board, and the 1944 convention, all of which upheld the trial committee. Thereafter he instituted a suit against the union, claiming $250 thousand in damages from the trial officers, including Shelton Tappes.

Ernest Goodman took the case and was opposed by Larry Davidow who, Sugar noted, since "Martin's journey into oblivion, when he has not been pursuing his futile effort to get elected to office on an anti-labor platform, has been looking under the beds for reds." The trial itself was a tough one: "Davidow used every known device (and some devices which . . . may previously have been unknown) to inject the deadly poison of prejudice into the case." All actions against O'Brien from the shop floor to the full convention "were pictured as part of a vast Communist conspiracy" involving Thomas, Addes, *and* Reuther (all of whom were subpoenaed), the entire executive board, Sugar, and anyone else Davidow could think of, including the judge, who finally directed a verdict of *not guilty.* Goodman, who usually "kept his cool," became so enraged at Davidow's abuse of the law, the court, and himself personally that he almost took a swing at Davidow at one point when the jury was not present.

But the case was more than another good Davidow story. It was the first time the full trial and appeal procedure had come under the scrutiny of the courts and it had passed with flying colors. Sugar wrote:

> In the ruling against O'Brien the court said that in the absence of a showing of bad faith, fraud, or illegal action, the union, being a self-governed voluntary association "has exclusive control over its own internal affairs in accordance with its constitution, by-laws, and practices." We may be proud that the democratic procedures which long characterized our International Union are so patently fair that the net result of this most vicious attack was the solemn approval of their fairness by the very court which was called upon to condemn them.

The O'Brien case was a landmark in the U.S. union's struggle for internal democracy. It also turned the tables on the red-baiters.[15]

The UAW thus remained in 1945 what it had been—a liberal, democratic union in which red-baiting was often in evidence but just as often backfired. It was, to be sure, increasingly bureaucratic with lots of protected positions and lots of competition for paid union jobs. The war had done a great deal to domesticate U.S. unions, but the agitation on the shop floors and the roaring battles at conventions proved there was fire left in the membership. Local meetings were still well attended, members still felt they were in charge, and suspicion of officers remained high.

But labor, and the UAW in particular, had gone, during the war, through an experience that greatly accentuated a condition of national life present since the Wagner Act (or at least since it was ruled constitutional in April 1937): the labor movement was enmeshed in the law. There was jubilation even when its own internal procedures got the stamp of approval of the courts! Labor, of course, was not the only movement or social institution to be wrapped in the constitution and its interpretations—the black struggle, led by the NAACP and its lawyer Thurgood Marshall, moved forward largely through the courts and would only begin to transform when legitimized by *Brown v. Board of Education;* the battle for female equality was waged primarily through the pursuit of legal goals, the Equal Rights Amendment being one more step along the way; family life and organization are thoroughly mixed up with the law and constitutional interpretations; even the individual right to die with dignity is deemed to be the business of the courts.

It is beyond the scope of this book to discuss the historical bases of the United States' absorption in the law, but the example of labor's experience should make activists in other fields (and labor itself) think twice before making legal sanction their principal goal. What happened in the most general sense was that the old fight *against*—through the use of the Bill of Rights and all its technical protections of liberties—increasingly became a fight *with the aid of,* where the law became a positive instrument for labor rather than a negative restraint on capital. But that in turn made labor dependent on the law-making process, on politics, which in fact it had never sought to control, although the Left, at least, understood that it should try. In fact, however, political power remained in the hands of a majority that for whatever reasons one might give— from capitalist hegemony to the "good sense" of individualistic U.S. citizens— was hostile to labor.

The political balance tipped briefly to the interests of industrial workers during the midthirties. By 1939 the NLRB was rendering decisions that made it seem that labor had taken a permanent place in the U.S. power structure. But then things shifted the other way. Fear fed upon fear and the U.S. business community began its comeback. The war only accentuated the trend. Labor fought back and effected a kind of stalemate through the law, while many rank-and-filers, through illegal strikes, shocked loyal citizens and embarrassed labor leaders. Roosevelt kept reaction from swinging too far, but with his death and with a man highly mistrusted by labor (the CIO had fought Truman's nomination tooth and nail) in the White House, the net of the law began to close around labor.

In his report to the January 1946 convention in Atlantic City, Sugar summarized the "dangerous trend of the NLRB in the last few years." While some success was still to be had in the federal courts (for example, Morten Eden's case in which the Supreme Court ruled in April 1945 that Republic Aviation could not prohibit solicitation of union members on company property if not on company time), the influence of Gerard Reilly on the board was becoming alarming, especially in regard to organizing and jurisdictional rights. During the war there was real pressure to keep plant guards separated from the union for security reasons. The union fought this and managed to get a two-to-one vote in its favor. After the war and with the replacement of Millis by Paul Herzog, the decision was reversed with Herzog joining Reilly on the grounds that protection agents were not production workers. The "national-security" question could no longer be at issue. The legal department saw this as "a serious threat against our union and against organized labor generally" for "the same kind of 'reasoning' may be held to apply to office workers, engineers and a great many other categories." The locals were put on notice not to negotiate any contract that specifically excluded categories of workers in the same plant and to be prepared to strike if necessary. Contracts containing such divisive clauses would not be accepted by regional directors.

In a case involving the Phelps-Dodge Corporation, the NLRB upheld a company plea that despite a long history of plantwide bargaining with the CIO and AFL skilled workers, they now be given the right to bargain with the AFL crafts individually. Millis, who dissented, saw this as a "new and unwarranted precedent."

284

What was most frightening, however, was the popularity of Reilly with congressional committees, especially because of his proposal that through an amendment to the act, "this board be given the same power to invoke the judicial process against recalcitrant labor organizations which it now possesses with regard to disobedient employers." As Sugar lamented, "What Reilly was really here seeking was an amendment to the Act to permit of proceedings against unions at the instance of employers, a consummation that employers have not only been wishing for, but fighting for, for many years." He concluded, "Frankness impels us to state that there can be no justification for membership on the NLRB of a person holding such views." Sugar's opinion, of course, was rooted in the decade of experience with a prolabor board, that that was the way the board was supposed to be. Such a public perception of the board's role would gradually slip away over the next two years.[16]

Sugar had an enviable record in overseeing the multiple legal affairs of the UAW during the war. His men had a string of Supreme Court victories, and the complex and trying battles with the War Labor Board and the NLRB had been fought to a standoff, at any rate. He had a highly competent staff, who groused occasionally about their own "starvation wages" but whose political and social commitment generally outweighed their unhappiness in this regard.

During the war, the range of Sugar's activities became so immense—as the catalog in this chapter shows (and only the surface has been scratched)—that he was largely an advisor, consultant, and political analyst for the union. He went to all executive-board meetings and generally to the major council meetings of the CIO. He was constantly going back and forth between Detroit and Washington. An incredible stickler for detail, he put in sixteen-hour days on a regular basis and expected the same of his men. Jack Tucker recalled that he even gave up going to Ann Arbor for football games because Saturdays were too busy. Only his trips to his beloved cottage on Black Lake in the north remained sacred.[17] Sugar had become a key link in a vast organization. In a certain sense he was a labor bureaucrat, although neither he nor any of the officers and the staff of the union matched the fifties image of the stable, staid, and self-satisfied labor leader. Still, the trend had begun almost as soon as the union won its last great victory at Ford. And even that depended as much on the manipulation of the law and the support of the NLRB as the militance of the workers.

But, at the war's end, the promise of that militance reviving, the continuing democracy within the union, and the holding at bay of the bogey of anticommunism augured well for keeping these bureaucratic tendencies in check. In what seemed like no time, however, militance was smothered, democracy misused and then truncated, and the road to a tightly run bureaucracy laid open. While the fundamental cause of this dramatic transformation, which also ended Sugar's career, was the reassertion of the political authority of U.S. capitalism, the key mechanism by which these ends were reached was anticommunism run rampant.

10 ❈ THE COMING OF THE NEW MODEL UNION

In the wake of the lockout of 1852, leadership of the machine-builders union, the Amalgamated Society of Engineers (ASE), gathered in London to consider their next step. The British labor movement had seen great movements come and go in the past two decades—the glory years of organization in the early thirties followed by repression, then revival, particularly on the political front, with the Chartist movement. In 1848 London bourgeois had armed themselves to fight against the revolution that never happened. Then, in the fifties, British capitalism set on a course of development that made England the undisputed economic (and political) power in the world for two decades.

Mid-Victorian England and Eisenhower's United States, while a century apart, had much in common. To prepare the way, both societies quickly shed their radicalism inherited from the earlier period. While physical-force Chartists suffered fates less dramatic than U.S. Communists, an anti-Socialist tenor beset England as surely as it did the United States a century later. Richard Cobden and Hubert Humphrey kept the fires of liberalism glowing by roasting the reds of their respective societies.

The beleaguered members of the Amalgamated Society of Engineers decided upon a different form of trade unionism. Explicitly condemning political radicalism while reinforcing ties with the Liberal party, emphasizing the importance of "responsible leadership," and, above all, stressing the building of union resources and avoiding strikes if possible, they made the best of a bad situation. Historians would call it the "new-model union." By the mid-1870s, ASE leaders and those of other like-minded unions who had formed the Trades Union Council were called the "junta." Their ranks, along with hordes of the unorganized, were increasingly restless.[1]

Historical parallels can always be overdrawn, so we shall stop. But union movements go through waves of change and they normally correspond to larger changes in the economic and political circumstances of the time. Walter Reuther

286

was hardly a William Allan (ASE general secretary), but the adjustments within the UAW and in its relationship to the society and politics of the postwar United States bear a striking resemblance to what happened in Allan's organization. Benefits, in terms of fringes, wages, and other economic guarantees, improved dramatically while worker power both on the shop floor and within the union deteriorated. The classic trade-off that ascendant capitalism always managed to effect in good times, money for authority, worked well in both cases. Neither Allan nor Reuther need to be viewed as villains (though many contemporaries of radical persuasion viewed them so): they followed their noses in a context where their moderate political principles, dedication to trade unionism, and thirst for personal power coincided with the trends in their booming economies. (How fleeting was the boom in the case of pre–Great Depression England is known; Americans are now facing the consequences of the Eisenhower-era freeways, suburbs, and gas guzzlers.)

Despite its hard-line, militant character, the GM strike of 1945–46, led by Reuther, itself represented the trade-off in action. Important gains in shop-floor autonomy made during the war were relinquished in the "reconversion," and the strike failed to address the issue. Money, instead, got all the attention. From a certain perspective, even Reuther's "open-the-books" demand posed a danger because in calling current profit levels "indecent" and demanding to expose them, it implied that there was a level that was decent.

It was within the union, however, that the changes wrought by the "new model" would become most striking. By 1951, Reuther had removed or co-opted most of his opponents (Local 600 remained a thorn in his side, and he ultimately put it under receivership, and his supporters there red-baited opponents before the House Un-American Activities Committee), revised the constitution to give increasingly greater power to the executive board, and ordained triennial conventions in the name of economy while multiplying the numbers of paid staff people beholden to him. The union ran efficiently and "served" its members well enough, much like a mutual insurance company serves its customers. To be sure, idealism remained, but its principal locus was at the leadership level, particularly among the key officers and department heads. Reuther himself came to be regarded as a "labor statesman," brushing shoulders with the main liberal and social-democratic leaders in this country and abroad and proposing grand schemes for social progress such as a national health plan.

For the rank-and-file, the main consequence of all this was withdrawal from union activism. Meeting attendance declined substantially, and union dues, increasingly "checked off" by most companies, became just another deduction box, like social security or group insurance, on a member's paycheck stub. Occasionally the ranks would mount a protest against their loss of power, but the majority remained complacent. They had good reason of course, because the union treated them well—wages and benefits increased with the boom in the auto market and with unheard-of programs like Supplemental Unemployment Benefits, instituted first in the 1955 Ford contract.[2]

Trade unionism in the postwar United States, if successful, operated on such principles, and there is certainly no guarantee that if the Addes-Sugar forces had won, the results would have been much different. But the *way* the winning occurred does require comment. Basically, Reuther combined the use of the anticommunism that ran rampant in the Cold War era with acquiescence to the legal shackles now replacing the legal aid of the past. Inasmuch as Sugar was at the heart of the story on both counts, his perspective and what happened to him personally help us grasp the entire problem.

The general framework of the UAW's last great factional fight is well known. Having taken a stand during the war that hedged a bit more on the no-strike pledge than the Addes forces and then proposing its repudiation for nonmilitary production, Reuther led the postwar General Motors strike to a successful conclusion. This momentum allowed him to mount a strong campaign for the presidency of the union, and at the Atlantic City convention in February 1946 he defeated R. J. Thomas in a close race. Addes had thought of running, too—and had told a number of people that he was "rather sick of Thomas"—but decided not to, largely because the CIO hierarchy again discouraged him. (One of the things that historians have little appreciated about Addes was that he really enjoyed his job as secretary-treasurer. He was good at it and confident in his abilities. The presidency was uncharted territory.) Reuther's victory, however, was incomplete because only seven of his people, including Emil Mazey (who was still in the armed service), were elected to the executive board. This gave Addes, Thomas, and Leonard, who emerged as the triumvirate opposed to Reuther, a solid ("automatic" said their detractors) majority of fourteen to eight. Under the anti-Martin constitution, this effectively contained the president.

Over the next year and a half, the struggle raged. It was the most publicized internal union fight in U.S. history. The daily press, news magazines, newsreels, and radio commentaries gave it full coverage. The bias was clearly toward Reuther, whose boyish good looks, intelligent manner of speaking, and consistent denunciation of Communists found wide appeal. Every executive-board meeting was a battleground, as Reuther tried to use his presidential power to remove this or that "red" staff member, while the Addes bloc tried to embarrass him at every turn. Every local union became a scene of factional bloodshed. The jockeying for position, the intrigues, dirty tricks, and vicious attacks in hundreds of local unions left marks that remain to this day. Little by little, the power of the presidency, Reuther's personality, his wider public support, the logic of his paycheck/security program, and the remarkable discipline of his army gained him the upper hand. The Addes faction was especially embarrassed by the support it gave to the strike by Allis-Chalmers Local 248 in Milwaukee, which the press characterized as a Communist conspiracy, an opinion Walter Reuther felt had sufficient validity to warrant ending the strike.

The anti-Reuther forces became desperate in the spring of 1947. They first attempted to merge the Communist-influenced Farm Equipment (FE) Workers into the UAW, a good idea two years before, but now grist for Reuther's publicity mill. The referendum vote on the FE merger in the summer showed just how much the Addes people had slipped and caused a stampede of the uncommitted to Reuther's side. In the last days of the campaign (the convention did not take place until November), the Addes-Thomas-Leonard coalition disintegrated, while they tried futilely to discredit Reuther as a stooge of U.S. capitalism.

This brief survey will suffice to set the scene. The story of the fight is well told elsewhere.[3] Its emotional content was perhaps best captured by novelist Clancy Sigal in *Going Away*. The sense of frustration and bitter enmity toward Reuther can be seen in this passage (Reuther appears under the name *Victor Hauser*):

> The people who hated Hauser most . . . were the militants and the old-line shop stewards: theirs was the clearest case. These old ones (in the auto industry you are old at thirty-five), with their memories, looked back to the thirties as the high point in their lives because they had a chance, for the first time, to fight back and give the front-office the well-deserved works, and now here was Victor Hauser, flanked by teams of social psychologists and campus economists, proposing replacement of this (granted, frequently anarchic) militance with a morbid philosophy of "sound labor-management relations," "centralization of union authority," "co-operation," "responsibility." Had a major employment crisis hit in '46 or '48 Victor Hauser would have gone down the drain. It didn't.

Those characterized here were the types Sugar respected and trusted most. They were the sit-downers, the Ford firees, and, for better or worse, many of the wartime wildcatters.

The factional fight was not the only—or even the main—thing affecting the union in 1946–47. In November 1946, U.S. voters elected the most conservative Congress since the early twenties. The campaign had been filled with fear of the Soviet Union and good old "Americanism" (including a massive dose of antiblack racism), and Truman was running scared. Robert Taft led the charge against labor, and before the cherry blossoms bloomed in 1947, the House had passed the Fred Hartley–sponsored version of the bill, and on May 13 the Senate overwhelmingly supported Taft's. They got together, passing a "compromise" that largely featured the Taft "moderate" bill. Although Truman vetoed it on June 20, he was overruled, and the Taft-Hartley Act became law at the very moment the bottom was falling out of the Addes campaign within the union.[4]

Sugar's relationship to both the factional fight and the rightward turn of labor law was intimate.

His feelings about Walter Reuther were conditioned by past experience. On occasion after occasion he had cringed at Reuther's opportunism and mistrusted his politics. Two more recent incidents seemed to confirm his opinions. The first occurred in 1943. Union officials often went to Washington to meet with the War Labor Board on various questions, and Sugar sometimes accompanied them as legal advisor. Only once, however, did Reuther ask him to go, and this was to a particularly sensitive discussion of possible ways around the wage-freezing Little Steel formula as it related to GM. Sugar recalled that Reuther's behavior was most unusual, because no sooner did they arrive at the conference room than Reuther headed for a seat as far away from Sugar as possible. Sugar, of course, made no move to join him, and that was clearly the way Reuther wanted it. Throughout the discussion, Reuther never once invited Sugar to contribute. The general counsel uttered not one word. The meeting adjourned without any progress being made and Reuther returned to Detroit empty-handed. The only reason Sugar could think of for Reuther's requesting his presence was so that the Left would know that "their man," Sugar, was also a party to the failure.

A more delicate situation arose during the General Motors strike. The issue was whether or not to mount a picket line of tool-and-die workers and thus risk a battle with police and an injunction. Both Reuther and Sugar knew that these skilled workers were so solid, and the possibility of finding scabs so remote that anything more than token picketing was not called for. Reuther had to talk to the leaders of the tool-and-die workers, who were generally leftists and came out of a strong confrontationist tradition dating back at least to 1933. So, again in an unusual move, he asked Sugar to come along to the meeting. Rather than taking the floor himself he did the even more unusual thing of calling first on Sugar to offer his opinions, legal and practical, on the question. Sugar did so, and Reuther then followed by agreeing that mass picketing would not be necessary.[5]

These instances demonstrated Reuther's deft political touch, but naturally left Sugar with the sense that he had been used. Combined with earlier experiences, they convinced him that Reuther was consumed by personal ambition and would stop at nothing to achieve complete power. With Reuther's election as president, Sugar therefore prepared to fight back.

Sugar was, perhaps, fortunate to be involved at all. At the Chicago board meeting (April 1946), the first confrontation between Reuther and the Addes majority almost ended Sugar's career as general counsel. Reuther certainly wanted to get rid of him, but since the board had to advise and consent on all appointments and Reuther wanted desperately to control the publicity and education departments, he "traded Sugar for Vic Reuther and Frank Winn," as board member Percy Llewellyn put it. This same board meeting saw a good deal more horse-trading and was the source of a policy statement from the board that condemned red-baiting. The fight was on, but Sugar was sorely dissatisfied with the first round. He was upset that compromises had been made. This created the framework for his blistering internal "Memorandum on the Existing Situation in the International Union," of May 23, 1946. This statement, essentially a list of instructions on how to fight Reuther, was not signed, and it circulated only among the top people in the Addes caucus. With it, Sugar became the chief strategist in the fight. It predicted the course of events with uncanny accuracy.[6]

After reviewing Reuther's long-range planning in the past, Sugar noted how he fell short of his objective at the last convention; "but no one who has the slightest knowledge of Reuther's personality could believe that he has changed in his objectives. . . . He proposes to 'take' [the officers and opposing board members] *at the next convention*." His first move, wrote Sugar, would be to try to eliminate more staff members, specifically Irving Richter (UAW lobbyist in Washington), George Crockett in fair employment, Allan Saylor in radio; and William Levitt in education. (This certainly was to be the case as time went by.) He would further try to undermine the board members' prerogatives in choosing their own International representatives. (This also happened—the following year at Louisville Reuther attempted to set a precedent by blocking the appointment by Region 1A director Percy Llewellyn of Chester Mullins, a somewhat mercurial figure by all accounts. Reuther failed.)

Sugar went on to give a pep talk, basically, for the officers to present to their board allies: "There must be no deals." The board had the power, it had to "be made to understand and feel that the *Board* is the highest authority in the union." Reuther had divided the membership and "been guilty of flagrant anti-Union conduct" by presenting his own program contrary to the program passed by the board. Reuther had already violated the board ruling on red-baiting by explicitly stating that he would eliminate the "10% of the Union who are Reds." (Reuther later attempted to beef up the innocuous anti-Communist clause in the Union's constitution passed back in 1941 by eliminating local-trial rights for "admitted" Communist officers. This move was blocked at the March 1947 Louisville board meeting by Addes using a constitutional law brief prepared by Sugar.)

Sugar felt that Reuther's red-baiting, his pronouncement of people *guilty* without proof was "a point of great vulnerability on his part. No one with a drop of fairness in his blood would even attempt to justify it." In this, Sugar was wrong, as were all who believed that constitutional guarantees, Anglo-American liberal concepts of equity, and old-fashioned fair play would condemn the red-baiters as they had in the past. A whole organization of alleged liberals dedicated to something other than "fairness" would soon be formed. The Union for Democratic Action, as it was first called, would have as charter members Walter Reuther and his friend Eleanor Roosevelt, who attacked board members for being "unfair" in trying to gag Reuther's anticommunism in Chicago. Phil Murray might condemn witch-hunts at two successive steel conventions, denounce the Taft-Hartley affidavits, and all the rest, but ultimately he would shake Walter Reuther's "good little hand" after Reuther wiped out the board at the next convention. Sugar, on page 10 of his memorandum, confidently urged,

"The contrast between Reuther and Murray must be exploited to the utmost. It is dynamite for Reuther."

Reuther took every opportunity to paint the Addes-Thomas-Leonard caucus with a red brush. He formed alliances with the Association of Catholic Trade Unionists and with the followers of the eccentric Trotskyist, Max Shachtman. The ACTU published a newspaper called the *Wage Earner,* the purpose of which became to extoll Reuther while minutely researching the "pinko" past of as many of his opponents in locals throughout the country as it could. Shachtman's associates, Irving Howe and B. J. Widick, did much the same in the widely disseminated newspaper, *Labor Action,* and later wrote a book justifying everything Reuther did.[7] *Walter Reuther and the UAW* (later shown to be in error on dozens of questions of fact by historian James Prickett) did demonstrate the Reuther strategy clearly: attack the Communists not because they represented a disruptive force in U.S. society, but on the grounds, first, that they were not really good trade unionists, having allowed Soviet foreign policy to dictate their stand favoring harmony with the bosses during the war and second, that now, while they might have toughened up, their association with the trade-union movement only hurt it, due to U.S. citizens' alleged hatred of the Soviet Union.

The Addes caucus, encouraged by Sugar, responded in kind, vilifying Reuther at every turn as a power-hungry opportunist with little concern for the true interests of the workers. The easiest—and ill-advised— path to follow was to emphasize that all the attention Reuther was getting from the "capitalist press" (there were hundreds of positive stories about him in the Luce publications *Time* and *Life, Colliers,* the *Saturday Evening Post,* and the mass daily press) meant that he was dancing to the corporations' tune. The final sally, prepared by Jim Wishart with the blessings of Sugar and the entire Addes leadership, proved a disaster: a pamphlet called *The Bosses' Boy* attempted to hang Reuther as a tool of capitalism by mixing accurate information with half-truths and downright lies. It was an unedifying conclusion to an unedifying campaign.

Reuther played for keeps. Jack Conway, Sugar's counterpart as chief strategist for the Reuther side, knew it well. Conway called the preparation for the convention triumph in October 1947 "a juggernaut."[8] The other side thought it was fighting a tough battle too, but they were not really in the same league and constantly had to deal with the "Communist question" gingerly. A good local-union example and the actions and attitudes of George Addes himself take us a long way toward understanding how hopeless the struggle actually was.

Bendix Local Number 9 in South Bend was one of the oldest and most militant locals in the UAW and a traditional Addes stronghold. Two incidents here in 1947 illustrate what was happening. Outstanding documentation allows us to give more detail than usual.

The first was the August 11 statement of Ralph Hershberger, a pro-Addes officer, read into the minutes of the third-shift meeting on the Farm Equipment Workers—merger referendum, which accurately reflected the oppressive anti-Communist atmosphere.

I have no more love for the communists' basic philosophy than they have for my basic philosophy.

The red hering [*sic*] is being dragged around over this merger issue. Some say anyone favoring this merger is following the party line. They may as well say that because the commies favor a wage increase, that anyone else who favors a wage increase is also a fellow traveller.

Let's face this matter on pure union principles and not let the matter of who is for or against it determine our vote and not let any phoney propaganda sway our judgement.

The merger lost in his shift twenty to three and seventy-eight to twenty-eight overall.

More complex was a successful power play by Reutherites based on charges of procompany, antiunion behavior. John Neff and Cyril Rogers, both pro-Addes, had been elected local vice president and recording secretary, respectively, the previous March in one of many spring elections that seemed to show a swing of the pendulum towards the Addes forces. The president, John Saxton, several other officers, and a number of committeemen were in the Reuther camp. On July 19, 1947, Neff was called to the plant by Brother Ladd, a Reuther committeeman, to check out a threatened wildcat strike in one department. When he arrived, Rogers also asked him to come to another department floor where it appeared that Florence Yates, who had done something to irritate her foreman, was about to be fired. Neff heeded Rogers's call first and ended up by berating Yates (in private) as a troublemaker. He also failed to deal with the other situation, which fortunately resolved itself. Yates then filed charges against Neff and Rogers for behavior unbecoming an officer (although she did keep her job) and shortly thereafter Saxton filed charges against Neff for trying to form "a rump group to oust Saxton unconstitutionally." He argued in meetings that Neff was tied to the Communists. Rogers resigned in the midst of the storm under agreement that Yates would drop her charges. He thus admitted his "guilt" and lost his credibility as a union leader.

Neff fought on. On August 14, the local voted him suspended of all duties and any eligibility for "elective or appointive office" until his trial. This meant (1) that his delegate credentials to the Indiana State CIO convention were voided and (2) that unless the trial were scheduled before September 21, he could not stand for nomination as a delegate to the UAW national convention. It was not. Only on October 2 was he tried and convicted on the grounds both of having "taken management's side" against Yates and for having failed to deal with the more serious—and potentially costly—wildcat threat. The matter did not end there. For on October 6, while nominees campaigned for slots in the delegation, the local magnanimously rescinded the conviction by a vote of 137 to 127! But no matter, the basic work was done: chalk up at least 28.66 votes more for the Reuther camp, that many fewer for Addes. Glenn Porter, Neff's friend, attempted to have the delegate election of October 21 declared fraudulent, but was simply ignored at the next local meeting.

293

Whether this was all a prearranged railroad or not (Yates and Ladd certainly might have been part of a plot), it allows us to penetrate the daily reality of union politics that year. Neff and Rogers may have exercised bad judgement and possibly sexist behavior, but did they deserve to be ousted from power? The keys to the Saxton strategy were those used by Reuther on the national level: keep the fear of communism percolating and appear to be taking a stand more militant than the Addes forces. They also knew how to go after the weak links: neither Neff nor Rogers, as demonstrated by this story, seemed particularly competent.

What happened here goes well beyond a mere example. Local 9 was the second largest in Region 3 (after Studebaker Local 5, also in South Bend). These two locals alone took the entire region into the Reuther column at the November 1947 convention. Local 5 had some shady elections, too. Arnold Atwood, located in Indianapolis, was the head of the region and a loyal Addes man. But in the end, because he saw the Reuther steamroller taking his region, he attempted to save his skin in a variety of ways.

The most important was of historic proportions, for in the October mail ballot on the Taft-Hartley Anti-Communist Affidavit sent to executive-board members, which Reuther recommended signing, Atwood cast the deciding vote in favor. Taft-Hartley, besides outlawing the closed shop and granting management a dozen other advantages, also stated that in order to receive certification from the NLRB, unions had to sign affidavits that their officers were not members of the Communist party. It was possible to refuse and a few unions, notably Lewis's United Mine Workers, did so, but the costs were great, particularly when one remembered how hard the battles to organize had been before the Wagner Act. Nevertheless, the vote in the UAW—with its strong anti-Reuther and anti-anti-Communist majority—was close. Two pro-Addes regional directors, O'Halloran of California and Kerrigan of the East Coast were fighting the International Association of Machinists–AFL, which had already complied, in major representation fights, and their shift to Reuther's side on the issue is somewhat understandable. But, with George Burt from Canada abstaining, one more vote was needed and it was Atwood's, thus aligning the UAW with the majority of the labor movement who complied. This was the last act before the convention in the Reuther drive to victory.[9]

Finally, even Sugar's closest friend in the UAW, George Addes, was not entirely immune to the enormous pressures the anti-Communist environment put on a union officer in 1946–47. After the 1946 state CIO convention in which his forces were soundly whipped, in part, he felt, because the Communists rode herd on the coalition and lost a lot of moderate votes as a result, Addes wavered for the first time. On June 27, 1946, Blair Moody, then labor editor of the *Detroit News,* reported that a meeting between Addes and several east-side Detroit local presidents had resulted in a "decision" to "purge reds" from the Union. Although he vehemently denied the allegation three days later, Addes still stressed that Socialists, Communists, ACTU people, and Trotskyists "all attempt to use the union as a vehicle for achieving . . . their political goals."

Addes demonstrated inconsistencies on the "Communist issue" right through to the end. He went down the line in support of the beleaguered Local 248 and its nine-month Allis-Chalmers strike in Wisconsin and never flinched in his determination to bring the Farm Equipment Workers and its Left-voting members into the UAW despite daily crimson badgering from Reuther. But other instances showed him in a different light. For example, at the Louisville board meeting (March 1947), Reuther had suggested that the two of them bury the hatchet because a Communist "spy hysteria" was soon going to grip the nation. The hatchet was not buried, but the thought, perhaps, remained. Oddly, Addes failed to support Percy Llewellyn's motion for a full, positive vote of confidence for Irving Richter, whom the board had just saved from Reuther's real hatchet. Then, on the fateful question of the Taft-Hartley affidavits, while Addes in the end voted not to comply, he took a legalistic, wait-and-see attitude, obviously disturbed at the prospect of losing members because of the loss of NLRB instruments. He also pointedly noted that his remarks were made "without advice of counsel"—meaning Sugar. Moreover, in contrast to Llewellyn and Paul Miley from Cleveland, he spoke out little in opposition to Reuther's red-baiting tactics at any of the board meetings.

At the same time, Addes maintains that he never knowingly violated the constitution by making interpretations that would benefit his caucus. "I was always fair and square. Integrity was always my watchword and I wasn't going to change then," he said in a recent interview. But Sugar did not either. A close examination of his constitutional advice during this period has not turned up a single instance to support Emil Mazey's charge that he had made legal and constitutional interpretations in a "factional manner."[10]

And this is the final point. Despite the shrillness of his instructions to the board, despite his massive mistrust of Walter Reuther, Sugar assumed that the high road would win out. This he shared with Addes. Expose Reuther's red-baiting and justice would take its course. Justice did not take its course, however, as a new red scare engulfed the nation. This assured that any Left-liberal alliance in the U.S. labor movement—one that would stand firm against the power of a corporate capitalism greatly enhanced by World War II—would not be politically viable.

For Maurice Sugar, who represented this alliance as clearly as anyone in the country, this course of events was a tragedy. Not only had all he worked for within the union collapsed in the face of the tactics that he believed basic U.S. morality would counter, but also the law, which he had been lured to believe could render positive aid to the labor movement, had turned on it and destroyed much of what he had worked to build. In the end, Sugar wanted to go back to square one: do not sign the anti-Communist affidavits and forget the NLRB. The union movement had lived without it before and could do so again. These sentiments were expressed at the Buffalo board meeting in early September 1947 by Paul Miley and William Stevenson, who relied on Sugar for advice. But the real thrust of Sugar's public pronouncements to the union membership

295

was to urge that they demonstrate against the act and join in the political fight to get it declared unconstitutional. By 1947 labor relations were so dependent on the law that it was almost unthinkable to return to a situation where the sheer will of labor militants could do the trick.[11]

The final phase of Sugar's relationship with the UAW was a personal tragedy as well. There was no question that Reuther would fire him once he had captured the board. But the recriminations and plain meanness that accompanied his dismissal established forever a wall of hatred between Sugar, his associates, and the entire old Left community on one hand and Walter Reuther and his friends on the other. The irony that the Walter and May Reuther educational facility would be located on Black Lake directly adjacent to Sugar's retirement home is multiplied by the fact that the man who was the main attorney for the nation's largest union for the first decade of its existence was never invited to the Reuther domain nor, save when Sugar was dying, did a single Reuther union official or appointee ever visit the Sugar place next door.

To read the board meeting minutes for November 29, 1947 is to understand why. This was the day Sugar was fired, and the debate lasted eight hours. Sugar himself was not present. Reuther set the tone: "On the question of Maurice Sugar, I frankly want to say this for the record, that I think Maurice Sugar is a competent attorney, but I don't think he is a brilliant attorney. I think we can get legal talent in America that is more competent than Maurice Sugar. That is number 1." Quite obviously, that was not number 1, and as the ensuing debate made clear, Reuther's main objection was that Sugar "had chosen sides within because he has chosen sides without." Reuther then went off the record to reveal a "secret" meeting that Sugar had arranged with Weinstone and B. K. Gebert, Communists. In fact, it was the one that Reuther and his brother had requested Sugar to set up after the state CIO convention in 1939! Reuther and his allies also made a great deal of the Tessmer case.

Reuther went on to reveal the mentality of the "new-model" union. Whatever Sugar's politics were, the president claimed, he was too involved in union affairs, too much "a part of the labor movement." After all, "When you hire an attorney, you don't hire him because he is part of the labor movement. That ought to be one of the prime requisites, sure, but you hire him to give you expert legal advice." Reuther went on to compare the ideal labor lawyer to a physician whom one would bring in for "professional" advice, a "technician" who could manipulate the law as a doctor manipulates his implements.

Thereafter, Emil Mazey, the new secretary-treasurer, undertook the task of proving (1) that Sugar and company were worthless in court because they were reds and (2) that Sugar was not only overpriced but that he and his staff were double-billing the union. Regarding the first, Mazey remarked, "Maurice Sugar and his entire staff are tainted in the courts of Detroit. If you want to get somebody convicted, just hire one of Sugar's attorneys." Most judges have no use for them "based primarily on what they consider the political leanings of Sugar and his staff." Not only was this patently untrue for Detroit, where their acquittals far outnumbered their convictions, despite the often controversial nature of their cases, but on appeals their record was admirable. Ernest Goodman and George Crockett (who joined the firm after being fired by Reuther from the union's FEPC division, thus creating the first integrated law practice in Detroit) had each logged two U.S. Supreme Court victories and would have several more. Judges may have disliked them, but they could not risk too many overturns; as we have seen in so many instances, Sugar and his associates knew the law.

The second charge was so vicious that it remains almost impossible to believe that a man of the stature and generally good reputation of Emil Mazey could have uttered it. But there they are in the verbatim minutes that Reuther himself instituted during the factional fight in order "to keep the record straight."

Mazey's conclusion was pure vitriol: "So those of you who may feel that Sugar had made a contribution to the labor movement, I wouldn't shed any crocodile tears over him because he has been more than amply paid for services that he has rendered to this union. He has received giant fees. He has built up a very lucrative practice, one of the most lucrative in the City of Detroit, and he can't deliver the goods." Regarding the question of his retainer, Mazey stated the truth when he said Sugar received twenty-five thousand dollars—a lot of money in 1947. What he failed to mention was that of that only eight thousand was his personal income. The rest went to pay the rent on his office, all the attendant office expenses, and the wages of secretarial help. He also received travel-expense payments from the union. These figures in fact put his salary at a lower level than all officers and board members, including the frugal Mazey. To be sure, he collected a 10-percent service charge from the fees of his attorneys, but specifically *not* from fees for their work for the International.

The most scurrilous charge, of course, was the double-billing accusation. Richard Reisinger and Paul Miley (the only real opponents of Reuther who managed to get reelected), vigorously denounced it: "Are you calling Maurice an out-and-out crook?" asked Miley. It would appear that George Crockett submitted a bill directly and that the same one was sent in erroneously by Sugar's secretary (and not paid). The implication was that Addes had been "taking care" of his friend Maurice. Mazey was in fact very short on particulars: the Crockett case was the only one with documentation. It was an incredibly bad show. This is perhaps the one incident in the entire factional battle for which no justification can be found.

To have read Sugar's voluminous files of correspondence with Addes is to know how careful he was not to overcharge the union. Moreover, he fought again and again with lawyers around the country to get them to reduce their fees in the name of the "cause." It usually worked. But the saddest thing of all was that after he learned of Mazey's attack (he was never allowed to respond, despite repeated requests to do so), Sugar spent countless hours in December and January culling through all the bills, gathering together all the correspondence, sorting out all the agreements with the union in order to deal with this muck. They were kept in that form and remain in a special file for all eyes to see.[12]

The shock of the Reuther blitz gave way, therefore, to personal attack. Sugar in fact reeled under it. He was fifty-seven and very tired. The old resiliency was not there. He barely took an interest in the Henry Wallace campaign of 1948, although Goodman and most of the firm's members were deeply involved. As the United States moved toward the dark night of McCarthyism, Maurice Sugar prepared to move north: he would go back to the woods, to Black Lake where he and Jane would live, retired, until their deaths in 1974 and 1985. While he helped Crockett in developing the defense of the Communist leaders tried under the Smith Act in the famous Foley Square trial and kept an active interest in contemporary affairs, it was over. Walter Reuther had won and with his victory an era of U.S. trade unionism, Sugar's era, came to an end.[13]

What, then, was the era of the man Len DeCaux called "Mr. CIO"? While in so many respects a unique figure, Sugar led a public life that placed him at the core of the U.S. labor movement for more than three decades, a period during which—despite the trough of the twenties—U.S. workers challenged capitalist authority more fundamentally than in any similar span in our history. Sugar's life helps us to understand why this was so. Obviously, in the most basic sense, workers make their own history, and Sugar was not a worker. He was a political activist and a lawyer. But his place in labor history—along with dozens of other nonworkers of the era from Debs, Hillquit, and Max Eastman to Browder, Lee Pressman, and Paul Robeson—was important, indeed critically so. What distinguished this era, especially the teens and the thirties, was the profoundly significant role of committed socialist activists within or in relation to the trade-union movement and the work of dedicated professionals—be they writers, artists, teachers, scholars, lawyers, or physicians—who simply became part of the workers' struggle. Although there was always some dissonance between "pure and simple" union issues and the larger goal of social transformation, socialist zeal gave a special urgency to trade unionist demands. And during the dark days of the late twenties and early thirties, it can almost be argued that socialist zeal kept trade unionism alive.

Lawyers were of particular significance because of both their obvious practical use to the labor movement and their natural political proclivities. By the late thirties, politically committed lawyers by the dozens had become involved in labor's struggles in the courtroom, on the hustings, and as trusted advisors to labor leaders. It was a fruitful marriage. That Walter Reuther should shun that commitment announced a new age.

Sugar's life, then, has allowed us to examine in some detail two key buttresses of the U.S. labor movement in the most dramatic era of its growth: left-wing politics and the law. It has also contributed to an understanding of how each, almost dialectically, became an impediment to labor's outgoing drive for power—in large part because of the remarkably resilient social system that had been forged over the last century and a half. In the end, Sugar—profound analyst of the American scene as he may have been—was fooled by this system. Sugar's misassessment is all the more important because it has nothing to do, as was so often the problem for Communist party members, with a new turn in Soviet international interests. His independence assured that what Browder called the "living struggle" between Leninist doctrine and U.S. realities normally tipped, in Sugar's framework of analysis, toward the latter. Essentially, Sugar remained a Debsian socialist who appreciated the U.S. Communist movement (at least until 1938) as the most effective instrument for the realization of labor's emancipation.

Let us now review the main steps on Sugar's way. From the beginning, the law, socialist politics, and the labor movement were intertwined. Contacted by the typographical union because he was a Socialist, Sugar put his legal expertise at the disposal of the union's struggle. He immediately established an approach that would distinguish his work and pay off in a way "bread-and-butter" unionists could applaud: detailed attention to "technicalities" won cases—or else lost them with practical positive results, as by delaying injunctions long enough to win strikes. He also established himself as an effective legal analyst and legislative critic with his work on injunctions and learned very quickly that politicizing even this issue was not to the liking of Samuel Gompers. But no matter: his work in the courtroom and on labor's behalf in public forums helped to generate a sympathy for him and the Socialist party that put the Detroit AFL substantially to the left of the national federation. Sugar also ran for public office for the first time in 1917. With Debs and the other Socialist leaders, he viewed electoral politics as an educational tool, above all, but was by no means averse to the idea that the Socialist party might become a mass party capable of challenging the Democrats and Republicans.

The First World War and the Bolshevik Revolution changed everything. Sugar's experiences in relationship to the dramatic events of 1917, 1918, and 1919 yield important insights into the evolution of U.S. Marxism during this period. In the first place he, a lawyer, consciously broke the law. Although he claimed a constitutional right to do so, he was in fact giving primacy to Marxist revolutionary theory over U.S. constitutionalism. He thus entered a phase in his own development that increasingly corresponded to the view of thousands of fellow Socialists—and, more important, hundreds of thousands of workers— that U.S. society might be transformed, that power to the working class was possible. And if the Constitution stood in the way—as it seemed to—then the Constitution be damned. As it turned out, of course, it was the other side that violated the Constitution with impunity as the new decade opened with the Palmer raids. Capitalist hegemony was reestablished by force. Sugar stood by helplessly as the system separated the Left from the labor movement, with plenty of leaders in both seemingly applauding the process. The charms of anti-communism had been discovered and dreams of a workers' America were shattered.

Then began a long, arduous period of rebuilding. Sugar in the 1920s provides fascinating commentary on this process. He remained firmly fixed on the emancipation of labor as the essential goal, but had to sort out the two key questions of *the law and labor* and *Left politics and labor* all over again. The complex dynamics of how he made his choices included important personal dimensions rooted in his past and his prison and postprison experiences. But they also had to do with world and national trends. Most fundamentally, Sugar made his peace with the Constitution, or at least with the Bill of Rights. This involved modes of thinking that seemed, at the time, at variance with Leninist orthodoxy and might most easily be interpreted as the pragmatic response of a lawyer who wanted to practice again. But Sugar was also reassessing the law and what it could do for the labor movement. The perspective he developed recognized the vast potential of "bourgeois" law as an instrument to use against the bourgeoisie and also made him leery of current Communist bravado and proletarian adventurism. This, combined with his personal disinclination to "belong" anywhere, kept him out of the Communist party in the late twenties.

With the coming of the Depression, Sugar radicalized along with the Party, but basically maintained about the same distance from it as he had before. He retained this separateness throughout the remainder of his career, emerging as one of the nation's better-known independent leftists. In this role, Sugar and others like him contributed to the American labor movement in ways that have been neither well understood nor appreciated. It was they, above all, who forged the renewed links between Left politics and labor, links without which the CIO and indeed the prolabor orientation of the Roosevelt administration might never have developed, at least in the same magnitude. In Sugar's activities from 1930 to 1939, we see how it worked.

Using his expertise as a lawyer who knew how to make the law work in harmony with workers' interests, Sugar blazed a trail of precedent-setting casework in Michigan. Victories were not always clear-cut, but real setbacks were rare. Judge Black and lawless Flint were exposed in 1930. The legal cover-up after the Ford Massacre, despite its outward success, did not fool thousands of Detroit workers, employed and unemployed. Working for the International Labor Defense, Sugar defended workers arrested in demonstrations and strikes. He defended—with exceptional success—black workers pilloried by the public and the courts in one of the United States' most racist cities. And with the emergence of MESA, he moved to the heart of the work that would occupy the rest of his career: lawyer, advisor, and strategist for organizing automobile workers. His many-sided role in the UAW culminated the process. As he developed the "unclean-hands" doctrine, justified the sit-down strikes, and broke the Dearborn ban on leafleting, the former inmate of the Detroit House of Correction made U.S. legal history, using the instruments of the law for the advancement of the class struggle.

While his work as a lawyer often reflected concerns of the Communist party, and he was sometimes drawn into cases by Party organizations or individual members, his liaison role was less evident here than in the political arena itself. Following the old Socialist-party dictum of education through electoral politics, Sugar, more than anyone else in Detroit, brought the message of the organizing autoworkers to the larger public. He did so with the tireless support of the Communist party and its various "front" institutions. But above all, beginning in 1935, he organized a labor presence cutting across party lines the likes of which had never before been seen in Detroit politics. Even the AFL split did not derail the fall campaign. Moreover, a variety of other community political and social efforts that Sugar helped to animate contributed to a growing awareness of labor's drive in "open-shop" Detroit. Through those bastions of black conservatism, the churches, Sugar and his allies began to spread labor's message and "Mr. Ford" began to realize that his ability to manipulate racial antagonisms might not last forever.

The glory years, the harvest, came from 1936 to 1939. Popular Front meant that Sugar's politics and Communist politics were virtually indistinguishable, at least until the Browder-led disaster of Cleveland, 1939. The new UAW had fights-a-plenty both against the bosses and within, and Sugar, despite his solid middle age, was like the grand old man of the struggles with his personal knowledge of virtually all the problem people in the great events, from Frank Murphy to the goons and spies in the plants, and his warm ties with almost all the militants, whatever their political persuasion or union affiliation. Certainly the UAW would not have developed as it did without him and his role in creating a framework of understanding between the Communists and such trade unionists as George Addes.

As critical as this activity was, Sugar's real place in the age of the CIO derived from his work as a lawyer. First as a critic of the old Blue Eagle and then as a gifted practitioner of the opportunities presented by the Wagner Act, Sugar emerged, along with Lee Pressman, George Abt, and a handful of other radical attorneys, as one of the key figures in the development of a complex and immensely important new branch of the U.S. legal system: labor law. During the Second World War it became even more complex and important. We have chronicled the many contributions of Sugar and his firm to the field. Seemingly, the law could work for workers, and the Constitution remained a reliable instrument of the class struggle.

Within the union Sugar helped to create an internal structure, a law, that reflected the ideals of the Bill of Rights and grass-roots democracy. If it meant factionalism and sometimes unruly behavior, it nevertheless meant that most voices could be heard. The annual conventions ruled all. The officers and the board were always on their toes. In 1939, even in 1941, it seemed that both internally and in the nation the constitutional frameworks in which the UAW existed were "progressive" and democratic. And in the latter year, the final triumph of the NLRB-supported drive to organize was won: Ford was theirs. Internally, despite massive anger against the Communist flip-flop and its often disruptive consequences for the union, the "traitors" were not all crucified, and

George Addes, proclaiming his opposition to purges and his belief in union democracy, was reelected. Sugar, despite his sadness at what had happened to his old friends Mortimer and Kraus, could nevertheless feel confident that the victory over Ford and the continuing vitality of the internal structures proved that democratic constitutionalism was still the road to follow.

These opinions, nurtured by success, were born in the great days of 1937. Homer Martin had to be laid to rest before either the full benefits of the NLRB or internal democracy could be realized, but after 1939 that road was opened. It is interesting, however, that Sugar stopped writing about the sit-down—which was declared unconstitutional early in 1939—during this period. There is no evidence that this was a conscious decision, but the very success with the NLRB in unfair-labor-practice cases and in jurisdictional battles seemed to make the legality of the sit-down a less important issue. The mood, in other words, was to go with the law because the law was on their side. In 1940, Sugar began to sense the trap into which labor was falling when he showed grave concern about the changing personnel at the NLRB, but it was only during the war, with the imperious attitudes of the War Labor Board and the reactionary direction taken in state law, that the danger became truly apparent. Unfortunately, because of wartime patriotism, a meaningful critique had become virtually impossible, doubly so because the strongest bastion of the U.S. Left, the Communist party, had turned superpatriotic, losing almost all critical capacities. Challenging the law's hold on labor became a dangerous business, as rebels like Matt Smith, Emil Mazey, and a variety of Trotskyists discovered. After the war, with the conservative tide mounting, fueled by the Cold War, the squeeze was even greater, and the Wagner Act was thoroughly revised, embedding labor in the law once and for all.

This all demonstrates what an immensely sophisticated instrument of social ordering the U.S. Constitution is. Sugar fought it, lived with it, and finally embraced it as it appeared, after 1936–37, that the Wagner Act was indeed "labor's bill of rights." However independent, critical, and intelligent a Marxist he might have been, Sugar was unable to see the dangerous potentials of being drawn too far into the net of the law. The bill of rights also meant that there was a bill of wrongs—clearest among the wrongs being "expropriation of the expropriators." Nobody seemed to think again of the often excellent articles in the pre–Popular Front *Daily Worker* attacking the Wagner Act as a bourgeois smokescreen.

The juxtaposition of the international threat of fascism, a slight internal economic recovery that gave new verve to an already burgeoning labor movement, and a remarkably intelligent group of proponents of an updated capitalism in Roosevelt's "New Deal" administration combined in 1935–37 to adjust the U.S. Constitution to the new circumstances of a maturing corporate capitalism. Labor was given a defined institutional niche in the revised constitutional system. The potential critics backed off due to the perceived need to create a united Left-liberal effort against fascism. (Indeed many Communists, with Browder, welcomed with open arms the chance finally to be "real Americans.") The way was thus left open for the New Deal synthesis that firmly reestablished capitalism in a new *social structure of accumulation* (to use economist David Gordon's phrase) that became known as the welfare state. This synthesis tolerated, indeed encouraged, appropriate trade unionism, but not as a movement whose goal was fundamental social change. Rather it would help define a small, privileged segment of the labor market.

In the new alignment of forces that followed World War II—in which the superpowers vied for world domination, proper patriotism became anti-Russian, and unprecedented prosperity created the illusion of equality of opportunity for the vast majority of white Americans—trade unionism, if it were to survive at all, had to accommodate, had to become a "new model" providing service to its membership, neatly regulated by public law like the electric company. Walter Reuther perceived what was happening, and his close friendship with Eleanor Roosevelt symbolized the place of the new-model union in the new social structure of accumulation that accompanied the New Deal. Those who sought to live outside the law by not signing the anti-Communist affidavits were part of a militant past that could no longer be. But their determination finally to say *no* to the law should not have been repaid by mindless persecution. It should certainly be remembered today, as we enter a new era of crisis in the history of capitalism. The new model has now become old. The voices from the Sugar era are beginning to make sense once again.

NOTES

Preface

1. The name of Walter Reuther adorns Wayne State University's outstanding Labor History Archives and has gained Detroit's special form of canonization: a freeway connecting the east and west suburbs has been named for him. For rather a long time, the popular history of the UAW was written as if it were a history of Reuther and his allies. That tradition was started by B. J. Widick and Irving Howe in their famous encomium, *The UAW and Walter Reuther* (New York, 1949). Frank Cormier and William Eaton's large biography, *Reuther* (Englewood Cliffs, NJ, 1970), solidified it, and Victor Reuther's *The Brothers Reuther* (Boston, 1976), a remarkably insightful memoir with a wide reading audience, provided the benediction of Walter's more radical and idealistic brother. Recently, though lacking the public impact of these earlier trade books, a variety of studies emphasizing the importance of other leaders, especially those associated with the Communist caucus in the union, have appeared. Roger Keeran's *The Automobile Workers and the Communist Party* (Bloomington, IN, 1981) is the most partisan, but contains much new information. A new, more balanced biography of Reuther by John Barnard, *Walter Reuther and the Rise of the Auto Workers* (Boston, 1983), takes much of this new research into account, but still ignores aspects of Reuther's activities that won him an "opportunist" reputation among the Left and nonideological leaders such as George Addes and R. J. Thomas.

2. This introduces, of course, a massive debate, one revitalized by the publication of Harvey Klehr's extension of Theodore Draper's history of U.S. communism (*The Heyday of American Communism: The Depression Decade* [New York, 1984].) The problem with Klehr is the problem with Draper: they are not writing the "history of American communism" but the history of a formal party organization and its activities. "American communism" included those millions who never joined the Party and did not want to. They fought on various "fronts" (it is amazing how words are altered—the term was converted by the anti-Communists into the concept of "false front," a cover organization) to advance a socialism rooted in Leninist Marxism for which the Soviet experience provided the only model available. Most were not stupid enough to think it was perfect. See the exchange between Klehr/Draper and their critics in the *New York Review of Books,* May 9 and 23, 1985.

3. This study was largely completed before the appearance of Christopher Tomlins's fine book, *The State and the Unions: Labor Relations, Law, and the Organized Labor Movement in America, 1880–1960* (New York, 1985). Its theme in this regard is identical, although reading Tomlins helped me to sharpen some of my perspectives and integrate them into a larger canvas. The relevance of the containment of labor under the law today could not be greater.

4. Full citations of the secondary studies mentioned above are as follows: Richard Dorson, *Bloodstoppers and Bearwalkers: Folk Tales of Canadiens, Lumberjacks and Indians* (Cambridge, MA, 1952, reprinted 1972); Melvin Holli, *Reform in Detroit: Hazen S. Pingree and Urban Politics* (New York, 1969); Olivier Zunz, *The Changing Face of Inequality: Urbanization, Industrial Development, and Immigrants in Detroit, 1880–1920*

(Chicago, 1982); Steven Meyer, *The Five-Dollar Day* (Urbana, IL, 1981); Jerold Auerbach, *Unequal Justice: Lawyers and Social Change in Modern America* (New York, 1978); Ray Ginger, *The Bending Cross: A Biography of Eugene Victor Debs* (New Brunswick, NJ, 1949); James Weinstein, *The Decline of Socialism in America, 1912–1925* (New York, 1967); Robert Murray, *Red Scare: A Study of National Hysteria, 1919–1920* (Minneapolis, 1955); Theodore Draper, *The Roots of American Communism* (New York, 1957); Nick Salvatore, *Eugene V. Debs, Citizen and Socialist* (Urbana, IL, 1982); Robert Dunn, *Labor and Automobiles* (New York, 1929); David Levine, *Internal Combustion: The Races in Detroit, 1915–1926* (Westport, CT, 1976); Sidney Fine, *Frank Murphy, the Detroit Years* (Ann Arbor, 1975); Bert Cochran, *Labor and Communism: The Conflict that Shaped American Unions* (Princeton, 1977); Sidney Fine, *The Automobile under the Blue Eagle: Labor, Management, and the Automobile Manufacturing Code* (Ann Arbor, 1963); *Sitdown* (Ann Arbor, 1967); Mark Naison, *Communists in Harlem* (Urbana, IL, 1984); August Meier and Elliott Rudwick, *Black Detroit and the Rise of the UAW* (New York, 1979); Henry Kraus, *The Many and the Few* (Los Angeles, 1947); Raymond Boryczka, "Seasons of Discontent: Auto Union Factionalism in the Motor Products Strike of 1935–36," *Michigan History* 61 (1977): 3–32, and "Militancy and Factionalism in the United Auto Workers Union, 1937–1941," *Maryland Historian* 8 (1977); Nelson N. Lichtenstein, *Labor's War at Home: The CIO in World War II* (Urbana, IL, 1982); Clancy Sigal, *Going Away: A Report, a Memoir* (Boston, 1962); Steve Nelson, James R. Barrett, and Rob Ruck, *Steve Nelson, American Radical* (Pittsburgh, 1981); Klehr, *Heyday* (see Preface, n. 2); Maurice Isserman, *Which Side Were You On? The American Communist Party during the Second World War* (Middletown, CT, 1983); John Howell Harris, *The Right to Manage* (Madison, WI, 1983).

5. This book is designed to reach the general reader as well as the specialist and I have thus attempted to keep the scholarly apparatus, especially detailed and extensive footnoting, to a minimum. The preceding pages outline the key source materials and those secondary works of greatest importance to me. Notes for the chapters that follow fall into two categories: those providing a more detailed overview of sources and the literature concerning each section of the chapter and those relating to obscure or controversial issues on which I take a stand in this book.

Chapter 1

1. The essential information about Sugar's boyhood environment has been drawn from the following sources: Brimley and Bay Mills manuscript census, 1900 and *Michigan Gazetteer and Business Directory* (Detroit, 1890–1908), s.v. *Superior* and *Brimley,* both in the Burton Historical Collection, Detroit Public Library (hereafter Burton Coll., DPL); Walter Romig, *Michigan Place Names* (n.d.; reprint, Detroit, 1986), 79; Charlotte Hamilton, "Place Names of Chippewa County," *Michigan History* 27(1943):638–43. Maurice Sugar, manuscript autobiography (hereafter *SAb*), written 1962–70, Sugar Collection, Reuther Library (hereafter Sugar Coll., RL), Wayne State University, Detroit, ch. 2; Interviews with Jane Sugar, July 11–12, 1978, Black Lake, Onaway, Michigan (notes and tapes in possession of the author). All quotations from Sugar in this chapter, unless otherwise noted, are from his long chapters 2 ("I Was Born") and 3 ("Detroit").

2. Dorson, *Bloodstoppers* (see Preface n. 4), 195–96. The outlook and values of the turn-of-the-century lumberjack are captured in this marvelous book in a manner unparalleled elsewhere. Of the literature on the north-woods jacks, much sparser than I expected, I also found these useful: Philip P. Mason, *The Lumbering Era in Michigan History, 1860–1900* (Lansing. 1956); Stewart H. Holbrook, *Holy Old Mackinaw: A Natural History of the American Lumberjack* (New York, 1943); Lewis C. Reimann, *When Pine Was King* (Ann Arbor, 1952) (the best, along with Dorson, for understanding the logger's mentality); John B. Martin, *Call It North Country* (1944; reprint, Detroit, 1986); David Olson, *Life on the Upper Michigan Frontier* (Boston, 1974) (boyhood reminiscences from the same period as Sugar's); John I. Bellaire, "Michigan's Lumberjacks: Manistique," *Michigan History* 26(1942):173–87; Ida M. Spring, "White Pine Portrait: Big Dave Ramson," *Michigan History* 31(1947):314–21; R. H. Maybee, *Michigan's White Pine Era, 1840–1900* (Lansing, 1973).

3. Sigal, *Going Away* (see Preface, n. 4). On Sugar's personality, interviews with Ernest Goodman (July 7–9, 1978), Jane Sugar and Emma and Gertrude Mayer (July 7–9, 1978), Jack Tucker (June 26, 1979), Nedwin Smokler (Aug. 28, 1979), Sidney Rosen (July 5, 1979), and John Safran (Sept. 22, 1979) were most useful, but all interviews and much more discussion with Sugar's friends and associates contribute to these assessments. For very hard work, Sugar did not expect, nor did he allow his legal staff to expect, much reward. For example, Ernie Goodman (Sugar's dearest friend) recalled on the subject, "As an illustration, I billed the Int. Union [UAW] at a rate of $5.00 per hour for all the work I did for it, beginning in 1939. Out of this I had to pay my own overhead. Without appearing egotistical about the value of my services, I think Sugar

got a real bargain. The $5.00 fee applied whether I argued the Thomas v. Collins case in the Supreme Court or defended a member in a local justice court" (Goodman to author [1980]). Goodman also noted that expenses were kept to a minimum (Sugar to staff, memo, Dec. 19, 1946 author's copy). A memo written by Sugar to the staff on June 15, 1943 shows clearly the kind of exemplary behavior he expected of them, which was nothing more than what he expected of himself. Addressed "To those on the staff to whom it applies (they will know)," he chastised his people for showing up late for appointments with clients, reminding them that for the latter, seeing his or her attorney might well be "the most important thing in his life." So "let's forget the big shot complex and not treat the client as an inferior who is in dire need of our help and to whom we, busily engaged in more important matters (such as lying in bed), will get around to in due course" (Memo in possession of the author from the files of Goodman et al., Cadillac Towers, Detroit).

4. *SAb,* ch. 2, 18–20. On fights, Dorson, *Bloodstoppers,* 190–95; on strikes, Dennis Valdes, "The Saginaw Valley Lumber Strike of 1885," Central Michigan University, 1970 (thanks to the author for a photocopy) and Holbrook, *Holy Old Mackinaw,* 95 ff.; Sugar's description of the Brimley strike, *SAb,* chap. 2, 16–17; on drink, Dorson, *Bloodstoppers,* 187–90 and Reimann, *When Pine,* 64 ff.

5. This analysis is based on the 1900 manuscript census, Brimley and Bay Mills. See also, for a comparable town (Lake Linden), Irving Rabideau "*Canadiens* in Copper Country: New Perspectives on the French Canadian Immigration Experience," Wayne State University, Department of History, 1986; *SAb,* ch. 2, 36 ff.

6. *SAb,* ch. 2, 17; Sugar, "The Handcuff King," *Student* (Central High School, Detroit) 5(Apr. 1909), Box 8, Sugar Coll., RL, p. 17; Dorson, *Bloodstoppers,* 23, 92, 94, 129–31, 148–49, 201–2, and in general, pt 1, "Indian Traditions"; Maybee, *Michigan's White Pine,* 5. On the general store, see Ferris E. Lewis, "Frederic: A Typical Logging Village in the Twilight of the Lumbering Era," Burton Coll., DPL. Lewis's father owned a store. Another store in town was owned by Harry Abraham, very likely a Jew.

7. Interview with Professor Sidney Glazer, Michigan historian and Jew born in Cadillac in circumstances similar to Sugar's, Apr. 14, 1979.

8. *SAb,* ch. 2, 43; Gordon, *Assimilation in American Life: the Role of Race, Religion, and National Origins* (New York, 1964).

9. *SAb,* ch. 2, 23–25, 27–29, 48–49; Sugar to Pressman, Sept. 12, 1939, Box 27, Sugar Coll., RL.

10. On Detroit in this period, see Zunz, *Changing Face* (see Preface, n. 4); Sidney Glazer, *Detroit: A Study in Urban Development* (New York, 1965); Holli, *Reform* (see Preface, n. 4); Robert Conot, *American Odyssey* (New York; reprint, Detroit, 1986), 101–79. On Jews, see Robert A. Rockaway, *The Jews of Detroit, 1762–1914* (Detroit, 1986), 51–96. The quote is from Holli, *Reform,* 61. It should be noted that the German Jews of Detroit were acculturating rapidly and moving out of the old neighborhood. See map and discussion in Rockaway, *Jews,* 97–100. For a good overview of labor in this era, see Steve Babson, *Working Detroit* (Detroit, 1986), 2–28.

11. *SAb,* ch. 2, 39–41.

12. Sugar, "Handcuff King," 17–20; Upton Sinclair, *The Jungle* (1905; reprint, New York, 1960), 264ff.; on racism and the struggle against it in the Socialist party, see James Weinstein, *The Decline of Socialism in America, 1912–1925* (New York, 1967), 63–74. Sugar's later statement is in his summation to the jury in the famous 1934 case of James Victory, a black man defended by Sugar against an assault accusation. Published as a brochure, *A Negro on Trial for His Life* (Detroit, 1935), Box 10, Sugar Coll., RL.

13. *The Student,* 6(Oct. 1909):22; (Feb. 1910):3, 24; (May 1910):15, 19–20. On the quality of Central, see the Oct. 1909 *Student,* which analyzes the previous graduating class. In a class of 250, a very high number for those days, 133, went to college—79 to the University of Michigan, 9 to State Normal (Eastern), 8 to Michigan Agricultural (later Michigan State). None went to Harvard or Yale, but 2 went to Cornell and Princeton, 1 to Columbia, 4 to Vassar, and 3 to Wellesley. Of the total, 42 women went to college, a significant percentage. Ethnically, the school was overwhelmingly of north and west European extraction. Jews, by Sugar's reckoning, were few in number and, though names do not tell us a great deal, this seems corroborated by the list of graduates. From pictures scattered through issues of the students, there are no blacks prominent enough to be included, although the school was not officially segregated.

14. *SAb,* ch. 3, 6–7, 22–24; *Michigan Gazetteer,* 1906–10; Brimley and Bay Mills manuscript census, 1910.

15. Wilfred Shaw, *The University of Michigan* (New York, 1920), 130–37, 179–80; Elizabeth Brown, *Legal Education at Michigan* (Ann Arbor, 1959), 68–225 (quotations, 207) for changing practices; for the larger framework, see Auerbach, *Unequal Justice* (see Preface, n. 4), 83ff.

16. On Jane Mayer's family background, interviews with her and her sisters Emma and Gertrude (Black Lake, July 10–11, 1978; Aug. 7–8, 1979) are the main sources, although a few family papers and a Bible in

their possession were useful, too. On German-American socialism, the furniture workers, and women see Richard Oestrreicher, *Solidarity and Fragmentation: Working People and Class Consciousness in Detroit, 1875–1900* (Urbana, IL, 1986), and Mary Jo Buhle, *Women and American Socialism* (Urbana, 1983). Marckwardt later taught at Wayne State. His papers include nothing from this period, but offer considerable insight into his personality and politics (University Archives, RL).

17. Marckwardt to Sugar, Dec. 18, 1912, reproduced in *SAb*, ch. 4 ("I Go to College").

18. Weinstein, *Decline,* ch. 2.

19. Ginger, *Bending Cross;* and Salvatore, *Eugene V. Debs* (for both, see Preface. n. 4); Ira Kipnis, *The American Socialist Movement, 1897–1912* (New York, 1972); Fred D. Warren, *Warren's Defiance* (Chicago, [1912]); George D. Brewer, *The Fighting Editor: Warren and the Appeal* (1910; reprint, New York, 1974), 64ff., 152.

20. This is from a speech Sugar delivered many times, "Law and the Prevailing Order," *SAb,* document labeled *6B.* He wrote it in 1916, but the sentiments expressed here were doubtless part of Sugar's developing sense of the place of the law in society.

21. Sugar details the books that influenced him in his memoirs (*SAb,* ch. 4). I read or reread several of them to familiarize myself with his evolving outlook and the interpretation offered here is the result of that effort. The roots and development of Marxist positivism (a subject treated with almost disdainful criticism in recent years) is best handled by Gustav Wetter, *Dialectical Materialism* (New York, 1958), George Lichtheim, *Marxism* (New York, 1961). In many respects, the break with such a perspective has been the most significant theoretical consequence of the revolt against Stalinism in contemporary Marxism.

22. Several copies of the ISS journal, the *Intercollegiate Socialist,* were in Sugar's possession. His membership card has also been preserved (Black Lake materials). On the general story of Sugar's years at Michigan, see his correspondence with Ann Fagan Ginger. *SAb* (files) (1960–61).

23. *SAb,* ch. 4 and "A Lecture Tour" (unnumbered).

Chapter 2

1. *SAb,* ch. 5 ("We're Off! I Get Arrested"). This is the first of many stories that Sugar tells in his memoirs for which there no longer exists corroborative evidence. For the most part, I have used them not as historical facts per se but as a guide to Sugar's development as a lawyer and activist.

2. Jane Sugar interview, Black Lake, Aug. 15, 1979; *SAb,* ch. 17 ("Heading for Prison"), 20–22.

3. Dubofsky, *We Shall Be All: A History of the IWW* (Chicago, 1969), 307 ff.; Henry Faigin, "The I.W.W. in Detroit and Michigan from the Beginning through the World War" (masters thesis, Wayne State University), esp. 88ff.; Robert Goldstein, *Political Repression in Modern America* (Cambridge, MA, 1978), 94ff.; Max Eastman, "Class War in Colorado," in *Echoes of Revolt: The Masses, 1911–1917* (Chicago, 1966), ed. W. L. O'Neill.

4. Babson, *Working Detroit* (see ch. 1, n. 10), 29–32; Meyer, *Five Dollar Day* (see Preface, n. 4); Jacob Solin, "The Detroit Federation of Labor, 1900–1920" (masters thesis, Wayne University, 1939); Jack Russell, "The Coming of the Line at Ford," *Radical America* 12, no. 3 (1978):28–47, (quotation, 31).

5. Sugar, "Law" (see ch. 1, n. 20) and *SAb* ch. 7 ("The Speech That Started a Career").

6. For Sugar's first labor case and the circumstances surrounding it, see *SAb,* ch. 8 ("How I Became a Labor Lawyer"), 1–24, and the *Detroit Labor News,* Dec. 10 and 24, 1915; Jan. 14 and Mar. 10, 1916.

7. Waldman, *Labor Lawyer* (New York, 1945), ch. 1; *SAb,* ch. 8, 42–43, also discusses why labor law (or *master-and-servant law,* as it was then called) was unattractive.

8. See n. 6. On Frank Murphy's role, see Fine, *Frank Murphy* (see Preface, n. 4), 32–33; *Detroit Labor News,* Apr. 21 and 28, 1916. Fine does not discuss this courtroom encounter with Sugar (though he notes the case) and in fact says virtually nothing about their ongoing relationship.

9. Sugar, "Working-Class Justice: The Use of Injunctions in Labor Disputes" (Detroit, 1916); *Detroit Labor News,* Mar. 3, 10, 17, and 24, 1916; and May 25, 1916 (speech by Sugar).

10. The story of the Mack strike and the antiinjunction drive goes well beyond Sugar's biography in importance. It is told here for the first time. The *Detroit Labor News,* Dec. 10. 1915 to Apr. 20, 1917 is the key source. *SAb,* ch. 8, provides the narrative of Sugar's role. The question of anecdotes, I think, is an ignored issue in labor history. Perhaps their significance requires an anthropologist's or folklorist's eye, but most labor historians bypass them in their analyses. On the Detroit ITU, see also Herman Koss, "A History of the Detroit

Typographical Union No. 18" (masters thesis, Wayne University, 1950). On local/national differences in the AFL, see John Laslett, *Labor and the Left* (New York, 1970), 294 ff.

11. Detroit and Michigan Socialist-party activities are poorly known and need a full-scale study. Sources for the foregoing discussion include (1) the Robert Westfall Papers—some correspondence, brochures, and above all the only extant run of the *Michigan Socialist,* July 14, 1916–Dec. 7, 1917—in the Labadie Collection at the University of Michigan; (2) the *Detroit Labor News;* (3) *SAb,* ch. 17 ("Heading for Prison"), a crucial source for the subject in general, Sugar's papers from the period (Box 9, Sugar Coll., RL) (sparse, but containing information of political campaigns), and interviews with Jane Sugar (cited earlier) and Stanley Nowak (Nov. 15, 1984). The last was very important in helping me understand the perspective of Keracher, Renner, and Batt, who would go on to form the Proletarian party, of which Nowak was a member in the early twenties. Also, see below, pp. 90–95. Of the voluminous secondary literature, the best sources for this period are David Kennedy, *Over Here: The First World War and American Society* (New York, 1980), ch. 1; Salvatore, *Eugene V. Debs* (see Preface, n. 4), 280 ff.; Weinstein, *Decline* (see ch. 1, n. 12) 119–76; H. C. Peterson and Gilbert C. Hite, *Opponents of War, 1917–1918* (Seattle, 1968); William Preston. Jr., *Aliens and Dissenters: Federal Suppression of Radicals, 1903–1933* (New York, 1966), 88 ff.; Draper, *Roots* (see Preface, n. 4), 50–96; and William L. O'Neill, *The Last Romantic: A Life of Max Eastman* (New York, 1978), 54–100.

12. The key sources here are *SAb,* ch. 18 ("The Sugar Conspiracy Case"); *Detroit Labor News,* Jan. 11 and 25 and Feb. 8, 1918; United States v. Sugar et al., 243 F. 423 (E. D. Mich. 1917), "Conspiracy Case" materials (clippings, memos, notes retained by Sugar), Box 9, Sugar Coll., RL; Sugar to Ann Fagan Ginger, Feb. 15, 1961, Box 7, Sugar Coll., RL; *SAb,* ch. 18 ("Barred from the Bar").

13. Weinstein, *Decline,* 145–70; Salvatore, *Eugene V. Debs,* 288–94; Debs's great Canton, Ohio, speech (June 15, 1918) was the catalyst—and the source of his prosecution under the amended Espionage Law.

14. Report of unnamed American Protective League spy, Sep. 18, 1918, U.S. Justice Department Papers, IWW Collection, RL (microfilm copy). The report was forwarded to Bureau of Investigation Chief A. B. Bielaski in Washington by special agent J. H. Cole on October 1. For the Debs story, see Bud Reynolds to Sugar, June 15, 1964 (Black Lake materials).

Chapter 3

1. Sugar's imprisonment had a profound impact on his life and work. We are extremely well informed about it because of his prison journal, some 250 manuscript pages of notes and thoughts that he kept in prison-office order books, and his correspondence while in the House of Correction, which was carefully preserved by Jane Sugar and then—as some was being weeded out—by Philip Mason during the process of collecting the Sugar papers at their Black Lake home. Sugar also "wrote up" his experiences shortly after his release, which he incorporated, with few changes, as a 143-page chapter 19 ("H. of C.—The Narrative") in his autobiography. The order books are also exerpted in typed form thereafter (pp. 144–247). This material is probably even more important as a guide to Sugar's evolving political thought—as we shall soon see—but the reform work was a proud achievement for him (interspersed with other matters in *SAb,* ch. 19, 8–89). The relations with other prisoners—several continued after his or their release—provide much insight into his personality and also help us to understand better the remarkable rapport he had with his working-class clients. Located in the Sugar Collection, Box 9. RL. I also consulted the *Detroit News,* Mar.–May, 1919; and the *Detroit Labor News,* all issues Nov. 1918–Dec. 1919; Westfall Papers, Labadie Collection, University of Michigan for originals of Westfall correspondence during this period. On treatment of political prisoners by fellow inmates, see Peterson and Hite, *Opponents* (see ch. 2, n. 11), 180 ff. and Salvatore, *Eugene V. Debs* (see Preface, n. 4), 308 ff.

2. On the 1919 revolutionary situation, see, among the hundreds of works one might cite, James Cronin and Carmen Sirianni, eds., *Work, Community, and Power: The Experience of Labor in Europe and America, 1900–1925* (Philadelphia, 1983), especially Cronin, "Labor Insurgency and Class Formation, 1917–1920" (pp. 20–48), Larry Peterson, "The One Big Union in International Perspective" (pp. 49–87), and David Montgomery, "Tendencies in Union Struggles in Europe and the U.S., 1916–1922" (pp. 88–116); David Brody, *Labor in Crisis: The Steel Strike of 1919* (Philadelphia, 1965); and Robert L. Friedheim, *The Seattle General Strike* (Seattle, 1964).

3. Again told here for the first time, the story of the Michigan home front in the Socialist wars needs deeper study, especially in view of the role of the Michigan people in Chicago later on. Sugar's responses and

ms. copy (with corrections) of the *Class Struggle* 3 (May 1919):178–87 article on the league are in Box 9, Sugar Coll., RL. For the April–June 1919 Michigan-NEC correspondence and other materials, see Reel 98, Series 3, State and Local Files 1897–1962, W-Michigan, Papers of the Socialist Party of America, Duke University (microfilm copy). On the general situation, see Weinstein, *Decline* (see ch. 1, n. 12), 201 ff. and Draper, *Roots* (see Preface, n. 4), 148 ff. For a view from Ann Arbor, where he was a student in 1916–20, see Oakley C. Johnson, "The Early Socialist Party of Michigan: an Assignment in Autobiography," *Centennial Review* 10, no. 2(1966):147–62. Johnson mentions Sugar as a key figure calling him "an intense dynamo of a man" (p. 159).

4. Sugar, Prison journal, selected May–June 1919 entries. The richness of this document must be underscored. There is little to compare with it, but it allows us to enter the mind of a man becoming a Leninist.

5. Sugar, "Dictatorship and Democracy," typescript, Box 9, Sugar Coll., RL.

6. We owe the identification of these people to Jane Sugar. It is quite important because it clearly delineates Sugar's friendship network.

7. Sugar does not discuss this in his notebooks, but does so in his "Narrative," *SAb,* ch. 19, 91bff. Also see the *Detroit Labor News,* May 2, 1919; *Detroit News,* May 3, 1919; *Detroit Free Press,* May 3, 1919; *Detroit Times,* May 24, 1919.

8. The essential guide through the labyrinth of 1919 Left politics remains Draper, *Roots* (see Preface, n. 4), especially pp. 159–96. See also Weinstein, *Decline* (see ch. 1, n. 12), 201–33. Neither fully appreciates the significance of the Michiganders' role or of their pouty response to the convention majority's position. *The Proletarian: Journal of International Socialism* 2(Oct. 1919) and Sugar's brochure [George Hamilton, pseud.] *The House of the Masses Trial* (Detroit, 1921) clarify their situation and the aftermath.

9. On the vitality of the Detroit labor movement in 1919 and the role of the DFL, see Babson, *Working Detroit* (see ch. 1, n. 10), 39–40 and especially the *Detroit Labor News'* detailed weekly coverage of events and editorial pronouncements throughout the year (May 9–Sept. 12, 1919, especially the editorial by Julius Deutelbaum in the last, "The Tide Cannot Be Stemmed").

10. On the AWU, see especially *The Auto Worker,* monthly issues May 1919–Apr. 1921 and Keeran, *Automobile Workers* (see Preface, n. 1), 32–35. On the Labor-party idea, see Weinstein, *Decline,* 222–30 and Shapiro, "Hand and Brain, the Farmer-Labor Party of 1920," *Labor History* 26(1985):405–22. For the Detroit response, see the excellent information and discussions in the *Detroit Labor News,* Aug. 18, 1919–Jan. 23, 1920. See also Sue Ellen Masty, "Labor and Radicalism in Detroit, 1919–1920" (masters thesis, Wayne State University, 1980).

11. Murray, *Red Scare* (see Preface, n. 4) remains the key study of this terrible interlude in U.S. history, although one senses that he feels that "public opinion" was generally responsible for the official as well as the popular excesses. His sources are largely newspapers, hardly the best guide to public opinion. On that problem, see Melvin Small, ed., *Public Opinion and the Historian* (Detroit, 1970). For Detroit, see Babson, *Working Detroit,* 39–40 and, above all, Sugar, *House of the Masses Trial.* The Palmer quote is cited by Murray, *Red Scare,* 219. See the Detroit daily press in Jan. and Feb. 1920 for local reactions. The best contemporary analysis was by Labor Secretary Lewis F. Post, *The Deportation Delirium of 1920* (Chicago, 1923)

12. I investigated this dramatic tale with some care. The "smoking gun," of course, is the letter from Blumenberg to Stedman of Jan. 5, 1920, which remains neatly arranged in the Papers of the Socialist Party of America (see ch. 3, n. 3). Sugar did not know about it when he researched the case for Pound or when he wrote the brochure on the trial. The latter includes much of the verbatim record of the trial, but the briefs of both lawyers contain further information. The *Detroit Labor News* carried stories on the trial, but the daily press ignored it. Interviews with Davidow (Aug. 18, 1979) and Jane Sugar (cited above) corroborated several facts and provided the information on the Sugar family situation. Anne Davidow, Larry's sister, would later marry Sugar's brother Vic. The main source is Hamilton/Sugar, *House of the Masses Trial.*

13. *SAb,* ch. 21 ("Back to the Bar"). Sugar would never forget Murphy's kindness, and they would remain friends until the latter's death in 1949. Sugar would deliver one of the eulogies at the National Lawyers Guild ceremony on that occasion.

Chapter 4

1. The following discussion, focusing on Sugar's development as a lawyer, is based primarily on brief chapters in his autobiography, each devoted to a single case that he felt was important in his growth or interesting in its own right. Other sources will be noted where appropriate.

2. *SAb*, ch. 11 ("Lewd and Lascivious Behavior"), 6a–b.

3. *SAb*, ch. 9 ("Use a Sharp Pencil") deals with a similar failure to provide evidence supporting the exact terms of a statute.

4. *SAb*, ch. 12 ("Technicalities—and Negotiations"), 2 and *passim; Detroit Labor News,* July 24, 1926.

5. *SAb*, ch. 35 ("An Unusually Unusual Judge"); Reynolds to Sugar, Apr. 30, 1960 and May 14, 1964, Black Lake materials.

6. Cochran, *Labor* (see Preface, n. 4), 20–42; Nelson, Barrett, and Ruck, *Steve Nelson* (see Preface, n. 4), 29–52 (the Weisbord interlude, however, was the cause of Nelson's departure for New York); *SAb*, ch. 35; Reynolds to Sugar, Apr. 30, 1960, Black Lake materials. Also Reynolds's account of the Martel intervention was sent to Sugar in 1964 and is located in Box 7, Sugar Coll., RL. Maurice Isserman, "Three Generations: Historians View American Communism," *Labor History* 26(1985):517–41 underscores the problem of local autonomy versus Moscow/New York control. It is perhaps the central issue of debate in the current literature on the U.S. CP. Harvey Klehr argues strongly for central authority and lockstep discipline among Party workers, wherever they might be, while many writers take a more nuanced perspective. The issue exploded in the pages of the *New York Review of Books,* May 30, 1985, as Theodore Draper mounted his steed in defense of Klehr's honor. Klehr, *Heyday* (see Preface, n. 2), nevertheless provides much useful information on the gyrations of Party central. For an excellent review of the problem and an example of greater local autonomy, see Bruce Nelson, "Unions and the Popular Front: The West Coast Waterfront in the 1930s," *International Labor and Working-Class History,* Fall 1986, 59–78. For the tens of thousands of Communists who were never in the Party, of course, "autonomy" was all the easier, a point that is central to this book.

7. On the ILD, see Klehr, *Heyday,* 6–7, 104ff. The Sugar-Reynolds connection can be gleaned from their later correspondence and from Sugar's autobiographical accounts of their work together (*SAb*, ch. 14). See also Nelson, Barrett, and Ruck, *Steve Nelson,* 29. Malvina Reynolds was a songwriter, a fact that made Sugar's personal friendship with them all the closer.

8. The standard study on the Sweet case and black Detroit in the twenties is Levine, *Internal Combustion* (see Preface, n. 4).

9. "Maurice Sugar," circular and Sugar campaign letter, Burton Coll., DPL.

10. Dunn, *Labor* (see Preface, n. 4). This little-used contemporary study is remarkable in its depth, thoroughness, and determination to ask the right questions. Dunn was a journalist close to the Communist party. For other aspects of the foregoing discussion see Keeran, *Automobile Workers* (see Preface, n. 1), chs. 2–3; Joyce Shaw Peterson, "Auto Workers and their Work, 1900–1933," *Labor History* 22(1981):213–36; Babson, *Working Detroit* (see ch. 1, n. 10), 48–54; Thomas Klug, "Management Strategies in the Labor Market: Detroit, 1900–1935" (Ph.D. diss., Wayne State University, 1988). Another important study of the industry, never published, was William E. Chalmers, "Labor in the Automobile Industry: A Study of Personnel Policies, Workers' Attitudes, and Attempts at Unionism" (Ph.D. diss., University of Wisconsin, 1932). The Sugar Collection Supplement (materials donated by the author), RL contains an excellent selection of the shop papers.

11. Clayton Fountain, *Union Guy* (New York, 1949), 36–37. *SAb*, ch. 28 ("The Ford Hunger March"), 12–15; Box 53. (Folder 9), Sugar Coll., RL.

12. This story, of special interest to Sugar, was reconstructed in his memoirs; Olds had turned the amazing transcript over to him. *SAb*, ch. 25 ("The Judge Was Black"); see below, pp. 194ff.

13. Christopher Alston, one of the first black organizers in the auto industry, remembered this as his first experience with the old Left. It won his respect and his commitment to industrial unionism (Alston interview, October 12, 1979). Browder quote is from the *Communist* 9(June 1930). On the unemployed councils, see Daniel Leab, "United We Eat: The Creation and Organization of the Unemployed Councils in 1930," *Labor History* 8(1967):300–317. Also, thanks are due to Ernst Benjamin for allowing me to look at his father's papers from those years. See Babson, *Working Detroit* for other examples of the councils' work and influence, especially in fostering black-white cooperation around questions of poverty and unemployment. On the same issue, see Scott Craig, "Black Workers and the Communists in Detroit, 1929–1941" (masters thesis, Wayne State University, 1986).

14. Interviews with Jane Sugar, Christopher Alston; *Detroit News,* Mar. 7–8, 1930; Sugar, *The Ford Hunger March* (San Francisco, 1980).

15. The story is recounted in detail in Sugar's memoirs. *SAb*, ch. 22 ("The Best Brains of the Depression"), 22–32. The original manuscript (from which this version is taken) is located in Box 53, Sugar Coll., RL.

16. Sugar, "Michigan Passes the Spolansky Act," *Nation,* July 8, 1931, 31–33; *SAb*, ch. 23 ("The

Foreign-born Are Reds"). Thomas Klug has recently analyzed the entire problem in "Labor Market Politics in Detroit: The Curious Case of the 'Spolansky Act' of 1931," *Michigan History,* forthcoming.

17. *New Force,* Jan. 1932, 2–3. This little magazine apparently did not last long. Sugar's collection of four of its issues may be the only copies in public archives. Box 117, Sugar Coll., RL, and Sugar Coll. Suppl., RL.

18. Sugar's detailed analysis, *The Ford Hunger March,* is the best-documented discussion of this tragic incident. See also his "Scrapbook," Box 117, Sugar Coll., RL. The legal aftermath was as shocking as the event itself. The account rendered here is drawn from Sugar's work, a careful analysis of the press during these months, and Sugar's correspondence, including the revealing letters to and from Roger Baldwin, Box 53, Sugar Coll., RL. See also Fine, *Frank Murphy* (see Preface, n. 4), 403–9; Josephine Gomon, interview, *Detroit Free Press,* Mar. 12, 1972; Babson, *Working Detroit,* 59–60; Keeran, *Automobile Workers,* 63–76; Alex Baskin, "The Ford Hunger March—1932," *Labor History* 13(1972). Anti-Communist sentiment among many historians has tended to downplay the significance of the Ford massacre in the standard accounts of the era. Anyone who has reviewed the press at the time and, above all, the repeated reference to the whole brutal process by organizers as the auto labor movement unfolded in later years knows very well that such relative silence is but a longer-range form of cover-up.

Chapter 5

1. In the chapter in his memoirs on the trip, Sugar clearly chose to report on cases that supported his sense that building a Socialist society seemed to override individual concerns, and they even have a ring of "Socialist realism" to them. They were undoubtedly those that he discussed in his speeches after his return (see *SAb,* ch. 30 ("A Trip to the Soviet Union"). For a profound critique of Socialist realism, see Herbert Marcuse, *Soviet Marxism* (New York, 1961), ch. 6. The Reuther letter is in Box 65, Sugar Coll., RL. See also Reuther, *Brothers* (see Preface, n. 1), chs. 9–11. Nelson, Barrett, and Ruck, *Steve Nelson* (see Preface, n. 4), ch. 5.

2. *SAb,* ch. 34 ("I Confer with My Client, Tom Mooney"); itinerary and crowd estimates in materials relating to the tour and "Free Tom Mooney," speech, Black Lake materials (copies in my possession). The school board incident recounted in *SAb,* ch. 30 ("A Trip to the Soviet Union"); *SAb,* ch. 31 ("The Board of Education Disapproves of Me"); and *Detroit Labor News,* Dec. 30, 1932.

3. This framework of analysis is provided by James Coppess, whose outstanding master's thesis, "The Briggs Strike, 1933" (Wayne State University, 1973) provides the foundation for the discussion of the 1932–33 strikes. See also Keeran, *Automobile Workers* (see Preface, n. 1), 77–95; Babson, *Working Detroit* (see ch. 1, n. 10) (again a marvelous summary), 62–63; and the interesting brochure by a participant, John Anderson, *The Briggs Strike, 1933–1983* (Cleveland, 1983). The quotations below are from Coppess, "Briggs Strike," 24–25, 66–69. Also, the press, including the *Detroit Labor News* and *Detroit Saturday Night,* carried many stories during the month of January. Finally, AWU files relating to the Briggs strike are found in Box 1, Henry Kraus Collection, RL.

4. Phil Raymond interview, transcript, Oral Histories, RL.

5. Keeran, *Automobile Workers* (see Preface, n. 1), 96–103; Fine, *Automobile* (see Preface, n. 4), 38–41.

6. Harry Dahlheimer, *A History of the Mechanics Educational Society of America in Detroit from Its Inception in 1933 through 1937* (Detroit, 1951); interview of Smith's long-time secretary, Elizabeth McCraken, Oral Histories, RL; *Colliers,* May 12, 1943.

7. On the national origins and role of militant tool-and-die men, see, above all, Steve Babson, "Class, Craft, and Culture: Tool and Die Workers and the Organization of the UAW" (paper delivered at the 1986 Social Science History Association Meeting, Saint Louis). His Ph.D. dissertation (Wayne State University, forthcoming) on this subject will provide rich detail on these issues.

8. Quoted in the *Detroit News,* Oct. 7, 1933. *SAb,* ch. 29a ("The Referee Was Fixed") provides many details on his activity and offers Sugar's perspective. Dahlheimer, *History,* 13–17 and Keeran, *Automobile Workers,* 104–7 both analyze the strike. The local press followed the events very closely and the clippings collected by Joe Brown are an excellent guide through the September–December 1933 period (Box 15, Brown Collection, RL). Fine, *Automobile,* 163–73 provides much information on the NLB's relationship to the strike.

9. The foregoing is from the official transcript of the meeting, a copy of which Sugar retained, included in *SAb,* ch. 29a, 11–15.

10. Sugar, *SAb,* ch. 29a, 16.

11. A major theme of this book, the mobilization of the Left community on behalf of the labor movement was certainly one of Sugar's key contributions. On the Buck Dinner, see "The Fiftieth Anniversary of the Buck Dinner," brochure, 1979, Supplement, Sugar Coll., RL.

12. See, above all, the *Detroit Labor News,* Mar. and Apr. 1934; Sugar, telegram, Mar. 16, 1934, Box 18, Metro-Detroit AFL/CIO Collection, RL.

13. Fine, *Automobile,* 231–32.

14. The *Detroit Labor News* covered the Henderson hearing carefully (see issue of Dec. 20, 1934). Sugar's testimony was reprinted in full in a brochure for his recorder's-court campaign, "Sugar Tells the Auto Labor Board Plenty" (Detroit, 1935) Box 10, Sugar Coll., RL. Waning enthusiasm for Roosevelt at this time was reflected everywhere in labor and on the Left. See Fine, *Automobile,* 372 ff. A good example is the *Nation*'s withering editorial, "Our Surrendering President," Feb. 20, 1935, 172.

15. Meier and Rudwick, *Black Detroit* (see Preface, n. 4), 3–33. My research on this question suggests a stronger role for the Left in changing black opinion than Meier and Rudwick allow. The problem was one that they were concerned about, but their research turned up little evidence of it. Their main problem, besides a pro-NAACP and anti-Communist bias (see especially how they slight the role of the National Negro Congress later on), is that they were not very familiar with the Detroit Left and its political history, particularly in the early and midthirties. This book fills some of that gap, but the reader is also referred to Craig's outstanding study, "Black Workers" (see ch. 4, n. 13).

16. See Snow Grigsby's remarkable contemporary study, recapitulated in "Detroit Civic Rights Committee Writes Open Letter to the Councilmen of the City of Detroit, Fourth Educational Letter," Box 11, Sugar Coll., RL. Sugar thanked Grigsby for sending this analysis to him remarking, "These are lessons of the kind I like to study," Sugar to Grigsby (cc), Sept. 21, 1935, Box 11, Sugar Coll., RL.

17. *SAb,* ch. 32e, "The Frame-up of James Victory" and a brochure, Sugar, "A Negro on Trial" (see ch. 1, n. 12), which includes Sugar's moving final speech to the jury.

18. The *Detroit Labor News,* Dec. 21 and 28, 1934; "Outline of Policy and Organization of the Campaign for Maurice Sugar," typescript report, Box 10, Sugar Coll., RL. The willingness of the Detroit federation to work with the Communist party is interesting and surprising. On Sept. 11, 1934, in its continuing battle against the reds, the national office issued a circular letter calling for the expulsion of all Communists and "cells" from all affiliated organizations "when it has been clearly established that such members . . . [are] carrying on communistic propaganda." It included both "every proven communist" and "communistic propagandist." (Box 1, Henry Kraus Coll., RL). The Detroit federation did not hesitate to follow orders either: we read on page 1 of the same *Labor News* that called for Sugar's candidacy (Dec. 21, 1934) a small article entitled "Communists Not Wanted in F. of L." that tells of the expulsion of William [Billy] Allan from his seat as a delegate of the Bakers Union Number 20 "for his communistic activities." Allan became the long-time Detroit correspondent for the *Daily Worker.* This coincidence dramatically underlines the role of a Maurice Sugar. Through figures like him, the Left could continue the struggle despite the most strident formal opposition to the CP from organized labor.

19. This detailed report ("Outline of Policy") is part of an important body of materials on this campaign and on Sugar's campaign later that year for city council, as will be seen in what follows. It provides marvelous documentation for understanding the work of the Left community in building prolabor sentiment in Detroit, especially among black citizens. Boxes 10 and 11, Sugar Coll., RL.

20. The best documentary source for the structure of these organizations in Detroit is a detailed FBI "Survey of Communist Activities in the City of Detroit and Vicinity," 1936, Box 1 ("Communism" file), Metro-Detroit AFL/CIO Collection, RL. Using this material, which goes well beyond formal and specifically Communist organizations, along with interviews (Stanley and Margaret Nowak, William Weinstone, Jane Sugar, Jack Tucker) and Sugar's invaluable "File: Recorder's Court Race," which includes a notebook of his daily activities through the campaign and considerable correspondence (Box 10, Sugar Coll., RL), allows a very close look at the problem posed in this section.

21. Fine, *Automobile,* 373 ff. provides the general story. See also, the *Nation,* Feb. 13, 1935, 181; *Detroit Labor News,* Feb. 1, 1935; MESA press release, Feb. 1, 1935, Box 11, Sugar Coll., RL.

22. This debate gives a taste of the themes in Sugar's campaign. Unfortunately, despite the excellent material on the progress of the campaign itself, we do not have copies or detailed reports on his speeches. Thus the quotations here are very important in apprising the mood of his rhetoric. Its radicalism is unequivocal, something that makes the positive results all the more interesting. *Detroit Labor News,* Feb. 8, 1935.

23. "Our Surrendering President," *Nation* (editorial).

24. Christopher Alston, interview, Oct. 12, 1979; LeBron Simmons, interview. September 28, 1979; Studs Terkel, *Hard Times* (New York, 1970), 500.

25. On the first two cases, see *SAb,* "The Cemetery Case" and "The Case of Munroe Brown and Charles Lee" and Sugar campaign literature (Box 10, Sugar Coll., RL). Sugar mistakenly puts the latter case in 1941. The Detroit *Tribune Independent* (Feb. 2, Mar. 2 and Mar. 9, 1935) reported on all three and the *Detroit Free Press* also had a story on the last.

26. The details on the timing of presentations are drawn from Sugar's campaign notebook, Sunday, Feb. 3, 1935–Saturday, March 20, 1935. The list of endorsements from black leaders that Sugar was proudest of is worth recording in full (from an undated list in the campaign file from late March):

Rev. William H. Peck, Greater Bethel AME
Rev. S. D. Ross, Greater Shiloh Baptist
Rev. Charles H. Hill, Hartford Avenue Baptist
Rev. R. L. Bradby, Second Baptist
Rev. J. B. Ford, Second Mt. Olive Baptist
Rev. R. L. Carson, Centennial Baptist
Dr. O. H. Sweet, physician
Dr. R. L. C. Markoe, physician
Dr. Julian J. Rucker
Mrs. Kate Johnson, president of the State Association of Colored Women's Clubs
Dr. W. E. Rainwater, dentist
Dr. J. A. Graham, physician
Dr. S. H. C. Owen, physician
L. C. Blount, vice president and secretary, Great Lakes Mutual Insurance Co. and president, Detroit Branch of the NAACP.
Mrs. C. S. Smith, member of the Administrative Committee of the National Association of Colored Women
Mrs. Cora Seymour. president, City Association of Colored Women's Clubs
Robert A. Crump, newspaper correspondent
Russell J. Cowan, newspaper correspondent

See also the endorsement letter of James Williams (chairman, East Side Progressive League), Mar. 26, 1935, Box 10, Sugar Coll., RL.

27. Louis Adamic, "The Hill-Billies Come to Detroit," *Nation,* Feb. 13. 1935; "Maurice Sugar, Labor Candidate vs. W. P. Lovett's City League," *Detroit Labor News,* Mar. 1, 1935; W. P. Lovett, (secretary of Detroit Citizens League) to Sugar, Feb. 7, 1935; Sugar to Lovett, Feb. 11, 1935 (typescript); Detroit Bar Association ratings for Recorder's Court, Mar. 1935; "The Fight Begins," campaign flyer, Mar. 14, 1935. The last four items are located in "File: Recorder's Court Race," Box 10, Sugar Coll., RL.

28. The leaflet and clippings are located in the "File: Recorder's Court Race," Box 10, Sugar Coll., RL. See also letters from Sugar and Weinstone, Box 1, Wayne County AFL/CIO Collection. *It's About Time!* 1, no. 1 (Mar. 26, 1935) carried the endorsements and remarks by Murphy. For details of the campaign operations, see Sugar's campaign notebook in "File: Recorder's Court Race," Box 10, Sugar Coll., RL.

29. *Detroit Labor News,* Apr. 6, 1935. The ward-by-ward breakdown was as follows (analysis made by Sugar campaign workers, Nov. 1935):

SUGAR VOTE

Ward	Recorder's Court	Council	Place in Council
1	2,863	2,352	10
2	1,059	728	15
3*	1,689	1,587	3
4	1,184	895	15
6	1,867	1,552	13
8	3,123	2,497	10

(*continued*)

(Continued)

Ward	Recorder's Court	Council	Place in Council
5*	1,954	2,105	3
7*	718	886	3
9	3,525	3,896	3
11	1,361	1,465	3
13	3,112	3,405	3
15	2,321	2,071	9

heavily black wards.

Chapter 6

1. Frank W. McCulloch and Tim Bornstein, *The National Labor Relations Board* (New York, 1974), 18–24 (quotation, 19). This is the opinion of a liberal board member (McCulloch). Christopher Tomlins, *The State and the Unions* (see Preface, n. 3) roots his general analysis in this framework; for the act itself, see pp. 119–47. The most exhaustive (if a bit exhausting) study is James A. Gross, *The Making of the National Labor Relations Board* (Albany, NY, 1974).

2. For an up-to-date discussion of this momentous development, see Robert H. Zieger, *American Workers, American Unions* (Baltimore, 1986), 41–46. More detail in Melvyn Dubofsky and Warren Van Tine, *John L. Lewis* (1977; reprint, Urbana, IL, 1987), 157ff.; Philip Taft, *The A.F. of L. from the Death of Gompers to the Merger* (New York: 1959), 140ff. On the historiography of the CIO more generally, see Zieger, "Toward a History of the CIO: a Bibliographical Report," *Labor History* 26(1985):485–516.

3. The reconstruction of the split between Martel and Sugar—a telling example of the growing alienation of the AFL from anything smacking of communism or Labor-party politics—has been made from the following documentation: ULCPA Continuations Committee, *Labor Holds the Key!* (Detroit, 1935); *Detroit Labor News,* Mar. 30 and May 3, 11 and 17, 1935; *It's About Time!* 1, no. 2 (Sept. 16, 1935); *Report on the Proceedings of the 55th Annual Convention of the A.F. of L.* (Atlantic City, 1935); Sugar correspondence, Box 18, Metro-Detroit AFL/CIO Coll., RL. The key document is *The Progressive Trade Unionist Bulletin,* Oct. 23, 1935, Box 10, Sugar Coll., RL. Also see ch. 5, n. 17. Sugar later assumed that the reason for his being "cut off" (for this meant no AFL business in the long run) was the rise of the CIO (*SAb,* ch. 8, 43–46). The split was coming, of course.

4. Peter Amann, "Vigilante Fascism: The Black Legion as an American Hybrid," *Comparative Studies in Society and History* 25(1983):490–524; Sheldon Marcus, *Father Coughlin* (Boston, 1973); Ernest Goodman interview (on Sugar moving his desk and obtaining a revolver); Dean testimony reported in the *Detroit Free Press, Detroit News,* and *Detroit Times,* July and August 1936. See below, n. 12.

5. Philip Bonosky, *Brother Bill McKie* (New York, 1953); *It's About Time!* 1, no. 2 (Sept. 16, 1935); David W. Shannon, *The Socialist Party of America* (Chicago, 1967). 240–48.

6. ULCPA Continuations Committee, *Labor; It's About Time!* 1, no. 2 (Sept. 16, 1935); *Detroit Labor News,* Sept. 20, 1935, for reactions to Sugar's claims and condemnation of the locals that bolted: "Local Endorsements Should Wait Until Central Body Acts," said a headline. The song was printed separately (Box 14, Sugar Coll., RL). Martel to Pattern Makers Association, Nov. 25, 1935, Box 8, Metro-Detroit AFL/CIO Coll., RL. Two unions—the Federation of Teachers and the Associated Auto Workers of America—protested that they had *not endorsed* the trio (letters to Sugar, one undated, one dated Sept. 17, 1935). Letters from MESA, the pattern makers, and others of support may be found in Box 10, Sugar Coll., RL.

7. Sugar to Grigsby, Sept. 21, 1935; Brochure: *On Equal Rights for Negroes; SAb,* "Turner Case" (unnumbered) and *North Detroit Herald,* Oct. 6, 1935; *American Guardian,* Nov. 2, 1935 (all in Box 10, Sugar Coll., RL).

8. *Detroit News,* Nov. 5, 1935; *Daily Worker,* Nov. 5. 1935; Sinclair to Sugar, undated (also an autographed copy of *The Flivver King*), Box 54, Sugar Coll., RL; *American Guardian* (Federated Press), Oct. 26, 1935; Ed Thal (secretary of the Detroit Building Trades Council) to Sugar, Oct. 15, 1935; *Detroit Saturday Night,* Oct. 12 and Nov. 2, 1935; *Detroit Free Press, Detroit News, Daily Worker,* Nov. 3–7, 1935 (correspondence and clippings in Box 10, Sugar Coll., RL).

9. On the Motor Products strike see Ray Boryczka, "Auto Union Factionalism and the Motor Products Strike of 1935–1936," *Michigan History* 61(1977):3–32; Box 4, Kraus Coll., RL and "Summary of the Motor Products Strike," Box 2, Martin Coll., RL; and especially Dahlheimer *History* (see ch. 5. n. 6), ch. 6. On the takeover and the events leading to the South Bend convention, the standard sources should be supplemented with a careful reading of Homer Martin's voluminous correspondence, Jan. 7–Mar. 29, 1936 (the Mortimer-Martin letters are especially fascinating), from which several of the details above are drawn (Box 1, Martin Coll., RL). A copy of the Toledo charter is in Box 2, Martin Coll., RL. See also Wyndham Mortimer, *Organize!* (Boston, 1971), 96–99.

10. This is the best reconstruction that I can make of this controversial issue. William Weinstone, in our interview, Mar. 9, 1979, presented a well-rehearsed version with all the details in place. But from all I and close friends like Ernest Goodman know about him, Sugar would never have escorted anyone to a Party meeting. Moreover, that Weinstone "remembered" *nothing* about the political campaigns of 1935 was indeed curious, since the details of the Reuther encounter were so vivid. Still, his remarks are useful. The key item, of course, was Nat Ganley's assertion that he collected CP dues from Walter Reuther. (See Martin Glaberman, "A Note on Walter Reuther," *Radical America*, Nov.–Dec. 1973, 113–17). Sugar's own discussion of these events ("My Relations with Walter Reuther," 1–3, *SAb* (Supplement) supported by the letter from the brothers while they were in the Soviet Union, Box 6, Sugar Coll., RL) ring true. The Ternstedt Left connection is well known and denied by no one. The point, however, remains that all these perceptions and suspicions are relevant only in that they help explain the origins of the mistrust that the pro-Soviet Left felt toward Reuther. Whether or not he was briefly a Party member is of no historical interest to anyone except red-baiters and (perhaps) the Party Historian (Weinstone's official title). As we shall see, Weinstone's other recollections were very helpful, and I thank him for his hospitality. See also Reuther, *Brothers* (see Preface, n. 1), 126–27; Keeran, *Automobile Workers* (see Preface, n. 1), 157.

11. *Call,* May 2, 1936. Among the dozens of studies and analyses of the Popular Fronts that emerged in 1936, the reader's attention is called to the special issue of *International Labor and Working Class History,* no. 30 (Fall 1986) on the Popular Front and to papers from a University of Michigan Conference on the Popular Front, Nov. 15–16, 1985 (Goeff Eley and Ronald Suny, University of Michigan, organizers). The issue of the CP role and the place of the Comintern in setting policy is central to several of the articles and papers in these collections. On Spain, see also Gabriel Jackson, "The Spanish Popular Front, 1934–1937," *Journal of Contemporary History* 5(1970).

12. The details on this bizarre, fascinating, and tragic story have been drawn from Sugar's own extensive collection of materials, the daily press, and the *Detroit Labor News.* Sugar kept an excellent clippings file and it was virtually complete with regard to the Black Legion. I went through the reels for the *Times, News,* and *Free Press* (along with the unmicrofilmed folio bindings of the *Labor News*) from the summer and fall of 1936 and found that Sugar had ignored nothing. The interpretation offered here has been checked from various angles and found accurate. It goes beyond the analysis provided by Amann and seems counter to his assessment that the Black Legion, because it was secret, mattered little as a force in the history of the era ("Vigilante Fascism," 517–19). Sugar's materials are found in Boxes 18–23, Sugar Coll., RL. See, above all, his "Memorandum on the Black Legion," undated 80-page typescript in Box 18, (Folder 1); on the threats to Sugar's life, see Sugar to Concealed Weapons Licensing Board, July 8, 1940, Box 19.

13. Wohlforth to Sugar, Jan. 29, 1937, and affidavit of Arthur Dobrzynski, Jan. 20, 1937, Box 54, Sugar Coll., RL. Dobrzynski, alas, would later himself become a company stooge. See Margaret Nowak, *Two Who Were There* (Detroit, forthcoming), ch. 10. On the LaFollette Committee and its work, see Jerold Auerbach, *Labor and Liberty: The LaFollette Committee and the New Deal* (New York, 1966).

14. Rather extensive materials on this campaign are located in Box 11, Sugar Coll., RL. On Left politics in 1936, see Klehr, *Heyday* (see Preface, n. 2), chs. 10–12; Shannon, *Socialist Party,* 244–48. Shannon argues that the election of 1936 marked the end of the Socialist party as a real political force; it was swamped by Popular Front and, above all, by Roosevelt (pp. 249–68.) See also Kenneth Waltzer, "The Party and the Polling Place: American Communism and an American Labor Party in the 1930s," *Radical History Review* (1980): 104–29.

Chapter 7

1. *Christian Science Monitor,* Feb. 8, 1937. Giussepe Maione, *Il Bienno rosso* (Bologna, 1975); Jacques Danos and Marcel Gibelin, *Juin 36* (Paris, 1972); Daniel Nelson, "Origins of the Sit-Down Era: Worker Militancy and Innovation in the Rubber Industry, 1934–1938," *Labor History* 23(1982): 198–225.

2. Jeremy Brecher, *Strike!* (Boston, 1972) ignores and simply misrepresents the positive role of leadership in the upheavals of the CIO years. This issue—which had long been central in the arguments within Marxism in particular—is also a major problem in interpreting the contemporaneous labor upheaval in France. See especially Herrick Chapman, "The Political Life of the Rank and File: French Aircraft Workers During the Popular Front, 1934–38," *International Labor and Working Class History* Fall 1986, 13–31, for a review of the literature and an important contribution. Steve Babson's forthcoming Ph.D. dissertation, Wayne State University, will examine the ranks/leadership problem in the development of the UAW, offering an interpretation paralleling and influencing my own.

3. Mortimer, *Organize!* (see ch. 6, n. 9), 84–125; Kraus, *Many* (see Preface, n. 4), 1–106; Fine, *Sitdown* (see Preface, n. 4), 100–48; Keeran, *Automobile Workers* (see Preface, n. 1), 148–64; UAW Executive Board minutes, Nov. 30–Dec. 5, 1936, Box 1, Addes Coll., RL; Carl Haessler interview, Oral Histories, RL; Interview with George Addes, Aug. 30, 1979. Davidow, of course, was also the brother-in-law of Victor Sugar and Maurice's old friend and confidante. Even at this point, politics had firmly separated them. As we shall see, Davidow, more or less following Martin, became a reactionary.

4. On Black see pp. 114–115. Davidow confirmed Sugar's account. Interview with Larry Davidow, Aug. 28, 1978; Sugar, "I Become an Attorney for the International Union," dictated to Bob Cruden, 1970, *SAb* (Supplement).

5. Like so many of the controversies regarding the Who's Who of the Flint strike, this one pits Social Democrats (proto-Reutherites) against Communists and friends. Kraus rooted for the latter, Fine for the former. The Davidow testimony (Aug. 28, 1978) is crucial, for had he been familiar with the controversy, his memory might well have been influenced by politics. What he does is corroborate Sugar's own account in "Item" (Black Lake materials, now at RL), Kraus, *Many* 113. Fine, *Sitdown* 193–94.

6. On Sugar's assessment of Murphy, see his memoirs ("I Become," 5); Fine, *Sitdown,* 48–55; Nowak, interview, Feb. 21, 1980.

7. Victor Reuther, *Brothers,* ch. 14; Claude Hoffman, *Sit-down in Anderson* (1968), Fine, *Sitdown,* 214–15.

8. Kraus, *Many,* 104–5; Box 14, Sugar Coll., RL; *New Masses,* Feb. 2, 1937.

9. *Detroit News,* Feb. 2, 1937; Fine, *Sitdown,* 266 ff.; Kraus, *Many,* 189ff.; and especially Sugar to Murphy (copy), Oct. 25, 1938, Box 25, Sugar Coll., RL (on who mentioned a "delay"—it was not Murphy, who explicitly asked Sugar not to do so). Schwartz v. Cigar Makers International Union, brief, Box 24, Sugar Coll., RL.

10. Sugar, "Flint, 1937," dictated to Bob Cruden, 1970; Sugar to Murphy, telegram (copy), Box 25, Sugar Coll., RL; *Detroit Times,* Feb. 4, 1937. (Sugar does not mention the singing of his song in his memoirs.)

11. Fine, *Sitdown,* 299–334.

12. Kraus, *Many,* 274–76. The final terms were reported verbatim in the *Detroit Free Press,* Mar. 13, 1937; see also Box 25, Sugar Coll., RL.

13. What follows owes a great deal to the pioneering work of Steve Babson, Dave Elsila, Ron Alpern, and John Revitte and their research for a labor-history site tour of Detroit, a project of Workers Education Local 189. Several publications and slide presentations were produced from this project (as well as numerous guided tours for visiting groups). The most accessible and first full account of the Detroit sit-down movement is in Babson, *Working Detroit,* (see ch. 1, n. 10) 72–91. Many of the photographs on these pages in Babson were published there for the first time. See also Carlos A. Schwantes, "The 1937 Non-Automotive Sit-downs in Detroit," *Michigan History* 58(1972): 179–200.

14. This strike (not highlighted by Babson) was reported fully in the local dailies, which now scrambled for every shred of news about the unfolding labor drama. Sugar's magnificent clipping collection picks up significantly from this point and provides one of the best sources for day-to-day UAW history that we have. Boxes 105–17, Sugar Coll., RL. Used in conjunction with the many collections deposited by the union and Sugar's own extensive collection of correspondence and other union business, the recreation of Sugar's relationship to the developing history of the auto labor movement in Detroit becomes relatively easy. On the other hand, it is also at this point that we lose Sugar's own recollection since, apart from a few vignettes, his vast manuscript cuts off.

15. There is no way to stress this point enough. It is a central theme of this book. Despite the strain between Martel and the Left and the CIO, the old lines of solidarity and friendship held AFL leadership in this city to a pattern far to the left of Green and his cronies.

16. Christopher H. Johnson, "A Forgotten World: The Women Cigar Workers of Detroit's Central Industrial Area," report prepared for the Poletown Historical Records Commission, Detroit, 1980. On the

Polish family, see above all, Paul Wrobel, *Our Way: Family, Parish, and Neighborhood in a Polish-American Community* (South Bend, IN, 1979).

17. Nowak, *Two* (see ch. 6, n. 13), ch. 13; *Detroit Free Press*, Feb. 20, 1937.

18. The foregoing is drawn largely from newspaper accounts—the *Detroit News*, the *Detroit Free Press*, the *Detroit Times*, the *New York Times*, the *Daily Worker*, and the *Christian Science Monitor*, Feb. 20–Apr. 23, 1937—preserved in Sugar's (over 500 articles) and Henry Kraus's clipping collections. Babson, *Working Detroit*; Schwantes, "1937"; interview with Stanley Nowak; Nowak, *Two*; and *Glos ludowy*, Nowak's Polish weekly, provided much information on the cigar workers' struggle and the response of family and community. The Murphy vacation with Joseph Kennedy was reported in the *Detroit News*, Mar. 9, 1937. The extensive quotations in the Chrysler injunction hearing are in the *Detroit Times*, Mar. 14, 1937; the *New York Times* (Russell B. Porter byline) ran much the same story and corroborated the sequences and the language.

19. Sugar to Murphy, Mar. 21, 1937 (photocopies) Box 25, Sugar Coll., RL; Russell B. Porter, "The Broad Challenge of the Sit-Down," *New York Times Magazine*, Apr. 4, 1937; Sugar, "Legality and Ethics of the Sitdown Strike," radio address, Box 25, Sugar Coll., RL; idem, "Is the Sit-down Legal?" *New Masses*, May 4, 1937, 19–24. See also Rep. John T. Bernard's (Farmer Labor Party–MN) speech defending sit-downs—which he was not permitted to deliver in the House—printed in the *Daily Worker*, Mar. 28, 1937. The *Detroit News* also carried a story (Apr. 17, 1937) noting that while Sugar predicted that the sit-down would become legal, strictly speaking they were not so currently. For a sense of reigning (negative) liberal opinion see Walter Lippmann's attack on Leon Green's "The Case for the Sit-Down Strike" (*New Republic*, Mar. 23, 1937), "After the Sit-Down, Then What?" *Detroit Free Press*, Mar. 30. 1937.

Chapter 8

1. On the opening salvo in the Ford fight, see the *Daily Worker*, Apr. 14, 1937; for Ford's opinions, the *Detroit Times*, Apr. 10, 1937 and Keith Sward, *The Legend of Henry Ford* (New York. 1948); and the *Detroit News*, May 14–15, 1937 for Ford's initial response to the union initiative. There was extensive coverage of the Yale and Towne strike from Apr. 10 to the end of the month in all three Detroit papers. For details on the conflict and its aftermath see especially the *Detroit News*, Apr. 15, 1937 and the *Detroit Free Press*, Apr. 16. The jail photos are in the *Times* and *News*, Apr. 29, 1937. The first hints of the impending fight with Homer Martin also surfaced in April as he opposed Bob Travis's ascendancy in Flint by fielding a conservative slate in the local election against the Travis/Roy Reuther men. See especially the excellent analysis by Martin Hayden in the *Detroit News*, Apr. 18, 1937 ("Two Tickets Emerge"). On the Power Strike and the Industrial Relations Bill, see the *Detroit News* and *Detroit Times*, May 4; *Detroit Times*, May 20; *Detroit Free Press*, May 21; *New York Times*, June 10—all 1937. The last provides a detailed analysis of the repressive Michigan law. The Murphy quote appeared in that article.

2. Jerold Auerbach provides the standard picture of the guild's founding and an excellent discussion of its make up and orientation in its early years (*Unequal Justice* (see Preface. n. 4), 198–204). This is virtually the only time in his entire autobiography when Sugar claims personal credit for an idea or development (that north-woods modesty would not permit it), so I am inclined to believe him. Morris Ernst does not refer to Sugar's role in his memoirs, *A Love Affair with the Law*, (New York, 1968), but his letter to Sugar seems conclusive. The story is in *SAb*, ch. 33 ("A Lecture Tour and an Idea"). Letter and Sugar, "Suggestions for an Association of Lawyers," 1933, Box 1, Papers of Maurice Sugar (all relating to lawyers guild), Meiklejohn Civil Liberties Institute, Berkeley, CA.

3. Among various press reports, see Jay Hayden, "Sit-downs under Fire in House and Senate," *Detroit News*, Mar. 20, 1937; William Green, interview with W. W. Chaplin, *Detroit Times*, Mar. 23, 1937; John L. Lewis's reaction to Green reported in the *Daily Worker*, Mar. 30, 1937 ("characteristically cowardly and contemptible," said Lewis, and quoted from *Hamlet*: "He bends the pregnant hinges of the knee that thrift may follow fawning"); *Daily Worker* editorial, "Our Answer to the Red-Baiters," Apr. 5, 1937; *Detroit News*, Apr. 23, 1937 (for the evolution of Frank Martel's attempts to mediate CIO-AFL differences and disciplinary action against him by Green); *Detroit Free Press*, May 25, 1937.

4. *Detroit News*, Apr. 18, 22, and 23 and May 2, 1937 (Martin Hayden and Archie Robinson bylines); Ternstedt statement, Box 1, Walter P. Reuther Coll., RL (another copy among Sugar's personal papers, Black Lake materials); Cormier and Eaton *Reuther* (see Preface, n. 1), 124 ff. On the CP shift in 1937, see Harvey Klehr, "American Communism and the UAW: New Evidence on an Old Controversy," *Labor History*

24(1983): 404–13. Unfortunately, Klehr knows nothing (or says nothing) about the Flint affair, which clearly is the origin of the conflict (not the Communist approval of wildcats), and, indeed, that was what sealed Weinstone's fate. The CP position reprimanding Weinstone made sense in any case, given the remarkable opportunity that the Ford beatings seemed to offer.

5. *Daily Worker,* Apr. 14 and 19, 1937; *Detroit News,* Apr. 14–15, 1937 for early Ford counterattack; *Detroit News,* Apr. 18–19, 1937; *Daily Worker,* May 24, 1937; *Detroit Free Press,* May 25, 1937 for the mounting UAW campaign. Sugar note and leaflet copy in Box 26, Sugar Coll., RL; *Daily Worker, Detroit News, Detroit Free Press, Detroit Times, New York Times* and *Time Magazine,* May 27–July 30, 1937 for the battle and its aftermath. Barnard, *Walter Reuther* (see Preface, n. 1), 51–53; Nancy Zimmelman, "The UAW Women's Auxilliaries: Activities of Ford Workers' Families in Detroit 1937–1949" (masters thesis, Wayne State University, 1987), 10–17 provides the best analysis of the particulars of the Battle of the Overpass and shows the preponderant role played by volunteers from the Women's Auxilliary. On the Monroe steel strike see the three Detroit dailies, June 7–14 (especially the outstanding photojournalism of the *Detroit Free Press* and *Detroit News,* June 11 and 12). Also, *SAb,* ch. 26 ("Ford Dislikes Handbills").

6. This important (and largely unnoticed) piece in the mosaic of the Ford struggle is reconstructed from Sugar to Brooks, July 23, 1937 and Sugar to Greene, Aug. 9, 1937, Box 26, Sugar Coll., RL and the *Detroit Free Press* and *Detroit Times,* Aug. 10, 1937. It is at this point (summer 1937) that Sugar's voluminous official correspondence and legal materials become the key source for our story. See also Sugar to Murphy, June 28 and July 23, 1937; Murphy's notes on dealing with the Dearborn situation and of Greene to Sugar, Aug. 6, 1937 (copy), Murphy Papers, Michigan Historical Coll. (photocopies in Box 26, Sugar Coll., RL).

7. On the economic/membership problems of late 1937, see the important contribution of Raymond Boryczka, "Militancy and Factionalism in the UAW, 1937–1941," *Maryland Historian* 8(1977): 13–25; on the CP, Keeran, "The Communists and UAW Factionalism, 1937–39," *Michigan History* 60(1976): 115–36; and Klehr, "American Communism." Most of the analysis laid out here, however, is drawn from Sugar's extensive legal files and even more extensive clipping collection relating to the factional fight. The Lovestonite connection was proved by Sugar through the "liberated" correspondence between Martin and Jay Lovestone. His detailed thirty-one-page brief (over the names of the five officers) is the key document. Perhaps the best source available for the factional-fight documents is to be found in Boxes 27–28, Sugar Coll., RL. A convenient summary is found in a "newspaper" published by the five officers and largely written by Sugar, *An Appeal to the Members of the UAW* (August 1938).

8. For campaign materials see Box 26, Sugar Coll., RL; Alan Strachan, "A History of the Political Action Committee in the Detroit Municipal Elections, 1937," Box 14, Sugar Coll., RL. Colored Citizens Committee for Support of the Labor Slate, *Campaign Express* 1, no. 1 (October 29, 1937) (copy in possession of the author).

9. Martin to Sugar, Box 27, Sugar Coll., RL.; Keeran, "Communists"; Klehr agrees but gets his chronology mixed up ("American Communism," 409–10; UAW executive board minutes, June 6, 1938; on Reuther and Martin, see Reuther's public statement, *Detroit News;* Tucker Smith to Norman Thomas, July 29, 1938, the Papers of the Socialist Party of America (see ch. 3, n. 3); Sugar, "Memorandum on the Existing Situation in the International Union," May 23, 1946 Box 1, Sugar Coll. RL; Sugar, "My Meetings with the Reuthers," 1971, Sugar Coll. Supplement, RL. Cormier and Eaton, *Reuther* (p. 138) and Barnard (*Walter Reuther*) stress the CIO election double-cross as the root of Reuther's anti-Communist perspective, thus putting the onus on the CP. This is perhaps understandable, but since the Party reversed itself in the name of unity and simultaneously moved Frankensteen away from Martin and since Martin then made it clear that he would destroy the union rather than give up power, and since the Socialist leadership would rather back a fool like Martin because he might back their line on U.S. foreign policy than join the fight to preserve a militant union movement in the auto industry, Reuther's equivocations *do* look rather opportunistic. These facts certainly help explain why large numbers of his opponents—whatever their politics—thought him to be so. See also, "Confidential Report of the Socialist Party of America (1938)," Box 41, Sugar Coll., RL.

10. For Sugar to Martin and other materials relating to the trial, see Box 42, Sugar Coll., RL; the press followed the outward events closely, especially the Dies Committee visit to Detroit. See Sugar's clippings, Box 49, Sugar Coll., RL.

11. See above all the long deposition of Ralph Rimar, a former Martinite, Box 54, Sugar Coll., RL. The Martin Coll., RL, is no help on this, or most, issues relating to the factional fight; he obviously weeded out any evidence that might show ties to the companies. The Ford Motor Company Library and Archives provides no information either, since Bennett, who would have arranged any deals, left no paper trail at all.

12. See Sugar's extensive papers relating to the legal aftermath of the faction fight and his correspondence with Taft, Boxes 3 and 46, Sugar Coll., RL. Again, press coverage provides much information.

318

13. The much discussed issue of the electoral maneuverings at Cleveland (see Cochran, *Labor* [see Preface, n. 4] 141–43; Keeran, *Automobile Workers* [see Preface, n. 1], 199–203; Mortimer, *Organize!* [see ch. 6, n. 9], 162–65) is here thrown in new light by our interview with Sam Sweet (a perceptive and well-informed union member and activist), then close, like Sugar, to the CP, (Dec. 10, 1979) and with George Addes himself, Aug. 30, 1979.

14. The reports (Aug. 9, 1937 and Apr. 24, 1939) are located in Box 1, Sugar Coll., RL. John Safran interview, Sept. 22, 1979. Christopher Tomlins analyzes with care the growing reliance of the entire CIO movement on the NLRB and stresses the importance of its jurisdictional battles with the AFL unions, which, for the most part, condemned such reliance. Tomlins seems to say that the AFL took a more principled (and wiser) stand on the question. Obviously their vested interest in pre–Wagner Act union structures had much to do with their position. Moreover, explicitly to blame the CIO for getting caught up in such a situation ignores the political realities of 1937–39 and beyond. Still, to witness a radical and most perceptive lawyer such as Sugar become drawn into the position laid out here shows how powerful the attraction was and, in light of later events, how fatal for the kind of labor movement he believed in.

15. Davidow, *The Genesis and Present-Day Methods of Communism* (South Bend, 1938); *Reford Record* (a weekly), 1939–50, for his regular column. For the trial record and all the supporting materials, see the voluminous file assembled by Sugar, "The Tessmer Case," Box 7, Sugar Coll., RL.

16. No honest memoir or history of communism in the U.S. (or anywhere else) denies the disbelief and profound shock that seized members and friends alike. Nelson, Barrett, and Ruck, *Steve Nelson,* 245–55 captures the mood very well. See also Vivian Gornick, *The Romance of American Communism* (New York, 1977); Jessica Mitford, *A Fine Old Conflict* (New York, 1978). Chaim Potok, *Davita's Harp* (New York, 1983), 241–52, explores the impact on a deeply committed Jewish Communist. The impact on membership was significant: as Cochran puts it, the Party "was shaken like a ship that had lost members of its crew in a storm" (*Labor,* 146). The Auden poem was first published in the *New Republic,* Oct. 18, 1939 and reprinted in Hilton Kramer, "The Summer of '39," *New York Times Book Review,* Aug. 12, 1979.

17. *Detroit News,* Mar. 4, 1939; Joseph Fardella, "The Origins of the Association of Catholic Trade Unionists" (masters thesis, Wayne State University, 1980); Barnard, *Reuther.* 71–73; *Proceedings of the Fourth Constitutional Convention of the UAW* (St. Louis, 1940).

18. Interview with Ernest Goodman, July 3, 1979; *Detroit News,* Nov. 10, 1939.

19. Much detail on both cases is to be found in the private records, consulted on the premises, of Goodman, Eden, Millender and Bedrosian. Also see the *Michigan Daily,* Nov. 10, 1940 (photo of Sugar also); *Detroit News,* Nov. 10 and 17 and Dec. 4 and 5, 1941; *Detroit Free Press,* Oct. 28 and Dec. 4 and 6, 1941.

20. *Detroit Free Press* and *Detroit News,* December 28, 1940. Tomlins offers much detail on the changing structure of the board, particularly the growing role of "neutral" Leiserson, (*State* [see Preface, n. 3], 204–24). (Tomlins chronology is somewhat incorrect.) On Lewis's break with Roosevelt, see Dubofsky and Van Tine, *John L. Lewis* (see ch. 6, n. 2), 243–67. Also the *Detroit News,* May 15–19, 1940.

21. Sugar's files on these cases are enormous. The Gallo Case ("Syllabus: Laughter on the Assembly Line not Misconduct under Act," Appeal Docket No. 5071) was one of hundreds (Boxes 54–55, Sugar Coll., RL). Again, press reports were numerous as well, fueling the publicity mill (Boxes 56–59, Sugar Coll., RL. See also Box 2, UAW Public Relations Dept., RL). Besides demonstrating the centrality of the legal work in the Ford fight these files contain fascinating personal histories of Ford workers.

22. Meier and Rudwick, *Black Detroit* (see Preface, n. 4), 82–107; Sumner M. Rosen, "The CIO Era, 1935–1955," in John Jacobson, ed., *The Negro in the American Labor Movement* (Garden City, NY, 1968), 188–208, esp. 194–99.

23. The fascinating depositions of former Ford spies may be read in Box 54, Sugar Coll., RL. Also Box 92, Addes Coll., RL for Rimar correspondence (Nov. 1941).

Chapter 9

1. Sugar kept a detailed account of the legal fee situation. See correspondence with Addes and attorneys like Johnson in Box 93, Addes Coll., RL. For the general financial situation, see Box 3, Addes Coll., RL. Among the other efforts Sugar made to save money for the union, after Louis Rosenzweig, a tax attorney, discovered that Local 157 could reduce its personal property tax from $155 to $12, Sugar then circulated the information to other locals and was of the opinion that such reductions were retroactive to the previous year

(Sugar to Addes, May 4, 1939, Box 3, Addes Coll., RL). The correspondence between Sugar and Addes on the financial state of the union in 1939 demonstrates clearly the devastating effect of Martin's idiocy. For the turnaround, see "President's report," in *Proceedings of the Sixth Constitutional Convention of UAW (Buffalo)* (Detroit, 1941); Addes interview, Aug. 30, 1979. On Ford legal work see also Box 92, Addes Coll., RL.

2. The Addes Collection is often regarded as boring by researchers because of the minor, "routine," questions the secretary-treasurer dealt with. But this was the test of union democracy: the fairness with which problems—especially nonpayment of dues—were dealt with. Trials for "antiunion" behavior, which often grew out of nonpayment, occurred all the time and required very careful oversight. Sugar and Addes showed themselves to be marvelous advisors. See especially Boxes 92–93, Addes Coll., RL, which contain the direct correspondence between Addes and Sugar about such matters; but the reader is also referred to the vast correspondence between Addes's office and the locals (along with many interoffice memoranda between legal and the secretary-treasurer), especially part 1, series 5 (Boxes 70–79) and part 2, series 2 (Boxes 7–9). Also, Box 64, Sugar Coll., RL. Advice to R. J. Thomas, Box 63, Sugar Coll., RL.

3. Cochran, *Labor* (see Preface, n. 4) 156–66. The Rubin "case"—*Detroit Times,* May 16, 1941; other examples: *Detroit Times,* May 13, 1941; *Detroit News,* May 21, 1941 (p. 2 ff.); *Detroit Free Press,* May 24, 1941; *Detroit News,* May 26, 1941; *Detroit Times* ("Charles Bondy, Charles Diggs, Ernest Nagel, Stanley Nowak, and Leo Wilkowski—Mark their names"), editorial, May 29, 1941; *Daily Worker,* May 30, 1941, quoting executive board of Flint Local 599 in regard to Reuther; Moody interview in the Detroit News, May 19, 1941; Pressman speech quoted in the *Detroit News,* June 1, 1941 and *Daily Worker,* June 2, 1941. For Sugar's loyalty-oath opinion on the Modine case, Box 93, Addes Coll., RL.

4. It should be noted that this is another clear instance where Sugar did not follow the CP "line." The Cleveland convention recommendation was another and more would follow during the war. On the North American Strike, Cochran, *Labor,* 176–82 sees the strike as a major CP faux pas, and in its consequences it certainly was; Keeran (*Automobile Workers*) focuses on the virulence of the UAW officialdom's reaction; Prickett, "Communism and Factionalism in the U.A.W.," *Science and Society* 32(1968), 257–77, stresses the ranks' enthusiasm for the strike; the additional interpretive elements added here are drawn from a close examination of the timing of Ford negotiating events and court cases (local press, June 10–14, Sugar's case materials, and Sugar-Addes correspondence) and from the testimony of George Addes—interview, September 12, 1979; *Life* magazine story and photos ("President Roosevelt breaks a Red Strike"), June 15, 1941, 32–34. Illustrating the contrasts and pressures under which Sugar was working are these articles in the *Free Press* on one day in June: (1) "Reds Reported Plotting Arms Tie-up in City" in which FBI agent John Bugas claimed to have uncovered a plot (meanwhile his people were watching Sugar, a "known Communist," according to the bureau, who had been in Russia in February–April 1937(!)—this from the fantasy-ridden FBI file on Sugar that I obtained through the Freedom of Information Act); (2) "Air Corps Urges Strikers to Return to Bohn Plants," which a semiofficial stoppage after a negative National Mediations Board decision had closed for a day; (3) "UAW Sues for Pay Lost after a Strike," a suit filed by Sugar and Smokler in circuit court in Saginaw; and finally and critically (4) "Ford Hearing before NLRB Delayed Again," a further story on the impact of the legal threat in the progress of Ford negotiations: "Both Mr. Capizzi and I," Sugar said, "advised the examiner [Horace Cranefield] that progress was being made." The *Detroit News'* "CIO Officers Battle Reds" carried the actions of UAW's top brass (including Addes's *no comment*) to Frankensteen's actions in California on June 10, 1941; also, Earl Freitag, interview transcript, Oral Histories, RL.; Mortimer, *Organize!* (see ch. 6, n. 9), chs. 11–12.

5. Art Preis, *Labor's Giant Step: Twenty Years of the CIO* (1964; reprint, New York. 1972), 133–41; on the Buffalo convention, see Cochran, *Labor,* Keeran, *Automobile Workers,* and the press; the key articles: Archie W. Robinson, "UAW to Push Fight on Reds," *Detroit News,* Aug. 1, 1941; "Addes Counts on Lewis Aid; Catholic Unionists Join Ouster Fight," *Detroit News,* Aug. 2, 1941 (Addes was a practicing Catholic, remember); "Purge Stirs UAW Battle," Aug. 3, 1941; Edwin Lahey in the *Buffalo Evening News,* Aug. 6, 9, and 11, 1941. *Buffalo Courier Express,* Aug. 15 and 16, 1941; Coughlin in the *Detroit Free Press,* Aug. 16, 1941; Roy Hudson, "Some Lessons of the Auto Convention," *Sunday Worker,* August 31, 1941, which summarizes the total about-face of the Party on defense and foreign policy issues, chastising the union for not taking stronger stands.

6. These well-known developments are discussed in all our key sources but most perceptively by Maurice Isserman, *Which Side Were You On? The American Communist Party During the Second World War* (Middletown, CT, 1983). On the movies, see Melvin Small, "Buffoons and Brave Hearts: Hollywood Portrays the Russians, 1939–1944," *California Historical Quarterly* 52(1973): 326–37.

7. On Addes, a very poorly known and understood figure in the historiography of the UAW, see, above all, Michael Kroll, "George Addes and the Auto Workers, 1933–1947" (masters thesis, Wayne State

University, 1981). My own interviews with Addes, deep reading in his routine daily activities and the thinking that these reveal (the Addes Collection and the Sugar Collection contain thousands of letters, interoffice memos, and directives from and to Addes), and an analysis of his speeches, most of them sent to Sugar for comment and emendation, help to establish the perspective on his politics here asserted. There remains a great deal more work to be done on this key figure in U.S. labor history.

8. The preceding is drawn from material (especially the Ternstedt clipping) in the "Reuther file," Box 65, Sugar Coll., RL; "My Relations with the Reuthers," Black Lake materials, (copy in Sugar Coll., Supplement, RL; Sam Sweet to Sugar, June 15, 1971, in Black Lake materials; interview with Sam Sweet, Dec. 10, 1979. This discussion again offers new insights into Reuther that I believe useful in understanding the man and the perceptions of many of his opponents, whatever their politics.

9. Sugar, "Legal Department Report," *Proceedings (President's Report)*, UAW Convention, 1942, Chicago (Detroit, 1942), 67–86 (RL); Studs Terkel, *The Good War* (New York, 1983); John Morton Blum, *V Was for Victory* (New York, 1976); Issermann, *Which Side;* Cochran, *Labor,* 206–12.

10. Sugar, "Report of the Legal Department," 1943 and 1944, Box 99, Addes Coll., RL and Box 69, Sugar Coll., RL.

11. These problems are laid out in Sugar's legal reports of 1943, 1944, 1945, and 1946 (all in the proceedings from those conventions). His voluminous correspondence with the War Labor Board, the preparatory documents for the major cases, and the reports from around the country on antilabor legislation are again found in the Addes and Sugar Collections. The problem of the state-level antiunion law that developed during the war is little studied and deserves to be more so because it set the framework not only for the industrial flight to the south but for the general antilabor reaction that marked the immediate postwar period. For a good overview of the labor movement during the war, see Zieger, *American Workers* (see ch. 6, n. 2), ch. 3 and the outstanding article by Paul Koistinen, "Mobilizing the World War II Economy: Labor and the Military-Industrial Alliance," *Pacific Historical Review* 42(1973): 443–78. On the Texas adventure, see the *Detroit Free Press,* Sept. 10, 1943; Sugar's legal report of 1944, and above all, Ernest Goodman interview (videotaped), Feb. 10, 1986.

12. Dominic Capezi, *Race Relations in Wartime Detroit: The Sojourner Truth Housing Controversy of 1942* (Philadelphia, 1984); Meier and Rudwick, *Black Detroit* (see Preface, n. 4), 175–206; Nelson Lichtenstein, *Labor's War at Home: the CIO in World War II* (Urbana, IL, 1982), 125–26. The details on events and activities in which Sugar and his associates played a role are drawn from Sugar's outstanding clipping collections of the local press, national magazines (e.g. the *Harper's* article), and the national press, especially the *Daily Worker*'s coverage by Billy Allan, and from internal UAW correspondence: Boxes 5, 99–102, Sugar Coll., Box 22, Addes Coll., Boxes 2, 3, and 14, Thomas Coll., and Boxes 6 and 8, Reuther Coll. Also Shelton Tappes interview, March 24, 1979, and Tappes and Crockett interviews, Oral Histories (Labor and the Black Worker)—all RL.

13. Martin Glaberman, *Wartime Strikes: the Struggle against the No-Strike Pledge in the UAW during World War II* (Detroit, 1980) with a list on pp. 51–60 and Lichtenstein, *Labor's War,* 189 ff. argue that the International was indeed draconian in its response. The big problem remains the difference between words and action—and selection of a few nasty examples to prove a general point (e.g. Chrysler Local 490). My main sources are the Sugar-Addes correspondence, 1943–45, Box 64, Sugar Coll., RL and above all my long and probing interview with Addes on this question, Aug. 30, 1979. I have also made a careful analysis of response time, juxtaposing press reports and official union action (again Sugar's magnificent clipping collection shows its importance; see Boxes 102–5). Also, Sugar's legal reports for 1943 and 1944.

14. The press followed the issue closely. See Sugar's clippings, Jan. 11–Feb. 24, 1944. Addes interview, Aug. 30, 1979. In the wake of these events, new red-baiting occurred and new concerns were raised by members who wondered why the leadership only attacked fascism and rarely said anything negative about communism. One letter (Feb. 11, 1944, from J. H. Blake of South Bend Local 5 to Addes) put the matter pointedly and Addes asked Sugar to prepare a reply. It is a fascinating document that captures the spirit of the Addes caucus in wartime and stands as a monument of the old union in face of what was soon to come. Addes 1944 folder, Box 69, Sugar Coll., RL.

15. Sugar, "Legal Reports," 1944, 1945, and 1946; Addes, "Report," May 31, 1944 (with charts and graphs of membership growth and reserve funds assets); Sugar, "Legal Report," 1946 (O'Brien case, 107–9—more details in Goodman interview, July 3, 1979 and his brief for the case in the files of Goodman et al., Cadillac Towers, Detroit). All reports in *Proceedings* of UAW Conventions for those years. See also Sugar's "Davidow File," Box 3, Sugar Coll., RL. On the operations of the UAW and the vast amount of practical work and benefits brought to members in this period, (as well as internal union discipline issues), the Addes Collection is inexhaustible; his principal internal correspondent is Maurice Sugar. My own research has only

scratched the surface on these subjects. The problem of union bureaucratization/service during the war has yet to be fully explored—it is much needed in light of the finger pointing with regard to "when-the-*movement*-died" controversies.

16. Sugar, "Legal Report," 1946, 99–103. See the outstanding study of this problem and the changing board, Tomlins, *State* (see Preface, n. 3), 197–281.

17. On staff relations and Sugar's personality, see ch. 1, n. 3.

Chapter 10

1. For the emergence of the "new-model" unions of mid-Victorian England, see G. D. H. Cole and Raymond Postgate, *The British Common People, 1746–1946*(London, 1961), 367 ff.; for an interesting discussion with relevance to what follows—especially regarding the significance of the term *political discourse* in relation to changing sociopolitical structures—see Gareth Stedman Jones, *Languages of Class* (Cambridge, 1983), chs. 2, 4, and 6.

2. The main guides here are Lichtenstein, *Labor's War,* (see ch. 9, n. 12), ch. 11 ("Reconversion Politics"); Seth Wigderson, "The UAW Convention of 1951" (paper presented to the Mid-America Historical Conference, Springfield, MO, 1980) and idem, "The UAW in the 1950s: the Triumph of Service Unionism," (Ph.D. diss., Wayne State University, forthcoming); C. Wright Mills, *The New Men of Power* (New York, 1948); and the great paean to the "New America," Frederick Lewis Allen, *The Big Change* (New York, 1952). For the general evolution of the U.S. economy, David Gordon, Michael Reich, and Richard Edwards, *Segmented Work, Divided Workers* (New York, 1982); for how business management changed with it, Howell J. Harris, *The Right to Manage* (Madison, WI, 1982); on the GM strike, Barton Berstein, "Walter Reuther and the General Motors Strike of 1945–46," *Michigan History* 49(1965): 260–77. For a thought-provoking alternative vision, see Mike Davis, *Prisoners of the American Dream* (London, 1986).

3. The essential study is that of Martin Halpern, *The Disintegration of the Left Coalition in the UAW, 1945–1950* (Albany, NY, 1987); see also Cochran, (see Preface, n. 4), *Labor* 272 ff.; Keeran, *Automobile Workers,* (see Preface, n. 1), 250–89; Barnard, *Walter Reuther* (see Preface, n. 1), 101–17; William Andrew, "Factionalism and Anti-Communism: Ford Local 600," *Labor History* 20(1979): 227–55.

4. Sigal, *Going Away* (see Preface, n. 4) 329; Tomlins, *State* (see Preface, n. 3) 275–30; on the general political atmosphere and the struggle of liberals to stay the course, see Alonzo L. Hamby, *Beyond the New Deal: Harry Truman and American Liberalism* (New York, 1973), 53–186; in general see Robert J. Donovan, *Conflict and Crisis: The Presidency of Harry S. Truman, 1945–1947* (New York, 1977).

5. Both incidents are related by Sugar in his "My Meetings with the Reuthers" (Black Lake materials).

6. Llewellyn interviews (Oct. 21, 1978 and Aug. 17, 1979); confirmed by Addes (Aug. 30, 1979); V. Reuther says he was traded for R. J. Thomas's acquisition of the competitive shops department, (*Brothers* [see Preface, n. 1], 259–60); International executive board minutes, April 1946, Box 90, Sugar Coll., RL; Sugar, "Memorandum on the Existing Situation" (see ch. 8, n. 9); Addes confirmed what had been long assumed, that Sugar wrote this guide to the faction fight for their side. The original of this document is in the files of Sugar's law office, but several copies exist in the UAW archives, notably in Box 1, Sugar Coll., RL.

7. Such positions abound in both journals, full runs of which exist in the Reuther Library and have been consulted for all of 1946 and 1947.

8. Copies of all these materials and much pertinent correspondence are located in Boxes 71–74, 109–10, and 117, Sugar Coll., RL; Conway, interview transcript, Oral Histories, RL.

9. Box 56 (Neff case), 71, and 72 (membership meeting minutes), Local 9 Coll., RL; Appeal Case, Glen Porter, Box 70, Addes Coll., RL; International executive board minutes (Buffalo), Sept. 1947, Box 7, R. J. Thomas Coll., RL. George Burt interview, July 20, 1979; Carl Haessler, interview transcript, Oral Histories, RL.

10. *Detroit News,* June 27, 1946; International executive board minutes (Louisville) Mar. 23, 1947, Box 90, Sugar Coll., RL pp. 183–202.

11. Sugar, "Report on the Taft Hartley Law" (draft of radio address), Box 73, Sugar Coll., RL.

12. International executive board minutes (Detroit), Nov. 29, 1947, pp. 223, 226, 229, 238 for the specific quotes, pp. 223–75 for the entire debate. Sugar's expenses analysis occupies approximately 400 pages in his collection. The copy of the board minutes and his work are found in Boxes 94, 5, and 75–78 (bills), Sugar Coll., RL. See also Boxes 4 and 12, Mazey Coll., RL. Sugar's notes on the board meeting are in Box 4,

Sugar Coll., RL. The multiple strands of documentation demonstrate clearly that the charges of bilking the union were false.

13. On Sugar's later life, a variety of collected clippings (Black Lake materials), show him reflective and at ease. See also his "personal" files, Boxes 15–17; Sugar Coll., RL, especially Box 17 dealing with his work in conservation and the legal work relating to the Alverno Dam project in the 1960s.

❖ INDEX

Murray, Robert, 93
Music, song, 33. *See also* Sugar, Maurice
Muste, A. J. (Musteites), 169
Myer, Gustavus, 46

Nash-Kelvinator strike (1937), 206–7
National Association for the Advancement of
    Colored People (NAACP), 276–77, 283
National Automobile Chamber of Commerce,
    111
National Automobile Dealers Association, 111
National Automotive Fibers Company, 186–87
National Business Alliance, 66
National Civic Federation, 51, 68
National Industrial Recovery Act (NIRA), 135,
    138, 140, 141
National Labor Board, 140–41
National Labor Mediation Board, 261
National Labor Relations Board (NLRB), 155,
    165–66, 201, 218, 223, 224, 225, 226,
    236, 239–40, 245–49, 262, 263, 270,
    283–85, 294–96
National Lawyers Guild, 217, 221, 261, 274–77
National Negro Congress, 161, 275–76
National Recovery Administration (NRA), 139–
    45, 155
Nazi-Soviet Pact (1939), 13, 242–44
Nearing, Scott, 12, 32, 61, 62, 69, 83, 99, 101,
    105
Neff, John, 293
Negro Baptist Ministerial Conference, 160
Negro Methodist Ministerial Alliance, 160
Nelson, Crawford, 153
Nelson, John, 114
Nelson, Steve, 107, 134, 242
Nelson, Walter, 72, 115, 188
Neuenfelt, Lila, 246
New Union Theatre (Contemporary Theatre),
    154, 199
Nicol, Henry, 206–7
Norris, George, 66
North American Aviation strike, 261–64
No-strike pledge, 266, 270, 278–81
Novy mir, 67
Nowak, Helen, 210
Nowak, Stanley, 90, 180, 186–87, 192, 197,
    208–11, 244

O'Brien, Arthur, 282–83
O'Brien, Patrick H., 115, 228–30
O'Camb, Fay, 167, 171–74, 188
O'Hare, Kate Richards, 67, 84, 95
Olds, Nichol, 114–15
Oneal, James, 62
Osborn, Chase, 51

Osborn, Laura, 174
Otis, James, 115
Owens, Edgar, 109

Packard Motor Company, 183–84
Palmer, A. Mitchell, 92–94, 121
Pannekoek, Anton, 45
Pathfinders, 79–80
Pattern Makers (AFL), 59, 169
Peck, Rev. William H., 159, 161
People's Council for Peace and Democracy, 68,
    69–70
Perkins, Frances, 148, 198, 279–80
Pettibone, George, 43
Picard, Frank, 261
Pickert, Heinrich, 120, 176, 182, 185, 214–15,
    220, 229
Pieper, Fred, 193, 230
Pinchot, Cornelia Bryce, 226
Pingree, Hazen, 34, 51
Pinkerton Agency, 185, 187
Pobedonostsev, Constantine, 35
Polish-Americans (Detroit), 34, 158, 186–87,
    208–11
Poole, Charles A., 182
Popular Front, 134, 152, 165, 174, 179, 180,
    221, 232
Porter, Glenn, 293–94
Porter, Russell B., 216
Pound, James, 89, 96–97
Pound, Roscoe, 39
Powell, Dan, 64
Preis, Art, 280
Pressman, Lee, 14, 32, 194–96, 200–206, 238,
    261
Prickett, James, 262, 292
Procedure, legal, 102–3
Progressive Trade Unionist Bulletin (1935), 168–
    69
Prohibition, 62, 73, 97
Proletarian, The, 75–76
Proletarian Party (Proletarian University of
    America), 76–77, 90, 94–95, 107, 123,
    169, 180

Quill, Mike, 269

Racism, 31–32, 36–37, 149, 229–30, 244,
    274–78. *See also* Anti-Semitism
Raskin, Jack, 275–76
Raymond, Philip, 107, 112, 135, 137–38
Reading, Richard, 228–30, 243
Reed, John, 83, 84, 86, 89–90
Reed, John, Club, 100, 119–20, 154
Reilly, Gerald D., 270, 284–85

Reisinger, Richard, 238, 297
Renner, Al, 63–64, 74, 77, 89–90, 94–96, 180
Reuther, Roy, 179–80, 192, 196–200, 222
Reuther, Victor, 133–34, 178–80, 192, 196–98, 211, 220, 222, 231–32, 267, 290
Reuther, Walter, 6, 11, 12, 14, 133–34, 178–80, 188, 198, 207, 220, 222, 223–34, 238, 242–43, 249, 261, 277, 282; political outlook of, 266–68; as "Right-wing" UAW coalition leader (1941–45), 264–69, 277–80; as UAW president, 286–98
Reynolds, Bud, 76, 85, 105–8
Reynolds, Harry, 225
Rice, Frank, 183
Richard, C. L., 142
Richter, Irving, 291, 295
Riebe, Alex, 94, 97
Rimar, Ralph, 235, 249
Roberts, LeRoy, 238
Robeson, Paul, 244
Rogers, Cyril, 293–94
Roland, James, 168
Romney, George, 16
Roosevelt, Eleanor, 291
Roosevelt, Franklin D., 142, 146–49, 155, 156, 165, 169, 175, 188–89, 200, 202, 204, 221, 245, 246, 249, 259, 260, 261–62, 263–64, 268, 270, 281, 284
Roosevelt, Theodore, 43, 66, 73
Root (Elihu) Commission, 68
Ross, Rev. S. D., 160
Roszel, Francis A., 186–87
Rovin, Dr., 75–76
Rubin, Joseph A., 260
Rubin, William, 59–60
Rubinoff, Charles, 247–48
Ruskin, Dr. I. W., 188
Russell, Charles Edward, 46, 68
Russell, Jack, 52
Russian Revolution (March), 67; (Bolshevik), 74–75, 105
Ruthenberg, Charles, 67–68, 84, 90
Rzembowska, Anna, 215

Sacco-Vanzetti case, 108
Safran, John, 240
St. Louis, Missouri (Special Convention of the Socialist Party, 1917), 67–69, 70
St. Matthew's Protestant Episcopal Church, 160
Sam's Department Store, 145
Sanderson, William, 199–200
Sanford v. Newell, 214
Saxton, John, 293–94
Saylor, Allan, 291
Scavrada, Caesar, 114–15
Schmies, John, 139

Scholle, Gus, 262
Schwartz, Bernard, Cigar Company, 201, 207–10, 215–16
Scottsboro boys case, 108, 154
Second Baptist Church, 160
Seltzer, Joseph, 71, 88
Seney, Michigan, 25
Seton, Ernest Thompson, 66
Shachtman, Max, 292
Shapiro, Stanley, 92
Sheffield, Horace, 248, 275, 278
Shenk v. U.S. (1919), 72
Shipley, Carl, 167
Sigal, Clancy, 26, 289
Silver, Paul, 281
Simmons, LeBron, 158, 159, 161, 172
Simons, A. M., 68
Sinclair, Upton, 37, 45, 68, 175–76
Sit-down strike: as a tactic, 191–92; in Flint (1937), 192–206; in Detroit (1937), 206–16; and the law, 211–12, 216–18, 220–21
Sloan, Alfred P., 198, 199
Smith, Edwin S., 245, 262
Smith, Gerald L. K., 275
Smith, Matthew, 138–48, 155, 167, 172, 185, 188, 206–7, 269
Smith, Tucker, 179, 233
Smokler, Nedwin, 245, 272, 274–76
Socialist Labor Party, 124
Socialist Party of America, socialists (U.S.), 12, 27, 37, 62, 67–69, 83–85, 89, 109, 138, 171; in Detroit, 49–50, 61–67, 69–77, 84–85, 94–97, 99, 107, 123–24, 152, 171, 179–80; "Militants," 188; "Old Guard," 171; and the Russian Language Federation, 74–75
Socialist Workers Party, 263–64
Sojourner Truth Housing Project, 274
Soviet Union, 131–35, 178, 262, 289, 292
Spanish Civil War, 231–32, 245
Spargo, John, 44, 67–69
Spencer, Harry, 142
Spies: company, 59, 106, 109, 111, 148, 155, 183–85, 186–87, 200; government, 75–77; union, 55–56
Spolansky, Jacob, 118–19
Stalin, Joseph, 242, 244, 265, 272
Stedman, Seymour, 94–97
Steel Workers Organizing Committee (SWOC), 225
Steele, James, 62
Stevens, Mary Thompson, 80
Stevenson, William, 295
Stone, Eve, 227
Stone, I. F., 197
Strachan, Alan, 228–30, 232

Christopher H. Johnson is Professor of History at Wayne State University. He has published widely in French social and economic history. His book, *Utopian Communism in France: Cabet and the Icarians, 1839–1851* (1974), was nominated for the National Book Award in History. He is currently completing a study of de-industrialization in eighteenth- and nineteenth-century Languedoc.

The manuscript was edited by Michael K. Lane. The book was designed by Joanne Elkin Kinney. The typeface for the text is Galliard. The display face is Galliard Ultra. The book is printed on 50-lb. Arbor offset paper. The cloth edition is bound in Holliston Mills' Roxite Vellum.

Manufactured in the United States of America.